PRAISE FOR *SMALL TIME OPERATOR*

"The best of the genre. A remarkable step-by-step manual that is a delight to read."

—*Library Journal*, New York

"Very well done, and should be of great help to anyone starting their own small business."

—Director, U.S. Small Business Administration, Washington, DC

"Everything you need to know for opening day but don't know enough to ask. Particularly good on the basics of getting started."

—American Library Association, Chicago

"Kamoroff's book was recommended continually by the people we contacted who were in the business of helping others start their own businesses."

—*San Francisco Bay Guardian*

"Mr. Kamoroff has twenty solid years of experience as a tax accountant and advisor for started from scratch businesses, and he's done an amazing and praiseworthy job of boiling those twenty years down into a complete and very useful technical manual."

—*Mother Earth News/Back to Basics*, North Carolina

"Of the dozens of small-business how-to books, one book tops the list: Small Time Operator. *A phenomenal book, it offers a ticket to success. It is a must-read."*

—On the Economy, King Features Syndicate, Washington, DC

"The most requested, most recommended, and the best known small business guidebook in the world."

—Professional's Bookshelf

"The most successful book of its kind ever printed."

—Nolo Law, Berkeley, CA

SMALL TIME OPERATOR

SMALL TIME OPERATOR

How to Start Your Own Business, Keep Your Books, Pay Your Taxes, and Stay Out of Trouble

15TH EDITION

Bernard B. Kamoroff, CPA

Guilford, Connecticut

An imprint of The Rowman & Littlefield Publishing Group, Inc.
4501 Forbes Blvd., Ste. 200
Lanham, MD 20706
www.rowman.com

Distributed by NATIONAL BOOK NETWORK

British Library Cataloguing in Publication Information available

Library of Congress Cataloging-in-Publication Data

Names: Kamoroff, Bernard, author.
Title: Small time operator : how to start your own business, keep your books,
  pay your taxes, and stay out of trouble / Bernard B. Kamoroff, CPA.
Description: 15th edition. | Guilford, Conn. : Lyons Press, [2018] | Includes
  index.
Identifiers: LCCN 2018032151 | ISBN 9781493040209 (pbk. : alk. paper)
Subjects: LCSH: New business enterprises. | New business
  Enterprises—Management. | Small business.
Classification: LCC HD62.5 .K344 2018 | DDC 658.1/1—dc23 LC record available at
https://lccn.loc.gov/2018032151

∞™ The paper used in this publication meets the minimum requirements of American
National Standard for Information Sciences—Permanence of Paper for Printed Library
Materials, ANSI/NISO Z39.48-1992.

Printed in the United States of America

Please Read:
I have done my best to give you useful and accurate information in this book, but I cannot guarantee that the information is correct or will be appropriate to your particular situation. Laws, procedures, and regulations change frequently and are subject to differing interpretations. It is your responsibility to verify all information and all laws discussed in this book before relying on them. Nothing in this book can substitute for legal advice and cannot be considered as making it unnecessary to obtain such advice. In all situations involving local, state, or federal law, obtain specific information from the appropriate government agency or a competent person.

Thank you . . .

Jim Hayes, for the original idea for this book.

Jim Robertson, for the title and the encouragement.

Andy Blasky, for the dedicated editing.

And Sharon, who has lived this venture as much as I have.

Thank you also to all the people who have generously contributed through fifteen editions:

Jim Angell, Richard Benson, John Bobbitt, John Brenneman, Joe Campbell, John Cedarholm, Anne Cedarholm, Peter deFremery, Paul deFremery, Heather Stone Detrick, Key Dickason, James Dillehay, Charles Dorton, Kathy Ward Eisman, Jerry Eisman, Emily Ellickson-Brown, Pat Ellington, Dick Ellington, Will Emerson, Kat Emerson, Stephen Fishman, J'Ann Forgue, Cynthia Frank, John Fremont, Carol Gibson, Robert Greenway, Beth Hackenbruch, Tim Hanna, Steve Hargraves, Marcie Hart, Hal Hershey, Kathy Hoffman, Lance Hoffman, Larry Jacobs, David Kamoroff, Paul Klipfel, Laura Klipfel, Jeanne Koelle, Mary Lai, Jan Lowe, Jed Lyons, Mike Madson, Tony Mancuso, Bob Mathews, Michael McCaffrey, Bruce McCloskey, Don McCunn, Nick Mein, Sharon Miley, Joanie Mitchell, Dorcas Moulton, Terry Nemeth, Paul Paul, Jacki Pealatere, Tom Person, Jim Puzey, Tim Ramming, Dave Raub, Rick Rinehart, Leigh Robinson, Joe Sachs, Robin Shelley, Mike Simon, Alex Singer, Omaya Sisemore, Mike Snead, Lara Stonebraker, Patty Walsh, Brad Walton, John Weed, Paul Williams, and Jan Zobel. And Crystal, Julia, Colleen, and Corrina.

The book is dedicated to John Muir, the Mechanic.

In this world, a person must either be anvil or hammer.

—Henry Wadsworth Longfellow

BRIEF CONTENTS

DETAILED CONTENTS

Chapter 2: Keeping Records

Chapter 4: Taxes

Chapter 5: Home-Based Business

PREFACE
Be Your Own Boss

You can be your own boss. All it really requires is a good idea, some hard work, and a little knowledge.

"A little knowledge" is what this book is all about. *Small Time Operator* will show you how to start and operate your own business.

Small Time Operator is also written for anyone who is self-employed: professionals, freelancers, artists, consultants, independent contractors, and workers in the "on-demand" economy. You may not consider your occupation a "business," but the laws, rules, procedures, records, taxes, and most everything else you need to know to be successful are pretty much the same.

And *Small Time Operator* is, hopefully, the road map to your success.

Small Time Operator is a technical manual, a step-by-step guide to help you set up the machinery of your business, the "business end" of your business, and keep it lubricated and well maintained. It is written in everyday English so anyone can understand it. You will not need a business education or an accounting dictionary to grasp the concepts or do the work.

Many people think that businessmen and businesswomen all come out of business school, kind of like F-150 pickups coming out of a Ford assembly plant. This just isn't true. I know many people in business, and most of them had no formal business education and little or no experience.

Some new small business owners are people who just got tired of the "nine-to-five" life, tired of working for someone else, and who decided to go into business for themselves.

Some are people—hardworking, talented people—who lost their jobs due to corporate downsizing and outsourcing.

Many new businesspeople are still holding on to their regular jobs, but starting a part-time, sideline business, probably at home, to bring in some extra income, or to make a little money at something that started out as a hobby, or to experiment with their business ideas and learn the ropes before going at it full-time.

And just as many people start their own businesses because they are the kind of individuals who want to control their own destiny, to find independence, to succeed on their own terms.

Small Time Operator comes out of my experience during the past twenty years as a consultant and accountant for small businesses, and from operating three of my own small businesses. I've learned from successes and I've learned from mistakes, my own and others'. Now I hope to teach you what I've learned.

Small Time Operator will show you things to do and things not to do. But like any book, it can't do more than that. You've got to go ahead and do it yourself. Bilbo Baggins said, "One should always begin at the beginning." That's where you are now. Other people, many others, run their own small businesses.

You can too.

The journey of a thousand miles begins with a single step.

—Lao Tzu

Chapter One
GETTING STARTED

Trying seems to be a start for getting things done
You get to know the right way by doing it wrong
And when you cross a bridge over shallow water
Does it always mean you're afraid to get wet
When you ought to?

—BARBARA PACK

GETTING STARTED: BASICS

A Small Time Operator: A True Story

When I first met Joe Campbell several years ago, he was working as a switchman for Union Pacific. He liked working on the railroad. Didn't love it, but it was a job.

Joe's hobby and one of his great pleasures in life was electronics. He especially enjoyed troubleshooting and repairing computers. Through experimenting, studying, and trial and error, Joe acquired a good technical knowledge of both hardware and software. It was not long before he started fixing his friends' and neighbors' computers.

Gradually, Joe's hobby developed into a business. He moved slowly at first, helping customers on evenings and weekends. He started with computer platforms he was familiar with, and slowly expanded to more complex equipment, and then smartphone repairs. Joe was a good technician and repairman, he didn't charge much, and he gave his customers fast service. And Joe's business grew. He soon found himself with more business than he could handle in his spare time. He started working fewer hours for the railroad, then quit altogether and set up a small computer service of his own.

Joe is a success, but not just because he makes his own living. Joe has shaped his life around his interests. He enjoys his work, and his customers recognize and appreciate the personal interest he takes in what he's doing. Joe "made it" because he worked hard to develop his interests and because he had the ambition to learn his trade. It never just comes naturally. Prior experience? He had none. A business background? None. Money? He spent a few hundred dollars on test gear and parts, not much more.

Find a need and fill it.
— Lettered on a cement truck, Oakland, California

The most important lesson to learn from Joe, I feel, is that you can start out easily and simply. You don't have to make the Big Plunge, selling everything you own and going into debt. More than two-thirds of all new businesses are started as part-time or weekend ventures, started by people still holding on to a job while they experiment with their new business. Start slowly, try it out, and learn as you go. You'll get there.

Things worked well for Joe. But if they had not— if he really did not have it in him to be in business for himself, or if he just picked the wrong thing at the wrong time—he could easily have stopped anywhere along the way with little or no loss. And maybe try it again sometime.

What Kind of Business?

Joe's computer repair business is an example of what is commonly called a "service" business. He does something for his customers and they pay him for his services. You can also support yourself by selling something, or by manufacturing or making something, or renting something. Many businesses combine several of these aspects, such as sales and service.

A **service business** is the easiest to set up. It requires the smallest initial investment and the simplest recordkeeping. It is also the easiest kind of business to operate out of your home. On the other hand, you will have to be competent at the service you offer. More than any other business, a service business will require some experience. A service business is more likely to be subject to state licenses and regulations.

If you do something well—fixing things, painting or decorating, writing or editing, cutting hair, catering—these are but a few possibilities for your own service business.

Self-employed professionals and tradespeople are all operating service businesses. And so are entertainers: musicians, DJs, storytellers, party clowns, and magicians. *There's no business like show business . . .*

And if you are good at something, consider teaching those skills to others, as a self-employed instructor, speaker, or seminar leader. Be imaginative. Don't ignore your own resources.

A **sales business** can take many different forms: retail, wholesale, storefront, direct sales, multilevel marketing (MLM), internet sales, or some other approach.

Your own sales business allows you to select and handle merchandise that reflects your own interests and tastes, and the interests and needs of your community. Most sales businesses will require inventory (stock on hand), which means a bigger investment than a service business. You may need a storefront or showroom to display your goods and attract customers. You will have to keep inventory records. The recordkeeping is a little more complex.

Sales businesses, however, offer more flexibility than service businesses. Service people are often limited by their training and experience. With sales, as your interests change and as the fashions change, it is easy for your sales business to change with them.

Manufacturing, for many small businesses, means crafts: leather, clothing, pottery, jewelry, and furniture, to name a few. Crafts offer, probably more than any other business, an opportunity for the craftsperson to do what he or she enjoys for its own pleasure, and get paid for it, too. But again, you have to be good at what you're doing. Nobody wants an ugly necklace or a chair that falls apart. And more than with a sales or service business, you may have a harder time finding a steady and reliable market for your product. But if you have imagination and talent, you might discover that what you think of as your hobby can become your source of income.

Conventional manufacturing often requires a large investment in machinery. But you would be surprised how many successful manufacturing businesses started out in some inventor's garage with homemade, experimental equipment, on a surplus store budget.

Rental businesses have expanded from the traditional car rentals, equipment rentals, and tuxedo rentals to renting out just about anything. Self-storage businesses are everywhere, and most of them are locally owned operations. Party rental businesses can be found in most towns. Amusement businesses rent foosball tables, jukeboxes, and pinball machines for parties. Weekend entrepreneurs rent out mobile bounce houses and climbing walls. There are stores that specialize in renting wedding ensembles, stores that rent designer clothes, galleries that rent out works of art. Some of these businesses also have subscription services, offering an endless rotation of items for a monthly fee.

Mobile businesses have been around since the wheel was invented. Just about any service can be operated out of a truck. Traveling vendors and entertainers spend every summer going from one event or show to the next; it's a gypsy lifestyle that's very appealing to a lot of people. And even the smallest towns have food trucks.

Pop-up businesses are short-term, temporary businesses and seasonal businesses, selling gifts for Christmas, or costumes for Halloween, or sunglasses at the beach. Or maybe someone has a stock of goods bought at an auction or bankruptcy sale that they'd like to sell. The businesses can "pop up" anywhere that people congregate: a vacant storefront that you can rent for a week or a month, a booth at some special event, or just a table at a farmers' market. A pop-up business is a fast, low-cost way to test out your business ideas and your business talents in a real-life situation.

Online business. Just about every business in the country has an online presence, and many small businesses are only online. It costs next to nothing to have a website, join an online marketplace, sell on social media, or all the above—all at the same time.

Mike Madsen owns Mike Madsen Leather, manufacturer and seller of handmade leather goods: "Look around, figure out what you want to do, and then try to sum up your business in one sentence or a paragraph at the most, no more. Business is just like life in a lot of ways, and you take things step by step. You don't become a big business overnight. You build it little by little, every day you walk into the building. You get started through your own will and determination and have a little fun at it.

"You can learn a lot by observation. If you own a business, try to visit other people who are in similar businesses. When I was in Argentina I went to seven leather factories. They're very willing to show you something when you're not in direct competition, and they're pleased to show off their business. But if you and I lived in the same city, you might be less willing to show your manufacturing process to a future competitor.

"Small business is the backbone of this country. Big businesses provide mainline products, but it's small business that provides all the little things that make your life interesting. I think it's also the kind of people who are in small business, those of a pioneering spirit. We built a country on pioneering spirit. That's just what being in a small business is, being a pioneer."

Business Failure Rate

The well-known statistic often spouted by the Small Business Administration and other business organizations—that 60 percent of all new businesses fail the first year—is totally misleading. First of all, I think it is a flawed statistic. Nobody, not even the Internal Revenue Service, has been able to come up with a failure rate for businesses.

But even if the failure figures are accurate, just because 60 percent of new businesses fail, this does not mean your own business has a 60 percent chance of failure. There are some businesses, businesses that just weren't well thought out, that are virtually guaranteed to fail. There are some businesses, ones that were well thought out and planned, that have an almost 100 percent chance of success.

Your chance of success or failure has a lot to do with the kind of business you are starting, your ability to find and keep customers, your talent at running a business, and how well you prepare yourself for this new venture.

THE SUCCESSFUL BUSINESS TRIANGLE

There are many factors that make a business a success, or a failure. But there are three major points, three major keys to success, that every business should have. You might think of it as a triangle. If you remember your high school physics, the triangle is the strongest structure that human beings can create. The same applies to business, and the strength comes from all three corners of that triangle.

One corner, and the most obvious, is the product or service you are offering. The more quality and the more value you offer your customers, the more likely you will stand out from the crowd. Offer a product or service that's better, more reliable, more useful, and more appreciated than the cheap products in this mass-produced world of ours.

The second corner of your business triangle, and possibly the biggest one, is marketing and promotion: spreading the word about your business, finding and keeping customers. Marketing can take many different approaches, and is often trial and error, finding what works for you. Many business owners devote as much as half their working hours to marketing. And for many business owners, it's a real challenge. But without marketing, no customers. Without customers, no business.

The third corner of your business is the "business end": the legal and tax issues, the permits and licenses, the office work and recordkeeping that's required of every business, every self-employed individual. It's the grease that keeps the machinery running, the glue that keeps it all from coming apart at the seams. It's the least loved part of business, yet not difficult to learn and manage. After reading this book and spending a few months at it, the "business end" of your business should become almost second nature.

CAN YOU DO IT?

There is another important factor in the success of your venture: you. Can you do it?

You don't have to be an expert in the line of business that you're thinking of going into, but you do have to be willing to learn. There are people who actually try to start a certain business because it's a "sure thing," a "guaranteed" big seller, and they know absolutely nothing about the field. Some of these people are, of course, real hustlers, but there are a lot of honest dopes in this group. They think that a little money and some good intentions are all they need to get started. And most of them soon wind up with neither their money nor any intention of ever being in business again.

I've known a lot of people in business, some who made it, some who didn't. And while nobody has a guaranteed secret for success, I believe that there are a few basic characteristics that you've got to have or be willing to develop if you're going to start any business.

Organization: The first and most important characteristic, I feel, is a clear head and the ability to organize your mind and your life. The "absent-minded professor" may be a genius, but he will never keep a business together.

In running a small business, you are going to have to deal with many different people, keep schedules, meet deadlines, organize paperwork, pay bills, and the list goes on. It's all part of every business. So if balancing your checkbook is too much for you, or you just burned up your car engine because you forgot to check the oil, maybe you're not cut out for business. If you are someone who can never find your keys, or your tools, or important documents, you may find running a business more of a struggle. The work in a small business is rarely complicated, but it has to be done, and done on time. Remember, this is going to be *your* business. It's all up to you. Being organized is your key to sanity.

Reading carefully: A second important characteristic is the ability to read carefully. Most of your business transactions will be handled on paper or online, and if you don't pay attention to what you're doing, you could miss out. You may receive special orders for your product. You will be billed by suppliers in all kinds of ways, sometimes with discounts if you are prompt in paying. You will have to fill out a lot of government forms. Government agencies cannot exist without forms, and the instructions for these forms are sometimes tricky. If you mess up, these agencies have the most aggravating way of telling you that you have to do it all over again.

Numbers: A third important trait is, if not a "head for numbers," at least a lack of fear of numbers. Tax accountants get rich off of people who look at a column of six numbers and panic. It doesn't have to be that way. The math involved in running a small business is mostly simple arithmetic—addition, subtraction, and some multiplication.

Personality: If you plan to operate a retail store, a service business, or any other business where you will be in regular contact with the public, you should be a person who likes to deal with people. Are you friendly and outgoing, pleased to talk about your products—and the weather, the ball scores, and the latest neighborhood gossip? Do you like selling, solving people's problems, listening to complaints, answering the same questions over and over again? Do you look forward to running a store five, six, or even seven days a week, keeping regular hours, stocking shelves, doing repetitive tasks every day?

There are many fine people, potentially excellent businesspeople, who are not the outgoing type, who would never survive behind the counter, and who certainly shouldn't be running a retail operation. And fortunately, there are many businesses that don't require these personality traits. Internet businesses, manufacturing, some service businesses, businesses where you don't face the public every day, where you know all your customers, where you do custom work for only a few people—these businesses do not rely so much on your personality, and they won't require that you constantly act and dress a certain way.

Treating your customers well: Customers and clients come back to businesses that treat them in a friendly way and with respect. You don't have to be everyone's best buddy; just don't be surly, and don't make negative comments, even to customers you'd rather never see again. Because those customers are going to tell their friends and neighbors about your business, and word of mouth can mean success or failure for many businesses.

If you get a complaint or make a mistake, don't just fix what went wrong, add something extra as an apology, even if it wasn't your fault. You'll turn an angry customer into a loyal customer.

ONE MORE KEY TO SUCCESS . . .

Pay your bills on time. In fact, pay your bills early. Your suppliers, your landlord, your bank, everyone you do business with, will love you. They'll go out of their way to help you. You'll be "one of our best customers," and you'll get priority treatment.

What's more, if you pay your bills as soon as you get them, you don't have to keep an unpaid bills file, and you don't have to remember that a bill is due. It's one less chore to worry about.

GET SOME HELP

Is all of this too much for you? Still feel you have a good product or a good service to sell but, oh, all this paperwork!

If you are alone in your venture, there is no alternative. You just have to learn to do it. Very often, however, the future business owner with no business moxie is blessed with a spouse, a partner, or a friend who has all those fine traits and is just itchin' to be part of it all.

Mike Madsen, Mike Madsen Leather: "You talk to people who are working on a salary, they don't understand what being in business is all about. They're not risk takers. They're not striving to make a whole number of things work simultaneously. They go to work in the morning and have a prescribed routine, they get off at five o'clock, and they go home, and their business is done. But if you're in business for yourself, you don't turn off the switch when you go home. You're constantly thinking about it."

Your Idea, and the Market

Every person who has ever started a business, I imagine, thought he or she had a good idea. It's the smart person, and the rare person, who tries to find out the most important thing: Do *other people* think it's a good idea? The majority of new businesses fail because the majority of new business owners never looked past their own desires and dreams, gave no real forethought to their ventures, no "market research," which is just a fancy term for "Look before you leap."

Do people really want what you have to sell? Can you find these people and convince them that they should buy from you instead of from someone else—someone else who may have a better product, a better price, a better location, a good reputation?

No matter how good your business idea is, you still must have a "market"—someone who is willing to buy your product or pay for your services. Talk to your friends; they're consumers. How many of them would buy what you have to sell? Then look around your community. Does your product or service fit the social, economic, and ethnic makeup of the area? Will your product appeal to these people? Can they afford it?

How many other businesses in the area are doing the same thing? How well are they doing? Is there room for one more business of this type? Can you improve upon what's already out there?

As important as it is to do research, don't let it stand in the way of trying things out. Instead of spending the next six months researching the market, you could begin to spread the word, run a few ads, set up a website or Facebook page, and know more about your market and whether you have a viable business than any research will tell you. You'll know whether you have something people want and are actually willing to pay for.

Mike Simon, Metric Motors Auto Repair: "There are some people who want to work for themselves, and they're not going to be happy working for anybody else. And then other people don't like the responsibility. They want to go in and work their nine to five and not have to worry about it when they go home. It takes a certain kind of person to run your own business, to accept the responsibilities and be thinking about it all the time. The first two years I worked, I worked seven days a week from seven in the morning until seven at night. Now I take Sundays off. But I wouldn't have it any other way. I could have made more money working for somebody else, but I'm happy with the way it is. And I think in the future it will be to my advantage. As for the guy who's working nine to five, I'll be better off than he is. Of course, he thinks he's better off than I am."

BUSINESS TERMINOLOGY

Sometimes, half the battle in learning business concepts and understanding business and tax regulations is just knowing the terminology. Familiar words and expressions in the non-business world often mean something totally different in the business world. Even within business, there are different terms and different words for the same thing.

What's even more fun, businesspeople are making up new words and expressions regularly, sometimes to describe a new type of business or new way of doing business, but sometimes to hide details they'd rather you didn't know. And sometimes they just don't know what they're talking about.

Terminology is even more important in tax law. Words have very specific meanings that sometimes apply only to tax laws. Be particularly aware that terms such as "up to" and "as much as" mean that the dollar amounts shown are maximums in some circumstances and not in others. The term *"may* be required" (as opposed to *"must* be required") means that there are a lot of variables in that particular law. These terms usually show up in complicated laws with too many exceptions to list here.

Throughout the book, I try to define every word that may have multiple meanings or may be unfamiliar. But if any terminology is confusing or unclear, if you do not understand a word, a definition, or an explanation, it is important that you stop and take the time to understand its meaning before using the information.

Here are a few important definitions you should know:

- **Self-employed individual.** Self-employed individuals work for themselves. They are sole proprietors. They may not consider what they're doing to be a business, but they are, in fact, in business for themselves. There is no legal difference between owning a business and being self-employed.

- **Independent contractor.** Independent contractors (also called outside contractors) contract their services to other businesses. Independent contractors are self-employed individuals.

- **Employer/employee.** The employer/employee relationship is a formal, legal relationship, with many federal and state regulations. Self-employed individuals and independent contractors are not employees. This book is careful to distinguish between employers, employees, and self-employed individuals (nonemployees).

- **Tax deduction (tax write-off).** A tax deduction and a tax write-off are the same thing. It is a dollar amount that is subtracted from your total business income (your total sales) to arrive at your taxable income, your net profit. The dollar amounts that you can deduct are also known as "allowable business expenses."

- **Tax credits.** Tax credits are different than tax deductions. A tax deduction reduces the net profit from your business. A tax credit does not reduce your net business profit; it reduces your taxes, directly. After you figure your profit and calculate your taxes, you can apply any tax credits to lower the taxes. An item is either a tax deduction or a tax credit, not both. Tax credits are a real gold mine.

- **Personal versus business.** A personal expense is a non-business expense, and is not deductible on a business tax return. However, in tax law, the term *personal* has a second meaning. "Personal property" is any property other than real estate, and includes machinery, equipment, furniture, and other assets a business owns. This "personal" property is actually business property, a business expense.

- **Capital.** *Capital* refers to equity, or money invested in a business. An "undercapitalized" business does not have enough money to operate successfully. In tax law, the term *capital* (as in "capital assets") refers to business assets of a permanent nature, such as equipment and machinery. *Capitalize* in tax law refers to the method of deducting the cost of capital assets.

- **Credit.** The word *credit* has several meanings. *Credit* refers to whether people pay their bills on time or not, whether they have good credit or bad credit. To "buy on credit" means a customer has made a purchase but not yet paid for it; the business has "extended credit" ("sold on credit") to the customer. To "credit your account" means adding money to your account. *Credit* is a bookkeeping term, as in debits and credits, which can get confusing (and, fortunately, which I avoid in this book).

BUSINESS LOCATION

For retail stores, retail service businesses, restaurants, and other businesses where customers come to you, location is critical. A bad neighborhood, a street that's hard to find, a location away from other shops or where it's difficult to park, a store too far away from the kind of customer you seek—any of these factors can easily lead to business failure, quickly. Do not underestimate the importance of the business location. Do not settle for a poor location. Do not compromise.

Is the location in a good business area? How many people shop nearby? Is there adequate parking? Do the neighboring businesses attract the kind of customers you are looking for?

Before you rent a storefront, find out why it's vacant. Try to locate former tenants and ask why they moved. Talk to other shopkeepers in the area and learn as much as you can about the area and its shoppers. A nearby supermarket or large retail establishment is usually a plus because they draw a lot of people to the area.

Be wary if there are several unoccupied buildings for rent. Besides being a general sign of a poor business area, vacant buildings make poor neighbors. Shoppers tend to stay away from them, and from you.

Spend a full day or two observing the area. A steady stream of pedestrians passing your door is the biggest single help a store can get. Avoid side streets, even if they are right around the corner from a main shopping street. Most shoppers will not go out of their way, even a few feet, to check you out. And get a first floor location. Second floor shops are less accessible, less visible, and less inviting. Customers who don't know you will not make that commitment, will not walk up a flight of stairs.

A location on a street that many people use going to and from work will make you even more visible, especially a street with a slow speed limit. If people are whizzing by at 55 miles per hour, you're just a blur in the rearview mirror. Being close to a well-known landmark will help because it is a point of reference people can easily remember.

Finding a Business Location

Once you know the general area where you'd like to locate your business, drive around and look for empty storefronts, and for signs advertising sale or lease of the building. Even if a sign just says "For Sale," you might call anyway in case the owner is willing to consider leasing the building. Look for going-out-of-business signs.

Check business rental listings in the local newspaper and on the internet. Contact real estate offices in the area. The local chamber of commerce may have a list of available business rentals. If your city has a business development office or economic planning department, call or visit them.

MALL BUSINESSES

Renting space in a busy mall, or inside another much larger business (such as a coffee shop in a large retail business) will guarantee the customer traffic you want, but the lease payments may be high, and there may be common area maintenance (CAM) fees in addition to the rent. You probably will have to conform to rules regarding signage and appearance, and you will not be able to keep your own hours.

NON-RETAIL BUSINESSES

For businesses that don't rely on customers coming to the door—manufacturers, wholesalers, workshops, many service businesses—the location is no longer of critical concern. You can find a place suitable to your own needs: close to home, inexpensive, close proximity to your suppliers and the services you require, easy access for deliveries and pickups.

In many cities, small businesses are finding excellent facilities in old and formerly rundown industrial areas of town. Real estate developers are buying abandoned commercial and industrial buildings, fixing them up, dividing them into smaller offices, shops, and warehouse spaces, and renting them at prices much lower than the busy shopping areas.

BUSINESS INCUBATORS

Some developers offer what they call "business incubators," also known as executive suites, business centers, and serviced offices. These facilities provide, in addition to a location, shared support services such as clerical help, management counselors, conference rooms, office equipment, truck docks, and other amenities.

As the term implies, incubators are often first-step locations for new businesses. After a few years, you no longer need nor care to pay for many of the support services. You are ready to be on your own. You've been hatched, so to speak.

Some incubators are simply a rental situation: You rent space and shared services. Some incubators also offer investment financing. The individual or company providing the incubator invests in your business, participates in management, takes part ownership of your business, and shares in—and sometimes takes most of—the profits.

RENTING BY THE HOUR

If you don't need a permanent business location, but occasionally need an office to meet with a client or hold a conference, or just need to get away from an overloaded desk or too many distractions, you may be able to rent business space by the hour or by the day. In many cities and larger towns, companies that own or lease business buildings, and even some hotels, rent out business space on a temporary basis. Some of these rentals are for shared spaces. Find a seat, open your laptop. Of course, there's always the local coffee shop . . .

POP-UP BUSINESSES AND SEASONAL BUSINESSES

Location is obviously important: you need to be wherever people already are. But all the details you should consider when finding a permanent location are no longer very important. You are not stuck with a lease or a significant investment in fixing up the store. If the location turns out to be lousy, if the roof leaks, or if the building inspector suddenly shows up with a nasty grin on his face, you just move on.

THE BUILDING

Before you sign a rental agreement, be sure the building is right for you. Is it large enough, or is it perhaps too large? Measure the square footage yourself. Landlords often give out incorrect square footage information. Will the building require extensive remodeling? Make sure the roof doesn't leak. Test the heating and air conditioning. Do you control your own heating and air conditioning? How expensive will it be to heat and cool the building? Are your utilities on a separate meter from other tenants in the building? Check out exterior lighting around sidewalks and parking areas. How good is the building security?

Learn all you can about the other tenants. If their behavior and activities annoy your customers, you may lose business. Ask neighbors how they feel about the location. Are people hanging out on the corner? How will that affect your business?

Have the store examined by the local building inspector, and if you plan to serve food, by the health inspector. You don't want to learn after you've moved in that you have to spend a thousand bucks to bring the premises up to code. Don't rely on the previous tenant or the landlord for this information. Building violations are often ignored or just not noticed by the inspectors until a new business moves in.

Americans with Disabilities Act (ADA). Is the building ADA compliant? Every business that has customers who come to the premises is required to have a building that meets all ADA requirements. This is a *major* issue for businesses. The ADA laws are lengthy and very detailed, and there are lawyers who will not hesitate to sue you if your door is too narrow, or the wheelchair ramp is too steep, or the counter is too high, or . . . the list goes on and on. Do not rent a building until you see written proof of ADA compliance. If your business is not open to the public and you do not have employees that fall under ADA laws, you do not have to meet ADA requirements.

ZONING AND PERMITTED USES

Before you sign a lease, check with the local zoning department to make sure the building is zoned and permitted for your use. Just because a building is a commercial property in a commercial area doesn't mean that any type of business is allowed to operate in that location. Even if a similar business previously occupied the same building without zoning problems, it is no guarantee you'll have no problems. The old business may have been there before current zoning laws were in effect (called "grandfathering"), or the former business may have had a variance, one that may or may not be transferred to you. Find out if there are any special requirements, such as off-street parking or sign limitations. Don't rely on the landlord for any of this information.

If there are zoning or permitting problems, don't give up right away. If a certain kind of business is not permitted, see if you can structure your business in a way that fits whatever the city or county requires. Sometimes, just the wording describing your business can make the difference between being approved or rejected. Even if you don't meet the exact requirements of the zoning, zoning officials often have authority to negotiate variances, to make exceptions to the rules. Be sure to get any variance in writing.

Find out if your city requires you to conduct a "neighborhood notification," mailing notices about your proposed business to nearby residents, and giving them a legal right to challenge your proposed business if they think it does not belong in their neighborhood. Typically, neighborhood notification is required for businesses setting up in residential neighborhoods, and for businesses serving or selling alcohol (and in some states, cannabis), live entertainment venues, and massage parlors. A neighborhood notification process can take several months; in the meantime you are paying rent on an unoccupied and possibly unsuitable building.

THE LEASE

Can you get a suitable lease? Without a lease, the landlord can, with little or no notice, evict you or arbitrarily raise the rent to any amount he or she pleases. Don't count on oral agreements with a landlord. Get a written lease that covers all the details, options, and who's responsible for what. Never assume anything.

There is no such thing as a standard lease. Every provision in a lease is negotiable, and you should read and understand every word. You may have to live with it for years.

How many years will the lease run? Is it renewable, will the rent increase, and by how much? Can you get out of the lease if your business fails or if you want to move? Can you sublet? If you sell the business, can you transfer the lease to the new owner? If the landlord sells the building, will you be at the mercy of the new owner, or will the old lease be legally binding on the new owner? Can you get a protection clause in which the landlord agrees not to rent adjacent space to a competitor? Can you get first refusal if adjacent space becomes available?

Who is responsible for repairs, maintenance, janitorial, and garbage? How quickly will a problem be fixed? Who is responsible for damage due to fire, or a broken water pipe, or any other calamity? Do you have to pay rent if you are forced to close temporarily due to damage to the building? Are there restrictions on parking, or signs, or hours of use? Can the landlord enter your premises without your permission?

Most leases require tenants to have liability insurance, naming the landlord as additionally insured, to protect the landlord in case one of your customers is injured at your business. Many leases require you to have property insurance on the landlord's building and insurance covering other tenants in the building.

Lara Stonebraker owns Cunningham's Coffee, a retail store: "As far as I'm concerned, location is everything. That can make or break a business. If you don't already have an established reputation, nobody will go looking for you in some obscure place. You have to be where there is a lot of foot traffic, and you have to be located next to some other established business that already has a clientele you can draw on.

"The corner is the best choice, and you usually have to pay more rent for it. The middle of the block is less desirable because there isn't as much visibility or parking. Parking can be a great problem. I've known fine businesses to fail because people would just get exasperated not being able to find a parking space and never go in them.

"One of the things we did at every location we looked at was spend a day just sitting around, hanging around, and watching the traffic flow, the patterns of the way people walk, where they stopped, and how many people came in and out of different stores in order to assess the desirability of that location.

"Talk to the building inspector and the health inspector and find out what the building and health codes are for your particular business. We made the mistake of seeing them after we signed the lease and then discovered that we had to put in a load of

improvements that rightfully should not have been our responsibility. That was a large amount of money that was just lost. The inspectors don't check old businesses, but they check every new one. You apply for a permit, you have to get a business license, then they know what kind of business it is and they send out their people. If you're doing any construction inside, any electrical work, the plumber has to get a permit, the electrician has to get a permit. You can't get away from it."

Joe Campbell owns Computer Connection. He recently moved his shop away from a high foot traffic area to a more remote part of town: "In a service business, especially a technical service business, customers don't have the slightest idea how to determine even the most rudimentary things about their computer. If it doesn't work, they don't have the means of determining what is wrong. So you get an incredible amount of people who come in and just go on and on, like an old Kenmore on the spin cycle, about some problem which is extremely minor and usually is a hookup problem. They've just got it hooked up wrong, which means they didn't read their instruction manual. But it's hard to convince them of that, and they all want detailed explanations.

"If you're in a high foot traffic area, you get the guy who's going to the restaurant next door for lunch, and as he walks out he thinks, 'Ah, there's a computer shop. I'll stop in here and ask this guy about my problem . . .,' and he comes in and there's twenty minutes gone. Just enormous time and energy sinks. Those people don't spend money. The kind of people who spend money are the people who walk in the door with computers under their arms, and say, 'Fix this mother, it doesn't work, and call me when it's ready.'

"My traffic was never off the street. It was from referrals from computer sales dealers. I took around cards and there was such a big demand for a reasonable, good repair shop that they'd send people by.

"You don't need those twerks who walk in off the street. You need the people who have the confidence in you and, by reputation, know that they can dump it in your hands. Now, when somebody walks through that door, they've either got a computer under their arm or they're picking one up. If they're there to pick it up, that means when they leave you're going to have money in the cash register. If they're coming in the door with one, that means one week later you're going to have money in the cash register. Those are the only two reasons you want that front door to open."

ANOTHER ROADSIDE ATTRACTION: RURAL BUSINESSES

It's a dream many people have—to move to the peace and quiet of the countryside and start a relaxed, prosperous little business. Unfortunately, a large percentage of these rural shops fail. The main reason? There are not enough people and there is not enough money in rural communities to support anything but the most basic businesses.

A tropical fish store is not going to survive in West Pork Chop, Oklahoma. Nor will an art gallery or a leather crafts workshop. The business just isn't there.

Service businesses, repair shops, and trades have the best chance of survival in a rural area. But even these have to compete with established locals who know everyone in town and have all the business.

When you have a particular area in mind, get to know the area and its residents first before you try to set up a business that caters to them. Ideally, you should live in the area awhile, and then try to judge what product or service the people need. Most country people are not wealthy; they don't spend money on things they have no use for.

Many successful rural businesses do not depend on local customers. They "export" their products and services out of the area. Manufacturing and crafts businesses have retail accounts in nearby metropolitan areas. Internet businesses, publishers, designers, and some professionals and consultants can do all of their business via the internet and the phone.

However, if your country town is a tourist destination, or on a highway leading to a tourist area, an attractive little shop may do quite well. One store I knew was an instant success thanks to a sign in the window: "Restrooms inside."

HOME-BASED BUSINESSES

Over 50 percent of all small businesses in the United States are operated out of the owner's home. Depending on the kind of business you operate, the kind of customers, and the size of the business, your home may be the ideal location to start a new business. See the chapter Home-Based Business.

FINANCING

How Much Do You Need?

How much money you need depends a lot on the type of business you are starting and the type of person you are. If you are willing to work hard, make a few sacrifices, and live on canned beans for a while, you can start a successful business for little or no investment.

Every service business I know started with almost no money. I started my accounting practice with my computer, an adding machine, and a stack of business cards. My friend Joe Campbell started Computer Connection with $500 worth of parts and test equipment. Another friend's graphic design business was started with $50 in supplies. Self-employed carpenters and repair people often start with their box of tools, period.

If you start a crafts business, you will need, besides your tools, materials to make your product. But you do not have to stock a large supply of inventory, and if you hunt around you can always find good deals on remnants and closeout materials. All of the crafts business owners interviewed for this book started with less than $2,000 initial investment.

A retail store requires a good stock of inventory, which will cost at least a few thousand dollars, often a good deal more. A retail business can sometimes save on initial inventory costs by taking goods on consignment, as in a custom dress shop, or by having only samples on hand or on your website and taking orders for the goods.

In addition to the money you need to get started, you will need "working capital" (for day-to-day expenses) to operate the business until it becomes profitable. The money always seems to keep going out long before it starts coming in.

Mike Simon owns Metric Motors, a repair shop: "I started with basically nothing and built from that. I had a box of hand tools and some jacks, nothing very impressive. If I had to have a tool, I'd buy it, and then I'd have it. A lot of garage owners buy $20,000 worth of equipment right at the start and don't have the clientele to pay it off. I'd say starting out small would be a smart thing to do. Find some place that's not expensive to rent, like this place. Don't put a lot of money into tools or inventory, and try to keep your costs down to a minimum until you can build your business up."

Lara Stonebraker, coffee store owner: "The worst thing you can do is start a retail business on a shoestring. If you're undercapitalized, your store will not be impressive when you open because it will be empty.

There's nothing worse than walking into an empty store. It's bound to fail because it embarrasses people. If you don't have your shelves just crammed with stuff, if you don't have an attractive, prosperous-looking store, you might as well forget it. And you ought to have not only enough money to open the doors, but enough to run the business for the first six months, because you'll be running it at a loss for sure."

Start-Up Capital: Financing a New Business

There are three typical financing arrangements for new businesses: (1) self-financing: You put up your own money; (2) debt financing: You borrow money; and (3) equity financing: You take on an investor, a partner, or a stockholder, an individual who acquires an ownership interest in your business in exchange for start-up money.

SELF-FINANCING

Just about every new business is at least partly self-financed, and many are 100 percent self-financed. A lot of new business owners cannot find anyone to loan them money or to invest in their untested and obviously risky ventures.

Many new business owners self-finance simply because they do not want outside financing and the risk and pressure of having to pay off a loan, and do not want to worry about, or share the profits with, a partner or co-owner.

DEBT FINANCING (LOANS)

When someone lends you money, you promise to pay it back, often with a high interest rate. Most business loans are also personal loans: You, the owner of the business, personally guarantee the loan, and you must repay the loan whether your business succeeds or not, out of your personal non-business assets if necessary. This is quite different from equity financing, where you acquire a partner or an investor who only gets paid back if the business succeeds.

You have to invest in yourself. If you don't invest in yourself, how can you expect anyone else to? You have to believe enough in yourself when you're starting out to put up some time and money. You can't expect someone to come along and drop a fortune on you.

—Musician and songwriter Dick Wagner

PRIVATE LOANS

Most loans to new businesses come from relatives, friends, and acquaintances. Banks and commercial lenders don't often make loans to first-time businesspeople. Quite often, someone you know or someone you can be introduced to has some extra money and might be willing to take a chance on your business, if they like you and your idea and the terms of the financing.

There are no real standards when it comes to this kind of informal financing. People lending money will most likely want a better interest rate than they would get from a bank or from a more conventional investment. Often they already have a good idea of the rate they would like to get. The repayment terms are entirely between you and the lender.

Private loans should be in writing and should include the names and addresses of the lender and borrower, the amount, the date the loan was given, the interest rate, and the payback terms, and be signed by both parties. This is especially important for loans from relatives, so it is clear that this is a loan and not a gift. If you are unable to repay the loan, the lender can take a bad-debt tax write-off without risk that the IRS will try to say the loan wasn't really a loan, but a nondeductible family gift.

Most loans are paid back over a period of months or years, with equal periodic payments. Some loans are repaid all at once at the end of the loan period (a balloon payment). The terms are entirely up to the lender and borrower. You may want a clause allowing you to pay off the loan early without penalty if you, the borrower, so desire.

If the loan agreement is kept simple, you can write it up yourself. If the agreement gets complicated, with late-payment penalties, collateral, provisions for death of one of the parties, or other details, you will probably want help from a lawyer or a paralegal to draft the agreement.

Find out if your state requires a notary's endorsement, filing or registering the loan papers, or other requirements. Your state's secretary of state office or the county clerk can probably give you more information.

When the loan is paid off, have the lender write "Paid in full" on all copies, sign and date them, and return them to you. If the loan is recorded with the state or county, the final payoff ("reconveyance") should also be recorded.

BANK LOANS

For new businesses, bank loans are hard to get. The banks are less willing than ever to take chances on new and untested businesses and new and untested entrepreneurs. Many new businesses are looking for very small loans (small, that is, by bank standards), and banks don't make any money on those. It's a lot of time and paperwork, not to mention the risk, for little return.

Banks, however, do sometimes make small business loans, and a bank just may make one to you, if you can convince the bank that your business has a good potential for success, that you are competent and reliable, and that you have a good plan to repay the loan.

Not all banks are alike, so try several. A young progressive bank is more likely to be interested in you and your needs than staid old First Conservative, Est. 1833. The bank's advertising may indicate its willingness to do business with you.

If you have done business with or obtained a loan from a particular bank, that bank is a good place to start. When a bank knows you, knows something of your willingness and capability to repay a loan, it will be more willing to give serious consideration to your ideas. If you know influential people in the community, have them put in a word for you. "Who you know" goes a long way in all business dealings.

When you meet a banker, come well prepared. Bring a résumé that includes your general and educational background and your prior experience. Read the section on business plans at the end of this chapter, and create one. Bring a personal financial statement and a statement projecting income and expenses of your business for the first six months, or year. The section "Profit and Loss Statement" in the Keeping Records chapter will help you prepare the projections.

The bank will expect you to have some of your own money invested in your business, typically a third to half of the starting capital.

You will most likely need collateral, security to give the bank. The bank may want a mortgage on equipment or even a second mortgage on your home. This is called a "secured" loan, the only kind usually available to new businesses. "Unsecured"

loans, ones that don't require collateral, are usually available only to successful, proven businesses who are longtime bank customers.

But stop! Are you ready to risk your home or other valuables on your new business? When you borrow money for your business, you are personally liable to pay it back. If the business fails, you will be required to repay the loan from your personal funds. In taking out a loan, you are making a big personal commitment. Be sure you are not getting yourself in over your head.

When you get a loan, read the fine print. Look out for loan fees, late-payment charges, and prepayment penalties. Be very wary of any loans with variable interest rates, meaning rates that can go up after a specified period of time. Many people have been hurt badly, and many people have lost their businesses, when the interest jumped and the monthly payments suddenly doubled.

OTHER POSSIBLE LOAN SOURCES

A surprising number of people finance their new businesses with their personal credit cards. This, of course, is an expensive method, given the high interest rates most cards charge.

If there is a credit union nearby, they may be more receptive than a bank. Commercial finance companies lend to small businesses, although at high interest rates. If you own stocks and bonds, ask your broker about borrowing against the securities. If you have a retirement plan from a job or another business, you may be able to borrow from the plan or get the funds out of the plan. If you own a life insurance policy, you can borrow on the cash value of the policy.

If you buy equipment, most equipment dealers have financing plans and installment sales. Your wholesalers or suppliers may extend short-term credit. But a new business may have to operate COD (cash on delivery) with your suppliers until you are better established.

Some communities have "revolving loan" or "seed loan" funds for local businesses. Check with the chamber of commerce or city hall.

SMALL BUSINESS ADMINISTRATION (SBA) LOANS

The U.S. Small Business Administration has over a dozen different loan programs for businesses, with loans ranging from a few thousand dollars up to as much as $5 million. Some SBA loans are available to new businesses, and some loans are only for

---

If you're determined to succeed, you can find a way around any obstacle, even money.

—Nancy Ridge, Ridge Tech Company

established businesses. Some SBA loans have limited uses, such as only for purchasing buildings or equipment or only for working capital. There are special SBA loans for businesses being started by veterans, businesses in economically depressed areas, businesses in rural areas, and businesses that export. Despite the word "small," most of the SBA loan programs are available to businesses with as much as $30 million in yearly sales and as many as five hundred employees. There are a lot of big businesses in these small business programs. However, one SBA loan program is specifically geared for very small and new businesses, the Micro-loan Program, which typically makes loans under $10,000.

SBA loans do not actually come from the Small Business Administration. The SBA makes no loans to businesses. Regular banks, commercial finance companies, and community nonprofit organizations make SBA loans. The SBA guarantees these loans. If you cannot repay the loan, the SBA reimburses the lender for most of its loss.

To get an SBA-guaranteed loan, you apply to a bank or organization authorized to make SBA loans. It is up to both the lender and the SBA to decide if you'll get the loan. You will have to convince the SBA and the lender that you have the ability to operate a business successfully and that the loan can be repaid from the business earnings. Most SBA loans will require you to put up collateral, usually equipment or real estate. The lender, not the SBA, sets the term of the loan and the interest rate, within SBA limits. Most SBA loans have a 2 to 3 percent loan fee—a fee the lender charges you to make the loan. And look out: Those loan fees can run in the thousands of dollars.

SBA loans come with strings attached. The agency has a set of operating guidelines you must follow. The SBA may periodically audit your books, which can be both a help and a nuisance.

Log on to SBA.gov or contact an SBA office to find out which of their loan programs might fit your business, what the requirements are, what the loan will cost you, and how to apply. The SBA has an online application called LINC (Leveraging Information and Networks to access Capital) that matches

If you open them all the same day, they'll all be approved.

—Karen Behnke, Pacific Wellness Company, on using seventeen credit cards to finance her new business

you up with a possible lender that fits your needs. There is no charge to apply, and it does not commit you to anything.

Pat Ellington, co-owner of Kipple Antiques: "There's no point in even going to a bank unless you can say, 'Well, we've been operating now for two years, and we've established a track record, and we want to expand. We've got our books, our balance sheets, we've got good references, some people do extend us credit.' I know that from my own experience. If you go there armed with a certain amount of paperwork, a certain kind of history, you'll have fewer problems dealing with them.

"I have mixed feelings about SBA loans. Sometimes they can be gotten easily, but it's sort of like by magic. And other times, no matter what you give them, no matter what sound business approach you give them, it seems they're deaf to you. That's discouraging. It's like grantsmanship. There's a whole lot to applying, and if you don't have the art, you don't get the loan."

INTERNET LOANS

There are several well-known internet lenders, commonly known as "marketplace" or "peer to peer" (P2P) lenders. They solicit investments from individuals and then use those funds to make loans. Unlike banks and private lenders, internet lenders don't use any of their own money. They are not really lenders at all, they're brokers. Internet lenders seem to be more willing to take chances on loans that conventional lenders will not, possibly because the internet lender's own money is not at risk. And most internet loans do not require collateral. Some of the best known internet lenders are Lending Club, OnDeck Capital, Funding Circle, Kabbage, and Prosper Marketplace, but there are several others as well.

Every internet lender has its own requirements, but most of them make both business loans and personal loans. The terms are misleading, as personal loans can often be used to start businesses. What the lenders call "business loans" are usually available only to businesses that are at least one to two years old and bringing in at least $75,000 to $100,000 a year, and the loans are often restricted to certain types of businesses. Personal loans are made to individuals, including individuals who are using the loan to start a business, any kind of business, no track record required. Each lender has its own rules and restrictions on how loans can be used.

Each lender has different loan maximums and different interest rates. Someone with good credit can get a loan for as low as 5 or 6 percent interest, but people in less than ideal financial situations might have to pay as much as 30 percent interest, which is exorbitant. You'd be better off using a credit card. Also, be aware that internet loans usually come with loan origination fees: You pay a fee to get the loan, which is usually a percentage of the loan amount, typically anywhere from 1 to 6 percent. This fee is in addition to the interest you pay.

It costs nothing to apply for a loan. If it does, go to a different lender. You will be giving out a lot of personal information on the loan application, including your Social Security number. If you are unwilling to provide personal information (and trust that it will be safe), you will not be able to get an internet loan.

Don't confuse internet loan companies with crowdfunding sites such as Kickstarter. Crowdfunding sites do not lend money nor do they help you find loans. The crowdfunding sites provide a platform for you to find people who might *give* you money, not lend you money, usually in exchange for something you are offering. Crowdfunding is covered below.

LOANS TO YOURSELF

For tax and recordkeeping purposes, there is no such thing as a loan to yourself (except for corporations). Any of your own money that you put into your business is considered personal funds. It is not taxable income, the repayment is not a tax deduction, and you cannot pay yourself interest on the funds. As far as the IRS is concerned, loaning money to your own business is the same as taking money out of your right pocket and putting it in your left pocket. The reasoning behind this law will make more sense after you read the section "Sole Proprietorship." Partners in partnerships and owners of limited liability companies (LLCs) come under the same law.

Corporations: If you incorporate your business, you can loan your business money and treat it as a regular loan. But be careful. Most states require corporations to have some amount of equity capital, called *minimum capitalization*, money that you, the owner, invest in the corporation. Before you loan money to your corporation, make sure you aren't

going to run afoul of your state's capitalization requirements.

GRANTS (FREE MONEY)

Small businesses occasionally (but truth to tell, rarely) find private or foundation grants to help start or expand a business, if the business is somehow related to the mission of the granting agency. It will take some research, and caution is highly advised. Be wary of anyone pitching grant money offers, especially anyone who wants to charge you a fee to process your application. Such offers are usually bogus.

Some cities have grant fund programs for local businesses, particularly main street retail shops, to remodel or paint or decorate the storefront, or to make the business more accessible to disabled people. Ask at city hall.

The Small Business Administration sometimes offers grant money to businesses wanting to enter exporting or expand an ongoing export business.

If your business is engaged in scientific research and development (R&D), you may qualify for a federal grant under three government programs: the Small Business Innovation Research Program (SBIR), the Small Business Technology Transfer Program (STTR), and the Federal and State Technology Program (FAST). Contact the Small Business Administration or log on to its website, SBA.gov, for more information.

EQUITY FINANCING (INVESTORS)

Equity means ownership. "Equity financing" is money put up by the owner or owners of the business or by investors in the business. Self-financing is, in fact, equity financing, even though I gave it a separate category in this chapter.

An investor is someone who buys into your business, who acquires an ownership interest in your business. Investors are not lenders. They are not lending you money. An investor is taking a risk on your business, just as you are, sharing in the profits if there are any, and risking losing their investment if the business fails. The owner of the business is not obligated to repay the investor out of personal non-business funds. The typical investor, like the typical lender, is usually a friend, acquaintance, or relative.

DIVIDING THE PROFIT

How the investor and the business owner share in the profits is negotiable. A 50-50 split is common.

I've known investors to accept as little as 30 to 35 percent of the profits; some may want a much bigger cut.

An important issue to make clear up front is how you define "profit." Income, less expenses, equals profit. But what income, and what expenses, are included or excluded in determining the profit?

What about payments to you? Will you be taking money out of the business or paying yourself a wage? If so, is that wage deducted as a business expense in figuring the profit? In other words, in a 50-50 arrangement, will you get a wage *and* half of the remaining profit? Or is your wage included in your share of the profit; that is, the profit that you and your investor divides would be the income less all expenses except for any money paid to you. This is something that is negotiated between you and your investor. You may find an eager investor willing to pay you a salary and also let you take half the profit.

If you are investing any of your own money in the business, is your own investment figured in the split between the investment and the business? In other words, does your investor still get 50 percent of the profit (assuming a 50-50 split) even though you have also invested in your business? Or do you get your 50 percent of the profit for running the business and also get some of the profit attributed to the investment, which means your investor will get less than 50 percent of the entire profit (since the investor's share of the pie would be a thinner slice), something an investor may or may not go for. I hope this isn't too confusing, because it is very important to spell out exactly how the money will be shared. A misunderstanding between you and your investor will lead to nothing but trouble for both of you.

PUTTING A TIME LIMIT ON AN INVESTMENT

Investments can be for a specified, limited time or for the life of the business. How long an investor can continue to be a part of your venture is a major issue to resolve before accepting an investment. If your business is successful and profitable, your investor may want to stay for the ride for as long as possible, while you, no longer needing the investor's money, may want to cash him or her out.

MULTIPLE INVESTORS

Some businesses seek only one investor; some businesses seek multiple investors. An investor may want to be the only investor in your venture, while some investors may be agreeable to being one of several. If you have multiple investors, usually each one has a separate agreement with you. The investors themselves are independent of each other. The profits are divided among all of the investors, which as you can imagine, can get complicated.

What you don't want to do is to mislead any investors about how much of the profit they'll receive. For example, if you have a 50-50 arrangement (50 percent for the investment, 50 percent for you), all of the investors would share the 50 percent, divided between them according to whatever agreement you have with them, usually their percentage of the investment: An investor who contributed 20 percent of the money invested would earn 10 percent of the profits (20 percent of the investment's 50 percent).

LEGALLY STRUCTURING AN INVESTMENT

Investments can be set up in a variety of ways, depending on how much the investor will or will not participate in the actual running of the business, and how much liability exposure the investor wants. The investor might become a full partner in a regular (general) partnership, a limited partner in a limited partnership, a stockholder in a corporation, or a member of a limited liability company (LLC).

Regular (general) partnership: The simplest way to structure an investment is for the investor and the owner of the business to be partners in a general partnership. It is simple and cheap to set up and requires no special licensing or government oversight. It is, however, the most risky way to structure an investment. There is full personal liability exposure for the investor, not just limited to the amount of money invested. A general partnership also can give an investor a lot more say in running the business than the owner of the business might want. General partnerships are covered in the Growing Up chapter.

Limited partnerships: Limited partners are not partners in the usual sense of the word. They are investors only, with no involvement in the operation of the business. Their liability is limited to the amount of their investment. Limited partnerships are very different from general partnerships, and are subject to much greater government scrutiny. Limited partnerships are registered with the county or the state. A limited partnership must have at least one general partner (you, the owner) with full personal liability, just like a sole proprietorship or general partnership. Very few small businesses are set up as limited partnerships because of the legal complications and the costs.

Corporations and limited liability companies (LLC): Due to the many restrictions on limited partnerships, businesses wanting investors often set up as corporations or limited liability companies. Corporations and LLCs are not as tightly regulated as limited partnerships, and they offer greater liability protection. Corporations and limited liability companies are covered in the Growing Up chapter.

Legally setting up an investment arrangement is, as you can see, a *job*. So you won't be surprised to learn that there are businesses that don't follow the rules. Businesses will sometimes take on what they call "silent investors" or "silent partners," people who give the business money in exchange for a percentage of the income, but otherwise have nothing to do with the business. It's all informal. No partnership agreements or stock certificates, no government filings.

The person who owns the business deducts the investor's share of the profit as an interest payment, as though the investor had made a loan to the business. The investor reports his share of the profit as interest income on his tax return. The IRS gets its tax money, and the risk of getting in legal trouble is very low . . . if everything goes well. But if something goes wrong, if someone sues the business, there's no telling what the outcome will be. An investor could discover that he is liable for much more than his investment. I do not advocate this type of investment arrangement.

VENTURE CAPITAL

Venture capital refers to money invested in companies, typically young, cutting-edge, high-potential companies, by investors called *venture capitalists*. Venture capitalists are a different breed of investor than the people who typically help finance small businesses, such as friends, relatives, and people in the community with some money to invest. Venture capitalists make their living as investors. Venture capitalists are usually only interested in businesses that have potential for huge growth and big profits within a few years, businesses that are likely to "go public" (make a public stock offering). The typical venture capitalist has no interest in most small businesses.

When you get financing from a venture capitalist, you will be taking on a partner who not only wants a percentage of the profits but may even want ownership control (at least a 51 percent interest) in the business, to be able to take charge of the business if the investor doesn't like the way things are going.

If you want to talk to a venture capitalist, you may be able to locate one through a referral. Ask a local banker or an accountant.

COMMUNITY DEVELOPMENT CAPITAL

A different type of venture capital, community development capital, is available from community development corporations, also called certified development corporations, or CDCs. Many CDCs are nonprofit, community-operated organizations, and many receive government grants. Their goal, in addition to making money on their investments, is to encourage small-scale local enterprises and to expand local job markets. To locate a CDC, contact a regional community action agency, SBA office, or state office of community affairs.

Venture capital is also available from small business investment companies (SBICs). SBICs are licensed by the Small Business Administration, but they are privately organized and privately managed firms. They set their own policies and make their own investment decisions. The Small Business Administration often makes loans to SBICs so they can turn around and invest the money in your business. The SBA publishes a national directory of SBICs.

ONE MORE SUGGESTION . . .

When looking for lenders or investors, start with the most unlikely prospects first, so when you say the wrong things and discover the holes in your plan, you won't have blown your chances with your best prospects.

CROWDFUNDING

Several sites on the internet offer platforms for people trying to raise money for just about anything, including starting a business. These sites, known as crowdfunding or crowd-sourcing sites, let you present your "project" or your "campaign," state how much you are trying to raise, and ask for contributions.

The contributors—customers really, getting in on the ground floor of something that sounds exciting and fun to them—are offered something in return for their contributions, usually the first in line to get whatever you're hoping to be selling, or maybe a "limited edition" or autographed copy of your product. The contributors are not loaning money to you and do not share in the profits. Neither the contributors nor the crowdfunding sites acquire any ownership interest in your business. It's still all yours.

The crowdfunding websites put a time limit on your fund-raising, usually no more than sixty days, and they take a cut of the money raised, about 10 percent. Some crowdfunding sites have an "all or nothing" requirement: You meet your goal or the money is refunded to the contributors. Other sites let you keep the contributions whether you meet your goal or not. On most crowdfunding sites, there is no charge to list a project and no fee if you don't raise any money. Crowdfunding sites are a painless way to ask friends and family to "invest" in your business without embarrassing anyone. It's easy to tell people about your venture and invite them to have a look. You don't have to ask for money and stand there while your brother-in-law squirms and wishes he was somewhere else.

Money raised from a crowdfunding site doesn't have to be the only source of money for your venture. You can still seek funds from other sources or contribute your own funds, and combine them with the funds that come in from the website. The crowdfunding sites take a cut only from funds that are collected through their sites.

A business that does acquire funds through crowdfunding has an obligation to deliver whatever it offered or refund the money. The crowdfunding sites make this a requirement of all projects. The sites, however, do not enforce the rules and do not bring any legal action against failed or fraudulent businesses. The likelihood a business that raised funds and then went bankrupt getting sued is remote. The crowdfunding sites are very careful to structure transactions so the sites themselves have no legal obligations to people who lose their money.

The problem with crowdfunding sites is that there are hundreds of projects/campaigns on each site, and it is not easy to stand out. You can easily get lost among the other businesses, and everyone else, looking for financing. The more clever and colorful and unusual your presentation, the more likely it will attract attention, even reaching a level where the crowdfunding site decides to feature you.

Obtaining crowdfunding is likely to require a lot of your time and energy, much like the work you would put into promotion and marketing. And, like marketing, some business owners find crowdfunding projects to be a lot of fun, and some don't.

Two of the best known crowdfunding sites are Kickstarter and Indiegogo, but there are quite a few more, including sites that specialize in different kinds of ventures. Log on to those sites, and do an internet search for other crowdfunding sites to see if your business idea might be a good fit.

Don't confuse the crowdfunding websites with a new, federally regulated financing program also known as crowdfunding, which allows businesses to acquire small investors through the internet. This investment program, known as Regulation CF (or A-plus), is complicated to implement, and requires filing with the US Securities and Exchange Commission (the SEC). The program is more appropriate for businesses trying to raise large amounts of investment money. You can learn more from the SEC's website, sec.gov, or from one of the internet platforms that broker crowdfunding, such as WeFunder.com and StartEngine.com.

LEGAL STRUCTURE

Every new business must decide if it will start as a sole proprietorship, partnership, joint venture, corporation, or limited liability company.

Sole Proprietorship

Most new one-person businesses and self-employed individuals start as sole proprietors, simply because sole proprietorships are the quickest, easiest, and least expensive form of business to start.

If you don't incorporate or set up an LLC, and if you don't have a partner, you are automatically a sole proprietor. The simple act of starting a business or becoming self-employed legally makes you a sole proprietor. It does not matter whether you filed any forms, got any permits or licenses, notified any government agency, or filed a tax return. Sole proprietorships are discussed below.

Partnership

If you have one or more partners and if you don't incorporate or set up an LLC, you have legally started a general partnership, also called a regular partnership. It's automatic, just like a sole proprietorship. Partnerships are covered in the Growing Up chapter.

Joint Venture

Married couples who start a business together can become a partnership or can instead elect to become a joint venture (officially known as a "qualified joint venture"). Only legally married couples can start a joint venture. The section "Married Couples" in the T.C.B.: Take Care of Business chapter explains the options for setting up a spousal business.

Corporation or Limited Liability Company

To become a corporation, nothing is automatic. You file incorporation papers with your state department of corporations, prepare articles of incorporation and bylaws, issue state-approved stock certificates, and pay registration fees and corporate franchise taxes.

A limited liability company (LLC) is similar to a corporation, but with different ownership requirements and tax structure. To set up an LLC, you register and file special LLC forms with your state. Corporations and LLCs are covered in the Growing Up chapter.

A business can start as a sole proprietorship, a partnership, or a joint venture and incorporate or become an LLC at any later date. In fact, most small corporations started as unincorporated businesses and incorporated after they were successful and found a real need to incorporate.

SOLE PROPRIETOR

The Traditional One-Person Business

A one-person business that has not incorporated is known as a *sole proprietorship*. There are over twenty million small businesses in this country, and most of them are sole proprietorships. This form of business has flourished because of the opportunities it offers to be the boss, run the business, make the decisions, and keep the profits. A sole proprietorship is the easiest form of business to start up. Despite all the regulations, it is the least regulated of all businesses.

Sole proprietors may call themselves business-people, shopkeepers, entrepreneurs, self-employed, artists, craftspeople, artisans, tradespeople, network or multilevel marketers, direct sellers, drop shippers, sales reps, manufacturers, inventors, employers, moonlighters, full-time, part-time, sideline, you name it. Legally, if you don't incorporate or form a partnership or an LLC, you are a sole proprietor; your business is a sole proprietorship.

Self-employed consultants, professionals, freelancers, outside and independent contractors, contingent workers, free agents, and people who are doing contract work for businesses (sometimes called outsourced work, virtual assistants, or external service providers) should understand that they are also sole proprietors. I can't tell you how many times someone has come up to me and said, "I don't have a business; I'm an independent consultant." It doesn't matter what you call yourself. Unless you are on someone else's payroll as an employee, with tax withholding and W-2 wage statements, you do have a business, you are a sole proprietor.

You, the owner of the business, the sole proprietor, are your own boss. You make or break your business, which may sound singularly appealing to those of you instilled with the entrepreneurial, pioneering spirit.

ON-DEMAND WORKERS

People providing services in the on-demand economy—also known as the sharing economy, gig economy, or 1099 economy (referring to the IRS form that their companies give them to report their income)—are self-employed. While on-demand businesses are often operated quite differently than conventional businesses, the on-demand workers are independent contractors just like any other self-employed individuals. You may consider yourself as working for Uber or Lyft or some other "platform," but legally, you are working for yourself. See the chapter On-Demand Economy.

LEGAL LIABILITY OF THE SOLE PROPRIETORSHIP

Legally, a sole proprietor (the owner of the business) and the sole proprietorship (the business itself) are one and the same. All business debts and obligations are the personal responsibility of the owner. Lawsuits brought against the business can be taken from the personal assets of the owner. Claims against the owner of the business, personal claims having nothing to do with the business, can be taken from business assets. In other words, a sole proprietor is fully and personally 100 percent liable for everything that happens to the business.

You should be fully aware of these legal aspects of the sole proprietorship. If you get your business into legal trouble or too far into debt, not only could you lose your business, you could lose your shirt.

The only way to avoid the unlimited personal liability of the sole proprietor is to incorporate or set up an LLC. Generally speaking, the debts of corporations and LLCs are limited to the assets of the business and are not the personal responsibility of the owner or owners. LLCs and corporations are covered in the Growing Up chapter.

TAXABLE PROFIT OF THE SOLE PROPRIETORSHIP

Sole proprietors file a Schedule C "Profit or Loss from Business" (or for some small businesses, a Schedule C-EZ) that is part of your 1040 return, and pay personal income taxes on the profit. Sole proprietorships are, to use the IRS's terminology, "pass-through entities": All the profits "pass through" the business to the owner, the sole proprietor, who pays the tax. The business itself does not pay income tax. The sole proprietor also pays self-employment tax, which is Social Security/Medicare tax, in addition to income taxes. These taxes are covered in detail in the Taxes chapter.

PAYING YOURSELF A WAGE

You, as the owner of a sole proprietorship, cannot hire yourself as an employee. This is a point of law often misunderstood by new businesspeople. You cannot put yourself on the payroll. You cannot pay yourself a wage and deduct it as a business expense. You may withdraw (that is, pay yourself) as much or as little money as you want, but this "draw" is not a wage, you do not pay payroll taxes on it, and you cannot claim a business deduction for it. The profit of your business, which is computed without regard to your draws, is your "wage," and is included on your personal income tax return.

For example, if your business made a $40,000 profit last year, you personally owe taxes on $40,000. If you withdrew (paid yourself) less than $40,000—or, for that matter, if you didn't even take a penny out of the business—you still pay taxes on $40,000. If you withdrew more than $40,000, you still pay taxes only on $40,000. Owner's draw is covered in more detail in the Keeping Records chapter.

CHOOSING A BUSINESS NAME

Thinking up a name for your business can be a lot of fun, an opportunity to let your creativity and your imagination take charge.

Business names can be descriptive (Computer Cave, Pinball Resource) or vague (Facets, Natural Choice), cute (We Be Stylin'), or professional (Julia Kaye Designs). Business names can be totally made-up words (Verizon, Intel) or real words whose meaning has nothing to do with what your business actually does (Apple) or a family name (JCPenney). Or your business name can be downright uncommunicative: "Acme Enterprises" tells people absolutely nothing.

Here are some considerations:

1. Choose a name that is pleasant, easy to pronounce, easy to spell, easy to remember. If your customers choke or stumble on your business name every time they mention it, fewer people will hear about you.

2. Customers who hear your business name once, or see it listed on the internet or in the yellow pages, form an immediate impression of who you are. Think like a customer. Does your name sound like a company a customer would want to contact?

3. If you want people to connect the business with you personally, using your own name as the company name may be the best choice.

4. Be wary of cute names and current popular expressions; they get stale over time. Be wary of intentionally misspelled words. "Kute Kids Klothes" may seem to be a clever name for a business, except for customers who spell it wrong and can't find you in the phone book.

5. Avoid a name that's similar to another business. Customers will confuse you with them. The town I live in has two local print shops, one called Printing Plus and one called Printing Xpress. I can never remember which is which.

6. Consider a name that starts with a word that describes your business (Dog Star Grooming, Flower Lady, etc.) so people who can't remember your business name might find it by looking up a "key" word.

7. If you will be doing business overseas, investigate whether your name may be offensive or otherwise embarrassing when translated or spoken in another country.

8. Avoid names beginning with articles, which can result in your business being listed under "The" or "An."

9. If customers are likely to look for you in a directory, there may be an advantage to being close to the beginning of the alphabet. Customers go to the yellow pages and start calling with the As, and stop when they find what they want.

10. Don't be trapped by a name that may limit future growth or change. What happens when Main Street Music moves to State Street? Or when The Silver Jeweler switches to gold or diamonds?

11. If you plan to have a website or a Facebook page, and if you want your domain name or your page to be the same as your business name, you should check first to see if the name is already taken.

12. Your state may restrict the use of certain words in business names. In many states, you cannot use words such as "Real Estate" or "Construction" or "Psychologist" or even "Barber" unless you are licensed.

Registering a Business Name

The next step is to find out if you can legally use the business name you've selected. There are local and state business name registrations, trademark laws, and internet domain name issues, and they occasionally overlap and conflict.

DBA: Doing Business As (Fictitious Name Statement)

When a business goes by any name other than the owner's real name, the business is being operated under a fictitious name, also known as an assumed name, an FBN, or a DBA—doing business as. Country Comfort Carpentry, Johnson Plumbing, and Ralph's Cleaners are all examples of fictitious names.

People doing business under a fictitious name are required to file a fictitious name statement (or assumed name certificate, or DBA, or whatever it's called in your state). In some states, the statement is filed with the state; in some states it is filed with the city or county.

Filing a fictitious name statement prevents any other business in the county or in the entire state (depending on your state's law) from using the same business name, with a few important exceptions covered below.

In addition to filing for the fictitious name, in some states you may be required to publish the fictitious name statement in a local newspaper, the theory being that the public has a right to know with whom they are doing business. The government office that handles fictitious names will provide you with a list of acceptable newspapers. Publication costs can be relatively low if your county or state has one of those newspapers that specialize in running legal notices (and little else). If not, small-time newspapers almost always charge less than large-circulation dailies. (And yes, times have really changed since most of these laws were passed. Newspapers are not read by most people anymore, and some states are reconsidering and updating their DBA laws.)

In most states, you will be required to renew your fictitious name periodically, usually once every five years. This is something you need to find out and remember. Your state may or may not send you a notice when your renewal is due. If you fail to renew, someone else can step in and file for your business name, and you will not be able to use it any more.

You usually don't have to register for a fictitious name if you use your real name as your business name, such as "Julia Smith." If, however, you are doing business as "Julia Smith Company" or "Julia Smith, Attorney at Law" or "Julia Smith's Bookstore," some but not all states consider this to be a fictitious name, subject to regular fictitious name rules.

Corporations and LLCs: Unless you are operating under a name other than the legal name of the business, you do not usually need to file a fictitious name statement. But you should verify this, as local rules vary from state to state.

Partnerships and joint ventures: In some states, these businesses must file a fictitious name statement unless operating under the full names of all the partners.

When you pick a name or several names you like, log on to the website for the county or state office that handles fictitious names or visit their office, and look at their alphabetical list of all names. If you live in a large urban area, you may find that your first, second, *and* third choices are all already taken. You can try to contact the person who owns the business name and find out if the business is still in existence. If it isn't, and if the owner of the name consents, an abandonment statement can be filed, whereby the prior owner gives up all rights to the name. You may simultaneously file a fictitious name statement for the name. The former owner will probably want you to pay the cost of filing the statement of abandonment and may even want you to pay him a fee for his trouble.

You should be aware of possible trouble if you select a business name that is already being used by an out-of-county or even an out-of-state business. Corporations are usually granted exclusive statewide use of a business name, assuming they were the first in the state to choose the name. Some states grant statewide trade name protection to businesses. Your state's secretary of state maintains a list of business names claimed by corporations and other businesses licensed by the state.

Trademarks and Business Names

Just because the county or the state approved your DBA or the state approved your corporate name, doesn't mean some other company can't stop you from using it if that company has filed a trademark on the name.

Most large businesses and many small businesses obtain federal trademarks. Trademark law is covered in the T.C.B.: Take Care of Business chapter, but generally, a business with a federally registered trademark sometimes has exclusive use of that name throughout the United States.

Locate a copy of the Federal Trademark Register (try your library) or search online at the U.S. Trademark Office's website, USPTO.gov, and look up your proposed business name.

In addition to federal trademarks, states issue in-state trademarks, valid only in the state where the business is located and the trademark is issued. Check your state's trademark database to see if anyone has claimed the business name you want to use. Your state's website probably can lead you to its list of in-state trademarks.

If your business name is the same as or similar to a trademarked name, you may have problems, particularly if your goods or services are similar to those carrying the trademark.

What happens if you start your business and find out later that some other business has prior claim to your business name? You will probably get a "cease and desist" letter from some lawyer telling you that you are in violation of the law and that you must cease using that business name, or else they'll take you to court, seek damages, etc., etc. At that point you can decide if you really are in the wrong, and right or wrong, do you want to fight it in court? There are few clear-cut answers in this area of law. Often, unfortunately, it comes down to who has the most money for lawyers.

Another suggestion: Check local telephone directories and national trade directories for your type of business. Type your proposed business name in a search engine and see what other businesses show up. Trademark or no trademark, try to avoid a business name already in use.

LICENSES AND PERMITS

The Pledge of Allegiance contains 31 words. Lincoln's Gettysburg Address, 268 words. The Declaration of Independence, 1,322 words. Federal regulations governing the sale of cabbage, 26,911 words.

When you open a new business, every government agency that can claim jurisdiction over you wants to get into the act. There are forms to file, permits and licenses to obtain, regulations and restrictions to heed. And, always, fees to pay.

Why all the government regulations? Why does water flow downhill? It's just the nature of government to regulate, license, permitize, officialize, "fees, fines, and forms" you to death.

Some of the laws were passed to protect the consumer public from unscrupulous or incompetent businesspeople. Some laws were created solely to provide additional revenues to the government. Some . . . well, who knows.

Most business licenses and permits are required and administered by local governments: the city, if you live within city limits; possibly the county. Some businesses must also have state and federal licenses. This chapter will describe the different

---

We thought it was a good enough name for a band. Plus, we might get sued by the Shell Oil Company, which would be worth millions of dollars in promotion.

— Jan Drees, of the band The Shell Corporation

licenses and permits typically required by states and municipalities and those currently required by the federal government.

Regulations vary from city to city and state to state, and they are changing all the time. You should contact state and local government agencies, anonymously if you prefer, to learn the current requirements and restrictions. All states, and most cities and counties, have their business requirements posted online. Many local and state government agencies let you file forms and get permits online.

To visit your state's main website, go to www .state.[your state's two-letter abbreviation].gov. For specific state agencies or for your city or county, type in the name of the agency, city, or county in a search engine. Just be sure you are getting your information directly from the government agency and not from another source, which may be inaccurate or out of date. If the website you find doesn't end in .gov you are probably at the wrong place.

Local Business Licenses

A local business license, if required, is merely a permit to do business locally. Most business licenses are simply a revenue-raising tax imposed on a business, offering no benefits to the business (other than that nice-looking piece of paper you get to thumbtack on the wall).

Some states, counties, and cities require all businesses to get a business license. In many states, no licenses are required at all. Some localities require licenses only for certain types or sizes of businesses. Some cities require "home occupation permits" or similar special licenses only for home-based businesses.

Local business licenses can cost anywhere from $30 or $50 to as much as several hundred dollars, and must be renewed monthly, quarterly, or annually depending on local requirements. The size and the type of business and the amount of income sometimes determine how much the license will cost. Ask about the fee structure, and see if you can define your business so it will fit into the least expensive category.

A few large cities issue "business registration certificates" in addition to a business license, charging for both.

In some states, the business license is a combined license, DBA, and sales tax permit.

Bob Matthews, owner of Country Comfort Carpentry: "I never filed a DBA. I liked the name, and right on the checks and letterheads it says 'Country Comfort Carpentry' with my name immediately under it. I felt that's good enough. I never got a business license. I'm in a rural area, twenty miles from town. I feel that business licenses are a tax on people who work in town, to make them conform."

Other Local Permits

Your business may be required to conform to local zoning laws, building codes, health requirements, and fire and police regulations. You may be required to get a use permit to operate your business in a new location.

I suggest that you contact your local government before you open your doors. If you do not get the proper permits or meet the local building codes, the city or county can shut you down.

Help from Local Government

Many cities, particularly smaller ones in economically depressed areas, are eager to help new businesses locate in their jurisdiction, especially businesses that will be hiring local people. The city will help you through the red tape, and they are likely to help if you have minor zoning or building code problems. Ask at city hall if they have any kind of economic development program or assistance.

Key Dickason, partner in Major Dickason's Blend, a coffee store: "My partner is an honest, law-abiding person, and he wanted everything A-OK. Then he found out that what the health inspectors required would cost $2,000: a three-compartment sink, molding all around the bottom of the restrooms. The sink could not be where we wanted it, it had to be in the storage room, and the storage room had to be repainted.

"The reason? Well, it's my opinion that the regulatory agencies are loaded with 'genus clerks,' and the only thing that they can see is the letter of the law. *Genus* is Latin for family. I say it's a subspecies of *Homo sapiens*, and you run across this type of person all the time. When they come in and you're serving coffee in paper cups, they look it up in their book and they say, 'Oh, serving beverages. It's a restaurant.' Then they say that you have to comply with this regulation, and they cite book and verse.

"We've been in business a year and haven't done any of the things they demanded. We didn't have the money. When the health inspector comes, he looks around, he says, 'The place is clean, it's nice.' That's it. There's no pressure to comply with the written directive. If they plan to shut us down, then they'd say, 'You have thirty days to comply.' Well, then you do it."

Jim McFeely, interviewed in *Inc.* magazine: "When my partner and I asked the city of Grand Rapids what was needed to open a business, we were told we needed only two things: a business license and a sales tax license. We obtained the licenses and opened a downtown flea market. We advertised our grand opening, offering nail polish for 25¢ and a package of noodles for 25¢.

"On opening day we got nailed by city licensing for not having a license to sell paint (nail polish), by grocer licensing for not having a day-old variance, and by the fire marshal for not having $900 in fire extinguishers. Two men showed up and demanded to inspect the freight elevator, which hadn't run since 1935. Inspection fee: $285. We received forms for business activity taxes, interim business taxes, and inventory taxes. When we hired a woman, we got this huge form from the unemployment office that looked like a wallpaper sample book.

"There were just the two of us. We closed our business forever. One week later we were cited for failure to get a going-out-of-business license. A week after that, the mayor appeared on TV saying, 'We have to seek new ways to attract business to Grand Rapids.'"

State Licenses

Most sales businesses (except those that sell alcoholic beverages or firearms), most manufacturing businesses, and many service businesses do not need state licenses.

States have traditionally licensed doctors, nurses, lawyers, accountants, architects, engineers, contractors, real estate and insurance agents, and other professionals. Many states also license auto mechanics, marriage counselors, psychologists, pharmacists, barbers, bill collectors, funeral directors, pest control businesses, private investigators, plumbers, travel agents, caterers, day care centers, tour operators, even dry cleaners, to name a few.

These occupational licenses are usually issued for one- or two-year periods and, as always, for a fee. Some of the occupational licenses require the licensee to pass a test. Some have education and experience requirements. Contact your state's agency for consumer affairs to inquire about possible licensing of your business. Every state agency has a website. Agencies have offices at the state capital and usually in the larger cities around the state.

SALES TAX

Every state except Alaska, Delaware, Montana, New Hampshire, and Oregon has a state sales tax. Many counties and cities (including some counties and cities in Alaska and Montana) also have a sales tax, which is usually reported on one combined statewide sales tax return. Merchants are required to collect sales tax from their customers and remit the tax to the states.

Some states have different names for their sales tax: sales and service tax, general excise tax (which should not be confused with federal excise taxes), retailer's occupation tax, transaction privilege tax, or gross receipts tax (not to be confused with an income tax that is also called a gross receipts tax, which is covered in the Taxes chapter).

Depending on the dollar volume of business, you will have to prepare monthly, quarterly, or annual sales tax returns, to report your sales and pay the taxes collected. Some states let you keep a portion of the sales tax you collect as a payment for the cost of collecting it.

Who Is Liable for Sales Tax

Every state with a sales tax requires businesses located in the state to report all in-state sales: in-person sales and all telephone, mail order and internet sales shipped or delivered to in-state addresses.

If your business makes sales to customers outside your state—telephone, mail order, or internet sales that are shipped to another state—your own state does not tax these out-of-state sales, but you may be liable for sales tax in the state where the goods are being shipped to. This is covered below.

If your business has a physical presence in more than one state—if you have facilities or employees in another state, or if you are making in-person sales in another state—you will be liable for taxes in the states where you are doing business. This is also covered below.

What Is Taxable: Retail versus Wholesale Goods

In every state with a sales tax, retail goods (goods sold to the public; and goods sold to businesses for their own use, not for resale or manufacture) are subject to sales tax. Wholesale goods are exempt from sales tax, except for Hawaii, which has sales tax on wholesale goods.

Special note: Don't confuse "wholesale" with "discount." Wholesale refers to goods that are sold by one business to another, to resell or to go into a manufactured product. The ads in the papers that say "Wholesale to the Public," "Wholesale—Factory to You," or some other misuse of the word are actually referring to discount retail sales, subject to sales tax.

If you pay sales tax on goods you purchase but then resell, you still have to charge sales tax to your retail customers. You can claim a credit on your sales tax return for the duplicate sales tax paid.

What Is Taxable: Services

Services such as repairs or construction, professional services, and labor charges are taxed in some states, exempt in others. In states where services are exempt from sales tax, some businesses have problems over the definition of what is a service (not taxable) as opposed to a product (taxable). For example, is expensive custom-designed software a taxable product or a nontaxable service? The same question applies to the work of freelance artists, graphic designers, and the like. Find out if your work is subject to sales tax. Sometimes the people in the sales tax office are unsure, so ask to see the rules in writing. A carefully worded contract or invoice that separately bills taxable and nontaxable items may be needed.

The time you or your employees put into manufacturing, fabricating, or assembling a product is not considered a service; it is part of the cost of the product.

What Is Taxable: More (and More) Rules

Many states tax restaurant meals but exempt groceries. Some states tax hot takeout food but not cold takeout food. (No, I'm not kidding.) Some states exempt shipping and handling charges, newspapers, magazines, prescription drugs, clothing, postage, manufacturing equipment, and printing. Goods used for samples, demonstration, or display are considered resale (nontaxable) by many states. Many states tax leased property and rentals. Downloaded music, books, and software are subject to sales tax in some states, and exempt in others. Sales to state and local government agencies are taxable in some states, exempt in others. Sales to U.S. government agencies are exempt from sales tax in all states.

Some states require that the price tag on taxable items include the words "plus tax" or a similar statement.

You've probably seen advertisements that say something like, "This Month Only: No Sales Tax." Well, there actually is sales tax, but the seller is absorbing it, paying it out of his or her own pocket, or lowering the actual sale price so the lower price plus the tax equal the advertised price. Some states, however, disallow this practice.

Building contractors: In some states, sales tax paid on building materials can vary, dramatically, depending on whether you have a "lump sum" contract or a "time and materials" contract. You should get information from your state sales tax department. The right wording may save you and your customers a lot of money.

Seller's (Reseller's) Permits

Every state that collects a sales tax issues seller's permits (also called a reseller's permit, resale number, resale license, sales tax certificate, certificate of authority, or something similar), and every in-state business that sells goods, parts, or taxable services must have one. In some states, seller's permits are good for as long as you own the business. In some states, the permits must be renewed annually.

Some states will require a security deposit from you before issuing you a seller's permit, which is the state's way of guaranteeing that you will file your sales tax returns and pay what is owed. After a year of paying your sales tax on time, you usually get your deposit back. In lieu of a deposit, most states will let you purchase a sales tax bond from an insurance company.

When a new business applies for a seller's permit, the sales tax people may ask you to estimate your taxable sales, and base the deposit on your estimate. Since you have no idea what your sales will be, no law requires you to be overly optimistic. Keep your sales estimate low, and you may avoid a deposit altogether.

Besides registering you as a seller, a seller's permit gives you the right to buy goods for resale, both finished products and the materials that go into products you manufacture, without paying sales tax to your supplier. Only goods that will be resold or manufactured in the normal course of business can be purchased tax-free (except in Hawaii, which taxes wholesale goods). You may not use your seller's permit to make tax-free purchases of office supplies, furniture, equipment, or goods for personal, non-business purposes.

Businesses that sell wholesale goods to other businesses without charging sales tax are required to keep a record of all customers who make tax-free purchases. Your customers must give you their resale numbers before you can sell to them tax-free. States often provide forms, called "exemption certificates," for this purpose. Usually, you only have to get one exemption certificate from each customer the first time you sell to that customer. You keep your customers' resale numbers and the exemption certificates on file. You don't send them to the county or state. Some states require you to verify your customers' resale numbers, by calling a toll-free number or logging on to a state website, before selling to them.

By the way, no business is *required* to sell goods tax-free to a business with a resale license. Some businesses just don't want to hassle with the paperwork, and require all of their customers, retail and wholesale, to pay sales tax (which is a fast way to lose your wholesale customers).

Sales Tax Rates

Some states have one sales tax rate that applies to the entire state. Most states, however, have different tax rates in different counties and cities. If you are selling goods locally, to a customer who lives in your city or who comes to your business in person to purchase goods, you charge the local sales tax rate.

If you are shipping goods within your state but outside of your local jurisdiction, what rate you charge depends on your state's rules. In a few states, you charge the tax rate where you, the seller, are located. This is known as "origin-based" rates, and it definitely makes tax calculations easy, as you only need to know your own location's sales tax rate. Origin-based states are Arizona, Illinois, Mississippi, Missouri, New Mexico, Ohio, Pennsylvania, Tennessee, Texas, Utah, Virginia,

and California, though California has a convoluted hybrid formula (it is California).

Unfortunately, the majority of states use what's called "destination-based" rates, requiring you to collect the tax at the tax rate where the goods are sent. In a large state, there could be a hundred or more different tax rates in the state. If you are in a destination-based state, you will need an app or a table to look up the rate for each destination.

Doing Business in Other States

If you have an office, warehouse, or store in another state, or if you or your employees are regularly traveling through and selling or servicing your goods in another state (what's called "nexus," a physical presence), you will be required to file sales tax returns in that state for all taxable sales made in that state. You do not pay the sales tax to both states, only to the state where the sale was made. States often refer to out-of-state businesses who have locations or make sales in their state as "remote sellers."

This law also applies to craftspeople and others who are traveling from state to state, selling at fairs and special events. Craft fair and trade show organizers usually have sales tax forms to fill out right on the spot, and they often will collect your money right on the spot, at the end of the show.

Drop shipping: Drop shipping means that you contract with another business to warehouse and ship products for you. If the business that is warehousing and shipping goods for you is in another state, you may or may not have to collect sales tax from customers in that state. Different states have different sale tax rules for drop shipments. Your drop shipper may know the answer, or you may have to contact the taxing agencies in the states involved. This is a different situation than renting and staffing a warehouse and shipping facility of your own.

Shipping Goods to Customers in Other States

Your own state does not charge sales tax for sales that you ship or deliver to out-of-state customers. But the states where your customers reside can, if they choose, require you to collect their state sales tax and remit the tax to those states.

This interstate sales tax requirement is new. For many years, no business was required to charge sales tax on out-of-state sales. The Supreme Court recently reversed a decades-old rule, and now every state will be figuring out how to collect sales tax from businesses all over the country. How states will try to enforce their sales tax laws on thousands upon thousands of out-of-state businesses is unknown right now. States will probably have to simplify their tax rates and reporting requirements. Some states will exempt small businesses with low-dollar sales in their states. Some states may establish elaborate systems for registering out-of-state businesses and enforcing laws. Some states may just accept whatever businesses decide to report and not do any follow-up.

What should you do? As this is being written, no one knows how individual state sales tax laws will be administered or enforced. I suggest that, for now, you follow the laws as they have been administered in the past: collecting sales tax (if required) on in-state sales and not collecting sales tax on out-of-state sales. If and when some state finds you and notifies you that you are required to collect their sales tax, first find out if there is an exemption for small businesses. If there isn't, well, you pay up.

What you should not do is charge sales tax to out-of-state customers until you know what to do with those taxes when you collect them. If you hold onto the tax money, that could be considered theft or fraud. And if you just send the money to the customer's state, they probably won't know what to do with it, and it will sit at the bottom of some clerk's in-box until he retires.

Use Tax

Out-of-state sellers may or may not charge sales tax, but in most states, buyers are required to pay sales tax whether the seller collects it or not. If a seller does not charge the tax, the buyer is supposed to pay the tax directly to the state where the buyer resides.

No, I'm not kidding. It is called a "use tax" (sometimes called a "compensating tax"). State income tax returns often include a line where you estimate the use tax you owe and pay it along with your state income taxes. This is not a well-known law, and, as you can imagine, it is not easy to enforce.

Purchases that businesses originally made for resale (purchased tax-free) but used for another purpose, such as personal use, are subject to the use tax. Your sales tax return has a line where you calculate the use tax you owe on these purchases and pay it with the sales tax you collected from your customers.

OTHER STATE REGULATIONS

To find out about other state requirements, contact the secretary of state or consumer affairs office. Most states publish booklets or provide online information for state requirements. Call or visit your state office or log on to your state's website. As I caution elsewhere, make sure you are on the government agency's site and not a private business or organization. Most government websites end in .gov. Here are a few common state regulations:

- States regulate finance charges imposed on customers.

- Some states regulate shipping and handling charges billed to customers.

- States have privacy laws protecting customer information, including information stored online.

- Truckers, taxicab operators, bus lines, and household movers must register with the state public utilities commission.

- Businesses operating factories or other potential air and water polluting equipment must meet state air- and water-quality requirements.

- Repair shops may need bonds or proof of solvency. Sellers of meat products, firearms, and alcoholic beverages may require state registration and permits. Many professionals and most financial services are licensed by the states. Many states require telephone marketers to be registered. (I think they ought to be jailed.)

- Employers may be subject to state wage and hour laws and occupational safety and health laws. State employment laws are covered in the Growing Up chapter.

- States have the legal right to restrict sales of regulated products (such as firearms, alcohol, and tobacco) sold to state residents, regardless of where the seller is located. If your business sells products that might be regulated, you may have to research and abide by the laws in all fifty states.

FEDERAL REGULATIONS

Federal Identification Numbers

Your business will be required to identify itself on tax forms and licenses by either of two numbers:

your Social Security number or a Federal Employer Identification Number (called FEIN or more often, EIN).

Sole proprietors can use either number, your choice, except in situations where you must get an EIN. You must get an EIN if:

1. You hire employees.

2. Your business is a partnership, corporation, or LLC.

3. You are required to file a federal excise tax return (covered in the Taxes chapter).

4. You set up a qualified retirement plan (covered in the Taxes chapter).

5. You purchase or inherit an existing business.

6. Your state or other government agency, a vendor or customer, your bank, or your insurance company requires you to have an EIN.

As you can see, although the federal identification number is called an "employer" identification number, the EIN is used by any business that needs a federal ID number, whether the business has employees or not.

Many sole proprietors get EINs even when not required, because the sole proprietors do not want to give out their Social Security number to customers and vendors.

The fastest way to get an EIN is online at IRS.gov or by calling the IRS toll-free at (800) 829-4933. You can also fill out and file Form SS-4 "Application for Employer Identification Number" with the IRS.

If you are getting an EIN but will not be an employer, be careful how you fill out Form SS-4. On line 13, for number of employees, put zero. Remember, you are not an employee of your own business unless you incorporate. Leave line 14 blank. For line 15, first date wages are paid, leave blank or put "not applicable," or N/A. (If you will be hiring employees, see the Growing Up chapter on filling out Form SS-4.)

You get one EIN per business, even if the business has more than one location. You keep the same EIN for as long as you own the business, even if you move. If you have more than one business, you should have separate EINs for each business.

Federal Licenses

Most small businesses do not need any federal licenses. The federal government licenses all businesses engaged in common carrier transportation; radio and television station construction; manufacture of drugs, alcohol, or tobacco products; preparation of meat products; manufacture or sale of firearms; and investment counseling. Contact the Federal Trade Commission, Washington, DC 20580, or online at FTC.gov.

Federal Agencies: Business Regulations

Although you may not need any federal licenses and do not need to register with any federal agencies, there are many federal laws regulating all kinds of businesses. The Federal Trade Commission and a dozen other federal agencies have laws that every business must follow. The agencies publish free booklets and list their business regulations on their websites. For general information, try business.usa.gov or, for the Federal Trade Commission (FTC), go to FTC.gov. Or type in the name of the law or agency in a search engine.

A few of the more important regulations:

Guarantees and warranties for goods must comply with the Magnuson-Moss Warranty Act. A *warranty* refers to the product itself: It will perform as promised for a given period of time. A *guarantee* is a promise of customer satisfaction: The customer can get an exchange or refund even if the product lives up to its warranty. You are not required by law to offer a guarantee or a warranty. But if you do, you are required to honor it. Some warranties must be made available to customers before they buy.

The Magnuson-Moss Act covers goods. Services are exempt from the act.

Internet, mail order, phone, and fax sales businesses must comply with the Mail, Internet, or Telephone Order Merchandise Rule, also known as the 30-Day Rule: Sellers must ship merchandise within their stated time, or if no time is stated, within thirty days. If there is a delay, the seller must notify the buyer of the delay, and give the buyer a cost-free option (a toll-free number, postage-paid reply card, or email) to cancel the order and receive a full refund within seven days.

Door-to-door sales businesses, and businesses that make face-to-face sales to consumers away from a regular business location (such as presentations at someone's home or at conventions), must give buyers three business days to change their minds and cancel their order. This is called the Cooling Off Rule. This rule does not apply to mail order or internet sales, sales to businesses, sales under $25, emergencies, vehicles, real estate, securities investments, or crafts sold at craft shows.

Telephone and fax marketers must comply with the Telemarketing and Consumer Fraud and Abuse Prevention Act, the Telemarketing Sales Rule, the Telephone Consumer Protection Act, and the Junk Fax Prevention Act. Unsolicited faxes are prohibited unless you have an established business relationship. Yes, all of those junk faxes are illegal.

Telemarketers are required to comply with many FTC restrictions, which of course they all do. Unsolicited telephone marketing is prohibited if people have signed up for the Federal Do Not Call list and during certain times of the day. (Ha ha ha. Last year, the Federal Trade Commission received over 300,000 complaints about unsolicited telephone calls.)

Packages and labels must conform to the Federal Fair Packaging and Labeling Act. Basically, a label must identify the product, list the manufacturer, packer, or distributor, and show the net quantity, both inch/pound and metric. The act specifies how the label must be printed and where on the goods it must appear.

Textiles, fabric, wool, furs, and clothing must be labeled according to a variety of FTC rules. Generally, a label must state (1) the fiber composition of the fabric; (2) country of origin; (3) names or registered identification numbers of the manufacturer and the business marketing the fabric; and (4) care and cleaning instructions. Warning labels are required on certain products that can injure people, or that may be unsuitable for children or may cause damage. The U.S. Consumer Products Safety Commission (cpsc.gov) has a list of products that require warning labels.

Even if a warning label is not required by law, you may want to include such a label if your product might cause harm or damage, to protect your customers, and possibly to protect yourself in case of a lawsuit.

Advertising, product offers, and claims in print and on TV, radio, and the internet are regulated by the Federal Trade Commission and the Food and Drug Administration (FDA).

Advertising may not be deceptive or misleading. (I am just quoting the law; at least half the advertising I've ever seen is deceptive or misleading.) However, bragging, generalized praise, and "puffery" are okay (well, they're legal). You can say that you sell the world's best cookies without getting sued for lying. But if you say something that sounds verifiable, you must have evidence to support your claims. If your advertising says that "Studies show . . ." or "Four out of five people prefer . . ." or "Experts agree . . .," you are required by law to have copies of the studies and documented statements from the experts. Be especially careful about medical and health claims, as the government tends to crack down hardest on these advertisements.

Environmental benefits cannot be exaggerated. Today, it seems that every product is "green," but how you define, or don't define, the word *green* might violate federal regulations.

If you are selling food products, the word *organic* is defined by law, but the word *natural* has no legal definition; any business can call any product "natural."

If you say something is free, it must be free. Sweepstakes are regulated. Misleading mailings such as ads designed to look like checks, and envelopes made to look like they came from government agencies, are prohibited.

If you are advertising a sale price, the item must have been previously offered at a higher price. If you compare your price to other businesses, it must be for similar merchandise.

Private mailboxes (PMBs) rented from mailbox stores (commercial mail receiving agencies, or CMRAs) must be carefully labeled in accordance with U.S. Postal Service laws. The mailbox store you rent from will have the rules.

Transportation safety regulations, administered by the Department of Transportation (DOT.gov), are imposed on truckers, transportation companies, commercial marine businesses, railroads, and aviation businesses.

Environmental protection regulations, administered by the Environmental Protection Agency (EPA.gov), are imposed on auto repair shops and metal finishing, printing, painting, chemical, agriculture, electronics, and transportation businesses.

Some food retailers, restaurants, and distributors are required to keep records of where food products came from. Food distributors and truckers are required to keep records of where food shipments are going. Manufacturers and sellers of fresh-squeezed juices must put warning labels on unpasteurized products.

Privacy policies are required of financial institutions, investment businesses, and retailers that issue credit cards. Any business that voluntarily issues a privacy policy is required to adhere to it.

Websites are prohibited from collecting personal information from children under the age of thirteen without their parent's permission.

Client and employee records with personal or credit information, when being discarded, must be destroyed.

Commercial email is regulated by the CAN-SPAM Act. Among other requirements, unsolicited email advertisements sent to someone you do not already have a relationship with, must state that it is an advertisement, have a legitimate email return address, have an honest subject heading, have an opt-out, and include your physical postal address. Harvesting email addresses from websites is prohibited—another law regularly ignored.

Although all businesses are subject to these federal regulations, enforcement is directed primarily at large companies that, due to their size, can and do take advantage of many, many people. Federal agencies usually ignore small businesses unless the agencies get a complaint.

INSURANCE

If you bought all the different kinds of business insurance available to you, you'd be broke before you made your first sale. First determine what insurance is required by law, what insurance is required by your landlord or by a lender, what insurance is extremely important, and what insurance you can do without.

Types of business insurance include:

Basic Fire Insurance. Covers fire and lightning losses to your building, equipment, and inventory. Fire premiums vary widely and are based upon the location of your property, the degree of fire protection in your community, the type of construction of the building, and the nature of your business and of neighboring businesses. If you move into a building next to a woodworking or dry cleaning shop, your fire premiums will be high even if your business is a low fire risk. A sprinkler system in your building will sharply reduce your premium.

Your computer may be covered under a fire insurance policy, but the data in your computer is usually excluded from coverage.

Extended Coverage. Protects against storms, most explosions, smoke damage, riot, and damage caused by aircraft or vehicles. Extended coverage sometimes includes vandalism, although this usually requires a separate policy. Vandalism policies cover physical damage to your business premises, but do not usually cover vandalism to websites or computer files.

Liability Insurance. Pays for claims brought against your business because of bodily injury: A customer or supplier or a delivery person slips and falls, breaks a leg, and files a $50,000 lawsuit; it's not uncommon.

Liability coverage is required by law in only a few states, but I consider liability insurance essential for any retail business. Many leases and rental agreements require you to have liability insurance.

Premiums for merchants usually are based upon the store's square footage. The bigger the store, the higher the premium. For manufacturers and contractors, premiums increase as payroll increases.

Liability insurance does not cover you, the owner, or any of your employees, though it would normally cover an outside contractor. It does not cover injuries caused by vehicles or by defective products.

Fire Legal Liability. Covers fire damage to your landlord's building—the portion you occupy only. The rest of the building can be covered by property damage liability insurance. Even if the landlord has fire insurance on the building, you may still be liable if your business caused the fire.

Property Damage Liability. Provides coverage for damage to property of others. There are two types of property damage liability: The first type is damage to property that is not under your control or in your custody. For example, a fire starts in your small office. The damage is minimal, but smoke and water destroyed $30,000 worth of Persian rugs in the business next door. Property damage liability covers this situation.

The second type of property damage liability is damage to others' property that is under your control or in your custody, such as property leased or rented to you and, especially important for repair businesses, property that belongs to your customers.

Products Liability. Covers products designed, manufactured, sold, or rented out by the insured once the product leaves the business's hands. It covers the business in case the user of the product sues for injury or property damage. The courts generally hold manufacturers strictly liable for any injury caused by their product, sometimes even when the product has been altered by the customer or not used correctly.

Distributors, wholesalers, and retail stores can sometimes be liable for products they sell, though not usually. If the products are in their original packages and if the retailer provides no assembly or advice, the risk is greatly reduced. Some manufacturers will indemnify retailers against product liability claims (sometimes called a "vendor's endorsement").

Rental businesses can also be held liable for injuries to customers.

Building contractors and tradespeople often get "completed operations insurance," a form of product liability insurance that protects you if someone is injured as a result of your work.

Malpractice. Also known as "errors and omissions" and "professional liability." Protects you from lawsuits and losses from professional, ah, *mistakes*. This insurance is often expensive and hard to find. It is sometimes available from professional societies or trade associations.

Internet malpractice—someone suing you over the contents of your website, is covered under some, but not all, malpractice policies.

Bonds. Surety bonds guarantee the performance of a job. If you do not complete a job, for any reason, your surety company must do so. Surety bonds are most often used in the construction industry and are always required on public construction projects. Surety bonds are difficult to obtain unless you have $30,000 or more in liquid assets, such as cash and inventory. The Small Business Administration (SBA) loan programs sometimes include financing for surety bonds.

Fidelity bonds are placed on employees, insuring the employer against theft or embezzlement by the bonded employees. Fidelity bonds also protect a business's customers if an employee of the business steals anything from the customer's home or business.

Theft Coverage. Covers burglary (theft from a closed business) and robbery (theft using force or threat of violence). The cost depends on the type of merchandise you stock, your location, and the theft protection on your premises, such as dead bolts, alarms, surveillance cameras, and bars on the windows. An investment in some security is certainly as important as buying theft insurance. Find out if coverage includes inventory and equipment away from your business premises, such as at a trade show or in transit to a customer.

Theft coverage does not include fraud, or losses due to customers who bounce checks or don't pay their bills. Theft insurance does not include lost data inside a stolen computer, nor does the insurance cover data stolen from your website by a malicious hacker.

THIS STORE PERSONALLY PROTECTED BY MR. LOWENTHAL HIMSELF!

Sale $1.99

Business Interruption. If your business closes due to fire or other insurable building damage, business interruption insurance will pay you approximately what you would have earned.

You can also purchase "extra expense insurance" that pays the added cost of keeping a business operating after a fire or other building damage, such as renting temporary quarters; "income insurance" that provides coverage if you are hospitalized or disabled and have to shut down the business; and "overhead insurance" that pays you for business overhead expenses you incur during periods of disability.

Business interruption insurance does not cover you if your website or your internet connection goes down, or if your computer crashes or is infected with a virus.

Business interruption insurance may seem to be something of a luxury, but if you have a fire or other disaster, it might be months before you are back on your feet, even with fire insurance. Most small businesses are not prepared to handle such a calamity, and many never reopen.

For tax purposes, some business interruption premiums are deductible, and some are not. The proceeds from an insurance claim may or may not be taxable to you, depending on what the insurance is actually covering. Your insurance agent should have complete tax information.

Workers' Compensation Insurance. Provides disability and death benefits to employees injured or killed on the job, or who become ill due to workplace conditions. If you will be hiring employees, read more about this extremely important insurance under "Hiring Help" in the Growing Up chapter.

You, the owner of the business, may or may not be subject to workers' compensation insurance, depending on your state laws. In many states, sole proprietors, partners in partnerships, owner-employees of small corporations, and owners of limited liability companies are not eligible for workers' compensation insurance. Some states make it an option; you decide if you want workers' compensation insurance for yourself.

In most states, you are not required to carry workers' compensation insurance for independent contractors. However, if an independent contractor is injured while working for you, you may be liable for the injury. Liability insurance usually covers this situation. If your independent contractor hires employees, verify that the contractor has purchased workers' compensation insurance for his or her employees. Do not let your contractor's employees come to your business if they are not insured by the contractor. If an employee gets hurt, you could be sued.

Health Insurance. Everyone in the United States is required to have health insurance. Business owners and self-employed individuals need to find out if their health insurance covers injury while at work. In some states, workers' compensation insurance, which covers employees injured on the job, also covers business owners and self-employed individuals, but in many states, it does not. If you are not covered by workers' compensation insurance, be sure you purchase a health insurance policy that covers you while you are working.

Employers with fifty or more full-time employees are required to purchase health insurance for their employees.

Vehicle Insurance. Liability coverage on all business vehicles is mandatory in most states. If you use your personal vehicle for business, check with your insurance company to make sure you have coverage that includes business use.

If your employees will be driving your vehicles, make sure their liability is included on your policy. If your employees will be driving their own vehicles on your company's business, you should have what's called "non-owned" auto liability insurance, which protects you if one of your employees injures someone or damages someone's property. This non-owned coverage does not protect the employee, who should have his or her own insurance as well.

Personal or business property inside a vehicle, such as merchandise you are delivering, is not usually covered by vehicle insurance.

Environmental Impairment and Pollution Liability. This is required by federal law for all gas stations and for businesses located at former gas station sites if the tanks are still in the ground. Other businesses that are at risk for pollution problems, such as quick lubes and even dry cleaners, sometimes purchase this insurance.

Computer and Internet Insurance. Most business insurance policies exclude coverage for internet- and computer-related problems. Regular business insurance policies often cover the physical damage, destruction, or theft of a computer, but these policies do not cover lost data, the consequences of lost data, or problems caused by a breach of security or stolen personal data.

Insurance is available for computer data problems. Called cyberinsurance, or net secure insurance, coverage may include reimbursement for computer mishaps, glitches, outages, systems failures, loss or theft or corruption of data, fraud, and breaches of security on the internet. Some policies protect you from liability, similar to malpractice insurance, should you accidentally spread a virus or cause other damage or loss to people accessing your site or using your service, or if you are sued over privacy issues. Some policies cover loss of income due to internet-related mishaps, similar to business interruption insurance.

None of the internet or computer insurance is required by law, and, truth to tell, some of it is so expensive, and deductibles so high, that most businesses just do without.

Insurance for Home-Based Businesses. Home businesses have special insurance needs and are subject to restrictions on some insurance policies. This is covered in the Home-Based Business chapter.

Is there more? Of course. There's vandalism and malicious mischief coverage. Patent owners' insurance. Key person life insurance. Breakdown insurance for equipment failures. Credit insurance for your accounts receivable. Damaged or destroyed records insurance. Specialized insurance (unusual kinds of coverage) for specific types of businesses and industries. Fiduciary insurance. Directors' and officers' insurance. Wrongful accounting insurance if you get sued by a shareholder for misstating your financial records (unintentionally, of course). Audit insurance if you get in trouble with the IRS—due to an honest mistake (there is no insurance if you get caught cheating). Website insurance. Copyright insurance. Export insurance. Identity theft insurance. Employment practices liability coverage if you are sued by an employee for wrongful treatment. Bad weather insurance, which covers losses if the weather ruins an outdoor event. There's even insurance that insures your insurance, called "umbrella" insurance, in case you aren't covered when you thought you were.

Purchasing Insurance

Where do you begin? Check with the state, your landlord, and your bank if you are getting a bank loan, to find out what insurance you must carry.

Most leases require tenants to carry liability, property damage, and fire legal liability. Banks usually require you to insure property purchased with loan money. Bank loans sometimes require you to carry life insurance naming the bank as beneficiary. Car and equipment leasing firms often require you to obtain liability or property insurance on leased equipment.

Over and above any mandatory insurance, liability coverage is the most important to any business where customers, clients, or delivery people come to your door. One lawsuit by an injured customer can wipe you out: your business, and you personally. Make sure the coverage pays attorneys and legal fees as well as any claims.

Beyond liability and mandatory coverage, how much insurance you have or don't have is entirely up to you. How much can you afford? How much do you want to afford? How much of a risk are you willing to take, and how comfortable do you feel with that risk?

Most insurance companies offer a business owner policy (BOP) or all-risk insurance, combining many coverages in one policy.

Some insurance companies offer industry-specific policies, offering special coverage to certain types of businesses. In fact, you might want to contact one of the trade associations for your type of business. Trade associations often offer reasonably priced insurance packages to members. To find a trade association, ask other people who own similar businesses or look on the internet.

Insurance companies are competitive, offering different rates, packages, and premium payment plans. Many insurance policies offer much lower premiums if you opt for large deductibles. For property and equipment coverage, find out if the insurance will reimburse your original cost, replacement cost, or current value at time of loss. These can be significantly different amounts. If you have more than one location, have your insurance agent explain the important difference between "blanket" and "scheduled" coverage.

It is a good idea to shop around. Pick an agent or broker who will devote time to your individual needs, who will at no extra cost survey your entire situation and recommend different insurance options, explaining the advantages and disadvantages of each.

Make sure you are dealing with a solvent, reliable company, one with a good reputation for settling claims. Your agent can show you the company's rating, or check with your state insurance department.

And finally, read the policy carefully before you pay for it, not after you've suffered a loss you thought was covered.

Self-Insurance

In an attempt to reduce insurance costs, business owners sometimes attempt self-insurance.

Basically this means you are not insured at all but have set aside funds to cover possible losses such as fire or theft or a liability claim against the business. Some people call these funds a "reserve." While self-insurance certainly saves on insurance premiums, the money set aside or in the reserve is not considered a business expense and is not tax deductible. Remember, too, that it is unlikely your self-insurance reserve will be large enough to cover a large loss or lawsuit. That's why people buy insurance in the first place.

Insurance required by law must be purchased from an insurance company. Self-insurance will not suffice.

Sustaining a Loss

If you actually sustain a loss that isn't covered by insurance, you may or may not have a tax write-off depending on the nature of the loss. Any loss covered by insurance is not deductible. The Taxes chapter explains how to deduct different kinds of losses.

THE BUSINESS PLAN

Business planning is essential to your success. I can tell you from firsthand experience, from seeing it happen too many times: Most new business failures are due to a lack of foresight, a failure to think things through. A failure to plan.

Although business plans are usually created to try to raise money, a good business plan is really for your own use. Business planning is a self-learning process. A business plan helps you to learn everything about your business, your industry, your customers, your competition. You especially need to think out how you are going to find customers or clients, and how you are going to market your goods or services to your customers.

The greatest benefit of a business plan is that, by writing everything down, you are more likely to see the entire picture, and you are more likely not to forget some important steps to prepare yourself for this huge venture. Launching a business without a business plan is much like building a house without blueprints. You can certainly do it, but when you discover a mistake in the foundation after the roof is shingled, you're really going to kick yourself.

Mission Statement

A good business plan starts with a short written statement of what your business is, what you want to do, and how you intend to get there. Sounds silly? Maybe, but many people wanting to start a business have not thought out their goals at all, and too many of these people quickly lose their direction and their interest. Although a mission statement can easily resemble a promo piece, keep in mind that this mission statement is for you, to help you visualize and verbalize exactly what you are trying to accomplish.

A Basic Plan

If you've read this chapter of *Small Time Operator*, followed through on the suggestions, done your market research, estimated your start-up expenses, tried your hand at the cash-flow guessing game (covered in the Keeping Records chapter), and wrote it all down, you would have yourself a respectable business plan.

Such an informal plan will help you to organize your thoughts and observations, show you problems that require more thought and analysis, and help you find all the jigsaw pieces and fit them together.

Don't create your business plan in a vacuum. If it seems appropriate to you, talk about your plan and your new business with as many people as possible. The best way to avoid wishful thinking is to get feedback from potential customers, clients, and prospects. Listen to their answers. If your new business is going to be successful, other people should be excited about it, and interested in hiring you or spending their money on your products. By creating a business that will give people what they want, a business that is structured to meet their needs, you have found the Secret To Success, the difference between an idea and a solid business.

It is important to understand the limits of a business plan, particularly one this early in the game. The ideas are only that: untested ideas. The numbers are guesses, your own inexperienced, optimistic guesses. Don't rely on them too heavily. Proceed with all caution, keep your eyes open, and let experience, not some written plan, be your guide.

Business planning is an ongoing process. After you've been in business awhile, you may want to draw up a new plan to help you make some major decision, such as reorganizing or expanding, or trying out some new idea. By then, you will know your business well, and you will be able to create a much more reliable plan.

Raising Capital

A business plan created just for yourself can be as informal as you like. But if you are trying to raise start-up capital from individuals or a bank, a more-structured business plan will help you get your ideas across to prospective lenders and investors.

Someone who is considering putting money into your venture will most likely want to see a written plan, one that includes:

1. Your business idea.

2. Your education, experience, business contacts, and other information to emphasize that you have knowledge and a background that will lead to success.

3. Where you plan to locate.

4. How you'll obtain or manufacture inventory.

5. How you will find and keep customers, and the status of the competition.

6. How much money you will need to start, and what the money will be used for.

7. How much time and how much of your own money you plan to commit to the business.

8. How much you will pay yourself.

9. How you will repay the loan or investment. This is a major key to the success of your plan and to raising funds. An investor wants to be confidant that your venture will net enough money, after all expenses, to have enough left over to pay back the investor.

Banks and investors may also want to see "pro forma" financial statements, which are projections (forecasts) of income and expenses and cash flow. These "projections" should be more honestly labeled "guesses" or even "hopes and dreams," because that's all they really are, and every banker and any savvy investor knows this.

Quite often, investors ask for a business plan just to see how good you are at preparing one, how well you understand business concepts. A good business plan tells an investor that you're serious about your venture, that you've taken time and effort to write down your ideas and your proposals, and that you

have the experience or talent to pull it off. A savvy investor can tell from a business plan if you know what you're doing or just talking through your hat.

Business plans can be and often are much more elaborate and detailed than what I've described here. Entire books are dedicated to the many considerations, formulas, options, and everything else you can conceivably fit onto graphs, charts, schedules, PowerPoints, and densely packed pages, to create some mighty impressive plans indeed, some of which are quite valuable and some of which are utterly useless. Sometimes, too much "information" will work against you, unable to see the forest for the trees.

Before you dive into anything, do a little research, write up a business plan, figure out if you're going to pay the mortgage or lose your shirt. Got an idea that is too hot to take the time for all that? Well, be prepared to fail.

—Walter Jeffries, *Flash* magazine

Research is everything. You've got to find where you fit into the puzzle.

—Mikal Ali, Sidestreet Inc. Greeting Cards

Statistics are no substitute for judgment.

—Henry Clay

The customer is always right—but who cares?

—Sign on Shady Nook Snack Bar, Laytonville, California

There are only two rules in customer relations:

1) The customer is always right; and

2) If the customer is wrong, reread rule 1.

—Business owner Stew Leonard

Customers are often right, and even when they are not, they think they are. We'll pretend they are, because it's not worth fighting to prove it to them.

—Jay Goltz, founder and owner, Artists Frame Service

I still go by the old rule that the customer is always right, even when he or she is clearly wrong.

—Business consultant Marilyn Ross

The customer is seldom right. But the customer is always in charge.

—Business owner Larry Taylor

The customer is always right. But the bartender decides who is still a customer.

—Sign in Granzella's Bar, Williams, California

Never tell a customer he's wrong. It's like putting gasoline on a fire.

—John Tschohl, president, Service Quality Institute, Minneapolis

No one ever wins an argument with a customer.

—Dale Carnegie

Chapter Two
KEEPING RECORDS

The best memory is not so firm as faded ink.

—CHINESE PROVERB

"If you take one from three hundred and sixty five, what remains?" asked Humpty Dumpty.

"Three hundred and sixty-four, of course," said Alice.

Humpty Dumpty looked doubtful. "I'd rather see that done on paper," he said.

—FROM *ALICE IN WONDERLAND*

WARMING UP TO AN UNPOPULAR SUBJECT

Recordkeeping—bookkeeping—seems to be the one aspect of business that so many people dread. Ledgers, columns of numbers, software you don't want to learn, printouts that make no sense, balancing the books (whatever that means), and "I'm a business owner, not an accountant."

Whenever I try to explain or defend the paperwork end of business to a new businessperson, I always feel I have two strikes against me before I even open my mouth. But once you understand why a business requires financial records and how these records can be kept with a minimum of time and effort, the fear vanishes, the work somehow gets done, and you are left with the satisfaction of seeing the total picture and of having done it yourself. And that's a nice feeling.

Recordkeeping is an integral part of business—of your business. To attempt a definition, recordkeeping—bookkeeping, accounting; they all mean the same thing—is a system designed to record, summarize, and analyze your financial activity: your sales, purchases, credit accounts, cash, payroll, inventory, equipment. Your records—your books, ledgers, reports, financial statements, whatever you want to call them—are the papers or software on which the recordkeeping activity is recorded, or "posted" (the two words mean the same thing).

Why Keep Records?

Why keep financial records? Well, number one, you need to keep records. And number two, you will want to keep records.

Number one: You need to keep records because the IRS says you need to keep records. The IRS requirement is short and blunt: "You must keep records to correctly figure your taxes." The IRS says that business records can be kept on paper, on a spreadsheet or accounting software, on a smartphone app, on a cloud server, or on any other physical or electronic platform as long as the information can be retrieved if the IRS requests it.

Number two: You will *want* to keep records so you know how much money you're bringing in, how much you're spending, and whether you are earning some money or going broke. Your records of income and expenses are your only source of complete information about your business. It is virtually impossible to keep all your financial dealings in your head. A good recordkeeping system will provide you with information essential to the survival of your business. Only with complete records will you be able to evaluate your business and make any needed changes and plans for the future. Only with complete records will you have a list of every expense, every tax deduction, to reduce your taxes. This is doubly true of a home-based business where personal and business expenses can get intermingled and confused. Good recordkeeping = more money in your pocket.

Business failures have been blamed, time and again, on a lack of accurate financial records. Don Willis, former owner of Booknews, a defunct bookstore: "Our biggest mistake was that we didn't keep a regular set of books. Half of our records were on scraps of paper and receipts. We didn't know whether some accounts were paid or not. We thought we were making a profit, but a good set of records would have shown us the truth: We were going broke. And you know, had I realized that, I could have taken steps to change things, to head us in a better direction."

Without a complete set of records, you find yourself trying to evaluate your business by looking at isolated areas, such as cash and inventory, these being the most observable, and also the most misleading. If, for example, you price your product based solely on its cost to you plus some arbitrary markup—a common mistake with beginners—you could be selling at a loss and not even know it. This happened at Booknews: "We knew what the books were costing us, but we didn't have any real idea of what our total overhead was—rent, insurance, supplies, utilities, payroll taxes, and the rest. We sold a lot of books because we sold at a discount, and I thought we were doing well. Do you know, it took me four months to realize that every single book we sold, we sold at a loss."

Joe Campbell, Computer Connection: "Everybody who runs a business should sit down and figure out what it costs them to turn the key in that door every morning. Overhead. I never knew until I sat down and calculated exactly what my expenses were, what it costs me to have that place down there. And it's eighty dollars a day! When you walk in there in the morning you know exactly what you gotta do before you start putting bread on the table. You gotta make eighty bucks for the man. And then you start making money for yourself."

Setting Up Your Financial Records

Where do you begin? How much recordkeeping do you need? If your business is a one-person operation, your records can be kept quite simple. A bank account, income and expenditure records, and a few worksheets are about all you need.

Do you sell on account? You will need records of each credit customer. If you hire employees, you need payroll records for each employee. Sales and manufacturing businesses need inventory records. Partnerships must keep records of each partner's contributions and withdrawals. Limited liability companies (LLCs) and corporations have even more requirements.

But let's take things one step at a time. None of the financial records need be too complicated for most people to set up, to keep themselves, and to understand.

MORE THAN ONE BUSINESS

If you have more than one business, the IRS requires that you keep a separate set of records for each business. However, if you are a sole proprietor (not a partnership, corporation, or limited liability company), instead of having multiple businesses, you can have separate "divisions" within one business, which will require only one set of records. This is covered in more detail under "Multiple Businesses" in the T.C.B.: Take Care of Business chapter. I suggest you read that section before you set up your records.

Recordkeeping: Keep It Simple

Your records can be very simple. There isn't anything complicated about most small business income and expenses. Simple records are easy to create, easy to use, and easy to understand. If your system is too cumbersome for easy use, chances are you just won't keep records at all.

If you don't like or don't want to learn business software, you can easily create a basic set of hand-posted ledgers. The software industry and the cloud computing preachers would like everyone to think that hand-posted ledgers are something from the past, as out of date as horse-and-buggy transportation. But the truth is that many new businesses use hand-posted ledgers the first year, and some never see a need for anything else. With hand-posted ledgers you don't need to master any software. You don't have to worry about files that disappear, websites that go down, hard drives that crash, and employees that snoop. You won't have to log on to an app every time you want to record an entry. Hand-posted ledgers cost next to nothing, never need to be upgraded, and no batteries required.

The majority of businesses, however, use some form of software. Once you master a software application, it's much faster than hand-posting. It does all the math for you, it can fix mistakes quickly, and it gives you many, many options that might take hours if you are doing them by hand. Software can give you daily, weekly, monthly, and annual totals in any category you want, and keep track of your bank balance at the same time. Tax accountants love accounting software because the accountants can download your records onto their computers to speed up tax preparation.

Technology has changed how businesses record their financial information, but the information itself, the income records, the expense records, the profit and loss, has never changed. The financial records produced by 21st-century software are exactly the same as the ancient ledgers Bob Cratchit kept for Ebenezer Scrooge.

Just remember, it's not the medium, it's the message. If you want to understand your business, you need to understand your records.

Don't want to do any of this? If this chapter has you gritting your teeth, getting nervous, and wishing you hadn't bought this book, skip down to "Hiring a Bookkeeper."

Hand-Posted Ledgers

You can easily create your own ledgers using accounting ledger paper (also called accountant's worksheets), available in any office supply store or website. The ledger paper usually comes in fifty-sheet pads and with anywhere from two to twenty-five columns, and is designed to go in three-ring binders. These sheets, however, are not sturdy and will not hold up well with repeated use. If you hunt around thrift stores and even antique stores, you might find an old heavy-duty post binder, probably still with unused ledger pages. These ledgers were well made; they'll last forever.

Spreadsheets

If you use and are comfortable with spreadsheets, spreadsheet software can easily be set up as a basic set of financial records. In fact, the word *spreadsheet* is an old accounting term that originally referred to a piece of ledger paper that had so many columns, it had to be folded over to fit in a binder. Today's spreadsheets are not much different. Spreadsheets and hand-posted ledgers are identical, except that spreadsheets can add and compute automatically (and you'll never have trouble reading the scribbling).

Most spreadsheet software comes with a set of recordkeeping templates, or you can create your own. You can easily copy the samples in this chapter.

Spreadsheets, however, are often limited in their interactivity. A financial transaction that needs to be recorded in more than one place in your records, such as a deposit that goes into your bank account and also gets posted to your income records, may have to be entered twice, in two different spreadsheet files.

Accounting Software

Accounting software is a complete recordkeeping system that can be as detailed or as basic as you want. Accounting software usually includes income and expense records, bank account records, inventory control, payroll, job costing, accounts receivable and payable, individual customer and vendor accounts, and many other business functions.

Accounting software is fully integrated. For example, when you record a deposit or a check you write on your bank account record, that entry can also post to your income or expense records, update customer or vendor information, and recompute year-to-date totals, all at the same time.

Accounting software looks very different from traditional bookkeeping ledgers. There are no columns of numbers, no lines running across the page, and nothing to add up. People with no accounting or bookkeeping knowledge can easily see and understand the records produced by the software. It is not difficult to learn basic recordkeeping using accounting software. You don't have to learn everything at once.

There are several different accounting software packages, some for sale, some available by subscription, and some for free on the internet, although free internet software often includes ads, which may or may not be a nuisance when you are trying to focus on getting your records posted. The best known and most popular accounting software is QuickBooks. It has managed to dominate the software market, and is used by most accountants and bookkeepers. QuickBooks is covered below.

QuickBooks and other software vendors offer a free trial period to try out their software. If you like the software, you can purchase or subscribe to it. If you don't pay for the software, at the end of the trial period it stops working, but you will be able to access your records for a period of time, usually ninety days, before it is deleted.

Most accounting software is for general business use, adaptable to a wide range of businesses. Some software is for specific types of businesses and specific industries, and usually includes specialized functions just for that type of business. There is also single-function software for specific purposes such as payroll, inventory control, or job costing. I suggest starting with general-use software. It's likely to be easier to learn, less expensive, and will probably be all you need for your business. Once you learn general-use software and discover its limits for your particular type of business, then look into specialized software. Again, try to find a vendor who will let you "try it before you buy it."

Accounting software can be a mixed blessing. By eliminating the mechanics of individually posting the ledgers, eliminating the step-by-step, think-it-through process, you create the dangerous possibility that you don't know where all of the numbers came from, that you won't examine the numbers as carefully as you should, missing some important information or failing to catch a serious error.

If your accounting software is producing documents you don't know what to do with, records you do not fully understand, numbers that don't seem right, stop! Go back to square one, take the time to figure out what you have, take the time to understand your accounting system.

Apps and Cloud Computing

Accounting software packages, in fact, all software applications, are being marketed more and more as subscriptions rather than something to purchase and install on your computer. You do not download the software, you access it online or through an app, and you store your records on the software company's servers. It is called *cloud computing*. Your records are out there in cyberspace, up in the clouds, so to speak. The argument for cloud computing is that if your computer crashes, you won't lose your records, and you can access your records from any internet-connected device. However, you are trusting your records, possibly your entire business, to an online service where you have no control over its use, privacy, security, and availability.

If you do subscribe to a cloud service, be sure you can download all of your records onto your own computer, so you have them to copy and print out any time you want, even if you cannot access the service. Find out what happens to your records if you miss a payment or if your credit card is rejected. Find out if you can transfer your records to a different service provider if you want to.

Smartphone apps that organize your business records may eliminate the need for some of the recordkeeping described in this chapter. Whatever recordkeeping system works best for you is the system to use.

Check Your Work and Back It Up

Print out income and expense reports every month, and look for items, particularly large-dollar items, that look wrong. It's very easy to enter, say, $4,000, when you meant to enter $40.00. The software is not going to flag the error. The software isn't going to pop up a box saying, "Isn't that a lot of money for an ink cartridge?" The accounting software will accept the $4,000 entry and not say a word.

Protect your records. Back up your work regularly. Yes, and floss your teeth every day and all that other stuff you really meant to do. The legendary ragtime pianist Eubie Blake, interviewed on his ninetieth birthday, said, "If I knew I was going to live this long, I'd have taken better care of myself." Same for your records.

Hiring a Bookkeeper

You don't have to keep records if you don't want to. You don't have to post ledgers, or struggle with confusing software, or despair if the computer crashes. There are independent bookkeepers and bookkeeping services in every city and just about every small town in the country: experienced, inexpensive, and eager to help you. However, even if you hire a bookkeeper, even if you never post a single entry in a ledger or spreadsheet or software app, I think it is essential to understand the basics of recordkeeping, to understand what is in your records and what the numbers mean. You can probably get excellent help from your bookkeeper, or you can read this chapter, or both.

If you do hire a bookkeeper, here is one important suggestion: Do not let your bookkeeper handle your money. Do not give your bookkeeper access to your bank account. Deposit your own income, write your own checks, and examine all of your bills yourself. Most bookkeepers are honest and trustworthy, but some of the nicest, sweetest, most sincere-sounding people turn out to be embezzlers.

BUSINESS BANK ACCOUNTS

As soon as you start your business, before you open your doors, go to the bank and open a separate business checking account. Keep your business finances and your personal finances separate. Nothing can be more confusing than mixing business with pleasure, financially.

Many states require you to have a DBA (fictitious name or assumed name statement) before you can open a bank account in your business name. Talk to your bank ahead of time and find out all the requirements. Some banks impose larger service charges and require larger minimum balances for business accounts.

Bank statements may be on paper or online. Most banks prepare monthly statements on the last day of each month, but some banks have a monthly cutoff date sometime in the middle of the month. I suggest you ask your bank to give you month-end statements—statements that cover the first to the last day of each month—because it's easier to organize your records month by month.

Some bank statements include a photocopy of each check that clears the bank, but some banks only list the check numbers and amounts. I suggest asking the bank to include photocopies, because, when you reconcile your account, it is so much easier to spot errors if you can see what you actually wrote.

Three Important Rules

There are three important bank account rules to follow:

Rule one: Avoid paying business bills in cash. Try to pay all business bills by check, credit card, debit card, or electronic transaction. Your expenses are more easily recorded, better documented, and unlikely to be forgotten when paid by a method other than out-of-pocket cash. Some payments, of course, will have to be in cash, but keep them to a minimum.

Rule two: Deposit all of your income, checks and cash, into the business bank account. You will have a complete record of your earnings. Deposit checks as soon as possible. Every day you wait increases the chances that the check writer will have overdrawn or even closed the account.

Rule three: Try not to use the business account to pay personal, non-business expenses. While it is legal for a sole proprietor to mix business and personal funds in the same bank account, the recordkeeping can get unnecessarily confusing when business and personal expenses are commingled. Partnerships, corporations, and LLCs should never combine business funds with the owners' personal funds. This can result in legal and tax complications you definitely want to avoid.

A few bank account rules of thumb:

1. Balance your bank account every month. It is too easy to make an adding error. You don't want to bounce a check on your most important supplier because you thought you were down to the last $10 when you were really down to the last dime. Never balanced a bank

account? The T.C.B.: Take Care of Business chapter explains how to do it.

2. Keep bank statements at least three years. They are the best documentation you have if you ever need to support your records. Three years is the normal statute of limitations set by the IRS for income tax audits.

3. Try not to write any checks payable to "Cash," as this leaves you no record of how the money was actually spent.

4. Expenses that are partly personal and partly business, such as automobile expenses, or rent and utilities for a home business, or your credit card bill if it includes business and non-business purchases, are partly deductible: the business portion. These expenses can be handled in one of two ways: (1) Pay these bills from your personal checking account, then post the business portion to your business records (explained below under "Recording Expenditures"); or (2) pay the bills from your business checking account; post the business portion to your expenditure record, and post the non-business portion to "Nondeductible" (also explained under "Recording Expenditures").

Tax and Legal Requirements for Bank Accounts

No federal law requires you to have a bank account. The IRS does not require you to deposit your business income in a bank account. The IRS *does* require you to report all income, whether deposited in a bank account or not.

Some states require businesses to deposit all checks payable to the business in a business bank account. In these states, cashing a business check is prohibited by law. So you may be required by your state law to have a bank account if you get checks payable to your business.

No law requires you to keep separate business and personal checking accounts (sole proprietors and joint ventures only; all other forms of business must have separate bank accounts). You can pay business bills from a personal checking account and get a full business deduction. You can deposit business checks into a personal bank account if your bank's rules don't prohibit such activity.

Most banks, however, will require you to set up a business bank account before they will let you deposit or cash checks made out to a business name. If your business name is the same as your name, your bank will probably let you deposit or cash business checks without setting up a separate business account.

Business bank accounts need to be protected from hackers. Your account can be hacked, and your money can be stolen. Read "Protecting Your Bank Account" in the T.C.B.: Take Care of Business chapter.

Joe Campbell, Computer Connection: "My problem was that I would look in our checking account, our one and only checking account, and I'd say, 'Wow, there's $1,000 in there. Let's buy the new tires we need for the car.' The kids need a new pair of shoes, and I buy them a pair of shoes. And I see we still have $600 in the bank; we're in good shape. Then all the parts bills come in, and I owe $800. I have to put creditors off. Having that parts money in a separate account tells you exactly where you are. It's security. Plus it's emergency cash if you have to go in and get it."

UNDERSTANDING RECORDKEEPING

How to keep your financial records depends on (1) the accounting method you use; and (2) the type of recordkeeping system you have. If you would like to understand the different accounting methods, read "Cash Accounting versus Accrual" below. If you would like to understand the different record-keeping systems, read "Single Entry versus Double Entry" below that. If you just want to get going, as I suspect most people do, you can skip the two explanations and jump down to "Defining Income."

Cash Accounting versus Accrual

All businesses must choose between two accounting methods, cash or accrual.

The cash method (also called "cash basis") does not mean all your transactions are in cash. *Cash method* refers to how you record your sales and purchases, and how you post your records. The word *cash* in cash method refers to all forms of payment (checks, money orders, credit cards, debit cards, electronic transactions), not just currency.

Under the cash method, income is recorded when the money is received, and expenses are recorded when paid, with a few exceptions explained below.

Accrual accounting, by comparison, records all income and expenses whether paid or not. Credit transactions—money you owe, and money owed to you—show on accrual records. (Credit transactions refer to credit you extend to your customers, or credit your suppliers extend to you; they do not refer to credit cards, which are treated as cash transactions.) This can get very complicated, as credit sales and credit purchases must be recorded twice—once when you make the transaction, and again when the money is paid.

Cash accounting is easier to understand and much easier to figure than accrual accounting, so almost all small businesses use the cash method.

Exceptions to cash accounting rules: Some prepaid expenses are not deductible the year paid; see "Prepaid Expenses" in the Taxes chapter. Purchases using a bank credit card are deductible the year charged, even if not paid until the following year; see "Payments by Credit Card" below. If you buy equipment or other business assets on time, making installment payments over several years, you may be able to write off the entire cost the year of purchase; you should ask your accountant how to record installment purchases.

Accrual accounting: Follow the same recordkeeping procedures that cash method businesses use, until the end of the year. On December 31 you will need to make adjustments for any unpaid and uncollected accounts. These adjustments are explained below. This simplified system will work fine as long as you don't need precise figures at the end of each month. Since you make adjustments only at year-end, at any time during the year, the figures may be off slightly.

Single Entry versus Double Entry

Financial transactions are recorded under one of two methods: single entry bookkeeping or double entry bookkeeping.

Under single entry bookkeeping, only one entry is made, either to income or to expenditure. Single entry bookkeeping keeps the paperwork to a minimum while still providing you with the basic information to manage your business and prepare tax returns.

There are two disadvantages to this simple bookkeeping system. Single entry bookkeeping will provide a record of your income and expenditures but will not automatically provide a complete record of inventory on hand, equipment, outstanding loans, or other assets and liabilities.

The other drawback to single entry bookkeeping is the lack of a built-in double-check of arithmetical accuracy. These disadvantages are partly offset by the additional asset records that the equipment and inventory ledgers provide, and by the total columns in the ledgers that provide a partial math double-check.

The alternative to single entry bookkeeping, the well-known and elaborate system called double entry bookkeeping, is a complete record-keeping system that posts multiple accounts with every entry, provides cross checks and automatic balancing of the books, and transforms bookkeeping from a part-time nuisance into a full-time occupation.

In double entry bookkeeping, every transaction requires two separate entries, a debit and a credit. These terms originated in double entry bookkeeping, along with the expression *balancing the books*: Total debits must equal total credits for the books to be "in balance."

Double entry bookkeeping is a science. It is the perfected bookkeeping system, and it requires a full semester in college to master. Simplicity is our goal. I find that most small businesses are better off without the refinements and the headaches of a double entry system.

Most hand-posted and spreadsheet ledgers are single entry ledgers, easy to set up, easy to use. Accounting software such as QuickBooks is double entry, but because the software does all the posting automatically, most users have no need to understand double entry bookkeeping. In fact, most people who use accounting software don't even know what we're talking about.

Defining Income

For recordkeeping and taxes, you must distinguish between "business" income and "non-business" income. Business income is what you earn from selling a product or providing a service. Only your business income is included on your income records. Non-business income is reported and taxes paid on it, but it is kept separate from your business income.

The differentiation between business and non-business income is not just academic accounting talk. Although business and non-business income are both subject to income tax, business income is also subject to self-employment tax (covered in the Taxes chapter). Non-business income escapes self-employment tax.

"Gross receipts" is your total business income before any expenses. "Net income" is the income after expenses have been deducted. The income discussed in this chapter is the total income (the gross receipts).

Rental income: Rental income is considered business income only if you are in the business of renting or managing property, or if you operate a hotel, motel, bed-and-breakfast, or similar lodging. All other rental income is non-business income. However, if you rent your home through a sharing app such as Airbnb, read the On-Demand Economy chapter for more details on this tax issue.

Interest income: Interest received on loans is not business income unless you are in the business of lending money. Interest received on accounts receivable (interest charges added to money your customers owe you) is business income. Interest from a bank account is non-business income, even though the business earned it.

Stock-market trading: People who buy and sell stocks are not usually considered to be self-employed. The money they make is taxable but does not come under the tax laws governing businesses. Stock traders, however—people who work at it full-time, making their living buying and selling stocks, are self-employed. They are running a business buying and selling stock. There may be a fine line here between a stock "investor" (not self-employed) and a stock "trader" (self-employed). You may want to discuss this with an experienced accountant. A significant amount of tax money is at stake.

Barter: If you barter or trade goods or services, you include the fair market value of what you receive as part of your business income. This is covered in the Taxes chapter.

Deposits and advances: If you take deposits or advances from your customers, they are considered income if they are not returnable. Returnable deposits and advances are not recorded as income.

Your own money, investments, and loans: Any of your own money put into the business, any money others invest in your business, and any loans received are not income to your business. You pay no taxes on this money. Do not include these amounts as part of your income.

Credit cards, debit cards, and electronic deposits: Merchants who accept credit and debit cards or electronic payments such as PayPal handle the transactions the same way as cash transactions. The T.C.B.: Take Care of Business chapter includes a section on becoming a credit card/debit card merchant.

RECORDING INCOME: STEP ONE—YOUR CUSTOMER'S INCOME RECORD

Income is recorded (or "recognized," which for recordkeeping purposes means the same thing) in two steps. Step one: At the time you make a sale, record the sale on an invoice, cash receipt, or cash register tape. Step two will be to record the sale in your income records.

Some software automatically combines steps one and two, but it is still best understood as a two-step procedure. I can't overemphasize how important it is that you understand your bookkeeping completely, which means understanding what your software is doing.

Let's examine step one. How you record each sale depends primarily on your volume of sales.

Low Volume of Sales

If your business has only a few sales each month, you can prepare a custom invoice for each sale. Include your name or business name and any other information you want your customers to have (your address, telephone, email); date of sale; customer's name and contact information; description of sale; the amount, showing sales tax separately; and a place to indicate when paid. Give or email the original invoice to your customer and keep a duplicate copy for your records.

Depending on your inclination and your finances, your invoices can be prepared on specially printed and custom-designed forms, or you can type the information on plain paper, or you can create most anything you like on your computer.

Medium Volume of Sales

Businesses with a larger volume of sales often use preprinted or computer-generated invoices. Most everyone is familiar with the cash receipt books and invoices many businesses use to record individual sales: pre-numbered forms in duplicate, one for the customer, one for you. You can purchase receipt books and invoices with your business name custom-printed at the top, or you can purchase a rubber stamp and mark each receipt individually.

Note: Don't confuse this book of cash receipts with other books labeled "cash receipts" that are in fact ledgers for recording income totals.

Throughout *Small Time Operator*, the terms sales slips, sales receipts, cash receipts, bills, and invoices are used interchangeably. They all refer to individual sales records. The term "statement," however, means something else to most businesses. A statement (or statement of account) is a summary of invoices and payments over a period of time. Some businesses issue statements, some don't. Most businesses don't pay from statements, so if the bill you give your customers says "statement" instead of "invoice," it may not get paid.

The procedure for using cash receipts or invoices is simple:

1. If the receipts are not pre-numbered, number them.

2. Use a separate receipt for each sale.

3. Make a duplicate copy of each receipt.

4. Write the date, amount, and description of the sale. Show any sales tax separately.

5. If your customer uses a purchase order (PO) number, that number should appear on your invoice in addition to your invoice number.

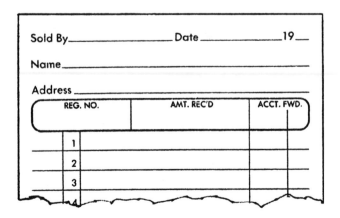

Sold By_____ Date_____ 19__		
Name_____		
Address_____		
REG. NO.	AMT. REC'D	ACCT. FWD.
1		
2		
3		

Pinball Alley
Box 640, Laytonville, CA 95454
We buy old Pinballs—Any Condition
707/984-6746

June 14
INVOICE TO:
B. Bear, Laytonville

Repair Gottlieb King Pin, 4 hours	$80.00
2 flipper coils	16.00
set of rubber bands	10.00
bulbs	8.50
sales tax on parts	2.50
Total	$117.00

6. If this is a credit sale (*not* credit cards), write "CREDIT SALE" on the receipt.

7. Include the terms of sale (see below).

Give the original receipt or invoice to your customer. Leave the duplicate in your receipt book. The duplicate copies will be summarized and posted to your income records.

If you void any invoice, do not throw it out. Mark it "VOID" and keep it in your receipt book. Although you should not include the voided receipt in your summary total, keep a record of it here, just so you'll know what happened to it.

Instead of a book of cash receipts, you can purchase individual two-part invoice forms from an office supply store or printer, with your name imprinted on them. These forms are used in the same way as the cash receipts.

Accounting and word-processing software can easily design and print invoices.

Terms of Sale

Spell out the terms of sale on your invoices.

If goods are being shipped, who pays shipping should be specified. Some businesses use an old term, FOB, which stands for Freight on Board. "FOB [shipper's city]" means the customer pays freight. "FOB [customer's city]" means the shipper (you) pay the shipping to your customer. Show shipping charges separately.

If you want to be paid immediately, include "Payment due on receipt." If you want to be paid within a certain amount of time, spell it out: "Payment due within 30 days." The term "net 30" means the same thing. If you offer discounts for prompt payment, these should be spelled out: "2 percent discount if paid within 10 days."

If the bill was prepaid, put that on the invoice: PAID. There are careless businesses that will pay a bill a second time, and then you have to send them a refund. If the bill was paid with a credit card, include the type of card (VISA, MasterCard, etc.) and the last three or four digits of the card number. Do not show the entire card number on the invoice, to protect the buyer should anyone steal the information from the invoice.

How you want to handle returns should be clearly spelled out: "Not returnable," "Money refunded if returned within thirty days," or "15 percent restocking charge for returns" (which, you probably know, always irritates customers). Or, if your returns policy depends on the individual situation or the individual customer, maybe it's best to not mention any returns policy on the invoice unless a customer asks.

If you offer credit terms (other than credit cards), federal law requires you to disclose, in detail, your credit terms and finance charges. See "Credit Sales" below.

Large Volume of Sales

Businesses with many sales each day—convenience stores, auto parts stores, hardware stores, and the like—will need a good cash register to keep track of sales. You can spend a small fortune on a new cash register, or you may be able to find a good used one. Keep an eye out for businesses that are going out of business. They are often selling *everything*.

If you will be accepting credit cards, credit card processors (banks and internet services that process credit cards for merchants) have business packages that include hardware that can be used instead of a cash register. See what systems are being offered by the credit card processors before investing in a cash register. Credit card sales are covered in the T.C.B.: Take Care of Business chapter.

Refunds

Refunds (returns) are handled the same as sales, just with negative amounts. The refund documents should include the same information as the original sale, showing sales tax and any other charges separately. Some people call refunds a "credit" or "issuing a credit," which is fine as long as you don't confuse the term (and the paperwork) with "credit" as in "credit sale," which applies to making a sale, not refunding money.

If you make a refund in cash or through a credit or debit card, combine the refund invoice or credit slip with your individual income records. The refund will get recorded in your records ("Step Two," below) along with your sales.

If you make a refund by writing a check, the refund is recorded differently, but the net results are the same. For hand-posted and spreadsheet ledgers, you will not be posting your income record, you will be posting your expense record, under a category called refunds or returns. If part of the refund was for sales tax, it gets a little complicated because you need to reduce the amount of sales tax collected.

You will need a category in your expense ledger for the refunded sales tax and then remember to include the refunded sales tax when preparing your sales tax reports. If you are using accounting software, these steps are automatic. The refund is posted directly to the categories it applies to. You don't have to remember anything.

RECORDING INCOME: STEP TWO— YOUR INCOME RECORD

Your income records—your income ledgers, spreadsheets, or accounting software—are summaries of your sales from your invoices, cash receipts, cash register tapes, and credit card processors. The income record is one of the most important business documents you have. It tells you—daily, weekly if you want, monthly, and at year-end—how much income you've earned and how much sales tax you've collected. It helps you to manage your business by showing you the days and the months that are busy or slow, so that you can better plan your expenditures, advertising, sales, even vacations. It is a guide to preparing cash flow information (cash flow and financial management are discussed at the end of this chapter). The income record saves you time preparing your sales tax reports and income tax returns.

Regardless of the type of income records you have—hand-posted ledgers, spreadsheets, or accounting software reports—you only record sales that you've been paid for. If you sell on account, if your customers have not paid yet, do not record the invoices until they are paid. If you don't receive the money, you don't record the income, and you don't pay taxes on the income. (This does not apply to businesses using accrual accounting.)

Accounting Software

If you use software such as QuickBooks (not spreadsheets), your income records are created automatically when you record your individual invoices. Every time you record a sale, the software updates the totals. There is no "step two." There is no income ledger to post.

Hand-Posting and Spreadsheets

If you use hand-posted ledgers or spreadsheets, you can easily create a simple income ledger. The sample here can be used as is or adapted to your individual needs and your state's sales tax requirements. You will be summarizing your individual sales from step one of recording income (see above), and posting the summary totals to this income ledger. Use a separate ledger or spreadsheet page for each month. Each page has eight columns:

1. Date. You may post daily or periodically. How often you post the income ledger depends on you and the volume of sales you have. (See below.)

2. Sales period. If you are posting daily, use the line corresponding with the date. If you are not posting daily, note the sales period here, such as "June 3–5." This is explained below. You can also use this column for any notations you want to make.

3. Taxable sales, excluding sales tax. If you do not have to collect sales tax, use this column for total sales and ignore the rest of the columns. All you need are the first three columns.

4. Sales tax collected.

5, 6, and 7.   Nontaxable sales. Some states require nontaxable sales to be broken down into categories such as labor, freight, wholesale, out-of-state sales, or other possible categories.

8. Total sales amount, including sales tax. This column serves as a double-check on your totals. The sum of the amounts in columns 3 through 7 should equal the amount in column 8.

DAILY POSTING

If you have a moderate or heavy volume of sales, you probably should post the income ledger daily. Add up your sales for the day and post your totals to the proper columns in the ledger. Compute separate totals for taxable sales (post to column 3), sales tax (column 4), nontaxable sales (columns 5, 6, and 7), and total (column 8). No need to make any entries under sales period (column 2).

After you have posted the ledger, add the daily totals in columns 3, 4, 5, 6, and 7 together. They should equal the total in column 8, which is the grand total for the day. The procedure is a lot simpler in the doing than in the explaining. You really should have no trouble getting the hang of it.

INCOME LEDGER Month of _June_

1	2	3	4	5	6	7	8
Date	Sales Period	Taxable Sales	Sales Tax	Non-taxable freight	Non-taxable Wholesale	Non-taxable Other	Total Sales
1		173.24	10.39				183.63
2		217.36	13.04	7.00			237.40
3							
4							
5	3rd - 5th	577.82	34.67	18.00			630.49
6		118.71	7.12				125.83
7	closed						
8		266.94	16.02	14.19	275.00		572.15
9							

Income Ledger   Month of: June

1	2	3	4	5	6	7	8
	Sales	Taxable	Sales		Non-Taxable Sales		Total
Date	Period	Sales	Tax	Freight	Wholesale	Other	Sales
1		$173.24	$10.39				$183.63
2		$217.36	$13.04	$7.00			$237.40
3							
4							
5	3rd - 5th	$577.82	$34.67	$18.00			$630.49
6		$118.71	$7.12				$125.83
7	closed						
8		$266.94	$16.02	$14.19	$275.00		$572.15
9							

Three examples of an income record. The hand-posted ledger (top) and the Excel spreadsheet (middle) are identical. The "Profit & Loss" (bottom) is a QuickBooks record that shows the same daily income totals as the top two ledgers, but without rows and columns.

Your Business
Transaction Detail By Account
June 1 - 8, 2017

Date	Memo	Amount
#3 Taxable sales		
6/1/2017	Deposit	173.24
6/2/2017	Deposit	217.36
6/5/2017	June 3-5	577.82
6/6/2017	Deposit	118.71
6/8/2017	Deposit	266.94
Total #3 Taxable sales		1,354.07
#4 Sales tax		
6/1/2017	Deposit	10.39
6/2/2017	Deposit	13.04
6/5/2017	Deposit	34.67
6/6/2017	Deposit	7.12
6/8/2017	Deposit	16.02
Total #4 Sales tax		81.24
#5 Freight		
6/2/2017	Deposit	7.00
6/5/2017	Deposit	18.00
6/8/2017	Deposit	14.19
Total #5 Freight		39.19
#6 Wholesale		
6/8/2017	Deposit	275.00
Total #6 Wholesale		275.00
TOTAL		**1,749.50**

POSTING EVERY FEW DAYS OR ONCE A WEEK

If you have only a few sales each day, you can post the ledger every few days or once a week. Total all your sales for the period, keeping separate totals for taxable sales, sales tax, and nontaxable sales. Enter the totals on the line corresponding with the last day of your sales period. For example, if the sales you are combining are for June 3 through June 5, post your totals on the June 5 line. Under sales period (column 2), note the period: "June 3–5."

Don't feel that you must stick to one method of posting once you have started. If daily posting becomes too tedious, try posting every three days or five days. If you post your income ledger every few days, and a busy time comes along, switch over to daily posting for the busy period.

The posting only becomes a nightmare if the paperwork is allowed to accumulate. All of a sudden there's a three-week backlog, all the receipts are mixed up, some billings are missing, and, Oh, how I hate bookkeeping! It doesn't have to happen that way if you keep your ledger up to date.

END-OF-MONTH PROCEDURE

No matter how frequently or infrequently you do your posting, run a monthly total at month-end, even though it may not be a full five or seven days since your last regular posting. Don't let a posting period cross months. You will often want, and some tax forms may require, monthly totals. As with your daily or period totals, your monthly totals in columns 3, 4, 5, 6, and 7 should equal the total in column 8.

YEAR-END PROCEDURE

Record the twelve monthly totals on the year-end summary page. Your yearly totals in columns 3, 4, 5, 6, and 7 should equal the total in column 8.

If you are keeping books on the cash method of accounting, that's all there is to it. No year-end adjustments are needed. You're done until next year. (If you don't know what the cash method is, don't worry; you're already using it.)

If you are keeping books on the accrual method of accounting, you add any credit sales you made this year that are not yet paid, money owed to you on December 31. "Credit sales" refer to credit you extend directly to your customers, not to credit cards you accept. When the money finally comes in the new year, you must remember not to post it to income, because you already posted it in December. If this sounds confusing, you're right, it is. It's one reason why most businesses avoid accrual accounting.

Altering the Ledgers

Feel free to alter the income ledger to suit your needs. Many businesses post taxable sales and sales tax (columns 3 and 4) as one combined figure in one column, and then back off the sales tax from the monthly totals. Some businesses want a separate column for each product or group of products they sell, or for different services they provide. You may not need the nontaxable sales information (columns 5, 6, and 7), or you may want to title them differently. And for some businesses, the total column may be all you want and need, period.

How to Record Sales Returns

Sales returns should be handled as if they were negative sales. Prepare a separate return invoice (or credit memo, or whatever you want to call it) for each return, and mark it clearly RETURN or REFUND. Write down all the information that was on the original invoice, including the sales tax. Record the return the same way you record current sales. You don't record the return on the date the original sale was made. The return is recorded when the return is made, not when the original sale was made.

Filing Your Sales Invoices and Receipts

Keep your sales invoices/receipts at least three years. These are the source documents that support your tax returns. If your invoices are not already bound, batch them monthly (staples, rubber bands, manila envelopes) before filing them away.

Installment Sales

Installment sales, where you receive periodic payments on account, are handled in one of two ways. If you are on the cash basis, post your income ledger as the payments come in. If you are on the accrual basis, you have the option to (1) record the income as the payments come in, same as cash-basis businesses; or (2) post the entire amount of the sale to your income ledger when you make the sale. Accrual businesses should get help from an accountant when making this choice. A lot of tax money may be at stake.

For all installment sales, set up a record to keep track of each sale: the full amount of the sale, the terms agreed upon, the payments, and the balance owed. This record is kept in addition to your income records. Installment sales are posted to both.

Returned (Bounced) Checks

If a customer's check bounces, your bank will return the check to you with an explanation. "Insufficient funds" means that there is not enough money in the customer's account to pay the check. Often, this is not an intentionally written bad check. Get in touch with your customer and find out when you can redeposit the check (better yet, ask the customer to come back and give you cash). If the check bounces a second time, the bank will not accept it a third time. Your bank will impose a service charge on you if your customer's check bounces; two charges if it bounces twice.

"Account closed" means just that. This is not a good sign. Honest people don't usually write checks on closed accounts. If the check came back from the bank marked "Stop payment," the customer deliberately stopped payment. Stop payments are usually used when checks are lost or stolen, but sometimes a customer gets mad or changes his mind after the sale, and stops payment in order to be sure he'll get his money back. In either case, try to contact your customer, find out what happened, and get payment. "Return to maker" is a general term; usually it means the same as "insufficient funds."

One possible way to collect on a bounced check is to "put it in for collection," a procedure that is very effective when you are dealing with well-meaning customers who are always down to their last penny. You give the bounced check back to your bank and request that it be held for collection. Your bank then sends the check back to your customer's bank, which will hold the check for up to a month. If any funds are deposited to the customer's account during this holding period, any checks held for collection will be paid first. Banks charge a fee for this service, so before you put a check in for collection (and hope it will eventually be paid), find out what it's going to cost you.

If all attempts at collection prove futile, you need to adjust your income or your expense record and your bank account record. For hand-posted and spreadsheet ledgers, you can do this in one of two ways: (1) Make a minus (negative) entry in your income ledger, reducing your income by the amount of the bounced check; or (2) record a bad-debt expense in your expenditure ledger by the amount of the bounced check. Either entry accomplishes the same thing. You also need to reduce your bank account balance by the amount of the bounced check. If you are using accounting software, record a minus bank deposit (a deposit with a minus sign in front of it), which will reduce your income and your bank account balance at the same time.

CREDIT SALES

Credit sales, also known as direct credit or selling on account, means that you, the business owner, extend credit to your customers. The term *credit sales* does not refer to accepting credit cards. Credit

cards are processed the same as cash transactions. There is a section in the T.C.B.: Take Care of Business chapter on how to become a credit card merchant.

Almost all wholesale businesses extend direct credit to their business customers. Some retail stores and self-employed individuals extend direct credit to regular customers and clients.

Direct credit involves more work and record-keeping on your part and a much larger expenditure of energy. You decide who you will and will not extend credit to and how flexible or inflexible your credit policy will be. It is a good idea to have a formal, written credit policy that applies to all customers, although you will find, time and again, that each customer is different and may require special handling. Any customer seeking credit should be made aware of your policy, which should clearly state: (1) maximum credit allowed; (2) payment timetable; and (3) any finance charges or late charges.

Adding finance charges, late charges, or interest to late payments may or may not be a good idea for your business. Customers who are always short of cash tend to give priority to bills that add finance charges. But many customers resent the implied threat, particularly when it comes from a small business where the customer knows you personally. There is something inherently unfriendly about late-payment penalties.

There's an old saying, you can catch more bees with honey than with vinegar (or something like that). Rather than threatening a penalty, offer an incentive for prompt or early payment: a small discount, or free shipping, or a "special" gift. Not only will you get a better response, you will generate more goodwill with your customers. And you can skip the rest of this credit section.

Federal Laws for Finance Charges

If you impose finance charges, you must abide by the federal Truth in Lending Act, Fair Credit Billing Act, and Equal Credit Opportunity Act.

The Truth in Lending Act requires that all customers be told the full details of the finance charges. Before the first transaction is made on any credit account, the creditor (you, the merchant) must disclose in writing (1) the conditions under which a finance charge may be imposed; (2) the method of determining the amount of the finance charge; (3) the minimum periodic payment required; and

(4) your customer's legal rights regarding possible errors or questions.

The Fair Credit Billing Act requires you to make prompt correction of a billing mistake.

The Equal Credit Opportunity Act prohibits discrimination against an applicant for credit on the basis of age, sex, marital status, race, or religion. If you deny credit, this act requires you to tell an applicant why credit was denied. You must keep all credit applications for a year.

These acts specify what information must be presented to the customer, right down to the exact wording and size of the print, and when the information must be made available.

In addition to the above laws, you may have to abide by the Consumer Credit Protection Act, Fair Credit Reporting Act, and Fair Debt Collection Practices Act. You can get information about all of these wonderful laws from the Federal Trade Commission, Washington, DC 20580, or on their website, FTC.gov.

None of the above federal laws regulate what interest you may charge your customers. Most states have usury laws that specify maximum interest, how it is to be calculated, and probably a hundred other details. Contact your state's department of consumer affairs for more information.

Credit Records

When you extend direct credit, you need to set up a record of each credit customer, purchases made, payments made, and balance owed. This credit record is in addition to your income records. Credit sales are posted to both. Businesses using the cash method of accounting (most small businesses) do not record credit sales in the income record until the money is collected, but you still want to keep track of what customers owe you. That's the reason for a separate credit record.

Accounting Software

If you use accounting software such as QuickBooks, you can create a customer file for each credit customer, but be careful that the entries in the customer files do not automatically transfer to your income records. (Reread the last paragraph if you don't understand why.) If your software doesn't seem to want to cooperate, if entries in customer account records are showing up in your income reports, don't use the software for customer

CREDIT LEDGER					
#1 Date of Sale	#2 Name of Customer	#3 Invoice Number	#4 Total Sale	#5 Date Paid	#6 Memo
1/18	Brenneman	113	$53.12	2/10	
1/23	S. Ross	128	$17.92		note sent 3/1
1/14	Rygh	134	$18.82	2/28	
2/12	S. Miley	186	$112.12		

records. Set up your customer credit records separate from the software. Follow the same procedures explained below for hand-posted ledgers and spreadsheets. Don't enter sales information in the software until you collect the money and record the sale, the same way you record all other sales.

Credit Ledger

If you don't have a large number of credit sales, you can easily set up a credit ledger to keep track of unpaid accounts (accounts receivable). You can use the sample credit ledger page as a prototype. The ledger has six columns:

Column 1: Date of sale.

Column 2: Customer's name.

Column 3: Invoice number.

Column 4: Total amount of sale including sales tax, shipping, and any other charges.

Column 5: Date paid.

Column 6: Memo, for any notes you want to keep.

Each credit sale should be recorded on a separate line on the credit ledger. Post columns 1 through 4 from the invoice, either when you make the sale or when you post your income ledger. Be sure to write the words "CREDIT SALE" on the invoice when you make the sale. Post column 5 when you get paid. At any time, you can glance down your credit ledger and, by looking at column 5, tell who still owes you money. Now, collecting that money—well, that's another story.

Remember, credit sales are also posted to your income ledger (after you collect the money) as well as to any credit ledger. The income ledger is your only complete record of income from all sales.

A Simple Alternative to the Credit Ledger

Instead of setting up a credit ledger, keep copies of your credit sales invoices in an "unpaid" file. When you receive payment, pull the invoice from the unpaid file, record the income, and file the invoice with your other paid invoices. Under this system, you can easily look through your unpaid invoices to see who owes you money.

Businesses that regularly make a large number of credit sales will need a more elaborate credit system. Stores with regular credit customers often keep a separate file on each customer with a complete record of sales and payments.

You and Your Credit Customers

The hardest part of direct credit is trying to collect past-due accounts from slow or nonpaying customers. I can think of no single aspect of

OUR CREDIT POLICY:

100% DOWN

No Monthly Payments!

business that is more upsetting than trying to deal with people who can't or won't pay their bills. You begin to resent the customers and they begin to resent you. Bad and sometimes bitter feelings build up. You decide for yourself where you draw the line, that the money is no longer worth the aggravation.

In fact, extending too much credit can destroy a business. I knew a small convenience store owned by a nice and eager-to-please couple that offered credit to everyone in the neighborhood. Quite a few customers ran up large bills they couldn't pay, until the shopkeepers finally cut off their credit. The customers, unable or unwilling to face the store owners, not only didn't pay their bills, they stopped coming in the store completely. They bought their groceries elsewhere. The poor couple not only never collected on the old sales, they lost out on new sales as well. The couple went broke and the store folded.

A few months later, a brand-new but much wiser owner reopened the store. And, lo and behold, all the old deadbeat customers came back to shop! It wasn't the new owner's responsibility to collect the old owner's debts; this was a new business. The new owner extended limited credit to reliable customers and never let the accounts get too high or too far behind. The owner had the rare talent of being able to look a negligent customer right in the eye, and say, friendly yet firmly, "Pay up." And they did. And she prospered.

Uncollectible Accounts

If you cannot collect what a customer owes you, there is no good news here. You don't get to reduce your income, because the income was never recorded in the first place. And you don't get a bad-debt tax write-off either. I know that doesn't sound fair, and it isn't, but that is how the tax laws are written. You are out the money you should have earned, and the IRS says "Tough luck."

RECORDING EXPENDITURES

Your expenditure records—your expense ledgers, spreadsheets, or accounting software reports—show all payments that you make: business expenses, payroll, loan repayments, personal draws (money you pay to yourself), and any other outlays.

The most important function of the expenditure record is to separate different types of expenditures into categories, such as inventory, supplies, rent, advertising, and so on. Each category of expenditure is recorded separately. For this reason, you cannot summarize a number of transactions on one line as you can with sales in the income records.

If you are keeping your records on hand-posted ledgers or spreadsheets, these records have columns of numbers, each column for a different category of expense. Accounting software does not have columns but instead has a list of expense categories. The software has the same information as a hand-posted ledger or a spreadsheet, the same expense categories, just arranged differently.

There are literally hundreds of different categories of business expenditures. The Taxes chapter lists a hundred of the more typical items. But you certainly don't want to post a ledger with 100 columns, or even with 50 or 25 columns. If you are using accounting software, you don't want to scroll through a hundred categories of expense. Neither is necessary. The secret is to know which expenditures need their own categories (their own columns in a ledger) and which expenditures can be combined.

Some expenditures need to have their own category because they are required to be shown separately on your income tax return. Some types of expenditures should have their own categories because they are used repeatedly or in large dollar amounts. You will want to know where your big dollars went, and so will the IRS. Occasional or small expenses can often be combined under "miscellaneous" or any other category that seems appropriate.

The sample expenditure ledger has eleven categories, each in its own column, specific enough to give you a good idea of how your money was spent and to provide information for preparing your income taxes, yet general enough to make the ledgers useful to a large variety of businesses.

Although these expenditure categories have worked for many businesses, they may or may not fit your particular business. Feel free to rename categories, and to add or delete columns.

If you are using accounting software, the software will include a selection of categories that are similar to the ones in my sample, or you can make up your own categories.

Here is a recommended system of posting:

Payments in currency: Get a receipt if possible. If you don't have a receipt, write down what you spent. This way you will have a record of your purchases, you won't forget that you spent the money, and you will have a reminder (the receipts) to record the expenses. I suggest that you record the expenses in your expenditure record as soon as possible, before you lose those receipts. Mark your receipts "posted" or "recorded" or "entered" (so you'll know later that, yes, you did post the receipts to your records) and keep the receipts in a file or envelope.

Payments by check: When you write a check, record the information in your checkbook (check register): check number, date, amount, paid to, and a brief description of what the payment is for. If you are using accounting software, and if you have access to the software at the time you are writing a check, you can just enter the check information directly into the software banking record.

Try to get an invoice or receipt for every bill you pay. Keep one copy as a record of your payment. Destroy duplicate copies so you won't mistakenly pay an invoice twice. Write the check number on each receipt or invoice before filing it. If there is ever a question about the bill, the check number will tell you that, yes, the bill was paid, and here's a record of the check to prove it.

Copy the information from your checkbook into your expenditure ledger, or into your software banking record, if you haven't already done so. How often you sit down and copy the information depends on your time schedule and the volume of checks you write. Whatever schedule you choose, stick to it. Don't get behind in the paperwork.

You can pay business expenses from a personal bank account or your business account. You are entitled to a full tax deduction (sole proprietors only; partnerships, corporations, and LLCs should pay their bills from a business bank account).

Payments by debit card: Debit card payments are handled the same way as payments by check or currency. Business expenses paid with your debit card are fully deductible, even if the debit card is from your personal, non-business bank account (sole proprietors only). However, you will simplify your recordkeeping tremendously if you pay your business expenses with your business bank account debit card, and not combine business and personal expenses on the same debit card.

Debit card charges are, as you know, deducted directly and immediately from your bank account. It's mighty easy to run up a bunch of debit card bills and not notice how much you're spending

until the monthly statement comes in—or until the card is suddenly over limit. Normally diligent business owners who record checks in their expense records when the checks are written will not record debit card purchases until the bank statement comes in at the end of the month. There is nothing wrong with this system, as long as you are sure you have enough money in the bank account to cover all of your expenses. Just be sure all business-related debit card payments get recorded in your expense records at least every month. And try to get receipts for all business purchases. If you don't have receipts, note on the bank statement (if it is a paper statement) what the purchase was for.

By the way, you should not use your bank statement to record checks that you've written. Checks, unlike debit cards, do not always clear the bank immediately. Your expenditure record should show all checks you write, not just the checks that have cleared the bank.

Payments by credit card: Record credit card purchases from the individual receipts or from your credit card statement, whichever is easier. If you are making partial payments on your credit card bill, you will have to figure out an easy method of allocating those payments. Any system that eventually gets all of your business expenses posted to your expense records will work.

Purchases made with bank credit cards such as VISA and MasterCard are deducted the year you make the charge, not the year paid, even for cash-basis businesses. So you can post your entire credit card bill each month, whether you pay it or not. This rule does not apply to store credit cards or gasoline company cards.

If you are a sole proprietor, you don't need a credit card in your business name. You can use your personal credit card for business purchases and get a full tax write-off for the business purchases, and for the business portion of any credit card fees and interest. If you want to keep the bookkeeping simple, you can get a separate credit card that you use only for business purchases. Credit card issuers have no restrictions on what you can and cannot purchase with a personal credit card. It's your card to use as you wish. And the IRS does not care what name is on the credit card; if the purchase is for business, it is deductible. Again, this applies only to sole proprietors. Partnerships, corporations, and LLCs should not pay bills from a partner's or an owner's personal credit card.

When acquiring a credit card, don't be seduced by flashy advertising and luxurious-looking cards. No one who accepts your card will care about its name or how it looks. Get the best deal you can find.

Electronic payments: Payments that are automatically deducted from your bank account often appear only on your monthly bank statement. The easiest system is to post these payments to your expenditure record once a month when you get your bank statement. Just don't forget, if your cash is tight, that your bank account wrote itself a check, and there is less money in that account than your checkbook might indicate.

Checkbook and Ledger Combined?

Probably some of you are already asking: Why have both a checkbook and an expenditure ledger? The expenditure ledger provides you with information that your checkbook does not show, such as expenditures paid by cash and credit card. The ledger makes it easy to summarize and review categories of expenditure. Your checkbook cannot readily show you how much you spent on inventory or parts last month, or on office supplies; it doesn't even show the total combined expenditures.

Your checkbook, on the other hand, shows your running bank balance and has space for ticking off the canceled checks, for recording void checks and adding errors, and for posting deposits.

Accounting software integrates the checkbook record and the income and expense records. The software eliminates the two-step procedure, which will save you time and reduce the possibility of errors copying one record to another one.

There are also hand-posted bookkeeping systems, often called "one-write" systems, that combine the checkbook and your ledgers. Even in today's electronic world, many small businesses use and like the simplicity of the checkbook-ledger.

Posting the Expenditure Ledger

For people using hand-posted ledgers and spreadsheets, here is how to record expenditures in the ledger. For people using accounting software, the categories in columns 1 through 11 are good ones to set up in your records.

First column: Date.

Second column: Check number. If you pay by currency, write "cash" in this column, or "MO" for money orders, "debit" for debit cards, "credit" for credit cards, "electronic" if the payment was automatically deducted from your bank account.

Third column: Who the money was paid to.

Fourth column: Total amount of the payment. This column will provide a double-check of your monthly and year-end totals. Post all payments to this "total" column and to one or more of the following expenditure columns:

Column 1—Inventory. If you make or sell a product, this will be your most important column. Record in column 1 all the goods you purchase for resale or for manufacturing, including any delivery charges. Include all the related materials that go into or are consumed in the process of preparing your product for sale, such as a jeweler's solder or a dressmaker's thread. Include packaging materials if they are an integral part of your product. If your packaging costs are only occasional or incidental, record them in column 2. Do not include in column 1 office supplies, tools, equipment, or any material purchased for reasons other than resale.

Column 2—Supplies, Postage, etc. These are expenses incidental to your work: office supplies, paper, pencils, coffee, small tools that will not last more than a year. Do not include the supplies that become part of your product or are consumed in making your product; such expenses are considered part of inventory and belong in column 1. Draws for petty cash should also be posted to column 2. Petty cash is explained later in this chapter.

Column 3—Outside Contractors. For independent contractors, consultants, and other individuals who are not employees on your payroll, see "Hiring Help" in the Growing Up chapter). Also use this column for professional services such as a bookkeeper and tax accountant.

Column 4—Employee Payroll. You record employee payroll both here in column 4 and in a separate payroll ledger (discussed in "Hiring Help" in the Growing Up chapter).

				Col. #1	Col. #2	Col. #3	Col. #4	Col. #5	Col. #6	Col. #7	Col. #8	Col. #9	Col. #10	Col. #11
Date	Ck. #	Payee	Total	Inventory	Supplies	Outside	Employee	Advertising	Rent	Utilities	Taxes &		Misc.	Non-
					Postage	Contractors	Payroll				Licenses			Deductible
6/1	1202	R&R Realty	450.00						450.00					
6/4	1203	PG&E	65.40							65.40				
6/7	cash	Coast Hdwr.	14.44		14.44									
6/10	1204	CRK Supply	224.65	224.65										
6/16	debit	Staples	47.13		47.13									

Your Business
Expenditure Ledger

The separate payroll ledger shows the full detail of the payment: gross pay, amounts withheld, and net pay. Column 4, however, should show only the net pay, the actual amount of the payroll check (the employee's take-home pay).

Payroll taxes that you withhold from your employees are also recorded in column 4, but only at the time you pay them to the government. Withheld taxes include income, Social Security, Medicare, and possibly state disability.

Don't confuse these withheld payroll taxes with payroll taxes that you, the employer, pay, such as the employer's portion of Social Security and Medicare, and federal and state unemployment taxes. Employer-paid payroll taxes are posted to column 8 (taxes and licenses). This is a confusing area because the employee and employer taxes are reported to the government on the same form and paid with the same check.

Payments to yourself should not be recorded here unless you have incorporated and are an owner-employee of your corporation. As a sole proprietor, a partner in a partnership, or an owner of a limited liability company, your own wage is not an expense of your business, and is posted to column 11 (nondeductible).

Column 5—Advertising. You can include promotion expenses in this column, such as brochures and business gifts.

Column 6—Rent. Rent on business property is fully deductible except for lease-purchase contracts. If you own the building your business occupies, you depreciate the building (covered in the Taxes chapter).

Home-based businesses: Rent on an office, workshop, or other business space in the home is deducted on your tax return as a separate category just for home businesses. The rent is not included in the rent category on your tax return. So if you are posting home office rent to column 6, be careful to separate it out when preparing your tax return. See the chapter Home-Based Business.

Column 7—Utilities. Power, water, garbage, heating oil or propane, etc. Your telephone expenses can be included in this column or given their own column.

Home-based businesses: The information about home-based businesses under column 6 above also applies to home utilities, except for telephone. Telephone expenses are not considered part of the home business tax deduction, and can be deducted separately, under utilities. The business portion of your telephone bill should be posted here in column 7.

Column 8—Taxes and Licenses. Record any tax payment or license fee here except withheld payroll taxes (see instructions under column 4). Note in the "paid to" column what the payment is for; you will need this information for your income tax return.

Sales tax: The only sales tax posted to column 8 is the amount you remit to the state, collected from your sales. Any sales tax you pay when purchasing goods should be included as part of the price of the goods purchased. For example, if your business cards cost $40.00 plus $2.40 sales tax, you should enter $42.40 in column 2. Nothing should be entered in column 8.

Column 9—*is blank*. I cannot possibly foresee all of your needs, so here is one extra untitled column to use or not to use as you see fit.

Column 10—Miscellaneous. The ol' catchall, for unusual expenditures and expenditures that do not recur enough to justify their own column. For example, this column can include payments for insurance, dues and organization fees, out-of-town travel, education expenses, minor repairs, or any of the dozens of one-time expenses you incur. Interest payments can be posted here, but repayment of a loan principal should be posted to column #11—Nondeductible. A more detailed list of items to post to column 10 can be found in the Taxes chapter.

Any expense that you are posting to column 10 that starts to recur regularly should be moved to its own column. Use column 9 or another column you are not using. Feel free to change the heading of any column in the ledger to suit your needs.

Column 11—Nondeductible. Use for:

1. Personal draws: money you pay yourself.

2. Furniture, tools, equipment, machinery, buildings, and other fixed (depreciable) assets. These expenses are deductible but may have to be depreciated over a period of years. Some people post these assets to the miscellaneous column; some set up a separate column just for fixed assets. Whatever column you use, these purchases should also be recorded on a separate asset ledger, so that you have a record of every asset you purchase. You will need this record for your income taxes and for calculating profit or loss when you sell or abandon an asset. This is covered in the Taxes chapter.

3. Repayment of business loans—principal only. A loan is not income when received and is not an expense when paid. Any interest paid on a business loan is a valid expense and should be posted to column 10.

4. Fines or penalties for breaking the law, including traffic tickets. These may be "valid" business expenses, but they are not deductible for income taxes. Contractual or other

fines or penalties, if you did not violate state or federal law, are deductible.

5. Accounts payable. For businesses on the accrual basis, this is a year-end adjustment, explained at the end of this section. For businesses on the cash basis, you can ignore accounts payable. (If you don't know what this is about, you can also ignore it; you are using the cash basis anyway.)

6. If you write a check on your business account for personal, non-business expenses, or if you write a check for something that is part personal and part business, the non-business portion is not deductible and should be posted here. The business portion should be posted to the column it applies to.

Uncashed Checks

If a check you write is never cashed, lost in the mail, or stop payment issued, make a negative (bracketed) entry in your expenditure record, reducing the expense. Under "payee" make a note of what you are doing. Also go back to the original entry and note there what happened and the date you posted the negative entry. Just make a note; don't change the original entry.

Refunds

If you write checks to refund money to customers, the refunds need to be recorded separately from other expenses. If you have an unused column, label the column "refunds" or "returns" (which is the term used by the IRS on business tax returns). Otherwise, add another column. If the refund includes sales tax, you will need to do extra work so the sales tax refund is included when you prepare sales tax returns. See "Refunds" under "Recording Income: Step One."

Recording Vehicle Expenses

There are two ways to record car and truck expenses. You may keep track of actual expenses, or you can take a standard mileage allowance (also called the standard mileage rate). "Vehicles" in the Taxes chapter explains both methods. If you decide to take the standard mileage allowance, you do not have to make any entries in your expenditure record. If you plan to keep track of actual expenses, you should record all vehicle expenses as they are incurred. Use column 9 or another unused column in your expenditure ledger to record these expenses. Note that the cost of the vehicle and any major repairs should not be included in column 9. These costs may have to be depreciated along with other fixed assets. See column 11 above and "Business Assets" and "Depreciation" in the Taxes chapter. If you use the standard mileage allowance, however, you do not depreciate your vehicle.

Monthly Totals

Ledgers: For hand ledgers and spreadsheets, total all the columns of your expenditure ledger each month. Cross-check the monthly totals to the "total" column. Correct any errors.

Do not, however, start a new expenditure ledger page for each new month. If a month ends and only half a page is used, double-underline your total, skip two lines, and start the next month on the same page.

Software: If you are using accounting software, you do not have to do anything. The software will give you monthly totals—or for any other time period you want—just by clicking on the options offered, or entering the beginning and ending dates on the profit and loss record.

Year-End Procedures

If you are on the cash basis (most small businesses), the only additional entries you make at year-end are for purchases using a credit card that were made but not paid for by December 31. Purchases made with bank credit cards, such as VISA and MasterCard, are deductible the year charged, not the year paid, even for cash-basis taxpayers. Add these purchases to your December expenses. When you pay the bill in the new year, do not deduct the expenses a second time. Record the expenditure in column 11 (nondeductible). This law does not apply to store credit cards, which for cash-basis taxpayers are deducted when paid.

Ledgers and spreadsheets: Add up your monthly totals for the year.

Accounting software: You don't have to add up anything.

Accrual Businesses: Accounts Payable

Accounts payable ("payables") are unpaid bills and unpaid accounts that you owe, and expenses you've incurred but haven't yet been billed for. Businesses using the accrual method need to make year-end entries for year-end accounts payable: expenses incurred but not paid by December 31. Cash-method businesses (most small businesses) can happily ignore this.

Accrual businesses should list each unpaid bill in your expenditure record in the appropriate columns. As you record each unpaid bill, clearly mark it ACCOUNTS PAYABLE. Any other unpaid expense for the year just ended, such as payroll taxes, should also be recorded on this year-end summary, one to a line, even if you have not received a bill. Any unpaid credit card charges should also be included.

The accounts payable require special handling when paid the following year. These expenses are deductible the year they were incurred, which is the year just ended. They may not be deducted again next year, even though they will be paid next year. When the bills are paid (you will recognize them because you marked them ACCOUNTS PAYABLE when you recorded them), they are posted to column 11 (nondeductible).

Altering the Ledgers and Designing Your Own

After a year's experience with these ledgers, learning which categories of expense you need and don't need, you can easily design your own ledgers. Do you need the Outside Contractor column, or the Payroll column, or the Advertising column? Instead, you may want a separate column for equipment purchases, or freight charges, or travel, or some other category important to your business. Many small businesses set up their expenditure ledger to exactly match the categories on the income tax forms. For my own business, I try to use as few columns as possible to minimize my recordkeeping; and yet I've met business owners who felt they had to have twenty or more categories to keep their expenditures straight.

Asset Ledger

When you purchase business assets—equipment, machinery, furniture, and other permanent assets—you record the purchase in the expense record. You should also keep a separate record of all assets purchased, so you have a permanent record of each of your assets, when you purchased each asset, how the assets were depreciated or deducted on your tax return (covered in the Taxes chapter), and how and when they were sold or disposed of. This record will also be useful if your state has a tax on business assets and requires a list of them, or if you have an insurance claim.

List each purchase separately. Fill out the information when you purchase an asset, and you'll never have to hunt up the information a second time. Each item should include:

1. Date purchased, or date first used in business if purchased before going into business.

2. Description, detailed enough so it can't be confused with other assets you buy. If you have two or more identical items, include a serial number or a similar designation in the description.

3. Whether the asset was purchased new or used.

4. Cost, including any sales tax and any delivery or installation charges.

5. Percentage used for business.

6. Write-off method. This is how the asset was deducted or depreciated on your tax return. This is covered in the Taxes chapter.

7. Conclusion. Date the asset was sold, retired, destroyed, stolen, or whatever else happened to it, and proceeds if sold or if there was an insurance settlement.

This asset ledger may not be adequate for businesses purchasing and maintaining heavy machinery or expensive equipment. Manufacturing equipment, construction equipment, and the like may require separate records for each item.

A Brief Introduction to QuickBooks

There are several accounting software programs and apps, but one, QuickBooks, has managed to capture over 90 percent of the market. It is used by most accountants and bookkeepers and by most of the small businesses that use accounting software other than spreadsheets.

For people who are familiar with hand-posted ledgers and spreadsheet ledgers, QuickBooks can be puzzling when you first look at it. There are no ledger sheets to fill in. There are no columns of numbers. QuickBooks is a blank screen with dozens of actions to choose from.

The records QuickBooks produces (QuickBooks calls them "reports") have the same information that hand-posted and spreadsheet ledgers have, just arranged differently. People who don't know how to read ledgers will probably find QuickBooks reports easier to understand than traditional ledgers.

Like most good software, you can easily learn the basics of QuickBooks and get your business records set up and working, quickly. The software does live up to its name. But QuickBooks can get complicated and confusing just as quickly. For someone just getting started, especially someone with no accounting background, there are a few shortcuts, ways to avoid some of the complexity of the QuickBooks system.

TYPES OF ACCOUNTS

QuickBooks has several types of accounts, but the two QuickBooks categories that are most important to small businesses are the same two that are

Your Business Asset Ledger						
Date Purch.	Description	New/Used	Cost	Business %	Write Off	Conclusion
1/6/2017	Desk chair	New	$67.34	100%	Option #1	
3/4/2017	H-P printer #640	New	$95.55	100%	Option #1	
6/14/2017	Hooboy Printing Press	Used	$4,700.00	100%	Option #2	

most important in traditional ledgers: income and expense. QuickBooks also has asset accounts, liability accounts, and equity accounts, some of which will be useful to you and some of which you can ignore completely. But to get started, all you need to learn is how to record income and expenses and keep a record of your bank balance.

QUICKBOOKS LOOKS LIKE A CHECKBOOK

Basically, QuickBooks is designed to look like a checkbook register. It's actually a lot more than a checkbook register, but it's set up to look like one, and it helps if you think of it as one. You start by entering the amount of money you have in your business bank account. That's your beginning balance.

RECORDING INCOME

QuickBooks has different options for recording sales, but the easiest way is to enter the income on a form that resembles a deposit slip. You are not actually making a deposit to your bank account, but QuickBooks records it as a deposit. You can break the "deposit" down into different types of income, just like you would in an income ledger. QuickBooks adds the deposit to your bank balance and to your record of income. The procedure:

1. Under Banking, select Deposit.

2. Fill out the amount of the sale.

3. Enter the income account or accounts. The software has pre-labeled accounts, or you can create your own. You can use one or more of the categories shown on the sample income ledger.

RECORDING EXPENSES: CHECKS

When you write a check, you copy the information into QuickBooks on a form that resembles a check. The QuickBooks "check" is not a real check (although QuickBooks does offer real check writing as an added option), it just looks like one. You select an expense account category from the QuickBooks list, or create your own category. QuickBooks keeps a record of every payment you make, organized both by check number order and by expense category.

RECORDING EXPENSES: DEBIT CARDS

Debit card transactions go through your regular bank account, just like writing checks. When you want to record debit card expenses in QuickBooks, where it asks for a check number, write Debit Card; or if you want to have a quick reference of all debit card entries, include a number with each entry: Debit Card 1, Debit Card 2, and so on. Then fill in the expense information, the same as if you were writing a check.

NON-BANK TRANSACTIONS

A problem with QuickBooks, at least for beginners, is that many purchases are not made by check or debit card, and income is not necessarily deposited to a bank account. So how do you enter non-bank activity in QuickBooks software forms designed to look like checks and deposit slips?

There are two ways. One is confusing (the one QuickBooks recommends), and one is easy (the one I use). The QuickBooks method for recording income or expenses that don't go through a bank account is to create what they call "journal entries" for income and expenses, which requires a knowledge of debits and credits and double entry bookkeeping, a knowledge that most people don't have.

Instead of making journal entries, a much easier system is to create a dummy bank account in QuickBooks. Give the dummy bank account any name you like, other than the name of your real bank account. When you want to record income that does not go through a real bank account, go to the dummy account and "make a deposit" to that account. It's not a real deposit, of course, but it will result in a real record of your income in the QuickBooks income record. Likewise, when you want to record an expense that does not go through a real bank account, go to the dummy account and "write a check." Make up a check number, post the date, the amount, and the expense category. You haven't really written a check, but QuickBooks will use the "check" information to record the expense in the expense record.

If you'd like to keep separate records of transactions in cash as opposed to, say, credit card transactions, you can create a dummy bank account called CASH to record cash income and expenses, and another dummy bank account called CREDIT CARD for credit card purchases.

The result of setting up dummy bank accounts is that all income and expenses will get recorded correctly in the QuickBooks reports, but there also will be a report (a balance sheet) showing a bank account that doesn't really exist, with a dollar balance in the account, actually a negative balance, that is meaningless. Don't worry. Ignore it; it's not real. The fake bank account balance does not go on your tax return or on any other business records.

JOURNAL ENTRIES

If you do need to make journal entries in Quick-Books, here's the procedure to remember: If you are recording income, you *debit* cash and *credit* income. If you are recording an expense, you *debit* the expense and *credit* cash. Note that when you spend money, decreasing your cash, you *credit* the cash. These are bookkeeping terms, *debit* and *credit*, and are often confusing to people with no bookkeeping training, but QuickBooks uses these terms in their journal entries.

EQUIPMENT PURCHASES

When you purchase business assets such as equipment, machinery, a computer, or furniture, you have the option (with exceptions, explained in the Taxes chapter) of deducting the cost immediately or spreading out the deduction (depreciating the assets) over several years. Most small businesses write off the cost the year of purchase. For those businesses, in QuickBooks you should create an expense category called "business assets" or "equipment," or something similar.

You should not post the purchase to an asset account, because QuickBooks does not include asset account entries in the expense reports. If you don't enter the purchases as expenses, if you enter them as assets, it's too easy to forget that you made the purchases when you are figuring your income taxes or looking at your profit and loss statements (which do not include assets).

However, you should keep a permanent record of all assets purchased, in QuickBooks or on a separate asset record. See "Asset Ledger" above.

ACCESSING YOUR RECORDS

Any time you want, you can look up any of your records, for any period of time. Go to Reports, Company and Financial, and then Profit and Loss (for income and expenses) or Bank (for your bank account).

These are just a few tips to get you started in QuickBooks. There is a bit of a learning curve, but once you get used to the software, you'll understand why so many people like it.

PETTY CASH

A petty cash fund provides a systematic method for paying and recording out-of-pocket cash payments and payments too small to be made by check. ("Cash" in petty cash refers to currency, not to checks, which is just the opposite of my earlier definition. Nobody's perfect.)

I suggest, for starters, that you do not have a petty cash fund. It's more bookkeeping, more paperwork, and more procedures to remember. Pay the dollar here, dollar there expenditures out of what cash is on hand, and record the payments directly in your expenditure records. However, if you are always short of cash, or have employees or co-owners who often need cash, I have devised a relatively simple system for handling petty cash. It is a compromise between no system at all and a bookkeeper's dream, and it requires you to follow three rules:

PETTY CASH LEDGER

1	2	3	4
Date	Payee	Amount	Balance
3/1	(Beginning balance)		$50.00
3/12	Stamps	$12.50	$37.50
3/16	C.O.D. charge	$12.75	$24.75
3/17	Office Supplies	$6.99	$17.76
3/20	donation to Boy Scouts	$4.00	$13.76
3/31	coffee for the machine	$5.29	$8.47

1. Keep no more than $50 in the fund.

2. Make payments out of the fund only for miscellaneous supplies and postage, expenses that normally would be posted to column 2 in the expenditure ledger.

3. Use the fund only when there is no practical way to write a check or use a debit or credit card instead.

If you promise to follow those ground rules, here is the procedure:

1. Write a check payable to "Petty Cash" or to yourself for $50. Cash the check at your bank and put the money, a piece of accounting worksheet paper, and a pencil in a separate cash box or cigar box, whatever is handy and relatively safe.

2. Record the check as an expenditure in your ledger, posting it to column 11 (nondeductible).

3. Every time you make a payment from the petty cash fund, record the date, payee, and amount on your accounting worksheet, which has just become your petty cash ledger. Get receipts for the payments if possible and put them in the box with the cash.

4. When the fund starts to get low, total the payments recorded on the worksheet, and add up the remaining cash in the box. The worksheet total and the remaining cash should equal the amount that was originally in the fund ($50). If you are out of balance, you either made an adding error, recorded a payment wrong, failed to record a payment, or else you've been robbed. If you can't find an error, adjust the worksheet total so that your petty cash fund is back in balance. Staple all the petty cash receipts to the worksheet and file it away.

5. Write a check payable to "Petty Cash" or to yourself equal in amount to the total (or the corrected total if there was an error) from the worksheet. Cash the check and put the money in your petty cash box with a new worksheet. Sharpen the pencil.

6. Record the check in the expenditure ledger in column 2 (supplies, postage, etc.).

Thereafter, whenever your petty cash fund gets low, and also at year-end, repeat steps 4, 5, and 6.

FINANCIAL MANAGEMENT: USING YOUR FINANCIAL RECORDS

Your ledgers, spreadsheets, and software reports are more than just a record of your business activity and an aid to preparing income tax forms. They are valuable tools to help you manage your business successfully. You can use your income and expense records to learn how your business is doing, where you could cut expenses or improve income. Using your financial information to help you make decisions is sometimes called *cost accounting*, which is a generic term for just about any financial records you use to help you make decisions. The most important "cost accounting" records are a profit and loss statement and a cash flow statement, and if you buy and sell goods, an inventory record.

Profit and Loss Statement

Without a record of profit and loss, it is difficult for the owner of even the smallest business to determine whether or not the business is making a profit. Your cash balances and the day-to-day cash income and outgo, as important as they are, are not a good indication of profit or loss. Cash flow can, in fact, give you a totally misleading picture of how your business is doing.

Simple profit and loss statements (also called income statements or break-even statements), prepared monthly from your ledgers or printed from your software, can tell you a great deal about your business. A profit and loss statement is, basically, a schedule showing your income and your expenses and the difference between the two.

LEDGERS AND SPREADSHEETS
You create a profit and loss statement from your income and expenditure records.

Income. The income on the profit and loss statement is the monthly income total from your income ledger (columns 3, 5, 6, and 7). You should exclude sales tax, loan income, and any money you put into the business from your own personal funds.

Expenses. Expenses should be separated into two groups: inventory (column 1 in the expenditure ledger) and all other expenses (columns 2 through 10). Do not include column 11.

Profit and Loss Statement
Bear Soft Pretzel Company

January through September

	Month of September	Year to Date
Income	$6,095	$57,724
Inventory	2,077	18,723
Gross Profit	$4,018	$39,001
Other Expenses		
Rent	$400	$3,600
Supplies	32	340
Other	27	226
Total Other Expenses	$459	$4,166
Net Profit	$3,559	$34,835

"All other expenses" are your operating expenses and include everything in columns 2 through 10, except sales tax paid (recorded in column 8, taxes and licenses). Be sure not to include any expenditures from column 11 (nondeductible).

Your total income (gross receipts) less inventory purchases gives you what is known as "gross profit." Gross profit less all the other expenses gives you "net" profit or loss. (Note that in IRS terminology, "gross receipts" and "gross profit" are two different things.)

By showing both a gross and a net profit or loss, you can tell more easily how your expenses relate to income. If you are losing money, you can readily determine if it is the cost of the inventory (cost of goods sold) or the other expenses that are responsible for the loss.

A business that has no inventory does not have to compute gross profit. For such a business, income less "all other expenses" equals net profit or loss.

A statement prepared in the above manner will give you profit and loss information for the month just ended. Some business owners like to see a second column in their profit and loss statement that shows the year-to-date activity. The year-to-date column is prepared in almost the same way as the monthly column. Year-to-date income is the sum of all the monthly income totals in columns 3, 5, 6, and 7 from January 1 to date, including the month just ended.

"All other expenses" is the sum of all the monthly totals in columns 2 through 10, again excluding sales tax payments in column 8.

Your profit and loss statement should look something like the Bear Soft Pretzel Co. illustration. The Bear Soft Pretzel "illustration" is the Profit and Loss Statement (that is being replaced), not the cartoon of the pretzel vendor. The word "illustration" should be replaced with "statement." The cartoon should stay in its current location, not here, and I do have written permission to use the cartoon. This type of profit and loss statement is only approximate. It does not include unpaid expenses or expenses computed at year-end, such as depreciation, and it should not be used for preparing income tax forms.

ACCOUNTING SOFTWARE

Software can automatically produce profit and loss statements for any period you choose, in a variety of formats. You can view a summary statement (Quick-Books calls it "standard") for the month or with the year-to-date similar to the Bear Soft Pretzel example. You can see a statement with full details. You can see year to year comparisons. Just select what you want, select the period (today, this week, this month, last month, etc.), and click "enter."

CASH FLOW

One of the most damaging things that can happen to a business is a cash shortage. Here you are with a successful business, happy customers, and no cash. Whoa! How did that happen? I know of profitable businesses actually forced to shut down for a lack of immediate cash.

To help avoid a sudden cash squeeze, many businesses prepare monthly cash flow projections: estimates of cash that will be coming in and cash that will be spent during the upcoming month. These projections show approximately how much cash will be on hand during the month and alert you to possible cash shortages.

During the first few months your business is in operation, cash projections will be difficult for you to make. You cannot yet estimate how much income

will be coming in, nor will you be familiar enough with your regular expense requirements. But the first few months are a critical time for any business. You should make some attempt to estimate and be prepared for cash needs. Here is a way to project your first month's cash flow:

First, determine how much cash you will need to get your business off to a good start. If yours is a sales or manufacturing business or a service business that stocks parts, estimate how much additional inventory you will need during the first month of business.

Next, add expenses that will be paid during the first month, such as supplies and payroll, and those that will be paid by the first of the next month, such as rent and utilities. Be sure to include your own wage or draw. Then add another 20 percent for unanticipated expenses.

The sum of the above items should give you an estimate of your first month's expenses. Now, how much income do you anticipate during the first month of operation? Obviously, this can only be a guess, but be conservative. And once you've arrived at a good guess, knock it down by 25 percent. All new business owners are overly optimistic.

Estimated Cash Flow Projection
Month of June

	Cash In	Cash Out	Balance
First of Month			
Cash on hand June 1			$3,000
June 1 rent payment		$600	
June 1 utilities		$150	$2,250
Week #1			
Receipts	$1,000		
Inventory purchases		$2,000	
Supplies		$50	$1,200
Week #2			
Receipts	$1,000		
Payroll		$500	$1,700
Week #3			
Receipts	$1,000		
Supplies		$50	$2,650
Week #4			
Receipts	$1,000		
Payroll		$500	
Inventory Purchases		$1,000	
Personal draw		$500	$1,650

Comparing the "guesstimated" income to the projected expenses will give you some idea of your cash needs. It is a rough idea, admittedly, but it is better than no idea at all. Once you have a few months of actual experience behind you, cash flow projections will become easier and more accurate. A good procedure is to estimate income and expenditures week by week, showing the cash on hand at the end of each week.

The main purpose of a cash flow statement is to warn you in advance when cash might get dangerously low. If you know of a big cash outlay coming up next month, such as an insurance payment or a tax payment, or a predictable seasonal drop in sales, the cash flow statement will show you whether your regular income will provide enough cash to meet expenses.

If the statement predicts a cash shortage, you can plan in advance to avoid the problem. Postpone a payment that is not immediately necessary, or plan a sale to generate more income, or seek a short-term loan. Banks are usually willing to loan short-term funds (usually thirty or sixty days) to profitable businesses. What's more, the fact that you have actually prepared a cash flow statement indicates to a banker that you are knowledgeable about your business and, therefore, a better risk than someone who has no financial knowledge at all.

INVENTORY CONTROL

Any business that sells or manufactures goods, and any service business that stocks parts, needs some sort of inventory control, some way of knowing what has been ordered, what is on hand, and when it's time to reorder. For a very small business or one selling only a small variety of items, the inventory purchase records in your expenditure ledger (column 1) and your day-to-day observations of the stock on hand will probably provide you with the information you need to maintain adequate inventory control. A periodic count, or "inventory," is the easiest and quickest way to determine what is still on hand and what needs to be reordered. (In business jargon, "inventory" is both a noun and a verb).

Larger businesses and those selling a large selection of merchandise will need more formal procedures for controlling inventory. Such businesses should maintain a record of all stock ordered, received, and sold. "Perpetual inventory" records, as they are called, can be kept by hand, on a spreadsheet, or using accounting software. An up-to-date

and accurate inventory record can tell you at a glance your balance on hand, what is still on order, and how long it takes to receive an order.

How to Keep an Inventory Record

If you want to create your own inventory record, you can use the sample here as a guide:

1. When you place your order, record the date and the quantity of the order in the Ordered columns.

2. When you receive the order, record the date and the quantity received in the Received columns. Including the date received will give you an idea how long it takes your suppliers to send you an ordered item.

3. When you sell items, record the quantities in the Sold column.

On the sample inventory record, 50 silver buckles were ordered on January 31. A partial shipment of 35 arrived February 13. The back-ordered 15 buckles arrived on March 1. Fifty more buckles were ordered on March 12.

At least once a year, and preferably every six months, the perpetual records should be "proven" (verified) by taking a physical count. If there is a discrepancy, the records should be adjusted to agree with the count. If the difference is substantial, you know something is wrong. Either you have not been updating the records correctly, or your inventory is being stolen.

Inventory control, like cash flow, is a management tool only. It is meant to help you run your business. The method I described for inventory

INVENTORY RECORD

Item *#3 Silver Buckle*   Supplier *L. J. Silver Co.*

DATE ORDERED	QUANTITY ORDERED	DATE REC'D.	QUANTITY REC'D.	QUANTITY SOLD	BALANCE ON-HAND
1-31	50				0
		2-13	35		35
				13	22
				4	18
		3-1	15		33
				10	23
3-12	50				23

control is only a suggestion. Any system or non-system that works for you is probably a good one.

Inventory Software

Businesses with large or varied inventories have found that inventory software is extremely useful—some say essential. The software records should look similar to the ledger sample here, and the software should provide you with exactly the information you need. Software records should be verified by taking physical counts on a regular basis, just like hand-posted and spreadsheet records. The software is just as likely to be incorrect.

Larry Campbell, of Ingram Book Company, a book wholesaler whose customers are small bookstores: "One of the quiet, simple programs at Ingram seems to be a step back in time: the 'Card In Book' system. Booksellers pay 3¢ each for cards sent with each shipment, to go in each book. When a retail customer buys a book, the clerk takes the card. At the end of the day, the store can easily reorder sold titles. It's low tech. If you're a small store, you don't need computer inventory control, but you still need an inventory management program."

JOB COSTING

Service businesses, particularly construction, plumbers, electricians, and similar trades, need to keep a record of expenses for each job. Designers and freelancers also record expenses by the job, and so do custom manufacturers. If you are billing by the hour, you need to keep track of your time on each job. Even if you are not billing by the hour, it is a good idea, at least when you are starting out, to record the hours to see if you are charging enough for flat-rate jobs.

You are actually keeping two overlapping sets of records: income and expenditures for each job, and total income and expenditures for your business. This can get tedious, especially if you have bills from suppliers that may be for more than one job. I suggest writing down the job information on your supplier's invoice as soon as you get the materials, so you don't have to guess later.

If you use parts or materials that you previously purchased, you add these costs to the job sheet but, obviously, not to your expenditure record (because you already recorded the expenses when you purchased the materials). You will probably want to keep an easy-to-locate file of the cost of each part you already have on hand, so you can include the cost on the job sheet.

If you are keeping records by hand, you will be recording the expenditures twice, once on the job sheet and again on your expenditure ledger. Software applications like QuickBooks and some spreadsheet software have the ability to produce individual job records and your business's expenditure records with only one entry instead of two, but only for purchases made specifically for a given job. Previously purchased materials will have to be entered separately on the job record, as will the hours worked.

Individual job records will be more complicated if you are charging your customers a higher cost for materials than what you pay. You'll need an itemized bill to give to your customers, with different prices than the job cost record (which shows your cost, not what you are charging).

As you can see, it will be a bit of work to keep by-the-job records. But every business quickly figures out a system that works for them. A little trial and error, a few mistakes at first, but you will learn as you go.

Chapter Three
GROWING UP

Most people would succeed in small things if they were not troubled with great ambitions.
—HENRY WADSWORTH LONGFELLOW

BUSINESS GROWTH

LEARN the different methods and little-known techniques used today in building small companies into Powerful Places in Industry.

—from the cover of another book on starting a business

Well, maybe John D. Rockefeller did start with a two-pump filling station and some spectacular ambitions. After all, "bigger and better" has been a trademark of this big country of ours for as long as any of us can remember. For years we have associated big business and big industry with prosperity, happiness, and the good life.

But today it seems that America's "powerful places in industry" are just too powerful, and they are choking, not helping, our economy. In the last few years we have witnessed huge corporations laying off thousands of employees without warning, and doubling and tripling their prices and their profits, with us powerless to stop them. *Bigger* is no longer synonymous with *better*, and big business no longer seems to be able or willing to provide us a good way of life.

Small Time Operator is not going to be much help to the Rockefellers among you with dreams of building your business into "powerful places in industry." I feel that small business can offer you personal satisfaction and a good livelihood. But "small" does not have to mean that you are forever the one-person business, unable to grow. Business growth can be successful and profitable, beneficial to you and your customers. Business growth, however, can be mistimed and miscalculated, turning against you and doing you in.

Very often a business expands because a situation presents itself that the owner "just can't pass up": The adjacent storefront becomes vacant, and the landlord offers to knock out the separating partition and rent both stores to you. A competitor is failing and offers to sell his business to you, cheap.

Or maybe your customers have been encouraging expansion, suggesting that you offer some related product or service. And as frequent a reason for expansion as any, you're out to catch a bigger fish; success in your present business is tempting you on to bigger and better success (bigger and better?).

You should put in some real thinking time before making a decision about expanding:

1. Just as your present business was slow going at first, the expanded business will take time to get on its own feet. You will probably be making less money for a while, possibly even losing money for a year or two. Are you prepared for a repeat of the early, lean days?

2. Expansion is going to require more capital. It means investing your savings or borrowing. Far and away, the #1 reason successful businesses fail is because they took on debt to finance expansion and could not generate enough additional income to pay it back.

3. If you plan to acquire a second business location, be prepared for a major increase in the amount and type of work you will have to do. Someone must be hired to run one of the stores for you, and suddenly you will find yourself not only buyer, seller, bookkeeper, market analyst, and the rest, but manager also. Some real skills are required to manage a multi-store operation, not the least of which is being able to deal with employees: hiring, training, supervising, delegating authority, and sometimes firing.

4. The paperwork will just about double. How well do you handle it now?

He is well paid that is well satisfied.

—William Shakespeare, from *Merchant of Venice*

5. Your own leisure time away from the business will be reduced, possibly eliminated.

6. Repeating the warning about financial commitments: Legally, you and your unincorporated business are one and the same. Any liabilities of your business are also personal ones.

Do successful businesses grow every year? Most do, at least for a while, slow and steady for some, huge leaps for others. But at some point, all businesses reach their peak, or their maturity, where they reach the limit of what they can accomplish within the framework they've created and built. Where they go from there—well, that's the decision all business owners have to make for themselves.

Two hundred years ago, French philosopher Victor Hugo said, "Caution is the eldest child of wisdom." It is still true today. Think this decision through. Don't let any outside factors lure you into a move that you aren't ready for. Whether you choose to stay small or take a chance on expansion, be totally satisfied that you have made the right decision.

HIRING HELP: HOW TO SAVE TIME AND MONEY BY NOT BECOMING AN EMPLOYER

Hiring employees will just about double the amount of your paperwork. As an employer, you must keep payroll records for each employee; withhold income, Social Security, Medicare, and state taxes; prepare quarterly and year-end payroll tax returns; pay the employer's portion of Social Security and Medicare taxes and unemployment taxes; purchase workers' compensation insurance; and prepare year-end earnings statements for each employee. It's been estimated that the employer's taxes, workers' compensation insurance, and paperwork will cost you an additional 30 percent. In other words, if you pay a wage of $20.00 per hour, it's really costing you about $26.00.

Businesses hiring employees are more closely regulated than one-person businesses. The IRS and the states demand prompt payroll tax returns and require strict adherence to employment laws. If you are late filing your payroll tax return, if you don't pay the employment taxes when due, the IRS is likely to move quickly. Whenever you hear about the IRS padlocking a business and impounding the bank account, it's usually because of unpaid payroll taxes. And the penalties are severe.

Hiring Independent (Outside) Contractors

Many businesses get outside help without hiring employees. These businesses often hire people known as "independent contractors." Independent contractors are also called outside contractors, contract labor, or free agents. On-demand economy workers are independent contractors. Don't confuse the term *independent contractor* with building contractors and subcontractors.

Independent contractors are in business for themselves, people who sell their services to you. When you hire an independent contractor, you pay the contractor his or her fee in full. You do not withhold taxes, pay employment taxes, or file payroll tax returns. You can hire on an as-needed basis, and you don't have to worry about sick pay or vacation time or the trauma of laying off or firing an employee.

Who is an independent contractor? The IRS says, "Generally, people in business for themselves are not employees. [Individuals] in an independent trade in which they offer their services to the public are usually not employees." Independent contractors can accept or turn down work as they please.

A key determining point, as far as the IRS is concerned: Does the person perform services for more than one business? A person working solely for you is usually your employee. A person providing services to several businesses is probably an independent contractor.

Independent contractors usually have DBAs, business licenses, a business bank account, invoice forms, their own office, their own tools and equipment, a set of financial records, and similar indications of being self-employed. Independent contractors sometimes have employees of their own. Independent contractors are basically small business owners, just like the businesses hiring them.

Legislators have done their level best to create a legal environment that tempts us, when hiring, to focus on everything but finding the best person for the job.

—George Gendron, *Inc.* magazine

Who Is an Employee?

The IRS is likely to consider a person your employee and not an independent contractor if the individual: (1) uses your tools, materials, and equipment instead of his or her own; (2) receives on-the-job training; (3) must follow hours that you set; (4) is told not just what must be done but how the work is to be done; (5) hires or supervises your workers; (6) receives health insurance, sick pay, vacation pay, or similar employee benefits; (7) gets a regular paycheck.

Three other factors the IRS will consider are how similar workers are treated in other businesses, what the custom is within your industry, and whether or not you filed a 1099-MISC form for the contractor (covered below).

The employee/independent contractor guidelines—who is or isn't an employee—are in a state of flux, and the rules are likely to change. In California, the state supreme court has ruled that an independent contractor must be doing work that is outside the usual course of the hiring company's business. If, for example, you are manufacturing toys, you can hire an independent contractor to rewire your shop or repair your equipment; but if you hire someone to help make toys, that person is an employee.

Other states, and possibly the IRS as well, could follow with similar rulings. As Charlie Chan wisely said to Number One Son, "Pay attention."

A person who falls within the definition of an employee is an employee no matter what you call him or her. It also does not matter how payments are measured or paid, what they are called, or whether the employee works full-time or part-time.

If you are still unsure how to classify your worker, you can request a "Determination of Employee Work Status" from the IRS on Form SS-8. Not many businesses file this request because the IRS nearly always rules that workers are employees. In fact, many accountants suggest that businesses do not file Form SS-8. The accountants warn that, if you have already paid workers as independent contractors, and if the IRS rules against you, you will be subject to back taxes and penalties. You may want to talk to your accountant about this.

There is another and much more serious problem if you hire people and treat them as independent contractors when the law says they should be employees. If one of these people gets injured on the job and is not covered by workers' compensation

insurance, you could find yourself with medical bills and a large lawsuit.

Contracting with Your Contractor

When hiring individuals you plan to pay as independent contractors, be absolutely sure that the people you are hiring fully understand what you are doing: that they are not your employees, that they consider themselves to be self-employed, that they are not eligible for employee benefits or sick leave, that they are not covered for workers' compensation should they be injured on the job, that they know they are responsible for their own taxes and insurance and Social Security, and that they will not be eligible for unemployment insurance when the job is finished. I suggest a signed contract with independent contractors, clearly defining the work and the legal relationship.

Many small businesses have gotten into expensive trouble with the federal and state government because former "independent contractors" (who really should have been paid as employees) complained to the IRS when they were turned down for unemployment insurance or fined for not paying their own Social Security.

IRS FORMS FOR INDEPENDENT CONTRACTORS

For each contractor you paid $600 or more during the year, you are required to file Form 1099-MISC, "Report of Miscellaneous Income." The form shows the contractor's name, address, Social Security number or Federal Employer Identification Number (EIN), and amount paid. You include your business name, address, phone number, and ID number as well. One copy of the 1099 goes to the IRS and another to the contractor.

In addition, if your outside contractors are independent sales agents, you report, on Form 1099-MISC, each sales agent who purchased $5,000 or more in goods from you.

The 1099-MISC forms must be given to your contractors no later than January 31 of the new year.

The IRS copies of the 1099 forms are accompanied by a Form 1096, "Annual Summary and Transmittal of U.S. Information Returns." The 1096 and accompanying 1099s must be filed with the IRS by the last day in January.

The IRS provides a Form W-9 for your independent contractors to fill out, showing their name, address, and Social Security number or EIN. By signing the

PAYER'S name, street address, city or town, state or province, country, ZIP or foreign postal code, and telephone no.	1 Rents $	OMB No. 1545-0115	**Miscellaneous Income**
Monkeywrench Motors 7831 Claremont Berkeley, CA 95444	2 Royalties $	Form **1099-MISC**	

		3 Other income $	4 Federal income tax withheld $	
PAYER'S federal identification number 123-45-6789	RECIPIENT'S identification number 987-65-4321	5 Fishing boat proceeds $	6 Medical and health care payments $	**Copy 1** **For State Tax Department**

RECIPIENT'S name Crystal Rose	7 Nonemployee compensation 5,650	8 Substitute payments in lieu of dividends or interest
Street address (including apt. no.) 106 State Street	$	$
City or town, state or province, country, and ZIP or foreign postal code Santa Cruz, CA 95062	9 Payer made direct sales of $5,000 or more of consumer products to a buyer (recipient) for resale ▶ ☐	10 Crop insurance proceeds $
	11	12

Account number (see instructions)	FATCA filing requirement ☐	13 Excess golden parachute payments $	14 Gross proceeds paid to an attorney $

15a Section 409A deferrals $	15b Section 409A income $	16 State tax withheld $ $	17 State/Payer's state no. CALIF	18 State income $ 5,650 $

Form **1099-MISC**   www.irs.gov/form1099misc   Department of the Treasury - Internal Revenue Service

File a 1099-MISC for every outside contractor who received $600 or more during the year and for outside salespeople who purchased $5,000 or more in goods from you.

Do Not Staple   6969

Form **1096** Department of the Treasury Internal Revenue Service	**Annual Summary and Transmittal of U.S. Information Returns**	OMB No. 1545-0108

FILER'S name

Monkeywrench Motors

Street address (including room or suite number)
7831 Claremont

City or town, state or province, country, and ZIP or foreign postal code
Berkeley, CA 95444

Name of person to contact Samuel Thesham	Telephone number 519-555-1212	**For Official Use Only**
Email address	Fax number	☐☐☐☐☐☐ ☐

1 Employer identification number	2 Social security number 123-45-6789	3 Total number of forms 1	4 Federal income tax withheld $ 0	5 Total amount reported with this Form 1096 $ 5,650

6 Enter an "X" in only one box below to indicate the type of form being filed.   7 Form 1099-MISC with NEC in box 7, check . . . . . ▶ ☐

W-2G 32	1097-BTC 50	1098 81	1098-C 78	1098-E 84	1098-Q 74	1098-T 83	1099-A 80	1099-B 79	1099-C 85	1099-CAP 73	1099-DIV 91	1099-G 86	1099-INT 92	1099-K 10
☐	☐	☐	☐	☐	☐	☐	☐	☐	☐	☐	☐	☐	☐	☐
1099-LTC 93	**1099-MISC** 95	**1099-OID** 96	**1099-PATR** 97	**1099-Q** 31	**1099-QA** 1A	**1099-R** 98	**1099-S** 75	**1099-SA** 94	**3921** 25	**3922** 26	**5498** 28	**5498-ESA** 72	**5498-QA** 2A	**5498-SA** 27
☐	☒	☐	☐	☐	☐	☐	☐	☐	☐	☐	☐	☐	☐	☐

Return this entire page to the Internal Revenue Service. Photocopies are not acceptable.

Under penalties of perjury, I declare that I have examined this return and accompanying documents, and, to the best of my knowledge and belief, they are true, correct, and complete.

Signature ▶ *Samuel Thesham*   Title ▶ *Owner*   Date ▶ *1/31*

Form 1096 accompanies the 1099 forms sent to the IRS.

W-9 form, independent contractors certify to you that they are giving you correct information. You keep the form in your files; it does not get sent to the IRS. This W-9 form is optional. Independent contractors are not required to fill out the form, but they are required to give you their Social Security number or EIN if they are paid $600 or more in a calendar year. If a contractor refuses, you will probably be required to withhold taxes from the contractor's pay.

INCORPORATED INDEPENDENT CONTRACTOR

Some independent contractors incorporate themselves, setting up their own one-person corporation. When you hire an incorporated independent contractor, you are contracting with a corporation and not an individual. The incorporated contractor is an employee of his or her own company. Incorporated contractors are not your employees nor do they come under the independent contractor rules. You don't have to file 1099 or 1096 forms or any employment forms. You don't have to pay payroll taxes or workers' compensation insurance.

"Under the Table"/"Off the Books" Payments

And now, a word about paying a worker "under the table" (off the books). The term means that the worker is not on the payroll as an employee, payment is usually in cash, and no record is made of the payment. This is usually done to avoid payroll taxes and the expense of workers' compensation insurance, or to hire undocumented workers (non-U.S. citizens), both of which are illegal and can get you in more trouble than it's worth.

If the worker is supposed to be an employee, not only can you get in the same trouble as the independent contractor problems mentioned above, you also have no defense whatsoever when you get caught. At least when you are mislabeling employees as independent contractors, you can argue the issue and possibly minimize penalties.

If your "under the table" worker doesn't file taxes, that's fraud, and you could well be implicated. Again, an injury on the job could be disastrous. On top of all this misery, since you don't record the payment, you lose the expense deduction and pay more income taxes. Enough?

Special Situations

Subcontractors. Are subcontractors employees or independent contractors? For IRS purposes, the general rules regarding employees versus independent contractors apply to subcontractors. A subcontractor who is actually in business for himself, offering services to several building contractors, is most likely an outside contractor. Some states require contractors to purchase workers' compensation insurance for subcontractors if the subcontractors do not have the insurance themselves, even if the subcontractor is legally an outside contractor. Some states require subcontractors to be licensed.

Statutory employees. One strange exception to the above rules applies to people the IRS calls statutory employees: full-time life insurance salespeople; commission truck drivers who deliver laundry, food, or beverages other than milk; individuals working from their own homes who are hired by businesses to do work with materials provided by the businesses (typically seamstresses); and traveling salespeople working full-time, selling to businesses (not to consumers).

Statutory employees are subject to regular employee Social Security and Medicare taxes, and unemployment insurance, but otherwise are treated as outside contractors. They file Schedule C like a sole proprietor and are entitled to regular business deductions.

This is a confusing area of the law. "Curiouser and curiouser," as Alice said ("delivering beverages other than milk?"). If you are a statutory employee, or someone employing a statutory employee, you should get more details from the IRS or an accountant.

Statutory nonemployees. The IRS has another peculiar rule that applies only to certain commission salespeople: direct sellers, some delivery people selling consumer goods, licensed real estate agents, and some newspaper vendors. The IRS permits these salespeople, called "statutory nonemployees," to be classified as outside contractors, if there is a written agreement stating that they are independent contractors and responsible for their own taxes. The regular employee-versus-contractor tests do not apply.

Out-of-state residents. If you hire an outside contractor who resides in another state, who comes into your state to work for you, some states require you to withhold state taxes on the contractor. Check with your state income tax or employment offices.

Temporary help agencies. If you contract with a temporary help agency, where you pay the agency and they pay the laborers, the workers are not your employees nor are they independent contractors.

You are hiring a service, not a worker. But you should be sure the agency has filed all the correct papers on the workers, to avoid any problems if workers are injured on the job or have payroll tax problems.

STEPS TO BECOMING AN EMPLOYER

To meet the legal requirements of becoming an employer—hiring employees, not independent contractors—you will have to deal with the federal government and the state government, and you will probably have to obtain workers' comp insurance. These are one-time-only procedures, but they require quite a bit of time and paperwork. If possible, start these procedures a month before you plan to hire your first employee.

Federal Requirements for Employers

1. All employers must have a Federal Employer Identification Number (EIN or FEIN). You can obtain an EIN on the IRS website, IRS.gov, or by mail by filling out Form SS-4, "Application for Employer Identification Number."

   If you fill out Form SS-4, on line 13, if you don't know how many employees you plan to hire, estimate on the low side to avoid an avalanche of unnecessary IRS forms. One employee is enough. Check the box on line 14; you really don't know what your employment tax liability is going to be, so figure it's going to be low.

2. Order or download a copy of IRS Publication #15, "Circular E, Employer's Tax Guide." Publication #15 has detailed instructions for complying with federal requirements and includes federal withholding tables.

3. Order or download copies of Form W-4, "Employee's Withholding Allowance Certificate." Each new employee must fill out a W-4 showing marital status and the number of exemptions claimed. You keep the W-4s in your files.

4. All new employees are required to fill out Department of Homeland Security Form I-9, "Employment Eligibility Verification," stating that the employee is legally eligible to work in the United States, and that the employee has a Social Security number or an Alien Registration Number. The employer is required to examine the employee's documents and certify that the documents match the information on Form I-9. Employers do not send the forms to the government. Employers must keep the forms on file should a government agent request to see them. You can obtain or download copies of Form I-9 from the U.S. Citizenship and Immigration Service website, USCIS.gov.

5. All employers must comply with Occupational Safety and Health Administration (OSHA) regulations. If you have more than ten employees, OSHA requires you to keep routine job safety records (some retail businesses with low injury rates are exempt from this requirement). For more details, log on to OSHA.gov, or write OSHA, U.S. Department of Labor, Washington, DC 20210.

6. Most employers are subject to the Fair Labor Standards Act (FLSA). This Act sets a minimum wage for certain employees, and sets overtime pay (more than forty hours per week) at not less than one and a half times the regular rate of pay. Child labor laws, equal pay for men and women, comp time, and other regulations are included in the FLSA. The Act does not require vacation, holiday, or sick pay, or fringe benefits. It does not place any limit on the number of hours people work. Exempt from the Act are most executives, administrators, professionals, outside salespeople, and some amusement park employees, seamen, farm workers, and some computer-related work. Also exempt are unincorporated family businesses that

---

One thing I hate is staff meetings. And, you know, you read all these things about motivating people. I hate doing that. Why do I want to spend my time motivating people? I want to make some deals, make some money, and have a good time.

—Small business owner Sam Leandro

We prefer the no frills motivation style for our employees. If they want to do it, they do it. If they don't, I get somebody else, simple as that.

—Kevin Gallagher, partner, Quicksilver Messenger Service

employ only family members. For more details, log on to DOL.gov, or write U.S. Department of Labor, Washington, DC 20210.

7. The Americans with Disabilities Act prohibits job discrimination against certain disabled people, and requires employers with fifteen or more employees to provide reasonable accommodations for disabled employees.

8. If you have twenty or more employees, you must comply with the Age Discrimination in Employment Act, which forbids employment discrimination against anyone at least forty years of age.

State Requirements for Employers

1. Contact your state department of employment. Most states assign a state Employer's ID Number, in addition to your federal EIN. Some states issue federal EINs along with the state ID, saving you the extra step of dealing with the IRS.

2. Employers are required to fill out a New Hire Report for each new or rehired employee, and send the form to your state's employment department, usually within twenty days.

3. Every state that has an income tax on wages requires employers to withhold state income tax. The states publish employer tax guides that include state withholding tables. Some states have their own W-4 forms.

4. Most states have employer-paid state unemployment insurance, which is in addition to federal unemployment insurance (discussed below). The state will require you to submit an application and receive an insurance rating. The rates vary from state to state and from occupation to occupation.

5. Most states require employers to have workers' compensation insurance, which is covered below.

6. Many states have other payroll taxes or disability insurance for employers.

7. Some states, and even some cities, set their own minimum wage, higher than the federal minimum. Some states have paid family leave laws, required paid vacations, sick leave laws; the list in some states can go on and on. Be sure you know what's required of you as an employer before hiring your first employee. There is no avoiding these laws.

Separate here and give Form W-4 to your employer. Keep the top part for your records.

Form W-4
Department of the Treasury
Internal Revenue Service

Employee's Withholding Allowance Certificate

OMB No. 1545-0074

▶ Whether you are entitled to claim a certain number of allowances or exemption from withholding is subject to review by the IRS. Your employer may be required to send a copy of this form to the IRS.

1 Your first name and middle initial	Last name	2 Your social security number
Julia P.	Rose	222-22-2222

Home address (number and street or rural route)
106 State Street

City or town, state, and ZIP code
Laytonville, CA 95454

3 ☑ Single ☐ Married ☐ Married, but withhold at higher Single rate.
Note: If married, but legally separated, or spouse is a nonresident alien, check the "Single" box.

4 If your last name differs from that shown on your social security card, check here. You must call 1-800-772-1213 for a replacement card. ▶ ☐

5 Total number of allowances you are claiming (from line **H** above **or** from the applicable worksheet on page 2) ..... **5** | 1

6 Additional amount, if any, you want withheld from each paycheck . . . . **6** $

7 I claim exemption from withholding for 2016, and I certify that I meet **both** of the following conditions for exemption.
• Last year I had a right to a refund of **all** federal income tax withheld because I had **no** tax liability, **and**
• This year I expect a refund of **all** federal income tax withheld because I expect to have **no** tax liability.
If you meet both conditions, write "Exempt" here . . . . ▶ **7**

Under penalties of perjury, I declare that I have examined this certificate and, to the best of my knowledge and belief, it is true, correct, and complete.

Employee's signature
(This form is not valid unless you sign it.) ▶ *Julia P Rose*   Date ▶ 4/08

8 Employer's name and address (Employer: Complete lines 8 and 10 only if sending to the IRS.)	9 Office code (optional)	10 Employer identification number (EIN)

For Privacy Act and Paperwork Reduction Act Notice, see page 2.   Cat. No. 10220Q   Form **W-4**

Federal Procedures and Taxes for Employers

Below are the basic federal procedures for most employers. These laws do change occasionally. You should get IRS Publication #15, "Circular E, Employer's Tax Guide," to verify these rules. Unlike income taxes, there is no "gray" or questionable area where payroll taxes are involved. There is only one way to do it: their way.

These payroll laws and taxes apply regardless of how you pay your employees. You cannot avoid the taxes by paying in goods and services instead of cash, by bartering or trading, or by paying the money to a third party.

Income tax withholding. The IRS requires that you withhold income tax from each employee's paycheck. The amount is calculated from the tables in Publication #15.

Social Security and Medicare tax. Employees pay Social Security tax, also known as FICA (Federal Insurance Contributions Act) or OASDI (Old Age, Survivors, and Disability Insurance), and Medicare tax, that you withhold from their pay. The Social Security tax the employees pay is 6.2 percent on each employee's earnings, up to an earnings maximum of $128,400. The Medicare tax is 1.45 percent on each employee's earnings, with no maximum. So for employees earning $128,400 or less, you withhold 7.65 percent of their pay.

You, the employer, are also liable for an employer's portion of Social Security and Medicare taxes in addition to the taxes withheld from your employees. This is money you pay out of your own pocket on behalf of your employees. The employer's share of the tax is the same as the employee's share: 6.2 percent Social Security tax and 1.45 percent Medicare tax (7.65 percent total) on each employee's earnings up to $128,400. Do not confuse this employer's tax with the self-employment tax discussed in the Taxes chapter. They are different taxes.

Part-time employees, employees hired for a short period of time, and employees who also work for other employers are treated the same as full-time employees for withholding income tax and Social Security/Medicare tax.

Earned Income Credit. Many low-income employees are eligible for an Earned Income Tax Credit (EIC or EITC), reducing their income taxes. For some employees, the Earned Income Tax Credit is greater than the income tax owed, reducing income tax below zero. In these cases, the credit is "refundable," becoming in effect a negative income tax. If any of your employees are eligible for the "refundable" credit, instead of waiting until they file their tax returns to claim the credit, they can request to receive a part of it in advance, in their paychecks, increasing their take-home pay during the year. Employees fill out a Form W-5, "Earned Income Credit Advance Payment." Employers increase the take-home pay accordingly. IRS Publication #15, "Employer's Tax Guide," has instructions and tables to compute the Advance EITC. The Earned Income Credit is for employees, not for employers. The employer does not get the credit.

Payroll tax returns. You file a federal payroll tax return for taxes withheld from your employees (federal income, Social Security, and Medicare) and the employer portion of your employees' Social Security and Medicare. Do not include your own self-employment tax.

If the total employment taxes for the year, employer and employee combined, are under $1,000, you file an annual return, Form 944.

If employment taxes are over $1,000 a year, you file quarterly returns, on Form 941. Quarterly returns are due on April 30, for January, February, and March; July 31 for April, May, and June; October 31 for July, August, and September; and January 31 for October, November, and December.

In addition to filing the Form 941, you may also be required to make periodic deposits of the payroll taxes. As long as the total payroll taxes due, combined employee and employer portions, are less than $2,500 (for the year to date), the entire amount can be remitted with the return. If, however, the total payroll taxes due get to be $2,500 or more, you must deposit the full amount by the fifteenth day of the next month.

Deposits can only be made electronically, using the Electronic Federal Tax Payment System (EFTPS), which you can access through the IRS website, IRS.gov, or through a bank, a tax accountant, or a payroll service.

W-2 and W-3 statements. You fill out a Form W-2, "Wage and Tax Statement," for each employee, reporting their income and deductions for the year, and deliver or mail the W-2s to the employees by January 31 of the new year. One copy of each W-2 is sent to the Social Security Administration (the SSA), accompanied by Form W-3, "Transmittal of Income and Tax Statements," no later than January 31.

Unemployment tax. As an employer, you are subject to federal unemployment tax (FUTA) if during the year you (a) paid wages of $1,500 or more in any calendar quarter, or (b) had one or more employees for some portion of at least one day during each of twenty different calendar weeks (better reread that slowly). Note that "unemployment tax" is also known as "unemployment insurance." The tax is collected to provide the insurance. The two terms are often used interchangeably.

Unemployment tax is imposed on you, the employer. It is not deducted from your employees' wages. An annual return is filed on Form 940, "Employer's Federal Unemployment Tax Return," on or before January 31 of the next year. The rate is 6 percent of the first $7,000 of wages paid to each employee during the year. You may receive credit of up to 5.4 percent for state unemployment taxes you pay, so your net federal tax could be as low as 0.6 percent. You are required to make quarterly deposits of federal unemployment tax if the accumulated tax exceeds $500.

Restaurant and nightclub owners. Employees must report their tips to you, if the tips are $20 or more a month. You must withhold income and payroll taxes, and pay employer's payroll taxes on the tips, just as you do on wages. Restaurant owners may claim a special tax credit equal to the employer's portion of Social Security and Medicare taxes paid on tips, to the extent tips and wages exceed the minimum wage.

Agricultural employers come under different federal laws, particularly regarding Social Security and Medicare taxes, minimum wage, and overtime pay. See IRS Publication #51, "Agricultural Employer's Tax Guide."

Workers' Compensation Insurance. Workers' compensation insurance (also just called "workers' comp") provides disability and death benefits to employees injured or killed on the job, or who become ill due to workplace conditions, regardless of who is at fault.

Most but not all states require employers to carry workers' compensation insurance for all employees even if they are occasional or part-time. You, the employer, pay for your employees' workers' compensation insurance. Although a few states do not require workers' compensation insurance, the employer is still legally liable for injuries an employee incurs on the job. Legally required or not, workers' compensation insurance is essential to any business with employees.

Some states allow businesses to self-insure rather than purchase a workers' comp policy, but for most small businesses, the required bonds or cash reserves are prohibitively expensive.

Workers' compensation premiums for your employees are fully deductible. Workers' comp for yourself is deductible only if your state requires you to have workers' comp insurance on yourself. If the coverage is voluntary, the premiums are not deductible (except for corporations).

The minimum premium to obtain a workers' compensation policy, even for one part-time employee, can cost several hundred dollars a year. The high cost of workers' comp is a major reason so many one-person businesses struggle along doing everything themselves instead of hiring someone to help.

Premiums increase as your payroll increases (giving an employee a raise may increase your premium), and vary dramatically with the occupation. Workers' compensation premiums for a roofer are about thirty times higher than for a clerical employee. So be sure the insurance company doesn't misclassify you in a high-risk, high-premium category.

You can keep your initial premium at or near the minimum, particularly for part-time and hourly employees, by giving the

22222	**a** Employee's social security number 222-22-2222	OMB No. 1545-0008		

b Employer identification number (EIN) 68-1234567	**1** Wages, tips, other compensation 4,300.00	**2** Federal income tax withheld 327.50

c Employer's name, address, and ZIP code Music Photo Service 640 Bell Springs Road Laytonville, CA 95454	**3** Social security wages 4,300.00	**4** Social security tax withheld 267.70
	5 Medicare wages and tips 4,300.00	**6** Medicare tax withheld 62.35
	7 Social security tips	**8** Allocated tips

d Control number	**9**	**10** Dependent care benefits

e Employee's first name and initial Last name Suff. Julia P. Rose 106 State Street Laytonville, CA 95454	**11** Nonqualified plans	**12a** c o d e
	13 Statutory employee ☐ Retirement plan ☐ Third-party sick pay ☐	**12b** c o d e
	14 Other	**12c** c o d e
		12d c o d e
f Employee's address and ZIP code		

15 State Employer's state ID number CA 61444	**16** State wages, tips, etc. $4,300	**17** State income tax $64.70	**18** Local wages, tips, etc.	**19** Local income tax	**20** Locality name

Form **W-2** **Wage and Tax Statement**

Department of the Treasury—Internal Revenue Service

Copy 1—For State, City, or Local Tax Department

33333	**a** Control number	For Official Use Only ▶ OMB No. 1545-0008

b Kind of Payer (Check one) ▶	941 ☒ Military ☐ 943 ☐ 944 ☐ CT-1 ☐ Hshld. emp. ☐ Medicare govt. emp. ☐	**Kind of Employer** (Check one) ▶	None apply ☐ 501c non-govt. ☐ State/local non-501c ☐ State/local 501c ☐ Federal govt. ☐	Third-party sick pay (Check if applicable) ☐

c Total number of Forms W-2 1	**d** Establishment number	**1** Wages, tips, other compensation $4,300.00	**2** Federal income tax withheld $327.50
e Employer identification number (EIN) 68-1234567		**3** Social security wages $4,300.00	**4** Social security tax withheld $267.70
f Employer's name Music Photo Service 640 Bell Springs Road Laytonville, CA 95454		**5** Medicare wages and tips $4,300.00	**6** Medicare tax withheld $62.35
		7 Social security tips	**8** Allocated tips
		9	**10** Dependent care benefits
		11 Nonqualified plans	**12a** Deferred compensation
g Employer's address and ZIP code			
h Other EIN used this year		**13** For third-party sick pay use only	**12b**

15 State Employer's state ID number CA 61444	**14** Income tax withheld by payer of third-party sick pay

16 State wages, tips, etc. $4,300.00	**17** State income tax $67.70	**18** Local wages, tips, etc.	**19** Local income tax

Employer's contact person Sam Leandro	Employer's telephone number 707-984-7117	For Official Use Only
Employer's fax number	Employer's email address	

Under penalties of perjury, I declare that I have examined this return and accompanying documents and, to the best of my knowledge and belief, they are true, correct, and complete.

Signature ▶ Sam Leandro   Title ▶ Owner   Date ▶ 1/21

Form **W-3** **Transmittal of Wage and Tax Statements**

Department of the Treasury Internal Revenue Service

insurance company a low payroll estimate, since you really don't know how many hours your employees will be working. Once or twice a year, the insurance company will examine your payroll records, comparing your actual payroll to your original estimate. Your premium will be adjusted retroactively. Some insurance companies pay dividends (refunds) after the end of the year if you have no claims.

Some states offer workers' compensation insurance through a state-operated insurance fund or risk-sharing pool. In some states, the rates are comparable to or lower than rates from regular insurance companies, particularly if you are hiring only one or two employees. In other states, the state fund is insurance of last resort, for businesses that cannot get coverage from a regular insurance company, and the state coverage may be more expensive. To locate the state-operated insurance fund, look in the yellow pages under "insurance," or contact the state employment office or human resources department.

A special warning if your employees will be working at their own homes (not at the employer's home): Your workers' compensation premium will probably be triple the normal rate. The insurance companies view this as a high-risk situation because the employee is at the workplace twenty-four hours a day, and can too easily claim that any injury at home is work-related.

A warning if you have personal health insurance for yourself: Check with your health insurance company about on-the-job coverage. Some health insurance policies do not cover any on-the-job injuries.

Building contractors. If you hire subcontractors, some states hold you responsible for the subcontractor's workers' comp coverage if the subcontractor does not have the insurance. Ask to see a certificate of insurance from each subcontractor.

Family Employees

If you plan to hire your spouse, the section "Married Couples" in the T.C.B.: Take Care of Business chapter will explain your options and tax consequences. Generally, putting your spouse on the payroll will neither increase nor decrease your combined income or payroll taxes.

You may have a significant tax savings if you hire your children to help out in the business. You can pay each of your children up to $12,000 a year, and write it off as a business expense. The children pay no federal income taxes and do not have to file an income tax return. Neither the children nor the parents pay Social Security, Medicare, or federal unemployment taxes. The children are usually exempt from federal minimum wage and child labor requirements. Here are the rules:

1. Your business must be a sole proprietorship, joint venture, one-person LLC, or a spousal partnership.

2. Your child must be under the age of eighteen.

3. The child must perform legitimate work to justify the salary earned. The work has to be business related: You can't hire your seventeen-year-old to babysit your three-year-old and then take a business deduction. You should document the job, keep time records, and write regular paychecks.

4. If the child has bank interest or other "unearned income," it cannot exceed $1,050.

5. The child's total income from all sources combined cannot exceed $12,000 per year.

6. You are required to file payroll forms W-2 and W-3 like you would for any employee. You do not have to file payroll tax forms 941 or 944.

If your child is eighteen or older, or earns more than the above maximums, you still may be able to hire your child and save on income and payroll taxes. But the rules start changing, with a lot of variables. IRS Publication #15, "Circular E, Employer's Tax Guide," includes a chart that explains what federal payroll taxes are required for children on the payroll.

You should check your state employment laws before you hire your children. Many states have laws similar to the IRS, and impose no state income or payroll taxes, nor require workers' compensation insurance on your children. Check your state employer tax guide. Do not rely on verbal information from state agencies. People who work at state employment departments are often unaware of child employment laws.

If children hire their parents, the parents are considered regular employees, subject to all regular employment and income taxes, except federal unemployment tax (FUTA). Parents are exempt from FUTA tax.

Payroll Records

Every employer must keep payroll records that show all the details of every paycheck for every employee. If you have only one or two employees, you can keep the records by hand or on a spreadsheet without a lot of work. However, if you have several employees or have a regular turnover of employees, calculating tax withholding and payroll deductions for each employee, every paycheck, can get complicated and time consuming. I highly recommend that you use payroll software if you are up to learning how to use it. If not, hire a bookkeeper or a payroll service to prepare your payroll. You can still write your own checks, so you maintain control over your bank account.

Payroll records should be permanent. Keep them as long as you own the business, longer if possible. Long-gone employees can come back to haunt you years later, usually when there's some problem with Social Security retirement.

SETTING UP PAYROLL RECORDS
If you do want to keep payroll records yourself, by hand or on a spreadsheet, each employee should have a separate ledger or spreadsheet page. Each record should identify the employee, and the employee's hourly or monthly rate of pay. If the rate changes during the year, show the new rate as well as the old, and the date of change. The payroll record should have a column for each of the following:

1. Date of paycheck.

2. Check number.

3. Payroll period.

4. Number of regular hours worked.

5. Number of overtime hours worked.

6. Gross pay.

7. Federal income tax withheld.

8. Social Security taxes withheld.

9. Medicare taxes withheld.

10. State income taxes withheld.

11–12. Columns for other withholding: state requirements, retirement, health insurance, and any other withholding.

13. Net take-home pay. The net pay is also posted to your bank records and your expenditure records.

Employee records should be confidential and protected as best you can from people who should not have access to them, and from hackers who might gain access to your computer. You can take precautions like locking up your files, copying and removing prior years' files from your computer, and

PAYROLL LEDGER												

Name:_____ Social Security:_____
Address:_____ Pay Rate:_____
_____

1	2	3	4	5	6	7	8	9	10	11	12	13
PAYCHECK DATE	CHECK NO.	PAY PERIOD	HOURS REG	O/T	GROSS	F.I.T.	SOCIAL SECURITY	MEDI-CARE	STATE INCOME	OTHER WITHHOLDING		NET PAY

having as many software protections as reasonably possible.

Mike Madsen, M. Madsen Leather: "When you're first getting started you don't always hire the best people. You don't know what you are looking for. You might hire somebody who is sympathetic to you or flatters you or somebody who is good looking. But they might not fit the job. You've got to think in terms of what the job is, and hire people for the job, and not hire friends. I'd say it's better to make friends of the people that work for you, but never hire friends."

Nick Mein, Wallpapers Plus: "A person's gotta be happy if he or she is going to work for you. The people working for me were terribly unhappy. This one woman who worked for me, who I really liked, was a great saleswoman. She'd been going to a shrink, and he told her, 'Work's bad for you.' So she called up and said, 'I won't be in.' A lot of jobs depended on her charm; she brought a lot of people in the store. And she just gave up on it. That's irritating. No 'stick-to-it-ivity' my father calls it; no perseverance.

"It's difficult to be nice to your employees because they're going to take advantage of you. They're going to start coming in late. All the people who worked for me are perfect examples. I'd say, 'Get in at 9:30, do what ordering needs to be done, and open the doors at ten. I want you to be ready to sell at ten.' And they do that for a while, but then they say, 'I want to get in a little later because there's no ordering to do, there's no backlog.' I say okay. And then eventually, they're coming in at eleven. Because they felt nobody was coming in the shop until 11 or 11:30. If you're not on it every day, you get screwed. You have to be on it all the time. And then, they leave early.

"If you have somebody working for you you've got to make it absolutely plain that they're being paid for the specified hours. I find that really hard to do, keep people to that, because I'm a little bit like that myself. On a really slow day, I'd say, 'Go ahead, go home early.' Then it always happens: next day somebody would call and say, 'I came by your shop at 5:20 and you weren't there.' That's bad service."

PARTNERSHIPS

Partnerships offer opportunities often not available to the one-person business: more capital, more skills and ideas, the extra energy generated when two or more people are working together. Partnerships are the traditional meeting ground of the "idea" person and the "money" person. Having a partner can relieve the sole-proprietor pressures of having to do everything yourself. And, at last, you can take a little vacation without having to shut down the business.

Most partnerships are planned as a long-term relationship, to last the life of the business (hopefully). But many partnerships are temporary arrangements, often on a project-by-project basis. When the project is completed, the partnership dissolves, and you move on to the next venture.

Partnerships have drawbacks as well. The independence and sole decision making that only the sole proprietor has is now shared. There is more paperwork. Interpersonal relationships with your partners may require both time and tact. Most important, the legal consequences of having one or more partners can be serious.

General versus Limited Partnerships

There are three kinds of partnerships. The kind covered in this chapter, the typical business partnership, is called a *general partnership*.

There is also a *limited partnership*, which is not a partnership in the usual sense. A limited partnership is an investment financing arrangement, with one general partner who operates the business, with full legal and financial responsibility, much like a sole proprietor, and one or more limited partners, who are investors only. The limited partners have no involvement in the management of the business, and usually have no personal liability beyond their investment.

A third kind of partnership, a *limited liability partnership* or LLP (not to be confused with a limited partnership), is used almost exclusively by legal and accounting firms. LLPs are covered in the "Limited Liability Company" section.

LEGAL ASPECTS OF GENERAL PARTNERSHIPS

When two or more people start a business together, and do not incorporate or set up a limited liability company (both described later in this chapter), the business is a general partnership. It is automatic. The only exception to this is a married couple who goes into business together, who have options other than setting up a general partnership. This is covered under "Married Couples" in the T.C.B.: Take Care of Business chapter.

In a general partnership, individual partners can be held personally responsible for the debts and legal obligations of the partnership. Most important, all partners can be held personally, individually liable for the acts of any partner acting on partnership business. If your partner, representing the business, goes out and gets a bank loan, you can be personally responsible to repay the debt, even if you didn't sign the papers yourself, even if you didn't know about the loan. If your partner gets into legal trouble while on partnership business, you may also be in legal trouble. Creditors of the partnership can go after any partner they choose. If there is a lawsuit filed against the partnership, all of the partners can be held personally liable.

The only way out of this unlimited liability is to incorporate or set up a limited liability company (LLC). Both are covered in this chapter.

Like sole proprietors, partners cannot be employees of their partnerships. Partners can draw a "wage," called a "guaranteed payment," or the partners can merely share in the profits of the partnership, or some combination of the two. Profits and guaranteed payments are taxable to the individual partners. Partners are subject to self-employment tax (covered in the Taxes chapter).

Partnerships can hire regular employees, but the partners themselves cannot be employees. A partnership must have a federal identification number (an EIN). You can obtain an EIN on the IRS website, IRS.gov, or you can obtain an EIN by mail by filling out Form SS-4, "Application for Employer Identification Number." If you do use Form SS-4, be careful how you fill out line 13 (number of employees). If you have none, write "NONE" or "0." On line 15, first date wages are paid, leave blank or put N/A. This will alert the IRS not to send you payroll tax returns.

Partnerships file a partnership income tax return, on IRS Form 1065, although the partnership itself pays no taxes. Partnerships are "pass-through entities": All of the profits, to use the IRS's terminology, "pass through" the business to the partners, who pay the tax. Each partner pays personal income tax on his or her share of the profits, on Schedule E of the regular 1040 tax return. Each partner is taxed on his or her full share of the profit whether distributed to the partners or not.

Partnerships get the same licenses, permits, and DBAs as any other business. In some states, partnerships must also be registered with the county clerk or a state office.

UNIFORM PARTNERSHIP ACT

Partnerships are governed by state law. Every state except Louisiana bases their partnership laws on the Uniform Partnership Act (UPA) or the Revised Uniform Partnership Act (RUPA). There are important differences between UPA and RUPA.

Under RUPA, partners can sue their partnerships, and partnerships can sue partners for misdeeds. This is not allowed under UPA, where the partners and the partnerships are legally one and the same. You couldn't sue yourself. Whether this new RUPA provision is a step forward or a step backward remains to be seen.

There are many other provisions, but the good news is that you can avoid UPA and RUPA laws (and if you're in Louisiana, whatever law Louisiana created) by having a written, signed partnership agreement that spells out how your partnership is governed. Generally, a partnership agreement takes legal precedence over state partnership laws.

PARTNERSHIP AGREEMENTS

This sample agreement is bare-bones basic. The agreement gives equal rights to all partners. The agreement allows the partners to change or expand the details of the agreement at any time in the future. The agreement obviously leaves out many important details that could be—some attorneys would say *should be*—included in the agreement, including several of the items I mention in the text.

PARTNERSHIP AGREEMENT

[NAME OF BUSINESS]

1. [name of your business], a general partnership, was formed on [month, day, year].

2. The partnership address is [address where the partnership will receive mail].

3. The partners are: [List full name of each partner].

4. All partners have equal ownership of the partnership and will share equally in the profits and losses of the partnership.

5. All partnership business activity shall be decided by [majority] [majority plus one] [unanimous] vote of the partners.

6. If any partner leaves the partnership or dies, the partnership shall continue with the remaining partners.

7. In the event of the dissolution of the partnership, partners shall decide by [majority] [majority plus one] [unanimous] vote who will acquire the rights to the business name.

8. This partnership agreement can be modified at any time by [majority] [majority plus one] [unanimous] vote of the partners.

[Signed and dated by all partners]

But when a business is just starting out, sometimes it's important to just get the basics in place, and then expand from there. You don't know what issues will come up, or how you will want to deal with them.

With this "starter" agreement, you don't have to make decisions until actual situations present themselves. With each decision the partners make, that decision should be written down and signed by all partners. The decision then becomes part of the partnership agreement. If a decision turns out not to be beneficial—it didn't work out quite the way you wanted—you can revoke or reword the decision at any time.

A partnership agreement is an "understanding" between partners as to how the business will be conducted. Many partnership agreements are nothing more than a handshake and a "Let's do it." Often such agreements turn out to be more of a *"mis*understanding" than anything else.

A written partnership agreement is not required by law, but if you don't have one, you are asking for nothing but trouble. What's more, without a partnership agreement, state law (UPA and RUPA), not the partners, can dictate how the partnership is run and how disputes are settled.

In most states, if you don't have a written agreement, state law says that each partner shares equally in the profits, regardless of the time or money contributed, and has equal voice in the management of the partnership. A partnership with a written agreement is not bound by these laws; you can make your own rules.

One important issue in a partnership is how decisions are to be made. If there are two partners, can one partner make decisions? Or will it require both partners to agree? And what if the partners don't agree? If there are three or more partners, do the partners vote on decisions? If there is an even number of partners, what happens if there is a tie vote? I don't know the answer to these questions. There is no one answer that fits every partnership. If the partners have an idea how they want to make decisions, put this in the partnership agreement. You can always change it later, after you see how the business is actually operating.

Partnership agreements are not binding on outside ("third") parties. A lender or a creditor or someone suing the business can go after any and all partners, no matter what the partnership agreement says.

A written partnership agreement should be signed by all the partners and should include:

1. The name of the partnership, the date the partnership began, and the names of the original partners.

2. A simple statement of business goals. Long-range goals should be included as well. For example, one partner may want a business that will provide a good livelihood for many years, while the other partner may be dreaming of building up the business and when it becomes successful and established, selling it for a big profit. These two partners obviously have a serious conflict of interest. If partners do not agree on the basics, the partnership is doomed from the start. (This item doesn't need to be in a written agreement, doesn't need to be in writing at all. But it definitely should be discussed before starting the business.)

3. How much each partner is to contribute, in cash, property, and time, and when the contributions are to be made.

4. How each partner will share in the profits and losses. The easiest and most common arrangement is an equal division of profits between partners. You may wish, however, to provide for an unequal division of profits to compensate for differences in time or money contributed or for differences in ability and experience. A partner can draw a wage to reflect actual time spent running the business. The wage is known as a "guaranteed payment to partner." It is not a regular employee wage for tax purposes. There is no withholding and no employee payroll taxes. It is part of the partner's total partnership income. Paying a wage is common when one partner works day to day in the business and the other doesn't, or when partners do not put in equal time. After the wage is paid, any remaining profit (or loss) for the year is then divided between the partners according to the partnership agreement. Specify any wage arrangement in the agreement.

5. How expenses will be handled. Who can approve them? Who can sign checks? Who has the debit card?

6. You may want a clause specifying the legal and management powers of each partner. Who can sign contracts? Who can hire or fire employees? Such a clause in the agreement is not binding on outside parties, and it will not relieve any partner of partnership obligations entered into by other partners. It only reduces the possibility of misunderstanding among the partners.

7. Procedures for withdrawing funds and paying profits, how much and when, to prevent partners from arbitrarily withdrawing money from the partnership.

8. Can a partner have a separate outside business? Can one of the partners compete with the partnership, possibly siphoning off partnership business?

9. Provisions for continuing the business if one partner dies or wants out. Without such a provision, in states with UPA laws (as opposed to RUPA laws), the partnership ceases to exist. Equally important, without this provision a partner can quit or retire any time the partner wants, sell his share of the partnership to anyone he pleases, or demand to be paid fair value for his or her share of the partnership. Your biggest problem is determining how much money the departing partner (or estate) should receive, and over what period of time. For example, the business may be worth a lot of money because it is established and successful, or because it owns a lot of inventory and equipment, but there may be little cash on hand to pay a departing partner. Insurance companies offer "key person" life insurance for partnerships to buy out a deceased or seriously ill partner.

Your buyout agreement, sometimes called a "buy-sell" or "cross-purchase" agreement, should state how a partner's share of the business is to be valued. Is it based on the value of the business assets—that is, what you actually have invested in the business? Or is it based on what the going business is worth on the open market, what an eager new owner might pay for it? And who will be the lucky person to determine this "worth"?

There are tax consequences to a partner buyout that vary depending on how the agreement is worded. The tax interests of the remaining and outgoing partners are often diametrically opposed. These tax aspects can be substantial; they will probably require professional help.

The agreement might include a non-compete clause so that a departing partner cannot engage in a similar business, though to hold up in court, the clause would have to be for a reasonable period of time and in a limited geographical area.

10. If the partnership dissolves, who will own the right to the business name?

11. Every partnership agreement should have a clause that allows the partners to change anything in the agreement at any time.

Obviously, there are a lot of issues that can be included in a partnership agreement, and not all of them are pleasant. It's up to you whether you want to discuss issues now, while the partners are in a good mood and cooperating with one another, or a time in the future when maybe partners are not as beneficent toward each other. The more issues you are willing to talk about now while everyone is in a good mood, and put in writing, the more likely you will be able to avoid disputes down the road.

There also will be issues that come up later, issues the partners didn't know about or think about when they drafted the agreement. And there will be clauses in the agreement that need to be changed or eliminated. All partnership agreements should have a provision allowing the partners to alter the agreement any time they want to change it.

Most of the professional advice I have heard suggests that you hire a knowledgeable lawyer (not all lawyers are familiar with partnership problems) or an experienced accountant to draw up any partnership agreement. I feel that you can avoid the expense, and draft your own agreement if it is a simple one (such as 50-50, equal sharing), if you consider everything in this chapter, and if you know your partners well enough to be confident in your plans.

YOU AND YOUR PARTNERS

My friend Rory said, "Having a partner is just like having a wife, only more so." Well, Rory is a longtime loner, but his words are basically true.

Partnerships are more than business. They are often complex interpersonal relationships. And like marriages, partnerships can bring out the best and the worst in people. By acquiring a partner you are adding a whole new dimension to your business venture, one you should be fully prepared to deal with.

Anyone who has lost a friend after an argument can realize the possible problems and complications of having a business partner. It is not uncommon for partners to have a disagreement, a difference of opinion, or worse. You may feel that your partner is not working as hard as he should, and he may be feeling the same about you!

When trouble arises between partners, the logical step is to try to work it out. Sit down with your partner, get the problems "out front," and get them solved. Much more easily said than done. Like divorces, partnership dissolutions are common and often just as problematical. The alternatives—dividing up the assets and going out of business, or one partner buying out the other—can be difficult even with a good written agreement, can require lawyers, and almost always cause the business to suffer.

Marriage counselors can sometimes save a marriage. But it's a little out of my field, and there is little advice I can give you retrospectively. Knowing that such things happen should warn you to take every precaution prior to going into a partnership to reduce the possibility of problems later on.

The best advice I can offer is to pick your partners very carefully. This may seem basic, just common sense, but a poor choice of partners is the root cause of many partnership failures. How well do you know your partners? Are you old friends? Have you worked together before? What business experience do your partners have? What is his or her track record? Is a partner having financial difficulties? Look at the way your partners treat their families, neighbors, and friends. It may be indicative of how they will treat you.

Partnership Recordkeeping

The recordkeeping for a partnership is the same as for a sole proprietorship. But partnerships also keep a record of partners' capital: each partner's financial contributions and withdrawals, and each partner's share of profit or loss.

Like other financial records, a record of partners' capital can be a simple handwritten record, a spreadsheet, or an accounting software file. For a spreadsheet or hand-posted record, the partners' capital ledger has two columns for each partner. One column shows activity in each partner's account: contributions, withdrawals, and the partner's share of profit or loss. The second column is the balance of the partner's capital remaining with the partnership.

Contributions and withdrawals should be recorded when they occur. Contributions are shown as positive amounts and increase the partner's balance. Withdrawals are shown as negative, bracketed amounts and decrease the partner's balance. If a partner is getting a guaranteed payment (wage), the payments are shown as withdrawals.

Each partner's share of the partnership profit or loss is posted to the partners' capital ledger once a year at year-end. A profit is posted to the activity column as a positive amount; a loss is shown as a negative amount. Profits and losses increase and decrease a partner's balance accordingly. The total balance column is the sum of all the individual partners' balance columns.

The sample partners' capital ledger shows activity for 2018 and part of 2019 for a new partnership, Wesley's Farm Fresh Eggs, owned by two partners:

Entry 1: The partnership began on January 1, 2018. Each partner contributed $2,000 to the business. Each partner's balance is $2,000, and the total balance is $4,000.

Entry 2: On March 31, Huck (Partner A) contributed another $800, and Pippi (Partner B) contributed another $400.

Entry 3: The partnership made a $7,000 profit in 2018. On December 31, 2018, the partners' shares of the profit were posted to their individual accounts.

Entry 4: On February 5, 2019, Huck withdrew $400 from the business.

Entry 5: On May 1, 2019, Pippi withdrew $350 from the business.

With each entry, the partners' individual balances and the total balance were adjusted.

In addition to keeping a record of partners' capital, large partnerships, those with $250,000 in sales or $1 million in assets, will need to include a balance sheet (assets and liabilities, net worth) on their tax returns. Balance sheets are explained in the T.C.B.: Take Care of Business chapter.

		Wesley's Farm Fresh Eggs Partners' Capital Ledger				
		Huck (Partner A)		Pippi (Partner B)		Total
Entry		Activity	Balance	Activity	Balance	Balance
1	Contribution 1-1	$2,000.00	$2,000.00	$2,000.00	$2,000.00	$4,000.00
2	Contribution 3-31	$800.00	$2,800.00	$400.00	$2,400.00	$5,200.00
3	Income for Year	$4,000.00	$6,800.00	$3,000.00	$5,400.00	$12,200.00
4	Withdrawal 2-5	($400.00)	$6,400.00		$5,400.00	$11,800.00
5	Withdrawal 5-1		$6,400.00	($350.00)	$5,050.00	$11,450.00

PARTNERSHIP POSTMORTEM . . .

Lara Stonebraker, former partner in Aromatica, a retail coffee store: "It's been my experience that partnerships rarely work, especially if there is an odd number of partners. Because it's always going to be two against one in all decision making. Unless you have such well-matched personalities that everybody is always good friends, it creates incredible hassles. That was the most anxiety ridden period of my life. There were three of us and I happened to be the odd one. I blotted out a lot of that whole experience."

Key Dickason, former partner in Xanadu, a computer service: "I was in a partnership once, and my partner and I disagreed—not on the running of the business, but on the way we handled employees. Jack and I disagreed on a philosophical—a better word is ethical—aspect of employee relationships. To Jack, an employee was somebody you used and discarded. To me, an employee was somebody you had an obligation and a commitment to. If you have this basic disagreement, no partnership agreement will handle it. Do you put in there, 'You agree to treat employees fairly?' Well, that doesn't mean anything. Because to Jack, Jack was treating them fairly. It eventually led to the dissolution of the partnership.

"The biggest mistake in the world is to start a partnership if there is disagreement in the beginning when you're laying the groundwork for the business. If you enter into a basic disagreement on ethics, management, or whatever the objective of the business is, you shouldn't go into business together. Putting your doubts about the situation into a partnership agreement doesn't accomplish anything unless you're prepared to fight, which isn't what it's all about."

Jan Lowe, former partner in Midnight Sewing Machine, a retail dress shop: "I went into business with my sister, who is a dear person, and who taught me everything I know. I didn't sew a stitch in my life before we bought this dress shop, and she handed me a pattern and scissors and said, 'I'm going to lunch now. If you have any problems, let me know.' So I started off real cold there, which is no way to do it. I'd run into problems when people would want something intricate done or they'd want something altered, and I wouldn't know how to handle it. I wasn't really prepared to do what I did for a living.

"One of our basic problems was non-communication. My partner would borrow money from someone and I didn't know about it, which I thought was a cheap shot. You've got to be in constant communication. If somebody's going to lunch, they've got to tell you. We didn't have anything in writing between us, how things were going to be run. That should be made clear right from the start, exactly what do you want to see happen, how is it going to happen, who's going to make what work, who is best at handling what; and stick to it.

"I think you should be willing to bend when that system does not work. Face it immediately and try something else. To hang on to a system that doesn't work can get you into lots of trouble."

. . . AND A PARTNERSHIP THAT WORKS

Pat Ellington is a partner in Kipple Antiques, a small antiques store: "Kipple is a made-up word that means, um, kipple, the stuff that you gather around you that you can't live without. When we first started, I was the only one with any business skill. Neither Miriam or Pam ever held an office job. Ann has been a housewife all her life. But we function pretty well as a four-way partnership. Everybody's really working part-time. But this way we can operate a full-time business.

"We've had personality troubles, but not serious ones, because we squashed them right away. The interpersonal stuff can be worked out if everybody agrees it's going to happen, that there's no blame attached to differences of opinion or feelings. We all agreed when we set out that everybody was going to make mistakes, some of them are going to cost us money, but no blame should be attached to anybody, and we would not throw it up to each other.

"When Ann joined us, Miriam made a lot of noises: 'She did this wrong, she never should have bought that.' Pam and I would say, 'Miriam, you made your mistakes too; back off.' And she slowly but surely got over that. She felt, being the one partner with the most money in at that point, like the business was hers. None of this was conscious. We all have moments of 'mine' mentalities: 'That's mine. She's threatening it.'

"Miriam is a crackerjack saleswoman. She can sell anybody anything. But she couldn't keep a set of books to save her soul. She can't balance a checkbook. But she can sell. That's a real asset. Pam's got a good eye when it comes to buying. Ann, who's much better organized than the other two when it comes to shows, she's the one who sits down and makes out a list: We need lights, display material, we need so much inventory. These are skills.

"And I'm the bookkeeper. And between the four of us, we can really operate."

YOU, INCORPORATED: CORPORATION PRIMER

The corporation is truly a misunderstood animal. People, even businesspeople, have more misconceptions about corporations than about any other form of business. Some small-time operations will benefit by incorporating, but many will not. In order for you to make an intelligent choice between "You" and "You, Incorporated," you will need a basic understanding of what a corporation is and what can and cannot be accomplished by incorporating.

"In Twenty-Five Words or Less"

A corporation is . . . just another business. The basic day-to-day operations, the management, keeping records, are virtually no different than the operations of an unincorporated business. A corporation can be as tiny as the tiniest unincorporated business. Most (but not all) states allow one-person corporations. Just as there are "gray suits and elevators" corporations, there are "blue jeans and T-shirts corporations," home-based corporations, and part-time corporations.

A corporation is just another business . . . but the rules of the game are different. Owners of corporations are the stockholders, also called shareholders. They own shares of stock, pieces of paper. Your corporation may have one or more stockholders (one or more owners) with one or more shares of stock, depending on your needs and your state's laws (discussed below).

A corporation is just another business . . . but some people are impressed when a business has Inc. next to its name. Some people think they're dealing with a large company instead of, well, just you. At least that's the pitch you hear from businesses that want you to pay them to set you up as a corporation. I really don't know whether a corporation impresses anyone or affects buying decisions. Do you notice, or care, if some business you buy from is a corporation or not?

Two Types of Corporations

There are two types of for-profit corporations: Regular corporations, often called C corporations (not to be confused with IRS Schedule C that is filed by sole proprietors); and S corporations, also known as Subchapter S or Sub S corporations, because they are covered in Subchapter S of the Internal Revenue Code. C corporations and S corporations are very similar in how they are structured and the liability protection they offer, but the two types of corporations are taxed differently, have different fringe benefits for the owners of the corporations, and have a few other different rules, all explained below.

Corporate Taxes

Corporate Myth Number One: You're going to lower your taxes by incorporating. Probably not. The fact is, most small businesses will not save tax money by incorporating. Even though corporate tax rates are sometimes lower than individual tax rates, small unincorporated businesses usually pay about the same amount of federal income tax as incorporated businesses.

C corporations and S corporations are taxed differently. C corporation profits are taxed twice: once as corporate income and again when distributed to the shareholders as dividends. S corporations do not have this double taxation. S corporations do not pay any federal income tax. S corporations are "pass-through entities"; all of an S corporation's profits "pass through" (to use the IRS's terminology) to the owners of the corporation, who pay individual income tax on their shares of the profits of the business.

These tax laws can get complicated, but the bottom line for most small corporations is that the total federal income taxes are about the same whether the business is structured as a C corporation or an S corporation.

Most states impose income taxes on corporations. Some states call their income tax an excise tax, not to be confused with federal excise taxes described in the Taxes chapter.

Many states impose an additional tax on corporations called a franchise tax. The franchise tax may be a flat annual fee, or may be a percent of income like a second income tax, or may be based on the value of stock or assets. In some states the franchise tax is really a minimum income tax: you pay your income tax or the franchise tax, whichever is greater. In most states, the franchise tax applies to both C and S corporations.

Corporate Limited Liability

Corporate Myth Number Two: A corporation will protect you from business debts and lawsuits. In certain situations, yes, corporate limited liability offers protection to the stockholders and officers, protection not available to sole proprietors and partners. But in many situations, and in most lawsuits, corporate limited liability will not shield you at all.

The main reason for corporate limited liability is to protect you from creditors—suppliers and others you owe money to in the normal course of business—should the business go broke. A corporation is recognized by law as a "legal entity," which means that the business is legally separate from its owners. If your corporation is unable to pay its debts, the creditors usually cannot get their money from your personal, non-business assets.

Your corporation's limited liability, however, will not usually protect you from repaying a business loan, because most lenders will not lend money to a small corporation unless the owner cosigns as a personal guarantor of the loan.

Most important, a corporation will not protect you from lawsuits. If your company is sued by an angry customer, or someone who was injured, or someone who suffered a loss, you as owner or officer of the business will also be named in the lawsuit. Professionals such as doctors and lawyers cannot hide behind a corporation to protect themselves from malpractice suits. Do not be fooled by this common and dangerous misconception about liability protection.

A corporation will not shield you from personal liability that you normally should be responsible for, such as not having car insurance, or acting with gross negligence, or if your company breaks the law. Limited liability will not protect you if your corporation fails to pay any income, payroll, or other business taxes.

A corporation will shield you from a malpractice suit brought against one of your co-owners. Partnerships often incorporate (or set up limited liability companies, covered below) to protect individual partners from possible losses and lawsuits resulting from the actions of other partners.

People who own more than one business sometimes incorporate each business separately so if one business fails, the creditors cannot grab the assets of the other corporations. But that protection is often challenged in court, especially when one individual owns and controls several corporations.

If you plan to incorporate primarily with the intention of limiting your legal liability, I suggest you find out first exactly how limited the liability really is for your particular venture. You may find that buying insurance instead of incorporating offers better and less expensive protection. Talk to a good lawyer or accountant.

Corporation Change of Ownership

Incorporating a business eliminates much of the legal and tax complications of a change in ownership. New shareholders can be added easily (within certain legal limits, discussed later). Selling a business, passing a family-owned business from generation to generation, giving or selling your employees an ownership interest, and taking on investors in the company are all much easier with a corporation than with an unincorporated business.

Sale of stock or death of a shareholder will not end the business. The same corporation can continue in business with new shareholders. By comparison, a sole proprietorship ceases to exist when the owner sells or gives away the business, takes on a partner, or dies. In some states, a partnership ceases to exist when one partner quits or dies. A sole proprietorship or a partnership can be sold or otherwise acquired by new owners, but the result, legally, is a new business requiring new records, new valuation of assets and liabilities, and new business licenses and permits.

Corporation Owner-Employees

A corporation is the only form of business that can hire its owners as employees. You are in the unique position of being your own boss and your own employee. How owner-employee wages are taxed is one of the significant differences between C corporations and S corporations.

In both C and S corporations, owner-employees are paid a wage, subject to regular payroll taxes and taxable to the owner-employees. In both C and S corporations, the wage paid to owner-employees (that is, the wage you decide to pay to yourself) is deductible in calculating the corporation's profit.

Any profit, after deducting the wages, is taxable, but differently for C and S corporations. C corporations pay corporate income tax on the profit. And, as explained above, when the profit is distributed as dividends, the shareholders (the owners of the corporation) pay tax on those dividends. C corporation profit is taxed twice: once to the corporation and again to the owners of the corporation when the dividends are distributed. For S corporations, however, profits in excess of the owners' salaries are taxable to the owners, not to the corporation. There is no double taxation. (C corporations can avoid the double taxation by increasing owner-employees' wages, something to discuss with an accountant if you are going to set up as a C corporation.)

In a C corporation, the owners do not pay taxes on the dividends until the dividends are distributed to them. These dividends are taxed as capital gains, which have a lower tax rate than regular income. S corporation dividends are taxable to the owners the year earned, whether the owners actually receive the money or not. S corporation dividends, unlike C corporations, are taxed as regular income, at the owners' regular income tax rate.

Now this is where tax law gets interesting. Keep in mind that you as an owner-employee of your corporation draw a wage, subject to all regular payroll taxes. Any business profit in excess of your wage is also taxable to you, but as a dividend. Dividends, unlike a salary, are not subject to employment taxes.

Since you decide how much of a salary you earn, you therefore also get to decide how much of the corporation's annual profit is subject to payroll taxes, and how much escapes payroll taxes as dividends. But look out: If the IRS thinks that your salary is too low and your dividends too high, they may declare that the dividends were a salary in disguise, and hit you for back payroll taxes and penalties. This is an area that gets close attention from the IRS. I suggest you discuss this with your accountant.

A big difference between C corporations and S corporations is how employee health insurance is taxed. Owner-employees of C corporations are eligible for employee health insurance, which is not taxable to the employees and is 100 percent tax deductible for the corporation. S corporations come under different laws, the same laws that apply to businesses that are not incorporated (sole proprietorships, partnerships, joint ventures, and limited liability companies). S corporations do not get a tax deduction for health insurance purchased for owner-employees. This is explained in "Health Insurance" in the Taxes chapter. If your health insurance costs

are high, this alone may be an excellent reason to set up as a C corporation. I suggest you discuss this with an experienced tax accountant.

Another reason to consider incorporating is if you are retired and collecting Social Security. You can lose part of your Social Security income if any outside income, such as earnings from a small business, gets above a certain level. By setting up a corporation, you may be able to pay yourself a low enough salary so it stays under the Social Security limits. This arrangement cannot be accomplished with a sole proprietorship, a partnership, or an LLC because all of the profits of an unincorporated business are considered personal income whether you take a salary or not. This is another area you should discuss with an accountant.

Employee business expenses: Your corporation can take tax deductions for any allowable business expenses, as long as the corporation itself spends the money. If you personally spend the money, out of your own personal funds, the only way to get the deduction is to have your corporation reimburse you, so the corporation gets the deduction. This will require that you have an "accountable reimbursement plan," which is a written policy that the expenses are business related and substantiated (you have receipts).

Another warning to owner-employees: If your corporation is not yet making a profit, I suggest that you do not pay yourself any wages until the corporation is making a taxable profit. Otherwise you'll be paying payroll taxes and personal income taxes on the salary but get no tax breaks for your corporation. A lose-lose situation. Talk to an accountant.

Corporation-Retained Earnings

One tax advantage for C corporations, but not for S corporations, is the C corporation's legal ability to retain up to $250,000 ($150,000 for personal service corporations) of undistributed profits within the company, and not pay the profits out to the owners. Though the corporation pays income tax on these "retained earnings" (also called accumulated earnings), the owners do not have to pay the "double" or second tax because the profits have not been paid out to them. Retained earnings can be reinvested in the business, distributed to the shareholders at a later date, or retained indefinitely by the company.

All other forms of business can also retain the profits in the business, but the owners pay income tax on the profits whether distributed to them or not.

This is the one situation where setting up a C corporation might reduce your taxes. If the corporate tax rate is lower than your personal tax rate (which depends not only on how much profit you earn, but also on marital status and how many dependents and personal deductions you claim), any retained earnings—profits you decide not to take out of the business this year—will be taxed at the lower corporate rate. If you reinvest those retained earnings in the business in a future year, you're fine. But if you ever withdraw the retained earnings, they become taxable dividends, and you are penalized with the double taxation.

Business Losses: C Corporations versus S Corporations

If a business sustains a loss, that loss can be carried back to prior years to offset prior years' taxes, bringing immediate tax refunds. This is explained in "Net Operating Losses" in the Taxes chapter. Any business, corporation or otherwise, can avail itself of operating loss carryback laws. But if a corporation is brand new and sustains a loss, there are no prior years to carry the loss back to. However, if the corporation is an S corporation, the loss passes through to the stockholders, and they can carry the loss back to their personal prior years' returns even though the business did not exist then. Losses that cannot be carried back can be carried forward to offset future years' earnings, for both C and S corporations.

Stock Restrictions: C Corporations versus S Corporations

A C corporation can have an unlimited number of shareholders (stockholders) with very few restrictions on ownership. An S corporation is limited to a maximum of 100 shareholders. A family is counted as one stockholder. S corporation stock ownership is limited to U.S. citizens, resident aliens, estates, certain trusts, and some tax exempt organizations. There are limitations on how profits are to be distributed, and how and when the election to become an S corporation is made. An S corporation can own a subsidiary S corporation, a legal maneuver that protects the assets of one of the corporations should the other corporation go bankrupt.

One drawback to S corporations is that, unlike regular C corporations, S corporations can have only one class of stock. C corporations can have voting stock and non-voting stock, so investors in the C corporation can be given non-voting stock that prohibits them from being able to vote on corporate decisions. This is not possible with an S corporation. If you want your investors to stay out of your business affairs, an S corporation may not be the best choice.

More Reasons to Consider Incorporating

If you are applying for a Small Business Administration (SBA) loan, the SBA seems to be partial to corporations.

If you are trying to get a home loan, lenders are leery of self-employed people who have no proof of income except their records and tax returns. Lenders like to see pay stubs and W-2 wage statements, which a corporation will provide. Even though the corporation is still "you" paying yourself, a corporate structure is more reassuring to some lenders.

Corporations are allowed a few tax deductions not available to unincorporated businesses: charitable contributions, some inventory deductions, and state and local income taxes.

Corporations are less likely to be audited by the IRS than unincorporated businesses, though the difference is only about 2 percent.

State Laws for S Corporations

For state income taxes, most states recognize the S corporation, but several states do not. As of last year, Arkansas, Louisiana, New Hampshire, New Jersey, New York, Tennessee, Texas, and the District of Columbia do not recognize S corporations for state income taxes. Of the states that do allow S corporations, some states impose franchise, income, or other corporate taxes on S corporations.

People who like the pass-through tax benefits of an S corporation, but do not meet the requirements or whose states make S corporations unattractive, should consider setting up as a limited liability company (covered below).

Close Corporations

Some states have a legal structure called a close corporation. *Close corporations* are limited to thirty (sometimes fifty) shareholders. The shareholders, not a board of directors, oversee the operation of the business. Stock sales are restricted. If a shareholder wants to sell his or her stock, the shareholder must first offer the stock to other shareholders. Close corporations are often less costly to set up and have fewer legal restrictions than regular corporations.

B Corporations

B corporations, also called benefit corporations, are C corporations or S corporations that have been certified by a private, non-government organization as meeting certain environmental or societal objectives. There is no IRS or state category for a B corporation, and there are no B corporation laws.

Nonprofit Corporations

Businesses generally cannot be nonprofit corporations. Nonprofit corporations are charities, foundations, schools, churches, community organizations, and clubs. Nonprofit corporations do make profits, profits that are exempt from income tax, but the purpose of a nonprofit corporation has to be a reason other than running a business.

Nonprofit corporations have no owners, no stockholders like regular corporations. Nonprofit corporations can have employees, but the wages paid to employees are taxable like wages paid to any employees. Nonprofit corporations are not exempt from payroll taxes and employment laws.

Some businesses refer to themselves as "not for profit," claiming that the business exists for reasons other than to make money. But "not for profit" is not a legal term. There is no IRS category called "not for profit." There is nothing illegal about claiming to be not for profit, as long as you are not using the term to deceive people into thinking that your business is a nonprofit corporation.

Steps to Incorporating a Business

The states, not the federal government, license corporations. The IRS does issue identification numbers (EINs) to all corporations (covered in "Licenses and Permits" in the Getting Started chapter), but other than that, state law dictates how corporations are to be chartered and what documents are required. The laws vary from state to state, as do the fees. Your state may have filing fees, organization fees, charter fees, license fees, qualification fees, and annual report fees, which can run from minimal amounts in some states to thousands of dollars in others. And unless you are willing and able to study all the corporation laws and file all the necessary forms yourself, add several hundred dollars for a lawyer's assistance.

Start by contacting the secretary of state, the office of the corporate commissioner, or whatever state office registers corporations. Ask for their instructions, forms, and fee schedules.

Although different states have different requirements, *all* states require corporations to have three basic documents: articles of incorporation, bylaws, and stock certificates.

The articles of incorporation (sometimes called certificate of incorporation, articles of association, or corporate charter) is a document that basically states that the corporation exists and is registered with the state. Many states have a simple, one-page, fill-in-the-blanks form for the articles of incorporation.

The articles of incorporation usually include:

1. **Corporate name.** The state can reject your proposed name if it is too similar to another corporation's name or if it is deceptive so as to mislead the public. Some states prohibit certain words in a corporation's name, typically words that might make the company sound like it is a government agency.

2. **Corporate purpose.** Use the broadest, most unspecific description your state allows, so as not to limit the scope of permitted activity. In most states, all you need is one sentence stating that the corporation has been formed to engage in any activity allowed by law. That's it. Most state forms already include the exact wording of this clause.

3. **Corporate address.** The location of the principal office of the corporation. The address has to be a street address, not a post office box. Much has been written about the benefits of incorporating in a state other than your own, particularly Delaware, where the corporate statutes are lenient and the filing fees minimal. This is another corporate myth. Most states require small in-state corporations, where the majority of stockholders are state residents, to incorporate in that state.

4. **Service of process.** States require that corporations provide a name and address for one individual who can accept "service of

---

Articles of Incorporation

Corporate Name:
[Your Business, Inc.]

Corporate Purpose:
The purpose of the corporation is to engage in any lawful act or activity for which a corporation may be organized in [your state].

Service of Process:
This is the name and address of a state resident who agrees to be your business's agent to accept service of process (legal papers) in case your corporation is sued. You may list any adult who lives in your state. Most states require a physical address, not a PO box.

Corporate Address:
You can use any street address that you can get mail at.

Shares:
This corporation is authorized to issue only one class of shares of stock. The total number of shares which this corporation is authorized to issue is _____.
You can list as many shareholders (owners) as you want. Not all shares have to be issued, so no harm in having extra shares authorized. You can also, if you want, issue more than one class of stock, typically voting stock and non-voting stock (C corporations only; S corporations can have only one class of stock).

Signatures:
Each original shareholder sign and date.

_____

_____

_____

The sample Articles of Incorporation is the minimum legal requirement for most states. Your state's secretary of state or department of corporations will have a downloadable or printable form that you can use.

process" (legal papers) if the corporation is sued. This individual is usually the corporation's attorney, if the corporation has an attorney, but it can be one of the stockholders, or any other adult living in the state. The address can be the same address as the corporation.

5. **Shares of stock.** The maximum number of shares of stock the corporation can issue, and the number of classes of stock. Stock is covered below.

6. **Incorporators.** Some states require that the names and addresses of the shareholders (called incorporators, subscribers, or promoters) be listed in the articles, but many states do not. If required, incorporators can use the corporation's address instead of their own.

Bylaws
Your Business, Incorporated
Incorporated [date of incorporation]

Section 1. Purpose
The purpose of the corporation is to operate a business and provide products and services.

Section 2. Location
The corporation is located at [address where you will get mail].

Section 3. Stockholders
The corporation shall initially have _____ stockholders, each stockholder having one share of stock. Each share of stock gives each shareholder one vote.
The initial stockholders are: [list all stockholders]

Section 4. Board of Directors
The corporation shall have _____ directors, who shall be elected by [majority] [majority plus one] vote of the Stockholders. Directors can be removed and replaced by [majority] [majority plus one] vote of the Directors.

Section 5. Officers
The corporation shall have _____ officer positions: President, Secretary, Treasurer, and [as many additional officers as you want].

Section 6. Meetings
Directors and Officers shall have meetings as needed or as requested by a [majority] [majority plus one] of the Directors.

Section 7. Records and Reports
Directors shall maintain all records and reports of the corporation.

Section 8. Amending Bylaws
These Bylaws can be amended at any time by [majority] [majority plus one] vote of the Directors.

Dated _____ and signed by the initial Directors of the corporation:

_____

_____

The sample bylaws are the minimum a small corporation should have. Most states require corporations to have bylaws, but the states usually do not specify what should be in the bylaws.

7. **Capitalization.** Many states require corporations to have what they call "stated capital" or "minimum capitalization," a minimum amount of money in the bank account that cannot be withdrawn. Some states require the amount of capitalization be specified in the articles of incorporation, but many do not. Capitalization is covered below.

In most states, corporations must have bylaws. Bylaws describe, in much greater detail than the articles, how the corporation is to be run: the rights and responsibilities of shareholders, directors, and officers; how decisions are to be made; when meeting are to be held. Bylaws have much of the same information you'd put in a partnership agreement (described under "Partnerships" above). Bylaws can be as detailed or as bare-bones as you want, and can be changed or expanded at any time the company directors want to change them. In fact, the bylaws should include the procedure for changing the bylaws. Unlike the articles of incorporation, which is a simple document that should never need revision, the bylaws can be revised and updated any time a business issue comes up that needs to be addressed.

Corporate Directors and Officers

Corporations have a board of directors who oversee the corporation, and officers who run the corporation. And in case you don't know the difference between directors and officers, between "overseeing" the corporation and "running" the corporation, well, you don't have to worry: In most small corporations, the directors and the officers are the same people.

Most states require corporations to have at least one director (the "board" of directors can be one person), though some states may require more. Most states require corporations to have at least three officers: a president, a secretary, and a treasurer, although in many states they can all be the same person.

There is no legal maximum number of directors or officers; you can have as many as you want. Corporate directors are required by law to have at least one annual directors' meeting, though it can be over the phone or the internet.

Corporate Stock

All corporations are required to issue stock certificates to every stockholder (shareholder). Some states have exact wording that must be on a stock certificate, but in many states, you can just make up your own.

Most small corporations are private or "closely held" businesses, meaning stock is not sold to the general public. The stockholders (shareholders) are the people who actually own and run the corporation, and possibly their family members, or investors, or employees. The corporation has what's called a "limited offering," with each original shareholder individually registered with the state where the corporation is chartered. After the initial issuance of stock, most states require you to register new stockholders when you sell new shares, or sell old shares to new stockholders.

Many states put a limit on the number of shareholders a closely held corporation can have, but there is no limit on the number of shares you can issue, or how many shares an individual can own. When you prepare your articles of incorporation, you get to specify the number of shares authorized, often an arbitrary figure. Not all authorized shares have to be issued.

This kind of private corporation, and the very specific state rules regarding stock ownership, is quite different than a public corporation, which can sell stock to anyone. Stock that people buy and sell on the stock exchange is from public corporations. Public corporation stockholders are not registered with the state. Public corporations pay much higher state fees than private corporations. Public corporations must also register with the federal Securities and Exchange Commission (the SEC), not required of private corporations. And public corporations are required by law to hire CPAs to prepare annual audited financial statements. Most private corporations are not required to have their statements audited, and, of course, most don't.

A homemade stock certificate like this one may be all a small corporation needs. Check with your state first to see if there is any specific legal wording that is required by the state.

CLASSES AND STATED VALUE OF STOCK

S corporations can have only one class of stock. C corporations can, if you want, issue different classes of stock, typically a voting class that gives the stockholders the right to vote on all corporate decisions; and a non-voting class, where the stockholders do not get to make any corporate decisions. Non-voting stock is sometimes issued to family members or people who are only investors in the business, who you don't want to be able to help you run your company.

C corporation stock is also classed as common or preferred. Holders of preferred stock have prior or "preferred" claim on corporate assets over common stockholders. Preferred stockholders are often just investors, with no interest in the corporation other than making money on their investment. Preferred stock is usually non-voting stock.

And there's more. Stock can have what's called a *par value*, a stated value per share where you say how much one share is worth; or a *no-par value*, where the value is not stated. You will probably avoid complications by issuing no-par stock.

Capitalization

Many states require corporations to have a minimum amount of money in the bank at the time of incorporation. This is another important decision that requires a knowledge of corporate equity, which is the actual dollar investment in the business. Corporate equity is comprised of "stated capital" and "paid-in surplus."

Stated capital is an amount of money that belongs to the corporation and cannot be paid out to stockholders until the corporation is liquidated. All corporations must have some stated capital. Most states specify the minimum that must be in the corporation's bank account. This is protection for creditors, to prevent stockholders from raiding the company's assets and making it incapable of paying its debts.

Corporations try to keep stated capital as small as possible. Paid-in surplus is money in excess of stated capital and generally not restricted.

As you can tell, there is a lot of legal terminology here, but the correct wording can make the difference between a complicated and an easy incorporation.

Acting like a Corporation

If you are going to incorporate, you have to play the corporate game entirely. It is important for even a one-person corporation to play by all the rules and to follow all the formalities.

Your corporation must have at least one stockholder. Some states require corporations to have more than one stockholder. The stockholders appoint directors. Directors appoint officers. Officers hire employees. In a small corporation, one person often wears all four hats: stockholder, director, officer, and employee.

Stockholders and directors must hold meetings and keep written minutes of the meetings, or if your state permits, take action by unanimous written consent. Even if you are the sole owner, corporation law says that you must hold a meeting with yourself (that should be fun) and write down what you decide.

Corporate minutes are much more than a legal formality. Many important decisions are made at directors' meetings, and the minutes are often the only written record of these decisions. If there are disagreements among directors, old minutes can often resolve the issues.

Always identify your business as a corporation, using "Incorporated" or "Inc." or "Corp." Make it clear to people you do business with, and anybody loaning money to the business, that you are an officer of a corporation, and not acting as an individual. In correspondence, writing checks, and signing contracts, sign your name "Julia Marie, President, Company Name Incorporated (or Inc., or Corp.)" rather than just Julia Marie. Do not sign "DBA" (doing business as) after your name, as this implies you are acting as an individual.

If you don't act like a corporation—issuing stock, holding meetings, maintaining minimum capitalization, keeping records, filing annual reports, and making sure all documents indicate that this is a corporation—a court could rule that creditors can ignore the corporate limited liability rules and go after your personal assets, like they can if your business is not incorporated. This is called "piercing the corporate veil" or "piercing the corporate shield." This is something you do not want to happen.

A corporation can lose its limited liability protection if it is undercapitalized, if the owners drain the business of cash so it has ongoing problems paying its bills, if the owners pay personal bills from corporate accounts, or if the owners commingle personal and corporate assets. If a corporation fails to file state tax returns or pay state taxes owed, your state may be able to suspend or revoke your corporate charter.

Incorporating an Existing Business

A business can incorporate when it first opens its doors or any time afterward. You can start your business as a sole proprietorship or a partnership, both of which cost much less to start and involve a lot less paperwork than a corporation, and incorporate the business later, after you know the business is going to be successful, and you can see a real reason to incorporate.

LIMITED LIABILITY COMPANY (LLC)

The limited liability company is a form of business that combines some of the most desirable features of corporations and partnerships. The limited liability company, like a corporation, is a legal entity separate from the owners, who are referred to as members. For LLCs, I use the terms *owner* and *member* interchangeably.

Joe's Janitorial, Inc.

We had a "credit manager," a "warehouse manager," the whole bit. I'd put people on hold, wait, and pick up again.

—John Egard, First Team Sports Co.

LLC Limited Liability

An LLC has the same limited liability for its members that a corporation has for its stockholders, with the same warnings about the limits of "limited" liability.

This limited liability is a major reason many partnerships are restructuring as LLCs. Not only are the members' personal assets protected, each member of an LLC is only personally liable for his or her own negligence and not the negligence of other members. In a partnership, all partners are personally and fully liable for the actions of all other partners. Still, even with the limited liability protection, when someone decides to sue, everybody associated with the LLC is likely to be a target.

LLC Taxation

The limited liability company is taxed like a partnership or sole proprietorship, what the IRS calls a pass-through entity. All of the profits "pass through" the business to the owners of the LLC, who pay individual income tax on their shares of the profits. The LLC itself pays no income taxes.

For federal income taxes, an LLC with two or more members is considered a partnership, and files a regular 1065 partnership tax return. A one-person LLC is treated as a sole proprietorship, and files a Schedule C tax return. The members of an LLC pay income tax on their shares of the profits, whether distributed to them or not, just like partners and sole proprietors.

LLC members, like partners and sole proprietors, and unlike owner-employees of corporations, are not employees of their business. Members of LLCs are subject to self-employment tax just like partners and sole proprietors. However, if a member of an LLC is only an investor, has no involvement in the operation of the business or in any decision making, the courts have ruled that the investor is exempt from self-employment tax. If your LLC includes this kind of member, I suggest you talk to an experienced accountant.

Members of LLCs come under the same health coverage rules as sole proprietors, partners, and owners of S corporations. This is covered under Health Insurance in the Tax chapter.

LLCs versus Corporations

LLCs are similar to S corporations except that owners of S corporations are employees of their business. LLCs offer more generous loss deductions than S corporations, allow more classes of ownership such as voting and non-voting, have more freedom in deciding how profits and losses are divided, and are not limited to the S corporation's maximum of one hundred shareholders, nor to the requirement that shareholders be U.S. citizens.

An LLC can expel a member. A corporation cannot expel a stockholder.

Depending on your state's laws, LLCs possibly are not bound by sometimes-troublesome corporate rules such as minimum capitalization. In most states, LLCs do not have to hold director or shareholder meetings, don't have to keep minutes, and don't issue stock certificates.

Unlike a corporation, 100 percent of LLC income is subject to Social Security and Medicare tax. An LLC cannot separate income into wages and dividends the way a corporation can, so an LLC cannot declare that part of the profit is a dividend, exempt from Social Security and Medicare tax, a tax maneuver that many small corporations attempt. For some businesses, there may be a significant difference in what an owner of a corporation pays in payroll taxes compared to a member of an LLC. This was explained above under "You, Incorporated."

An LLC can change its tax status and elect to be taxed as a regular corporation, if the members of the LLC see a tax savings to be gained. This option is not available to S corporations.

State Laws for LLCs

Limited liability companies are licensed and regulated by the states, and each state has its own LLC laws.

A few states put a limited life on LLCs, although the LLC can refile with the state and continue its existence. Many states restrict transferability of ownership of LLCs. One of the major reasons people incorporate is to get that ease of ownership transferability.

Some states make an important distinction between LLC owners who are active in the business and those who are investors only, requiring LLCs with inactive investors to register under state securities laws. If your LLC will have investors who are not active in the business, who have no say in how the business is run, you should check your state laws to see what, if any, securities rules apply to your company.

For income taxes, most states follow IRS rules and tax LLCs the same way they tax partnerships. A few states, however, tax LLCs as corporations. Before you set up an LLC, find out how your state will tax the business. LLCs are not popular in states that impose corporate taxes on LLCs.

Many states exempt LLCs from franchise taxes and organization fees that corporations must pay. But some states have special fees just for LLCs.

Setting Up an LLC

To become an LLC, you register with your state's secretary of state. An LLC must have articles of organization, similar to a corporation's articles of incorporation. Some states require LLCs to have an operating agreement, which is a cross between a partnership agreement and corporate bylaws, and is by far the most important document an LLC has. Regardless of state requirements, every LLC should have a written operating agreement.

Everything about how the LLC will be managed, who can be a member, how money is to be invested, how money is to be paid out, and just about everything else involving the LLC is contained in the operating agreement.

With the operating agreement, you get to make your own rules for your LLC. Many of the issues covered previously under partnership agreements apply equally to LLC operating agreements. If you do not have a written operating agreement, you are bound by your state's default rules, which may not be to your liking.

Members of LLCs, like owners of corporations, should make it clear to everyone you do business with that you are not acting as an individual but as a representative of a limited liability company. Include "Limited Liability Company" or "LLC" as part of the business name on all checks, stationery, contracts, business cards, and all other documents. As with a corporation, members of LLCs can lose their liability protection if they fail to follow the rules.

The sample operating agreement is the minimum an LLC should have.

An existing business can convert to an LLC at any time in the future, should you find it suitable to your needs. Converting an existing corporation to an LLC may cause tax problems, but most partnerships and sole proprietorships can convert easily.

LIMITED LIABILITY COMPANY ARTICLES OF ORGANIZATION

LLC Name:
[Your Business, LLC]

LLC Address:
You can use any street address that you can get mail at.

Purpose:
The purpose of the LLC is to engage in any lawful act or activity for which an LLC may be organized under the limited liability company laws of [your state].

Service of Process:
This is the name and address of a state resident who agrees to be your business's agent to accept service of process (legal papers) in case your LLC is sued. You may list any adult who lives in your state.

Management:
The LLC will be managed by:
[one manager] [more than one manager] [all LLC members] [some other arrangement?]
This is a decision the members make. See the comments in the sample Operating Agreement.

Signatures:
Each member sign and date.

The sample Articles of Organization meets typical minimum legal requirements for limited liability companies in many states. But you should verify this with your state secretary of state or Department of LLCs, which will have a downloadable or printable form that you can use.

OPERATING AGREEMENT

YOUR BUSINESS, LLC

1. [name of your business], a limited liability company (LLC), was formed on [month, day, year].

2. The LLC address is [address where the LLC will receive mail].

3. The members are: [List full name of each member].

4. All members have equal ownership of the LLC and will share equally in the profits and losses of the LLC.

5. All LLC business activity shall be decided by [majority] [majority plus one] [unanimous] vote of the members.

6. The LLC will be managed by [one manager] [more than one manager] [all LLC members] [some other arrangement].

This clause is a legal requirement in some states. The term "manage" is not defined, so if you choose one person to manage the business, this agreement should specify the person and the duties. If you are unsure, choose "All LLC members."

7. If any member leaves the LLC or dies, the LLC shall continue with the remaining members.

8. In the event of the dissolution of the LLC, members shall decide by [majority] [majority plus one] [unanimous] vote who will acquire the rights to the business name.

9. This LLC agreement can be modified at any time by [majority] [majority plus one] [unanimous] vote of the members.

[Signed and dated by all members]

LLCs versus Limited Partnerships

Some limited partnerships are restructuring as LLCs because LLCs offer limited liability protection to the operating partner, something not available in limited partnerships, and because LLCs usually have fewer state regulations than limited partnerships. Investors prefer LLCs over limited partnerships because they can legally take a more active role in managing an LLC. However, keep in mind that limited partnerships are closely regulated by the states. Your state may or may not allow a limited partnership to be structured as an LLC. (Don't confuse a limited partnership with a regular general partnership. They are not the same.)

Limited Liability Partnerships

Some states do not allow some professional firms, particularly CPAs and lawyers, to set up as LLCs. There is another business form, called a limited liability partnership, or LLP, created for these professionals. LLPs are similar to LLCs. If you can set up as an LLC, there is no reason to consider an LLP.

Do not confuse this limited liability partnership with a limited partnership. They have similar names, but they are not the same thing.

A FEW LAST WORDS ABOUT GROWTH . . .

Nerv Norvus, business owner: "There's a subtle tendency in our society to belittle the very small businessperson, to champion growth at the expense of other issues. In my view, there are people for whom growing bigger is a disaster, a promotion to incompetence.

"So I made a conscious decision to stay small, not because I couldn't get the business, but because it would have changed me in ways I really didn't want to change. Most importantly, if I had grown my business the way the 'experts' say, I would have lost the time to do the little things that make work so enjoyable to me, like taking my wife and children to the mountains for a long weekend."

Terry Dalton, owner, Unicorn Village Market: "A successful company is not a perpetually larger company with ever-increasing sales and ever-increasing demands on personal time. A successful business is one that gives you plenty of options. Bigger is not better."

Don Massey, owner, Gulf Coast Publications: "I have no interest in growing larger than a one-person operation. I have complete control over my business and my time. No bureaucracy. No staff reviews. No personnel problems. And I get eight hours of restful sleep every night."

Richard Melman, restaurateur, founder, Lettuce Entertain You Enterprises: "I'm comfortable taking one step at a time, getting it right, then moving on. I don't like thinking big. You'll never get hurt by taking a small step, making sure the ground is firm, then taking the next step. I got big by thinking small."

Arthur Lazere, Northgate Computers: "There is a brick wall out there waiting for everybody who grows too fast. It's invisible until you hit it."

Chapter Four

TAXES

If the adjustments required by Section 481(a) and Regulation 1.481-1 are attributable to a change in method of accounting initiated by the taxpayer, the amount of such adjustments, to the extent such amount does not exceed the net amount which would have been required if the change had been made in the first taxable year, shall be taken into account by the taxpayer in computing taxable income in the manner provided in Section 481(b)(4)(B) and paragraph (b) of this section.

—INTERNAL REVENUE CODE

As through this world I've rambled
I've seen lots of funny men
Some will rob you with a six-gun
And some with a fountain pen.

—"PRETTY BOY FLOYD" BY WOODY GUTHRIE

DEEP IN THE HEART OF TAXES

Throughout *Small Time Operator* I've made enough comments—maybe more than enough—about the intrusion of government into all our affairs. And an introduction to taxes is an ideal setting to get into it again. But rather than criticize or defend that Wonderful American Institution known as Income Taxes, I'd just like to give you some information to help you deal with it.

This chapter will discuss federal income, self-employment, and excise taxes; state income and gross receipts taxes; and a few other local taxes. However, I handle this chapter differently from the rest of the book. Rather than presenting a step-by-step "all you need to know" guide to taxes—which would require an entire library of unreadable legalese—this chapter will provide you with general information about taxes, including specifics of some of the basic and more important federal laws.

Many tax laws are too complex to explain in a few paragraphs, or require fine-print details and definitions, or have multiple options, or, well, *all of the above*. If an explanation gets too complicated, no one will read it. But some of those confusing tax laws could save you a bundle in taxes. This chapter lets you know about these laws, if they might apply to your business, and whether it will be worth your time and money to talk to a tax accountant.

Even if you take your tax problems to an accountant, I think you should familiarize yourself with the information in this chapter. There is more to taxes than just filling out the tax forms every April 15. Many of the tax laws outlined in this chapter relate directly to everyday management of your business. The federal income tax laws affect your

A tax is a compulsory payment for which no specific benefit is received in return.

—U.S. Treasury

recordkeeping and, through a knowledge of which expenditures are and are not tax-deductible, your business profit. What's more, you will be of greater help to your tax accountant, which means your tax accountant can be of greater help to you, if you at least have *some* familiarity with the federal income tax laws. In fact, the information here may help you find tax savings that your accountant may have overlooked.

The Tax Laws as They Apply to You

Many of the federal tax laws are designed solely to keep you from cheating the government out of what they think is rightfully theirs—your money. But a lot of these laws were enacted to save you money, to give you some sort of tax break. The Internal Revenue Service does make an effort to educate people about beneficial tax laws, but basically it's up to you to dig in and find out how to save yourself tax dollars. The problem is that income tax laws tend to overwhelm most people because of their complexity and because of their sheer volume: so many different possibilities, so many ifs, ands, or buts.

A lot of special effort has been put into this chapter to help you understand the tax laws without getting trapped in the octopus tentacles of exceptions. This is accomplished by a four-step procedure:

Step 1: The basic tax rules, those that apply to most small businesses, are explained as simply as possible, in plain English.

Step 2: Following the basic rules, any special situations, exceptions, or tricky catches in the law are explained. This is designed so you can skim over them rapidly and spot an area that may apply to you.

Step 3: Unusual and complex rules, most of which apply only to a minority of businesses, are mentioned in order to alert you to their existence but are not explained in detail.

Step 4: Free sources of complete tax information are listed so that you can more thoroughly study the subjects you need to know more about.

A Warning

This chapter does not provide complete information on all federal tax laws, nor was it ever intended to. It is meant to be a general guideline to help you wade through the maze of rules and regulations that our government in its wisdom has seen fit to enact into law. And remember, tax laws are in a constant state of change. Never assume that any tax law in effect last year is going to be in effect this year. It is your responsibility, and it could be to your benefit financially, to keep abreast of current tax law.

As additional help, you should get a copy of the IRS's "Tax Guide for Small Business" (Publication #334), free from any IRS office, or you can order a print copy or download a digital copy from its website, IRS.gov, along with a list of their other free, small business publications. These are all excellent, reliable, and readable references. If you use the IRS's tax guides in conjunction with *Small Time Operator*, you shouldn't go wrong. Hopefully.

The IRS has a toll-free help number just for small businesses (800-829-4933), but a warning about IRS telephone help: Although IRS publications are usually accurate and reliable, the same cannot always be said of tax information the IRS gives out over the phone or in person. The IRS people do, on occasion, give out totally incorrect information. Tax laws are vastly complicated, and even the experts make mistakes. Do not rely on verbal information unless you can verify it. Ask the IRS person for a reference in one of their publications, and look it up.

Keep in mind that these are federal laws, applicable to federal tax returns. For state returns, most state income tax laws are similar or identical to these federal laws; but some states have different laws, different ways to write off business assets, different deductions allowed or not allowed. Study the instructions that come with your state tax forms. You might find additional state deductions that the IRS does not allow, and save some money on your state taxes. State taxes are covered at the end of this section.

A WARNING ABOUT THE INTERNET
If you, like everybody else, are searching the internet for an answer, I want to warn you about tax

information on the internet. Many websites have incorrect or out-of-date tax information. If you see the information multiple times on multiple sites, do not assume it is correct. Websites often lift information from other sites, sometimes word for word, without bothering to verify its accuracy. Even if you are reading information provided by tax professionals, check to see when the information was written. It might be several years old. If you can't find a date, don't trust it.

The most accurate, reliable tax information on the internet is on the IRS website, IRS.gov, although it can be a challenge to navigate the site. It's easiest to enter what you're looking for in a search engine and then look for links to IRS.gov. I wouldn't rely on any other site.

Filing tax and registration forms online: Be sure you go to IRS.gov. The ".gov" means it is a real government website. If the website ends in .com or anything else other than .gov, it is not the IRS. It is a private business. These online companies file IRS forms for you and charge fees that you don't have to pay at the real IRS website. Most of the forms are easy to fill out. You don't need to pay some online middleman to do them.

Accounting Period: Calendar Year versus Fiscal Year

Every business must keep books and file tax returns based on what the IRS calls a "taxable year," which is either a "calendar year" or a "fiscal year." A calendar year begins on January 1 and ends on December 31. A fiscal year is a twelve-month period ending on the last day of any month other than December.

Most small businesses use a calendar year simply because it's easier. All of the federal and state tax procedures are geared to the calendar year: issuance of W-2s, 1099s, and dividend and interest statements, and publication of the new tax forms and instructions. Most changes in tax law occur on January 1.

The calendar year is also preferred by the Internal Revenue Service. They have strict and rather complex rules about who can adopt a fiscal year and when the decision must be made. The rules vary depending on how your business is legally structured.

Generally, sole proprietorships must use the same taxable year as the owner, which means the calendar year in most cases. The same rule applies to partnerships, S corporations, limited liability companies, and personal service corporations (corporations that primarily sell services performed by the owner-employees). The IRS will allow these businesses to adopt a fiscal year if there is a valid business reason for using a fiscal year. File Form 8716, "Election to Have a Tax Year Other than a Required Tax Year." Regular corporations can choose either a calendar or a fiscal year.

Why choose a fiscal year at all? Some businesses have definite yearly cycles and find that coordinating their taxable year with the business cycle better reflects actual income and expenses. Large retail stores have traditionally chosen a January 31 fiscal year so they can have their January clearance sales, to reduce their stock of merchandise on hand, thereby making the year-end inventory count much easier and less expensive. Corporations sometimes choose a fiscal year coinciding with the month the business first began operation, to avoid a short-period tax return and extra taxes the first year.

The tax laws discussed in this tax section apply to both calendar year and fiscal year taxpayers, except where otherwise noted.

Who Must File a Tax Return

Sole proprietors and joint ventures must file a federal income tax return if the net earnings from self-employment (the business net profit) is $400 or more. Partnerships, corporations, and LLCs must file a return no matter what the profit or loss is.

Income tax returns can be filed by mail or on the internet at IRS.gov.

Which Tax Return to File

Sole Proprietors: Most sole proprietors will have to fill out a Schedule C, "Profit or Loss from Business." Schedule C is part of your regular 1040 return. The profit or loss on Schedule C is combined with any other taxable income or loss on your 1040. If you have more than one business, file a separate Schedule C for each business. Sole proprietors also file Schedule SE, "Self-Employment Tax," with their 1040 return.

Some very small service businesses may only need to fill out the much simpler Schedule C-EZ, "Net Profit from Business," which truly is "EZ": one total figure for income (gross receipts), one total figure for expenses, and your net profit. That, and a few questions about your vehicle, is it.

Latest Revision For:

1040 Individual Income Tax Return

Department of the Treasury—Internal Revenue Service

Income — Please attach Copy B of your Forms W-2 here.

Your social security number

1. How much money did you make last year? .... ▶

2. Send it in . . . . ▶

Schedule C-EZ can only be used by sole proprietors who meet all nine of the following requirements:

1. Business expenses of $5,000 or less.

2. No inventory at any time during the year.

3. Did not have a net loss.

4. Had no employees.

5. Deducted no depreciation, amortization, or first-year write-off of depreciable assets.

6. Deducted no expenses for a home office.

7. Used the cash method of accounting.

8. Cannot own more than one sole proprietorship.

9. No prior-year passive-activity losses. (If you don't know what that means, you probably didn't have any.)

Joint Ventures: A joint venture is a business owned and operated by a legally married couple who do not officially set up a partnership, LLC, or corporation. The spouses in a joint venture file two Schedule C (or Schedule C-EZ) returns and two Schedule SE returns for self-employment tax, as described above under "Sole Proprietors." The spouses divide the income and expenses between them according to their respective participation in the business. See "Married Couples" in the T.C.B.: Take Care of Business chapter.

Partnerships: File Form 1065, "U.S. Partnership Return of Income." No taxes are due with this return. Each partner gets a copy of Schedule K-1 (1065), "Partner's Share of Income, Credits, Deductions, Etc." Partners report their individual share of the business income, whether distributed to them or not, on their 1040 return, using Schedule E, "Supplemental Income and Loss."

Limited Liability Companies (LLCs): LLCs with two or more members (two or more owners) are taxed as partnerships by the IRS and file partnership tax returns as described above under "Partnerships." One-person LLCs can elect to be taxed as sole proprietors, and file a Schedule C (or Schedule C-EZ) and Schedule SE for self-employment tax, as described above under "Sole Proprietors."

Corporations: Regular C corporations report income and pay taxes on Form 1120. S corporations file Form 1120-S, but like partnerships, pay no income taxes. Each S corporation shareholder gets a copy of Schedule K-1 (1120-S), "Shareholder's Share of Income, Credits, Deductions, Etc." Shareholders report their individual share of the S corporation income on their 1040 return, using Schedule E, "Supplemental Income and Loss."

Payments. Write on your check your name, tax ID number, and what the payment is for: tax form number and year. If you don't do this, the IRS can apply your payment to a different tax bill you may owe.

1099 Income

The IRS form 1099-MISC is discussed in several places in *Small Time Operator*. Any business or organization that pays an individual, a sole proprietor, or an LLC $600 or more a year is required to report that income to the IRS on Form 1099-MISC and send a copy to the individual or business that received the income (the payee). If the payee who received the 1099-MISC form is a business or running a business or is self-employed, the payment reported on Form 1099-MISC is part of the payee's business income for the year. Assuming that the payee is keeping income records, the money reported on the 1099-MISC is already recorded in the payee's income records. The money was received during the year and recorded when received.

Judging from questions I get, the 1099 form has confused a lot of people. They want to know how to report "1099 income." There is no such thing as 1099 income. The 1099-MISC is just a form some payors prepare and some payors don't prepare. The person or business that received the payment is not required to have a 1099 form, and the 1099 form is not attached to the payee's 1040 tax return. It does

not matter to the payee whether he or she receives a 1099 form or not.

This 1099 issue is especially confusing to workers in the on-demand economy, who have never run a business and suddenly find out they're being paid as independent contractors, and do not know what that means. The on-demand company just sent them a 1099-MISC for income they received, and now what? They need to understand that they're now in business, just like any other self-employed person. See the On-Demand Economy chapter for more information about on-demand businesses.

There is a different situation for people who earned money doing a brief, one-time-only job, not recurring, not seeking more work. In this situation, the IRS says that you are not self-employed, not in business. You report the income, whether you get a 1099-MISC form or not, on your 1040 tax return as "Other Income." You do not prepare a Schedule C business tax form, and you do not pay self-employment tax.

More Than One Business

If you have more than one business, you fill out a separate tax return for each business.

If your businesses are all sole proprietorships, you might consider combining them so they are one business, and file one Schedule C tax return. Your income and self-employment taxes will be exactly the same whether you have one or multiple sole proprietorships.

If any of your businesses are partnerships, corporations, or LLCs, each business must have its own tax return. Before you set up multiple businesses, however, consider the possibility of creating just one partnership or corporation or LLC instead of several.

There are advantages and disadvantages to setting up multiple businesses, covered in the T.C.B.: Take Care of Business chapter.

Filing Dates for Tax Returns

For calendar-year businesses, sole proprietorship and joint venture tax returns (which are part of the owners' 1040 tax returns) are due April 15. Partnership, LLC, and S corporation tax returns are due March 15. C corporation tax returns are due April 15.

Automatic extensions to file returns, but not to pay the taxes: Sole proprietors, spouses in joint ventures, partners in partnerships (not the partnership), members of LLCs (not the LLC), and owners of S corporations (not the corporation) can obtain a six-month extension, to October 15, by filing IRS Form 4868 and paying the estimated tax on or before April 15.

Partnerships, multi-owner LLCs, and S corporations (the businesses, not the owners of the businesses) can obtain a six-month extension, to September 15, by filing Form 7004 by March 15. Partnerships, LLCs, and S corporations pay no income taxes, so no taxes are due with the extension. One-person LLCs that file Schedule C tax returns (covered above) only have to file Form 4868 for the owner of the LLC, not for the LLC itself.

C corporations (not S corporations) can obtain a six-month extension, to October 15, by filing Form 7004 and paying the estimated tax by the April 15 due date.

All extensions must be filed by the original due date of the return and include payment for all taxes due. If you underpay your taxes by more than 10 percent, the IRS can hit you with a penalty.

Fiscal-year taxpayers: For sole proprietors and C corporations, the federal income tax return is due on the fifteenth day of the fourth month following the end of the fiscal year. Partnership, LLC, and S corporation returns are due on the fifteenth day of the third month. The same extensions described above are available to fiscal-year businesses.

(They could have made all that a lot simpler, the same rules for all businesses, but of course they didn't.)

State tax returns: Many states have the same due dates as the federal tax returns, but some are different. Check your state income tax website or tax instruction book.

TAX CALENDAR FOR BUSINESS

The tax calendar lists due dates for federal and state tax reports. Each date shown is the last day on which to perform the required action without penalty. If the due date for filing a return or making a tax payment falls on a Saturday, Sunday, or legal holiday, the date is moved to the next regular workday.

Tax deposits and other reports that are due weekly and monthly throughout the year are listed at the end of the calendar.

To help you spot the dates applicable to your business, the first word in each description will tell who the information applies to, such as employers, corporations, etc. "Individuals" refers to sole proprietors, partners in joint ventures and general partnerships (not the partnerships), corporate stockholders (not the corporations), and LLC members (not the LLCs).

These dates apply to calendar-year taxpayers. Businesses using a fiscal year must change some of the dates (see the end of the calendar).

These dates don't usually change from year to year, but they can. Verify them before relying on them.

January 1–March 16

Corporations that meet certain requirements may elect to be treated as S corporations during current and future years. Use Form 2553.

January 15

Individuals either pay the balance due on the prior year's estimated income tax (Form 1040-ES), or file an income tax return (Form 1040) on or before January 31 and pay the full amount of the tax due.

Farmers and fishermen may elect to file declaration of estimated income tax (Form 1040-ES) for the prior year and pay estimated tax in full, and file an income tax return (Form 1040) by April 15. If declaration of estimated tax is not filed, see February 28.

January 31

Individuals file an income tax return (Form 1040) for the prior year and pay the tax due, if the balance on their prior year's estimated tax was not paid by January 15. Farmers and fishermen, see February 28.

Employers give every employee Form W-2 showing income totals and tax deductions for the year, and file Form W-3, "Transmittal of Income and Tax Statements," with the Social Security Administration, along with Copy A of each W-2.

Employers deposit federal unemployment tax (FUTA) if the tax is more than $500. Use Form 8109. If the amount is $500 or less, add it to the taxes for the next quarter, due April 30.

Employers whose total annual withholding of employees' Social Security, Medicare, and withheld federal income taxes is $1,000 or less, file Form 944.

Employers who are not eligible to file Form 944 (see above) file Form 941 for income tax and Social Security and Medicare taxes withheld from employees for the fourth quarter of the prior year and pay any taxes due. If timely deposits were made, employers have until February 10 to file Form 941.

Employers subject to federal unemployment tax file an annual return for the prior year. Use Form 940. If timely deposits were made, employers have until February 10 to file Form 940.

Businesses liable for excise taxes file quarterly excise tax return. Use Form 720.

Businesses: Most state sales tax returns for the fourth quarter of the prior year are due.

Businesses issue Forms 1099-MISC, 1099-INT, and 1099-DIV to recipients. See "Information Returns" in this chapter for a list of Form 1099 requirements.

Businesses issuing 1099-MISC forms for independent contractors (nonemployee compensation) file summary Form 1096 with the IRS.

February 10

Employers who made timely deposits in full payment of all income taxes withheld and Social Security and Medicare taxes due for the fourth quarter of the prior year file fourth-quarter return. Use Form 941.

Employers subject to federal unemployment tax who made timely deposits in full payment of the tax file annual return for the prior year. Use Form 940.

February 15

Businesses issue Forms 1099-B and 1099-S to recipients. See "Information Returns" in this chapter for a list of Form 1099 requirements.

February 28

Restaurants with ten or more employees report tips on Form 8027 if paper filing. For internet filing, the due date is March 31.

Farmers and fishermen who did not file declaration of estimated tax on January 15 should file final income tax return (Form 1040) for prior year.

Businesses that issued 1099-MISC forms other than reporting independent contractors (nonemployee compensation) file summary Form 1096 with the IRS.

March 15

Partnerships and LLCs file Form 1065 tax return for the prior calendar year. For a six-month extension, file Form 7004. One-owner LLCs can file Form 1040 instead of Form 1065.

Partnerships and LLCs give each partner/member a Schedule K-1.

S Corporations file federal income tax Form 1120S. For a six-month extension, file Form 7004.

Corporations file state income tax returns for Alabama, Alaska, Arkansas, California, DC, Illinois, Maine, Massachusetts, Maryland, Minnesota, Mississippi, Nebraska, New Hampshire, New Mexico, New York, North Carolina, Oklahoma, Rhode Island, South Carolina, Vermont, West Virginia, and Wisconsin.

March 31

Restaurants with ten or more employees report tips on Form 8027 (for internet filing).

Corporations file state income tax returns for the following states: Connecticut, Delaware, Florida, Ohio, and Tennessee.

April 15

Individuals file a federal income tax return for the prior year. The tax due must be paid in full with this return. File Schedule C or C-EZ (Schedule F for farmers), and Schedule SE. If you desire an automatic six-month extension, file Form 4868 accompanied by payment of your estimated unpaid income tax liability.

Individuals file first installment of estimated income and self-employment tax for the current year and pay 25 percent of the tax. Use Form 1040-ES.

Individuals file a state income tax return for all states collecting income tax except Delaware, Hawaii, Virginia, Louisiana, and Iowa.

C Corporations file federal income tax return Form 1120 and pay the balance of tax still due. For a six-month extension, file Form 7004.

Corporations deposit first installment of current year's estimated income tax.

Corporations file state income tax returns for the following states: Arizona, Colorado, Georgia, Idaho, Indiana, Kansas, Kentucky, Missouri, New Jersey, North Dakota, Oregon, Pennsylvania, Utah, Virginia, and Louisiana.

April 20

Individuals in Hawaii file state income tax return.

Corporations in Hawaii file state income tax returns.

April 30

Individuals living in Delaware, Virginia, and Iowa file a state income tax return.

Corporations in Michigan and Iowa file state income tax returns.

Businesses: Most state sales tax returns for the first quarter are due.

Employers who are not eligible to file Form 944 (see January 31) file Form 941 for income tax withheld, Social Security, and Medicare taxes for the first quarter, and pay taxes due. If timely deposits were made, see May 10.

Employers deposit federal unemployment tax (FUTA) if the tax is more than $500. Use Form 8109. If the amount is $500 or less, add it to the taxes for the next quarter, due July 31.

Businesses liable for excise taxes file quarterly excise tax return. Use Form 720.

May 10

Employers who made timely deposits in full payment of income tax, Social Security, and Medicare taxes for the first quarter file first-quarter return. Use Form 941.

May 15

Individuals in Louisiana file state income tax returns.

Corporations in Montana file state income tax returns.

June 15

Individuals file second installment of estimated income and self-employment tax for the current year and pay 25 percent of the tax. Use Form 1040-ES.

Corporations deposit second installment of estimated income tax.

July 31

Businesses: Most state sales tax returns for the second quarter are due.

Businesses liable for excise taxes file quarterly excise tax return. Use Form 720.

Employers deposit federal unemployment tax (FUTA) if the tax is more than $500. Use Form 8109. If the amount is $500 or less, add it to the taxes for the next quarter, due October 31.

Employers who are not eligible to file Form 944 (see January 31) file Form 941 for income tax withheld and Social Security and Medicare taxes for the second quarter, and pay any taxes due. If timely deposits were made, date is extended to August 10.

Employers with an employee benefit, pension, profit-sharing, or stock bonus plan file Form 5500 for the previous calendar year.

August 10

Employers who made timely deposits in full payment of all income tax withheld and Social Security and Medicare taxes due for the second quarter file second-quarter return. Use Form 941.

August 31

Heavy-duty truck owners and operators pay the federal use tax on highway motor vehicles used on the public highways. Use Form 2290.

September 15

Individuals file third installment of estimated income and self-employment tax for the current year and pay 25 percent of the tax. Use Form 1040-ES.

Corporations deposit third installment of estimated income tax.

Partnerships and LLCs that received an automatic five-month extension for filing prior year's federal income tax return file Form 1065.

S corporations, partnerships, and LLCs that filed a six-month extension (on March 15) file tax return.

October 15

Individuals who received an automatic six-month extension for filing prior year's federal income tax return must file Form 1040.

C corporations that filed a six-month extension (on April 15) file tax return.

October 31

Businesses: Most state sales tax returns for the third quarter are due.

Businesses liable for excise taxes file quarterly excise tax return. Use Form 720.

Employers who are not eligible to file Form 944 (see January 31) file Form 941 for income tax withheld and Social Security and Medicare taxes for the third quarter, and pay any taxes due. If timely deposits were made, date is extended to November 10.

Employers deposit federal unemployment tax (FUTA) if the tax is more than $500. Use Form 8109. If the amount is $500 or less, add it to the taxes for the next quarter, due January 31 of the next year.

November

Employers should request a new Form W-4 from each employee whose withholding exemptions will be different next year.

November 10

Employers who made timely deposits in full payment of income tax withheld and Social Security and Medicare taxes due for the third quarter file third-quarter return Form 941.

December 15

Corporations deposit the fourth installment of estimated income tax.

Weekly and Monthly All Year

Corporations that meet certain requirements may elect, anytime during the year, to be treated as S corporations in future years. Use Form 2553. To be treated as an S corporation this year, see January 1.

Employers: Tax deposits of Social Security and Medicare (*not* self-employment) and withheld income taxes are required monthly (by the 15th of the following month) whenever amount due is $500 or more; required eight times a month whenever amounts due are $3,000 or more.

Businesses liable for excise taxes are required to make monthly deposits on the last day of the month when more than $100 in excise taxes is collected.

Fiscal-Year Taxpayers

Individuals: Federal tax return 1040 is due the 15th day of the fourth month after the end of your tax year.

Partnerships and LLCs: Federal tax return 1065 is due the 15th day of the fourth month after the end of your tax year.

Corporations: Federal income tax return 1120 or 1120-S is due the 15th day of the third month after the end of your tax year.

Corporations: Federal estimated tax payments are due on the 15th day of the fourth, sixth, ninth, and twelfth months of your tax year.

Corporations electing to be S Corporations file Form 2553 by the 15th day of the third month of the tax year.

Employers maintaining an employee benefit, pension, profit-sharing, or stock bonus plan, file Form 5500 by the last day of the seventh month after your tax year.

All fiscal-year businesses: Many states follow the same schedule as the federal government for filing state income tax returns, but some states have different dates. Consult your own state.

20 PERCENT BUSINESS INCOME DEDUCTION

The list of business expenses that follow below will reduce your business profit. There is also an important tax deduction that is not an expense at all, you spend no money to get it, but it will reduce your taxable income.

The deduction is for up to 20 percent of your business or self-employment net income (profit). After you figure your business profit (business income less deductible business expenses), you then take this deduction to further reduce your taxable income.

This deduction applies to all self-employed individuals and all types of businesses except C corporations: sole proprietorships, partnerships, joint ventures, and S corporations. C corporations are not eligible for the deduction. If you have more than one business, each business, as long as it is not a C corporation, is eligible for the deduction.

You can take the full 20 percent deduction if your total taxable income for the year, all types of income combined, is no more than $157,500 for single individuals or $315,000 for couples filing a joint tax return (before taking the 20 percent deduction). If your income is under these maximum amounts, the deduction is a simple, straightforward calculation, and a significant tax savings—as long as you remember to take it!

If your income exceeds these thresholds, the deduction is no longer simple or straightforward. You cannot take the full 20 percent deduction. Calculating the amount you can deduct depends on how much you pay in employee wages, the value of your business assets, and even what kind of business you operate. The formulas are complex and lengthy, and will require help from an experienced accountant.

Unlike other business deductions, the business income deduction is entered on a line on your personal 1040 return. The deduction does not go on Schedule C or Schedule C-EZ (for sole proprietors), or on the partnership, S corporation, or LLC tax return. The deduction does not reduce your business profit, and therefore does not reduce your self-employment tax (which is covered later in this chapter), but it does reduce your taxable income on your 1040 return.

BUSINESS EXPENSES

All legitimate business expenses, except those specifically disallowed by law (covered later in this chapter), are deductible in computing your taxable income, as long as they meet the IRS's three basic rules:

Rule One: The expenses must be "ordinary." Ordinary expenses are ones that are common or accepted in your type of business. They do not have to be recurring or habitual.

Rule Two: The expenses must be "necessary." A necessary expense, according to the IRS, is one that is "appropriate and helpful in developing and maintaining your trade or business." The word *necessary* in this context of IRS tax law does not have the same definition we usually associate with necessary, as in required, indispensable, must be done. It is not necessary that you buy a nice desk chair. It is not necessary that you air-condition your office. These are not mandatory requirements of your business, but they pass the "necessary" test.

Rule Three: The expenses, to quote the IRS, "must not be lavish or extravagant under the circumstances." Defining what is or is not "lavish or extravagant under the circumstances" depends on, well, the circumstances. The bigger the business and the more income the business earns, the more likely you can deduct large amounts of money and call the expenses "not lavish or extravagant under the circumstances." Full-time, ongoing businesses can usually get away with a bit more lavishness than part-time and new businesses.

Expenditures that are partly personal (non-business) and partly business can be prorated and the business portion expensed or depreciated. Your home and your vehicle often fall into this category.

For sole proprietors, business expenses are deductible no matter how you pay them. You can pay cash out of your pocket, pay with your personal credit or debit card, or pay from a personal bank account or through the internet. If it's a business expense, it's deductible.

Any asset that you originally purchased for non-business purposes or before going into business that you are now using for business, or using partly for business, can be depreciated as of the date you began using the asset in your business. (See "Depreciation" below.)

Payments to foreign firms and individuals come under the same income tax laws as domestic payments.

Try to get receipts for everything, and keep them. Receipts are your best documentation should questions come up or if you are audited.

Partners in partnerships, owners of corporations, and members of LLCs: Try not to pay business expenses out of your personal funds. Business deductions are sometimes disallowed when claimed by owners or employees, instead of by the companies themselves. If you do pay any business expenses out of your own pocket, have the business reimburse you, so the business itself can claim the deductions. The IRS requires that reimbursements be part of an "accountable reimbursement plan," which is a written policy that the expenses are business related and substantiated (you have receipts).

Multiple businesses: If you have more than one business, shared expenses such as the same office, telephone, computer, etc., should be split between the businesses. A 50-50 split (if you have two businesses) is common, but you can use any reasonable percentage that reflects how much each business uses.

Start-Up Expenses

Business expenses incurred before you start operating your business—what the IRS calls "start-up costs"—come under a different tax rule than expenses incurred once you are officially open for business. The IRS says that start-up costs are those that are incurred before "opening day," before the "active trade or business begins."

Start-up costs include expenses to research and investigate the business, including travel, advertising before actually opening your doors, salaries, consultant fees, professional services, and most any other business expenses that would be deductible if you were already in business.

Up to $5,000 in start-up costs can be deducted the first year of business. You can include costs incurred in prior years, but you take the deduction the year you start your business. Start-up costs in excess of the $5,000 are amortized (depreciated) over fifteen years.

The $5,000 deduction is optional. You can deduct less than the maximum this year, and spread the balance over fifteen years. If your new business hasn't earned much money and will owe little or no taxes for the current year, by spreading out the start-up costs over fifteen years, you will save on future years' taxes.

One more rule: The $5,000 start-up deduction phases out, dollar for dollar, if start-up costs exceed $50,000.

Start-up costs are often a problem for businesses. The IRS has often wrangled with taxpayers over which expenses are and are not start-up costs, and at what point a new venture is actually "in business." I suggest you put off as many expenses as possible until after the business is operating—that is, bringing in paying customers.

One way around the start-up cost limitations is to start your business at home if that's feasible, just as small an operation as possible. Once you have generated a little income, then spend your money on finding a new location, on furniture and equipment, and on accounting and legal advice. Since you are now officially in business, the expenses are deductible as regular business expenses, no longer subject to the start-up rules.

If you do incur start-up expenses but never actually start a business, the expenses may, in some situations, be deductible as a capital loss. You will probably need an accountant's help with this.

Corporations: In addition to being able to deduct the start-up costs described above, corporations can deduct an additional $5,000 in what the IRS calls "organizational costs." Organizational costs are expenses and fees incurred to set up the corporation, though not the cost of selling stock. The options and limitations on start-up expenses also apply to organizational costs. Corporations can deduct both.

If you are already in business: If you are expanding a business, adding a new division, or adding a second location, it is not considered a start-up. The expenses are deductible. If you are starting a second business, if possible try to structure it as an expansion of your current business to avoid these start-up rules.

Prepaid Expenses

Generally, prepaid expenses that do not extend beyond twelve months can be deducted when paid, even though the expenses may be for part of the next year. If, for example, you pay an insurance bill in December that is good until the following December, you can deduct the entire bill when you pay it, even though only one month of it applies to the current year. If you pay next January's rent bill in December, the payment is deductible when you pay it, even though it applies entirely to the next year. One exception to the twelve-month rule is prepaid interest expense, which cannot be deducted in advance.

I need to warn you that there are different interpretations of the twelve-month rule. Some tax experts say that some prepaid expenses do not qualify for the twelve-month rule and cannot be deducted until the year the payments apply to. The IRS has made this argument during audits, denying deductions for prepayments, but the tax courts have often ruled against the IRS, allowing the deductions. So, what do you do? I usually advise my tax clients to take the deduction. But if they are audited, the IRS might ask about prepayments and might deny the deductions, or might not: IRS auditors are usually looking for big or blatant errors on tax returns, not deductions that may have been taken the wrong year. Still, this may be something you want to discuss with an experienced accountant, especially if there is significant money at stake.

Prepaid expenses that cover more than twelve months cannot be deducted until the year the expenses apply to. Only the current year's portion can be written off this year.

One Hundred Typical Business Expenses

Below is a list of over one hundred typical business expenses that can be deducted on your income tax return. If you would like a much more extensive list of deductions, my book *475 Tax Deductions for Businesses and Self-Employed Individuals* lists and explains many more than I can fit into this book. Any business expense that meets the IRS's three basic rules (ordinary, necessary, and "not lavish or extravagant"), if not specifically disallowed, should be taken whether it is on this list or not. Expenses specifically disallowed are listed later in this section.

This list is also a guide to filling out your income tax return. The Schedule C tax form, "Profit or Loss from Business," lists only twenty or so categories of expense. These are broad, general categories. There are many legitimate, deductible expenses not listed on the tax form. To help you figure out your tax form, I've grouped the one hundred expenses by tax-return category.

But don't feel this is cemented in stone. It is not critical which expenses go on which lines on the tax form. The IRS is not going to be upset if an expense that belongs on one line winds up on another. Even I'm not sure whether some expenses should be called "office expenses" or "supplies." If you have an expense you don't know where to put on the tax return, just pick a reasonable category and put it there.

There is a line on the tax return called "Other Expenses" used for deductions that don't fit into any other category. Many deductions get labeled "Other Expenses" because there really is no appropriate category on the tax return. Deductions you do include as part of "Other Expenses" should be listed individually. The tax return provides a separate area for listing the deductions that comprise "Other Expenses." List each expense separately, then show the total on the "Other Expenses" line on the return.

It is a good idea to make a worksheet showing which expenses you combined for the tax return, and keep it with your copy of your return; there's no need to send it to the IRS. This will make things a lot easier should you ever face an audit, or if you need to check your figures later, or if you are just looking back a year later, trying to figure out how to fill out the next year's tax return.

The bold categories below are the expense categories listed on a recent Schedule C. The IRS redesigns Schedule C almost every year, so the categories could change, but the expenses are still deductible whether listed on Schedule C or not. The items listed under the bold headings are some of the expenses you can include in each category. Remember, this list is not complete. Any business expense, unless specified by the IRS as nondeductible, can be deducted on your tax return, under any Schedule C category that seems to fit the expense. The most common and most important of these expenses are explained on the following pages.

Inventory

Inventory

Freight and shipping for inventory

Supplies used in manufacturing

Advertising

Business gifts

Mailing lists

Promotion expenses

Car and Truck Expenses

Includes all types of vehicles that you own. If you rent or lease a vehicle, the expense goes under "Rent or lease," not here.

Commissions and Fees

Consultants

Sales commissions

Contract Labor

Freelancers

Independent and outside contractors

Subcontractors

Depletion

This is for mining and logging businesses.

Depreciation

This category also includes business assets that are written off under 100% Bonus Depreciation and Section 179 First-Year Write-Off. Business assets deducted under the De Minimis Safe Harbor deduction are listed under Other Expenses, not here. This is explained under "Business Assets."

SCHEDULE C (Form 1040)
Department of the Treasury
Internal Revenue Service (99)

Profit or Loss From Business
(Sole Proprietorship)

► Information about Schedule C and its separate instructions is at www.irs.gov/schedulec.
► Attach to Form 1040, 1040NR, or 1041; partnerships generally must file Form 1065.

OMB No. 1545-0074

Attachment Sequence No. 09

Name of proprietor: Samuel Thesham

Social security number (SSN): 123456789

A Principal business or profession, including product or service (see instructions): pinball machine sales and repair

B Enter code from instructions ► 4 5 3 9 9 0

C Business name. If no separate business name, leave blank. Bell Springs Pinball

D Employer ID number (EIN), (see instr.) 9 8 7 6 5 4 3 2 1

E Business address (including suite or room no.) ► P.O. Box 1240
City, town or post office, state, and ZIP code   Willits, CA 95490

F Accounting method: (1) ☑ Cash (2) ☐ Accrual (3) ☐ Other (specify) ►

G Did you "materially participate" in the operation of this business during 2015? If "No," see instructions for limit on losses ☑ Yes ☐ No

H If you started or acquired this business during 2015, check here ► ☐

I Did you make any payments in 2015 that would require you to file Form(s) 1099? (see instructions) ☐ Yes ☑ No

J If "Yes," did you or will you file required Forms 1099? ☐ Yes ☐ No

Part I Income

1	Gross receipts or sales. See instructions for line 1 and check the box if this income was reported to you on Form W-2 and the "Statutory employee" box on that form was checked ► ☐	1	32,364
2	Returns and allowances	2	0
3	Subtract line 2 from line 1	3	32,364
4	Cost of goods sold (from line 42)	4	2,008
5	Gross profit. Subtract line 4 from line 3	5	30,356
6	Other income, including federal and state gasoline or fuel tax credit or refund (see instructions)	6	
7	Gross income. Add lines 5 and 6 ►	7	30356

Part II Expenses. Enter expenses for business use of your home only on line 30.

8	Advertising	8	150
9	Car and truck expenses (see instructions)	9	480
10	Commissions and fees	10	
11	Contract labor (see instructions)	11	
12	Depletion	12	
13	Depreciation and section 179 expense deduction (not included in Part III) (see instructions)	13	136
14	Employee benefit programs (other than on line 19)	14	
15	Insurance (other than health)	15	650
16	Interest:		
a	Mortgage (paid to banks, etc.)	16a	
b	Other	16b	637
17	Legal and professional services	17	

18	Office expense (see instructions)	18	78
19	Pension and profit-sharing plans	19	
20	Rent or lease (see instructions):		
a	Vehicles, machinery, and equipment	20a	
b	Other business property	20b	4,850
21	Repairs and maintenance	21	218
22	Supplies (not included in Part III)	22	1,218
23	Taxes and licenses	23	1,267
24	Travel, meals, and entertainment:		
a	Travel	24a	
b	Deductible meals and entertainment (see instructions)	24b	
25	Utilities	25	221
26	Wages (less employment credits)	26	
27a	Other expenses (from line 48)	27a	70
b	Reserved for future use	27b	

28	Total expenses before expenses for business use of home. Add lines 8 through 27a ►	28	9,757
29	Tentative profit or (loss). Subtract line 28 from line 7	29	20,599
30	Expenses for business use of your home. Do not report these expenses elsewhere. Attach Form 8829 unless using the simplified method (see instructions). **Simplified method filers only:** enter the total square footage of: (a) your home: _____ and (b) the part of your home used for business: _____ . Use the Simplified Method Worksheet in the instructions to figure the amount to enter on line 30	30	
31	Net profit or (loss). Subtract line 30 from line 29. • If a profit, enter on both Form 1040, line 12 (or Form 1040NR, line 13) and on Schedule SE, line 2. (If you checked the box on line 1, see instructions). Estates and trusts, enter on Form 1041, line 3. • If a loss, you must go to line 32.	31	20,599
32	If you have a loss, check the box that describes your investment in this activity (see instructions). • If you checked 32a, enter the loss on both Form 1040, line 12, (or Form 1040NR, line 13) and on Schedule SE, line 2. (If you checked the box on line 1, see the line 31 instructions). Estates and trusts, enter on Form 1041, line 3. • If you checked 32b, you must attach Form 6198. Your loss may be limited.	32a ☐ All investment is at risk. 32b ☐ Some investment is not at risk.	

For Paperwork Reduction Act Notice, see the separate instructions.   Cat. No. 11334P   Schedule C (Form 1040)

Schedule C (Form 1040)   Page 2

Part III Cost of Goods Sold (see instructions)

33	Method(s) used to value closing inventory: a ☑ Cost b ☐ Lower of cost or market c ☐ Other (attach explanation)		
34	Was there any change in determining quantities, costs, or valuations between opening and closing inventory? If "Yes," attach explanation ☐ Yes ☑ No		
35	Inventory at beginning of year. If different from last year's closing inventory, attach explanation	35	100
36	Purchases less cost of items withdrawn for personal use	36	1,958
37	Cost of labor. Do not include any amounts paid to yourself	37	
38	Materials and supplies	38	
39	Other costs	39	
40	Add lines 35 through 39	40	2,058
41	Inventory at end of year	41	50
42	Cost of goods sold. Subtract line 41 from line 40. Enter the result here and on line 4	42	2,008

Part IV Information on Your Vehicle. Complete this part only if you are claiming car or truck expenses on line 9 and are not required to file Form 4562 for this business. See the instructions for line 13 to find out if you must file Form 4562.

43	When did you place your vehicle in service for business purposes? (month, day, year) ► 1 / 1 /				
44	Of the total number of miles you drove your vehicle during 2015, enter the number of miles you used your vehicle for:				
a	Business 880	b Commuting (see instructions) 150	c Other 10,450		
45	Was your vehicle available for personal use during off-duty hours?			☑ Yes	☐ No
46	Do you (or your spouse) have another vehicle available for personal use?			☑ Yes	☐ No
47a	Do you have evidence to support your deduction?			☑ Yes	☐ No
b	If "Yes," is the evidence written?			☑ Yes	☐ No

Part V Other Expenses. List below business expenses not included on lines 8–26 or line 30.

Pinball repair manuals	70
48 Total other expenses. Enter here and on line 27a	48	70

Schedule C (Form 1040)

Amortization of intangibles

Buildings (other than your home)

Business assets

Equipment, machinery, tools

Office furniture

Sales tax (added to cost of business assets)

Shipping (added to cost of business assets)

Software (purchased)

Employee Benefit Programs

This is for employee benefits other than pension plans. This is not for self-employed individuals, partners in partnerships, or members of LLCs.

Adoption assistance

Child care

Dependent care assistance

Group life insurance

Health insurance

Insurance

Includes all deductible business insurance except:

Health insurance for yourself or partners; see "Health Insurance"

Health insurance for employees; deducted under "Employee Benefit Programs"

Insurance on a home business; see "Home-Based Business"

Vehicle insurance; use "Car and Truck Expenses," but if you are taking the standard mileage allowance, you cannot deduct vehicle insurance; see "Vehicles")

Interest

Do not include mortgage interest on your home. See "Home-Based Business."

Credit card fees

Finance charges

Late fees

Loan interest

Legal and Professional Services

The IRS says that this category is for accountants and lawyers, though many businesses include other professional services here, such as:

Answering service

Bookkeeping service

Burglar alarm service

Business consultants

Cleaning and janitorial services

Computer assistance

Security service

Technical assistance

Office Expense

Include all office supplies and other office-related expenses that don't have their own category.

Do not include the cost of the office itself, which is deducted under "Depreciation" if you own the building, "Rent or Lease" if renting, and "Business Use of Your Home" if a home business (see "Home-Based Business").

ATM fees

Bank service charges

Books and publications

Business cards

Coffee service

Computer supplies

Credit card fees

Decorations

Fire extinguishers

First-aid kit

Internet access and web hosting

Ledgers

Lightbulbs

Magazines and newspapers

Office and computer supplies

Periodicals

Postage

Restroom supplies

Safe deposit box

Shipping (with exceptions)

Signs (if not expensive)

Software (if inexpensive or if subscribed to)

Stationery

Water service

This book

Pension and Profit-Sharing Plans

This is for employees. This is not for self-employed individuals, partners in partnerships, or members of LLCs. See "Retirement Deductions."

Rent or Lease

Rent or lease of a vehicle goes in this category, not under "Car and Truck Expenses." See "Vehicles." Do not include rent or lease of your home. See "Home-Based Business." Items that you "rent to own," often called a conditional sales contract, are deducted as purchases, not as rentals.

Buildings

Equipment

Vehicles

Repairs and Maintenance

Do not include major restoration, remodeling, or structural changes to buildings. These are depreciated along with the buildings, under "Depreciation." Do not include repairs and maintenance to your home. See the "Home-Based Business" chapter.

Cleaning

Computer problems

Electrical

Landscaping (other than for home-based business)

Minor building repairs

Plumbing

Supplies

This category refers to industrial supplies. Do not include manufacturing supplies or supplies that are part of inventory. Office supplies should be included under "Office Expenses."

Building supplies

Equipment and tools that wear out within a year

Replacement filters and similar consumables

Uniforms

Taxes and Licenses

Do not include federal income or self-employment taxes, which are not deductible. Do not include sales taxes on goods and services you purchase, which are added to the cost of the purchase.

Business license

Employer's taxes

Floor tax

Gross receipts tax

Inventory tax

License fees

Permit fees

Property taxes (other than home businesses)

Sales tax collected from customers

State income taxes (corporations only)

Travel and Meals

Do not include vehicle expenses. See "Vehicles."

Lodging

Transportation (other than your own vehicle)

Incidental expenses

Utilities

Do not include utilities (other than telephone) related to a home-based business. See "Home-Based Business."

Electricity

Garbage

Heating

Telephone (see "Home-Based Business" for restrictions)

Water

Wages

These are employee wages, not payments to sole proprietors or partners.

Payroll (the amount of money actually paid to employees, after deductions)

Withheld payroll taxes (employee portion)

Other Expenses

Any deductible expense that doesn't fit another category on the tax return can be included. "Other Expenses" are itemized on page 2 of Schedule C.

Business assets deducted under the De Minimis Safe Harbor method (see "Business Assets")

Collection agency fees

Credit bureau fees

Dues to business and professional associations and unions

Education expenses

Moving expenses

Business Use of Your Home

See "Home-Based Business."

DEDUCTING BUSINESS EXPENSES

Below are explanations of some of the most important, most common, and most asked about business expenses.

INVENTORY

Inventory is merchandise—goods, products—that you sell or manufacture. Inventory also includes repair shop parts and manufacturing parts, materials, and supplies that will go into the making of a finished product, and work in process (partly finished goods you are making).

Businesses using the cash accounting method (most small businesses) can deduct the cost of inventory when purchased. Businesses using accrual accounting deduct the cost of inventory when the inventory is sold, not when it is purchased, a calculation known as "cost of goods sold" (CGS).

The cash method can be used by any business with annual sales of $25 million or less. Once you choose a method, you cannot change it without special approval from the IRS. You cannot use cash accounting one year and accrual accounting the next.

If you are starting a new business and already have inventory on hand that you will be putting into the business, inventory you purchased before going into business, you can add the cost of that inventory (or the market value if less than cost) to the current year's purchases, even though you didn't buy it this year, and include it as part of your inventory deduction.

BUSINESSES WITH LARGE INVENTORIES

For businesses with substantial inventories, such as retail stores full of merchandise and manufacturers with warehouses full of parts, how you deduct your inventory—under the cash method (deducting the cost when you make the purchase) or under the accrual method (deducting the cost when you sell the goods)—will have a dramatic impact on your profit or loss for the year and on the income taxes you'll pay.

For example, let's say you own a retail store and you purchase $50,000 worth of goods to stock the store. And let's say that during the year, you sold $25,000 of those goods and still have $25,000 on hand at December 31. Do you write off the entire $50,000 this year (using the cash method)? Or do you only deduct the $25,000 cost of what you sold this year, writing off the $25,000 balance next year or whenever you sell the goods (using the accrual method)?

That decision will affect both this year's and next year's profit and taxes. If you deduct the entire $50,000 this year, you may find that you have more tax deductions than you need to minimize this year's taxes. You may benefit by postponing part of the deduction (in our example, the $25,000 of goods on hand at the end of the year) and take the deduction next year, to offset next year's income.

This is an important decision, and I urge you to investigate your options. A lot of tax money may be at stake. And keep in mind that once you choose a method, you cannot switch to the other method without approval from the IRS.

Again, this issue only applies to businesses with large-dollar inventory that is unsold at the end of the year. If you usually have little or no inventory on hand at the end of the year, you can ignore this warning. Use the cash method, and deduct the cost when you buy the goods. It is much simpler than calculating cost of goods sold.

CALCULATING COST OF GOODS SOLD

If you will be using the cash method, deducting your inventory when you purchase it, you can skip this calculation and all the rules explained below. If you will be using the accrual method, calculating cost of goods sold is a three-step procedure:

Step One: Start with the cost of your inventory on hand at the beginning of the year. If you had no inventory, you start with $0.

Step Two: Add all the inventory purchases made during the year. Beginning inventory (from Step One) plus your purchases during the year gives you the total inventory available for sale during the year.

Step Three: Subtract the ending inventory: the cost of inventory still on hand at the end of the year. The resulting figure is your cost of goods sold: Inventory at January 1, plus purchases during the year, minus inventory on hand December 31, equals cost of goods sold.

To accomplish Step Three, make a list of inventory on hand at the end of the year. This is called "taking inventory" or "taking a physical inventory." The word inventory refers to both the goods and to the procedure of counting the goods. Inventory on hand at year-end is usually valued at its cost to you and not at its sales price.

If for any reason your year-end inventory is worth less than what you paid, the inventory should be valued at this lesser amount. "Worth" refers to its retail value, what you can sell it for. If year-end inventory is totally worthless, it should be valued at zero. This inventory valuation method is known as "lower of cost or market": You value your year-end inventory at its cost or at its market value, whichever is less. Lowering the value of ("writing down") damaged or unsalable merchandise increases your cost of goods sold, thereby decreasing your profits—and decreasing your taxes.

If you do value your inventory at less than its cost, the IRS requires you to offer the devalued inventory for sale at the lower-than-market price, either before year-end or within thirty days after the year-end. You don't have to actually sell the inventory, but you do need to offer it for sale. If you have worthless inventory (valued at zero dollars), the IRS has stated that you must dispose of the inventory to get the deduction.

Inventory missing, stolen, or given away: The cost of stolen or missing inventory and the cost of samples given away are deductible as part of cost of goods sold. This missing inventory is not on hand at year-end, so it is not included in your year-end inventory count. It automatically becomes part of your cost of goods sold (even though it really wasn't sold—the term "cost of goods sold" really should be "cost of goods sold, lost, stolen, given away, damaged, unsalable, etc.").

Manufacturers and crafts businesses: The cost of inventory on hand at the end of the year includes not just your materials and manufacturing supplies (inventory you have not yet worked on) but also any finished and partially finished goods. Value your finished and partly finished inventory at its cost to you. That cost includes materials and paid labor. It does not include your own labor, unless you are an employee of your own corporation.

Consignment: Consigned inventory is merchandise one business or self-employed individual places with another business for the other business to try to sell. Consigned inventory belongs to the consignor (the business that produced the inventory), not the consignee (the business trying to sell the inventory). The inventory, if unsold at year-end, is part of the consignor's ending inventory.

A special note about deducting inventory: Prior to 2018, no businesses were allowed to deduct inventory when it was purchased. Even businesses on the cash basis were required to compute cost of goods sold, a requirement that was the law for fifty years or more. The new law, allowing the deduction without computing cost of goods sold, was the biggest change to a business tax deduction in history, and great news for most small businesses. But what Congress gives, Congress can take back. Verify the status of this new law before relying on it.

BUSINESS ASSETS

Business assets are possessions that you use in your business: machinery, equipment, tools, furniture, fixtures, office machines, computers, display cases, vehicles, buildings, and assets specific to the kind of business or profession you're in, such as a musician's instruments or a surveyor's transit. These assets are sometimes called capital, fixed, or depreciable assets. They are also referred to as "tangible assets," meaning physical, touchable. Business assets also include intangible assets such as patents, trademarks, and copyrights. I make the distinction because tangible assets often come under different write-off rules than intangible assets.

Business assets do not include inventory (goods you sell or manufacture to sell), supplies, or any assets that wear out or become useless in a year or less, which can be deducted as supplies.

Tax-Deduction Options for Business Assets

Most tangible business assets other than buildings can be written off the year of purchase, or, at your option, can be depreciated: written off over a period of years, deducting part of the cost each year. Most small businesses opt for the immediate write-off because the write-off is simple to calculate, while depreciation is quite complex, and also because businesses want the maximum deductions they can get this year, to pay the lowest taxes possible this year.

However, new businesses might save tax money by choosing depreciation over writing off assets all at once. Many businesses make little or no profit and pay little or no taxes the first year or two, when they're just getting started. These businesses may have no need for the higher deductions the immediate write-off brings. It might be better to depreciate the assets, deducting the bulk of the expense in future years when you can use it to save taxes in future years. Businesses might want to compare profit, and taxes, writing off assets versus depreciating assets before deciding which method to choose. If you bought several assets this year, you can depreciate some assets and write off others. It is not all one way or the other.

Most buildings and intangible assets must be depreciated; they do not qualify for first-year write-off. These assets, and how to depreciate them, are covered below.

SOME BASIC RULES
Business assets can be deducted in several different ways. Some assets can be written off the year

of purchase, and some have to be written off over a period of years. Regardless of the write-off method used, there are rules common to all business assets:

Determining cost: Cost is the purchase price and includes sales tax, shipping, and any installation charges. If you pay for an asset in installments, the cost is the total purchase price as if you had paid cash for it. Finance or interest charges are not included in the cost of an asset (except for some newly constructed buildings and some custom-built equipment). Finance and interest charges can usually be written off the year paid, completely separate from the cost of the asset.

Assets used partly for business: Generally, if an asset is used partly for business and partly for personal or non-business use, the business portion can be written off, though there are some exceptions for assets that are used less than 50 percent for business. Try to keep business use above 50 percent, and keep detailed records—dates, hours, miles, etc.—to prove it.

New versus used assets: Both new and used assets can be written off or depreciated, except for used assets you already own.

Assets purchased before starting your business: You cannot write off assets owned before you started your business, but you can depreciate them. The amount you can depreciate is the original cost or the current market value, whichever is less. Determining the "market value" for your equipment, your desk, or any other business assets you've owned for a while might be difficult. If these are high-dollar items, it probably would be worth having them appraised. Otherwise, use your best estimate and don't worry. The IRS is not likely to ever question your figures.

Selling assets: When you sell an asset that has been written off, or fully or partly depreciated, there may be a taxable profit on the sale. This is covered below, after "Depreciation."

SOME SPECIFIC RULES
Buildings: Most buildings must be depreciated, though there is an important exception for remodeling or renovating retail stores and restaurants (also known as "refresh" costs): 75 percent of the cost can be written off. Also, some livestock and horticultural structures and some storage buildings can be written off instead of being depreciated. If you have a home business, the building itself (if you own your home) can be depreciated, but see the "Home-Based Business" chapter for restrictions.

Land: While a building can be depreciated, the land the building sits on cannot. Land is considered a permanent asset that cannot be expensed until sold. If the cost of land and building are not separately stated, most accountants figure 80 percent of the cost was the building, 20 percent the land, but you can use any reasonable allocation. The cost of parking lots and cost of landscaping can be deducted or depreciated, so these should be separated out from the cost of the land.

Antiques: According to the IRS, valuable antiques and art treasures cannot be depreciated and cannot be written off until sold. The tax court, however, has ruled that antiques actually used in a business, such as an old desk or a professional musician's rare violin, can be written off or depreciated like other business assets. The IRS disagrees. If you have significant money at stake, I suggest you talk to your accountant.

Software: Software is considered a business asset if purchased, but different types of software have different tax deduction rules. See "Software" below.

Vehicles: Vehicles have special limitations. There are many tax deduction rules for different types and weights of vehicles. See "Vehicles" below.

Intangibles: Intangible assets (also called *intellectual property*) such as trademarks, copyrights, patents, and goodwill cannot be written off the year you acquire them. They must be amortized, which means the same thing as depreciated. The term *amortization* refers to intangible assets; *depreciation* refers to tangible (physical) assets. One exception: A trademark licensed from another business can be written off; it does not have to be amortized.

Original films and recordings: Motion picture films, videotapes, digital productions, and sound recordings—originals, not duplicates, for sale or rent—come under a different set of IRS rules. I suggest you talk to a knowledgeable accountant if you are a movie, TV, or record producer.

Rental businesses: Businesses that rent out equipment can depreciate or write off the equipment.

Farms, ranches, nurseries, and orchards: Plants, trees, agricultural fields, and farm and ranch animals come under a variety of depreciation and write-off rules that will require research in IRS publications or help from a knowledgeable accountant.

Writing Off Business Assets

The IRS has three different options for writing off assets the year you purchase them. The options can be confusing because many assets qualify for all three options. But you don't have to struggle. For all tangible assets except buildings and some building improvements, Option One: "100% Bonus Depreciation," is simple and straightforward, no special rules, no extra paperwork.

OPTION ONE: 100% BONUS DEPRECIATION

The term "depreciation" usually means that the cost of an asset is deducted over a period of years. Bonus depreciation, however, allows you to deduct the entire cost of an asset when you purchase the asset. You are not depreciating the asset at all. Bonus depreciation can be used for any tangible assets other than buildings, though some buildings do qualify, and many building improvements also qualify. Bonus depreciation has none of the restrictions of the second and third options below and is probably the simplest way to deduct assets. If you choose this option, there is no need to read any further.

Bonus depreciation is deducted on the tax return under "Depreciation." You also fill out IRS Form 4562, "Depreciation and Amortization."

OPTION TWO: ASSETS THAT COST $2,500 OR LESS

These can be written off the year you purchase them, under a law called the De Minimis Safe Harbor method. *De minimis* means trivial, insignificant, which I sure wouldn't call $2,500, but then the IRS and I live in different worlds. The $2,500 limit is per asset. You can deduct every tangible asset you buy that costs $2,500 or less. You cannot use this option for intangible assets; they must be amortized (depreciated).

This safe harbor deduction is optional. But if you choose this option, you must use it for all tangible assets that cost $2,500 or less.

You deduct these safe harbor assets under "Other Expenses," *not* under "Depreciation." You must also include a statement with your tax return listing the assets individually.

All the assets that qualify for this De Minimis Safe Harbor deduction also qualify for the 100% Bonus Depreciation option above. The bonus depreciation option has fewer requirements and is a better choice.

OPTION THREE: ASSETS THAT COST MORE THAN $2,500

These can be written off the year you purchase them, under a different law known as the First-Year Write-Off, or Section 179 deduction. This option has a maximum deduction of $1 million, all assets combined. Assets that exceed the maximum must be depreciated.

Actually, this option can be used for most tangible assets, including those that cost $2,500 or less. But this option has an annual maximum, and the other options do not. Businesses are better off using Option Two for assets that are $2,500 or less, leaving more of a deduction under Option Three for the more expensive assets.

Unlike the De Minimis Safe Harbor option, this Section 179 deduction is not all or nothing. You can write off some assets under this option and depreciate others. However, there are many restrictions on what assets can be deducted. They are listed below. Assets that cannot be deducted under this option can be deducted under the other options or depreciated.

Section 179 assets are deducted on the tax return under "Depreciation and Section 179 Expense." You also fill out IRS Form 4562, "Depreciation and Amortization."

Option Three restrictions:

1. If you have more than one unincorporated business, the $1 million is the maximum for all combined businesses.

2. Married couples are allowed a maximum write-off of $1 million between them.

3. If you purchase more than $2.5 million in depreciable assets in any one year, the $1 million maximum is reduced, dollar for dollar, by the amount in excess of $2.5 million.

4. The write-off cannot exceed your total taxable income. For sole proprietors, total taxable income is all income, both business and non-business, reported on your tax return (married couples combined if filing jointly). Any write-off disallowed because of this income limitation can be carried forward to the next year, and future years if necessary, until the assets are fully written off.

5. Automobiles and SUVs have a maximum Section 179 deduction. Some trucks and vans are not subject to this limitation. See "Vehicles."

6. If an asset is used 50 percent or less for business the first year, you are not eligible for this Section 179 deduction.

7. Assets must be placed in use in the current year. If you buy a piece of equipment and put it in storage for future use, you cannot take the Section 179 deduction for that asset; it has to be depreciated. Assets that are purchased one year but paid for in the next year, and assets bought in installments with payments over more than one year, can be written off under Section 179 the year you acquire and use the assets.

8. If you sell assets you've previously written off, or convert them to non-business use, you may have to "recapture" (add back into income) the amount you wrote off the year of sale or conversion, depending on how many years you own the assets.

All the assets that qualify for this Section 179 deduction, except some building improvements, also qualify for the 100% Bonus Depreciation option above. The bonus depreciation option has fewer requirements and is a better choice.

Depreciation

Instead of deducting the cost of assets the year you purchase them, you can spread the cost over several years, deducting part of the cost each year, a tax procedure known as *depreciation*. All assets that qualify under the three write-off options above can be depreciated instead of written off. However, some assets must be depreciated: most buildings, intangible assets, and other assets that do not meet the three options' write-off requirements.

There are several ways to calculate depreciation, and all of them are complicated. None of them are something most business owners want to struggle with if they don't have to. That's why most small businesses take the write-off options whenever they can. But if depreciation will save you tax money, or if depreciation is your only option, the depreciation rules and calculations are explained below. Personally, though, I suggest you get help from a tax accountant. All tax accountants have software that will automatically calculate depreciation and that can compare the tax difference between depreciating and writing off assets.

Depreciation is deducted on the tax return under "Depreciation and Section 179 Expense." You also fill out IRS Form 4562, "Depreciation and Amortization."

RULES FOR DEPRECIATION: WRITE-OFF PERIOD

Assets that are being depreciated are written off over a period of years, known as the "write-off period" (also called "recovery period" or "useful life"). Here are the write-off periods for assets most used by small businesses and farmers:

3 Years: Website design. Some software. Semitrucks (not trailers). Racehorses over two years old. All horses over twelve years old. Hogs.

5 Years: Office equipment and computers. Some electronic equipment. Farm equipment and machinery. Most equipment used for research and experimentation. Carpeting. Movable partitions. Appliances and furniture in residential rental property. Cars, trucks (other than semitrucks), buses, and trailers. Solar, wind, and some other alternative-energy property. Movable gasoline storage tanks. Farm machinery and equipment. Cattle, sheep, and goats.

7 Years: Machinery. Equipment. Tools. Furniture. Store fixtures. Small signs. Railroad track. Horses other than those listed under "3 Years."

10 Years: Boats, barges, and tugs. Single-purpose agricultural and horticultural structures. Fruit and nut trees and vines.

15 Years: Large outdoor signs. Gas stations, including their mini marts (with some exceptions). Intangible property such as goodwill, trademarks, trade names, franchises, customer lists, and covenants not to compete. Domain names purchased from a reseller. Patents and copyrights if acquired as part of a business you purchase (see "Other" below). Leasehold improvements. Many building renovations.

20 Years: Some farm buildings.

27½ Years: Residential rental buildings.

39 Years: All buildings other than residential rental property, farm buildings, restaurant and retail renovations, and some gas stations.

Other: Patents and copyrights are depreciated over the life granted by the government.

METHODS OF COMPUTING DEPRECIATION

There are four methods of depreciation. All four methods result in the same tax write-off eventually, but each method involves different amounts that can be written off in any given year.

GENERAL DEPRECIATION SYSTEM #1 (GDS #1)

The most commonly used depreciation system, GDS #1 (also called the 200 percent declining balance method) offers the fastest write-offs: larger write-offs in the first few years, smaller write-offs in later years. Most business assets other than buildings, intangibles, farm assets, and certain "listed property" can be depreciated under this method (see below for the exceptions).

At your option, assets eligible for this method can be depreciated under the other three methods described below. If you already have reduced your taxes down to nothing and don't need any more deductions this year, the other methods will bring larger deductions in future years.

GENERAL DEPRECIATION SYSTEM #2 (GDS #2)

Also known as the 150 percent declining balance method, this system is required for most farm buildings and equipment, and some land improvements. The method is similar to GDS #1 but with smaller write-offs in the early years.

STRAIGHT-LINE METHOD

This method must be used for intangibles, most buildings other than farm buildings, leasehold improvements, vineyards, and fruit and nut trees. The straight-line method distributes depreciation equally over the write-off period. Each year, the same amount is depreciated (except the first year, when only part of a year's depreciation is allowed; more on this later).

ALTERNATIVE DEPRECIATION SYSTEM (ADS)

This method is required for certain assets if used 50 percent or less for business (called "listed property"); vehicles (unless you take the standard mileage allowance, in which case you take no depreciation at all); boats; airplanes; cell phones; and computers (if you use the computer away from your business premises). The ADS method is required for assets used primarily outside the United States, and assets imported from certain trade-restricted countries.

Under ADS, the write-off periods are different than those shown above, and the depreciation runs over a longer period of years. If you are required or want to use ADS, IRS Publication #534, "Depreciation," lists the different write-off periods.

FIRST-YEAR DEPRECIATION

You are not allowed a full year's depreciation the year you acquire an asset. For assets other than buildings, you are allowed only a half-year's depreciation the first year. "Year" refers to the calendar year, not to the first twelve months you own an asset. Don't confuse this rule with the First-Year Write-Off rules above. This is a completely different rule and applies only to depreciation.

If you compute your own depreciation, just divide the first year's depreciation in half. At the end of the write-off period, you add the remaining half-year's depreciation. If you use the Depreciation Table (see below), the half-year is figured into it.

In effect, this "half-year convention" adds an extra year to the write-off period. A seven-year asset, for example, will be depreciated over an eight-year period: a half-year the first year, a full year the second through the seventh years, and a half-year the eighth year.

There is an important exception to the half-year rule. If more than 40 percent of your depreciable assets (other than real estate) are purchased in the last three months of the year, you do not use the half-year calculation. You group the assets according to which quarter of the year they were purchased and then make four separate computations.

Buildings: First-year depreciation on buildings is calculated building by building using what's called a "mid-month convention." Whatever month a building is acquired for business or first used for business, you are allowed a half-month's depreciation that month, and then full depreciation for the remaining months of the year. So if you purchased a building in April, you are allowed eight and a half

months' depreciation the first year. Then at the end of the depreciation period, you get an additional three and a half months' depreciation.

DEPRECIATION TABLE

This table will help you compute depreciation using GDS #1, GDS #2, and straight-line, and to compare the three methods. The fourth method, ADS, can't be included in a simple table because there are too many asset categories. In the table, "year" refers to the calendar year, not to the first twelve months you own the asset. Percentage is the percentage of cost you can write off that year. This table is only for assets qualifying for the half-year convention (see "First-Year Depreciation"). Do not use for assets requiring mid-quarter calculations.

SELLING AN ASSET

When you sell an asset that has been written off or fully or partly depreciated, there may be a taxable profit on the sale. This is known as "recapture" and is somewhat complex, depending on how many years you've had the asset, how much depreciation or write-off you've taken, and what method of depreciation you've used. No additional depreciation should be taken the year you sell the asset.

The basic concept: The cost of the asset is reduced by the amount you wrote off or depreciated, to come up with what's called *adjusted cost* (or *cost basis*). If the selling price is higher than the adjusted cost, you have a taxable profit. If the selling price is lower, you have a tax-deductible loss.

If you took the first-year write-off (Option One or Two above), your cost basis is zero. You've written off the entire cost, so the entire sale price is taxable.

If you did not take a first-year write-off, you must reduce the cost basis by the depreciation during the time you owned the asset.

DEPRECIATION TABLE

Year	3 Yr. Assets			5 Yr. Assets			7 Yr. Assets		
	GDS #1	GDS #2	St. Line	GDS #1	GDS #2	St. Line	GDS #1	GDS #2	St. Line
1	33%	25%	17%	20%	15%	10%	14%	11%	7%
2	45	38	33	32	26	20	25	19	15
3	15	25	33	19	18	20	17	15	15
4	7	12	17	12	17	20	13	13	14
5				11	16	20	9	12	14
6				6	8	10	9	12	14
7							9	12	14
8							4	6	7

For example, let's say you bought a piece of equipment a few years ago for $4,000, and you already deducted $3,000 of depreciation on prior tax returns. Your adjusted cost is $1,000 ($4,000 original cost less $3,000 depreciation). Let's say you sell the asset for $2,500. You will have a $1,500 taxable profit:

Original cost	$4,000
Subtract accumulated depreciation	(3,000)
Adjusted cost	$1,000
Sale price	(2,500)
Profit	$1,500

Now, let's change the example and say you sold the same asset for $600. You will have a $400 deductible loss:

Original cost	$4,000
Subtract accumulated depreciation	(3,000)
Adjusted cost	$1,000
Sale price	(600)
Loss	$400

Record the sale of a business asset in your income record the month of sale, but record it separately from your regular sales. Although the sale may be subject to income tax, it is not a regular business sale and should be shown separately. Profit on the sale of a business asset is taxable, and loss on the sale is deductible, but they come under different tax rules than regular business income and expenses. Also record the sale on your equipment ledger.

DISCARDING OR JUNKING AN ASSET

If an asset is fully depreciated or fully written off when it becomes worthless/useless/unsalable junk, that's as far as the taxes and recordkeeping go; there is no additional deduction, no profit and no loss. But if the asset is only partly depreciated, you can write off the balance of the cost (the undepreciated part of the cost) the year the asset becomes worthless.

For example, a piece of equipment cost $3,000 a year ago, and so far you've deducted $800 in depreciation. The thing burns up. This year you can write off $2,200, the undepreciated balance ($3,000 cost less $800 depreciation). This example assumes, besides no selling price, no insurance. If the asset is insured, any insurance payment is treated the same as income from the sale of an asset (see "Selling an Asset" above).

Software

Software that was packaged with your computer when you bought it is considered part of the cost of the computer, not deducted separately.

Any purchased software other than software that was custom-designed for your business can be written off when purchased; or at your option, the software can be amortized (depreciated) over three years. Custom-made software—software created just for your business—must be amortized over fifteen years.

Software that is subscribed to, usually a monthly fee, can be deducted as an office expense.

If you develop software programs, you can, at your option, write off the development costs as current expenses. You also have the option to depreciate software development costs over five years, using the straight-line method.

Apps are software and come under the same tax deduction rules.

Vehicles

Most expenses of operating a vehicle for business are deductible except regular commuting expenses between your home and your usual place of business, which are not deductible. If you operate a home-based business or have an office in the home, read about commuting in the Home-Based Business chapter.

How a vehicle is registered will make a difference in allowable deductions. If you are a sole proprietor, the vehicle can be registered in your own name or in your business name. Either way, you are eligible for the deduction. If, however, your business is a partnership, corporation, or limited liability company, how the vehicle is registered can affect the allowable tax deductions. You should talk to an accountant before purchasing a vehicle for your business.

Doing taxes is not an effective use of a business owner's time.

—Business executive Jane Wesman

Personal versus business use: If you use your personal vehicle for business, you are entitled to a business deduction for the business use (again, this applies to sole proprietors). The IRS requires you to keep a log of business miles driven, including time of day, destination, and business purpose. If you are audited and you don't have a daily logbook, or if you only have estimates or summaries, the IRS will disallow your deduction.

TWO METHODS OF FIGURING VEHICLE EXPENSES

There are two ways of figuring vehicle expenses. As in so many other situations, one is difficult and one is easy:

Method One: You can keep itemized records of all your vehicle expenses. These include gas, oil, maintenance, repairs, insurance, parking, tolls, garage rents, license and registration fees, interest on the purchase, even auto club dues. The purchase price of the vehicle can be depreciated, or written off the year of purchase.

Vehicle expenses are prorated between personal use (not deductible), and business use (deductible). The most common method of proration is based on the miles driven. For example, if you drove 10,000 miles last year, of which 2,500 were for business, 25 percent of all your vehicle expenses are deductible, and 25 percent of the cost of the vehicle can be depreciated or written off the first year.

Keeping itemized records of all your vehicle expenses is tedious work. The IRS realizes this also. In one of their rare helpful moods, they have come up with . . .

Method Two: An optional "standard mileage allowance" (standard mileage rate). Instead of recording each fill-up and every oil change, you may take a standard flat rate for every business mile driven (not including the commute). The current rate is 54.5 cents per mile. The rate changes every year. The standard mileage allowance is in lieu of depreciation and all vehicle expenses except parking, tolls, interest, and state and local taxes, which are deductible in addition to the mileage allowance (sales tax on the vehicle is not deductible).

You may not use the standard mileage allowance if your business operates more than four vehicles at the same time, such as having a fleet of vehicles. If you have more than four vehicles but are alternating vehicles, never having more than four being used for business at any one time, you can take the standard mileage allowance.

You may not use the standard mileage allowance if you take the first-year write-off deduction on the vehicle.

Business vehicles that do not qualify for the standard mileage allowance may still use Method One, itemizing expenses.

Using the standard mileage allowance reduces the cost basis of your vehicle, for figuring profit or loss when the vehicle is sold. You reduce the cost basis by 25 cents for each business mile driven. This rate also changes every year.

The method you choose the first year you use your vehicle for business determines what methods you can use in future years for that vehicle. If you use Method One (itemizing) the first year, you must stay with that method as long as you use that vehicle. If you use the standard mileage allowance the first year, you can switch back and forth if you want, itemizing some years and using the mileage allowance other years. If you do switch from the mileage allowance to itemizing, you must use straight-line depreciation.

If you choose Method One, depreciation is limited depending on the type and weight of the vehicle, on the cost, whether it was purchased new or used, and if the vehicle is used 50 percent or less for business. And when you sell or trade in the vehicle, you have to calculate gain or loss and cost basis of the new vehicle. The rules are complicated and may require the help of an accountant. These limitations do not apply if you take the standard mileage allowance.

Which method do you choose: Obviously, Method Two, the standard mileage allowance, is much easier to calculate; anybody can do it. But if you are driving an expensive vehicle, depreciating the vehicle under Method One will probably generate a larger tax deduction. It will be worth your time to compare the deductions under both methods. If you don't want to struggle with depreciation calculations, get help from an accountant. Tax accountants have software that can calculate vehicle depreciation.

Sole proprietors report vehicle expenses on the "Car and Truck Expense" line on Schedule C. You also report the expenses on Form 4562, but only if you are required to fill out that form for depreciation or first-year write-off of any assets.

If you rent or lease the vehicle, the rent or lease payment is reported separately.

RENTING OR LEASING A VEHICLE

The business portion of a vehicle rental or lease is deductible, with exceptions. You can deduct the actual expenses of renting and operating the vehicle, or use the standard mileage allowance.

If you lease an automobile for thirty days or more, your lease payment is not fully deductible. The IRS has a table, called "Inclusion Amounts for Cars" that shows how much of an auto lease can and cannot be deducted. The Inclusion Amount applies to automobiles and to some light trucks and vans that are primarily passenger vehicles. The Inclusion Amount does not apply to vehicles weighing 6,000 pounds or more, nor to trucks and vans specifically designed or outfitted primarily for business purposes. And again, the Inclusion Amount is only for rentals that run thirty days or more. The typical day- or weeklong car rental is fully deductible.

A lease-purchase is considered a purchase, and not a lease, for tax purposes.

To learn more about vehicle deductions, read IRS Publication #463, "Travel, Gift, and Car Expenses."

Repairs and Remodeling

Repairs on business property, buildings, and equipment are fully deductible.

Major repairs that involve structural changes, restoration, remodeling, or repairs that adapt an asset to a new or different use must usually be treated as a permanent (capital) investment and handled in the same manner as the purchase of a depreciable asset. See "Depreciation" above.

An important exception for retail stores and restaurants: 75 percent of remodeling ("refresh") costs can be deducted currently instead of depreciated. The 25 percent balance is depreciated over fifteen years.

The IRS often challenges businesses that deduct expensive repairs, particularly on buildings, arguing that the repairs are really capital improvements and must be depreciated. You may want to discuss this with your accountant.

Bad Debts

Some bad debts are deductible. These include customers' bounced checks and credit card chargebacks—charges customers refuse to pay.

If you sell on account to customers, uncollectible accounts are deductible, but only if they were posted to your income ledger when you made the sale.

Webster's World

ONE MILLION DOLLARS CHARGED FOR RETURNED CHECKS

Businesses using the cash method of accounting—which is the method used by most small businesses, recording income when the money comes in, not when the sale was made—cannot take a bad-debt write-off for uncollectible accounts, because the income was not recorded in the first place. If this does not make sense to you, read "Cash Accounting versus Accrual" in the Keeping Records chapter. And if this doesn't sound fair to you, you're right, it isn't, but that is how the tax laws are written. You were cheated out of the money you should have earned, and the IRS says "Tough luck."

Losses: Casualty or Theft

Business losses from fire, storm, or other casualty, or from theft or vandalism, are deductible, if the items destroyed or stolen have not already been deducted. Assets that have already been deducted (most machinery and equipment, inventory, supplies) cannot be deducted a second time as a loss. Assets that are being depreciated and not already fully written off (most buildings) can be depreciated further, but only up to the undepreciated balance. Loss or theft of cash is deductible. Cleaning and repairing damage is deductible.

Any loss covered by insurance is not deductible. If you have insurance, you are required to file a claim with the insurance company or you cannot take a tax deduction on any of the insured property.

Be sure to document your losses. Take photos, make a list of everything affected, and if theft or vandalism is involved, file a police report. Theft and vandalism losses are deducted the year discovered, regardless of the year they occurred.

Operating losses (your business loses money) are covered below.

Donations and Charitable Contributions

Businesses other than C corporations are not allowed a deduction for donations to charities or community organizations. However, if a donation results in favorable publicity for the business, and therefore a likelihood of increased sales, many businesses deduct the donations, not as charitable contributions but as a promotion expense.

This interpretation of tax law (taking a promotion deduction for a charitable contribution) has been fought by the IRS for years. But the Tax Court has ruled in favor of the deduction several times, and the IRS has allowed it in at least one case. Still, the IRS will challenge businesses that deduct charitable donations as sales or promotion expenses, *if* the IRS audits the business and discovers the deduction. You may want to discuss this with an accountant.

If you do take the deduction, how it is written off depends on what the business is donating:

Cash donations are deducted as promotion expenses.

Merchandise donated, such as a raffle prize for a fund-raiser, or a food store donating food or beverages for a charity or community event, was deducted when the inventory was purchased (assuming your business, like most small businesses, is on the cash basis). There is no further deduction.

Gift certificates and gift cards cannot be deducted because no additional expense was incurred. If the gift is a service you provide, there is no tax deduction because you cannot deduct the cost of your own time.

Sales proceeds or a percentage of sales proceeds donated to a charitable or community organization can be deducted as a sales expense.

Ads and sponsorships: An advertisement in a charitable organization's directory or event program, or sponsorship of an organization's team or event, is deductible. These expenses are not considered charitable donations. The IRS says they are legitimate promotional expenses. Instead of making a charitable donation that may or may not be deductible, place an ad or offer a sponsorship.

C Corporations: C Corporations can deduct charitable contributions and donations as a charitable business deduction, if the charities have IRS charitable nonprofit status. C Corporations can deduct up to 10 percent of their taxable income. C corporations that donate inventory to qualified charities can get a deduction for more than the cost of the inventory. They can deduct the cost plus half the difference between cost and regular sales price, up to twice the cost of the inventory. If all this is too complicated, corporations can follow the lead of the non-corporate businesses and write off the entire donation as a promotion expense, as long as you read the IRS warning above.

Political donations are not deductible, period. But, yes, large corporations have found ways around this law, as I'm sure you're not surprised to hear . . .

Interest Expense

Interest paid on business debts, including interest on credit card purchases, is deductible, with a few important exceptions:

> *Interest on loans to construct real estate* (if you are building a new building) must be capitalized—that is, added to the cost of the property.
>
> *Interest on back taxes* is not deductible, except for C corporations. That's right: If Walmart gets audited and hit with back taxes, the interest charges are fully deductible. But if you get audited and owe interest on back taxes, well, sorry about that.
>
> *Prepaid interest*, according to the IRS, is not deductible until the year it applies to.

BUYING A BUSINESS

If you borrow money to purchase an existing business, the interest deduction laws can get complicated. If the business is a sole proprietorship, partnership, S corporation, or limited liability company, part of the interest may be deductible as a current business expense, but part may have to be capitalized. Generally, the interest on the part of the loan that applies to actual business assets (equipment, inventory, etc.) is deductible. The interest that applies to intangibles (goodwill, trademarks, etc.) must be capitalized. If you are purchasing a regular C corporation (not an S corporation), you are actually buying stock, and the interest comes under a different set of rules, and is not deductible as a regular business expense. You will probably need help from an experienced accountant.

CORPORATIONS

If you are an employee of your own corporation, and you get a personal loan to purchase business assets, the interest is not deductible as a business expense. If the corporation itself borrows the money, the interest is deductible. How you structure corporate finances has a major effect on how much you pay in taxes. This is another situation where you should get help from an experienced accountant.

Business Gifts

Tax deductions for business gifts are limited to $25 per recipient in any one year.

Samples of your merchandise, given to prospective buyers or to people who might review or publicize your products, are not considered gifts and are not subject to the $25 gift limitation. You write off the cost of the samples as part of inventory.

Gifts to employees come under stricter rules. Gifts of nominal value, such as a Thanksgiving turkey, a bottle of wine, a framed photo of the boss, are deductible and not taxable to the employee. But any gift of significant value, and any cash gift, or cash equivalent such as a gift certificate, even for a small amount, is considered taxable wages to the employee, reported on the W-2, subject to all payroll taxes. The same rule applies to awards given to employees, except for some employee achievement awards or employee safety awards that are tax-free if they meet certain IRS rules.

Meals

Regular meals at work are generally not deductible.

Meals while traveling away from home on business are 50 percent deductible. See "Travel" below. Truck drivers who qualify under special Department of Transportation rules are allowed an 80 percent deduction.

Meals that you provide as part of a business meeting, sales presentation, or seminar are fully deductible. Food samples made available to the general public are fully deductible.

Meals with current or prospective customers and clients: May be 50 percent deductible, or may not be deductible at all, depending on how the IRS interprets a new law that prohibits deductions for entertainment. If the IRS allows the 50 percent meal deduction, you can take it only if business is specifically discussed at the meal and the cost is not "lavish or extravagant." Tips are considered part of the meal. The IRS requires that you have a receipt and write on it who you took out and why. If you are paying with a smartphone app or other electronic form of payment, print out a receipt or keep a record that you can print out if you get audited.

Employers: Meals provided to employees on a regular basis are considered taxable income to the employees, subject to all payroll taxes, and deductible by the employer as employee wages. However, if the meals are served on the business premises and are, to quote the IRS, "for the convenience of the employer," the meals are 50 percent deductible and are not taxable to the employees. There must be a substantial business reason for providing the meals, such as requiring employees to work through lunch or to be on call. You can take a 100 percent deduction (and tax-free to employees) for the cost of the annual company picnic, an occasional pizza party, or a holiday celebration.

Restaurants, caterers, food vendors: The cost of meals sold to your customers as part of your regular business is 100 percent deductible. Your expenses are not recorded on your tax return as meals. The food is inventory.

Child-care businesses can deduct the full cost of meals provided or can take a special "standard meal allowance."

Travel

If you are away from home overnight on business, you can deduct most of your travel expenses, though with exceptions.

BUSINESS TRIPS

A business trip within the United States that is 100 percent business is 100 percent deductible for the cost of round-trip travel, lodging, transportation, and incidental expenses such as laundry.

There are three important exceptions: Meals are 50 percent deductible. If you travel on a cruise ship or other type of luxury boat, the deduction for the travel is limited; check with the IRS or a knowledgeable accountant.

What about a trip that is part business and part vacation? You may be able to write some of it off, and you may be able to write all of it off, if you carefully follow the rules.

If the reason for your trip is primarily personal (more than half the days are for vacation), none of the traveling expenses to and from your destination are deductible. Only expenses directly related to your business can be deducted.

If your trip is primarily for business (more than half the days are for business), and it is within the

United States, the cost of the round-trip travel is fully deductible even though some of the trip is for pleasure. So you can tack a short vacation onto a business trip, and the only costs that aren't deductible are the non-business expenses, such as the extra days' lodging and meals.

And if you have a business trip that overlaps a weekend, requiring you to be there Friday and the following Monday, lucky you: You can write off the weekend as well as a business expense, even though all you did was sit on the beach and dance in the clubs.

When counting business versus vacation days, a "business day" does not require you to do business all day. Any day you put in at least four hours of work is considered a business day. Any day your presence is required, for any amount of time, is also considered a business day. And travel days count as business days.

If you take your spouse, the spouse's expenses are not deductible unless he or she is an employee or partner in the business and has a legitimate business reason for accompanying you.

TRAVEL OUTSIDE THE UNITED STATES
If you travel outside the United States, more stringent rules apply. If the trip is no more than one week or the time spent for pleasure is less than 25 percent, the same basic rules apply as a trip within the United States. But if the trip is more than a week, or if the vacation days are 25 percent or more of the trip, you allocate travel expenses between the business and the personal portion of your trip. When counting business versus vacation days, the same rules for travel in the United States also apply.

If you attend overseas conventions, seminars, or meetings, a deduction is allowed only if, in the IRS's opinion, there is a valid business reason for holding the meeting overseas. Some countries are exempt from this restriction. I suggest you talk to an accountant familiar with travel deductions.

THE IRS DOES NOT LIKE BUSINESS TRIPS
As you can tell from the generous way the law is written, it's a bit too easy to write off a business trip that is really a disguised vacation. The IRS knows this all too well, and they are forever suspicious of business travel expenses, particularly sole proprietorships where the owner is accountable to no one else: You feel like taking a business trip (and you can afford it), you take it. The IRS wants to be sure it's not a vacation in disguise. You want to be sure

you can prove, if audited, that the trip wasn't a vacation. A log of daily activities and business contacts is not required by law, but it may help convince a skeptical IRS auditor that your trip to the Bahamas or to New Orleans really was for business.

One tax client of mine who owned a retail coffee shop took an expensive trip to Scandinavia and wrote it off as a business deduction. When she was audited, which didn't surprise either of us, she was able to show the IRS auditor photos she took of coffee shops she visited throughout her travels. She showed the auditor Scandinavian coffee mugs that she is now importing. She got through the audit successfully.

KEEPING TRACK OF EXPENSES
For meals, you can keep a record of actual expenses or, at your option, you can use a standard per diem meal allowance set by the IRS: so much per day. If you do use the per diem meal allowance, only 50 percent of the allowance is deductible, because only 50 percent of meal expenses are deductible. The standard allowance varies from city to city. For lodging, corporations can use a per diem rate if they choose, but unincorporated businesses must use actual expenses. For current rates, see IRS Publication #1542, "Per Diem Rates."

Travel expenses, other than use of a vehicle, are deducted on your tax return under "Travel and Meals." Vehicle expenses are deducted under "Car and Truck Expenses." For more information, see IRS Publication #463, "Travel, Gift, and Car Expenses."

Living on the road: The deduction for expenses incurred while "away from home overnight" is often denied to people who make their living on the road, such as self-employed itinerant workers, traveling salespeople, touring musicians, and some long-distance truck drivers. The IRS says that "home" is your place of business, not where you live. In the IRS's harsh eyes, a traveling worker's place of business—the worker's "home"—is the road, so the worker is never away from home overnight and cannot deduct travel (other than vehicle expenses). These people are sometimes called "tax turtles," because as far as the IRS is concerned, they carry their homes wherever they go. The tax court sometimes agrees with the IRS on this hostile interpretation of tax law, but the court sometimes disagrees, and rules in favor of the taxpayer. If your business is of this nature and if travel expenses are substantial, I'd advise consulting a good tax accountant. If you are working away from home for over one year, the IRS automatically considers the road to be home, and disallows travel expenses.

Dues

Dues for business groups, professional organizations, merchant and trade associations, unions, chambers of commerce, etc., are deductible. Dues to community service organizations such as Rotary and Lions are also deductible. If part of your dues is for political lobbying, that portion of the dues is not deductible.

Dues and membership fees in clubs are not deductible. Even if you join these clubs solely to generate or discuss business, the dues are not deductible.

Dues are deducted on your tax return under "Other Expenses."

Shipping, Postage, and Freight

Business assets: Shipping charges for business assets you purchase are added to the cost of the assets, and written off or depreciated along with the assets.

Inventory: Shipping charges for inventory you purchase and for parts and supplies that go into goods you manufacture or build, are deducted as part of inventory.

Merchandise you sell: Shipping charges you pay on merchandise that you sell can be deducted as "Office Expenses."

Supplies and other purchases: Shipping charges for supplies (other than inventory) can be added to the cost of the supplies or deducted separately as "Office Expenses."

Education Expenses

Here is an opportunity to get some additional education and write off the cost on your business tax return, if you are careful in selecting your courses.

The cost of education is deductible only if the education maintains or improves a skill required in your business. Education expenses are not allowed if the education is required to meet minimum educational requirements of your present business or if the education will qualify you for a new trade or business.

A self-employed welder who takes a course in a new welding method can charge the expense to the business. A self-employed dance teacher who takes dance lessons can deduct the cost of the lessons. On the other hand, a leather craftsperson who takes a woodworking course cannot deduct the expenses; the education must be directly related to the business you already operate. Taking a course in pottery before opening your pottery shop is not deductible.

Any self-employed person can take a course in recordkeeping, or computers, or marketing, and deduct the cost.

Education expenses include tuition, fees, and books, and travel expenses while away from home overnight (with limitations). Education expenses are deducted on your tax return under "Other Expenses."

Employers: Employers can deduct up to $5,250 per employee for employer-paid educational expenses for the employees. The education does not have to be employment-related.

Insurance

Most business-related insurance premiums are deductible, with exceptions. Vehicle insurance is deductible if you don't take the standard mileage allowance. See "Vehicles" in this chapter.

Life insurance premiums are not deductible.

Premiums for business interruption insurance may or may not be deductible, depending on what the insurance covers. See "Insurance" in the Getting Started chapter.

Prepaid insurance, as long as it does not extend beyond twelve months, is deductible when paid. See "Prepaid Expenses" in this chapter.

Workers' compensation insurance is deductible for your employees. Workers' comp on yourself may or may not be deductible, depending on your state laws. See "Workers' Compensation Insurance" in the Growing Up chapter.

Insurance other than vehicle insurance, insurance for employees, and health insurance is included on your tax return under "Insurance."

Health Insurance

Sole proprietors, partners in partnerships, members of LLCs, and owners of S corporations can deduct the cost of health insurance, dental insurance, and long-term care insurance for themselves, spouses, and dependents. The deduction, however, is not considered a business expense. It does not reduce your business profit and is not included on the business tax return. The deduction is taken on your 1040 return. The deduction cannot exceed the net profit from your business.

To get the health insurance deduction, the IRS says that the insurance plan must be either in the name of the business or in the name of the self-employed individual. If your spouse is shown as the main insured on your policy, ask your insurance company to change the name on the policy. The change should not affect your coverage or premiums.

I also suggest you pay the health insurance premiums from the business bank account, even if the policy is not in the business name. Some tax experts have stated that this is an IRS requirement. I've never found this requirement in the IRS code or any IRS notices or publications, but it certainly will help in the unlikely chance that an IRS auditor might challenge the deduction.

The deduction is not allowed if you are eligible for employer-paid health insurance through your own employer (if you have another job) or through your spouse's employer.

Disability insurance that pays you for lost earnings if you are disabled, is not considered health insurance and is not deductible.

Medicare coverage: Medicare insurance premiums beyond the legally required coverage ("premiums you voluntarily pay" to quote the IRS) are deductible the same as health insurance premiums. It appears, however, that Medicare premiums required by law are not deductible, though this ruling has gone back and forth in prior years. It's also unclear whether Medicare premiums for a spouse are deductible, as the IRS has issued conflicting rulings in the past. If you or your spouse is receiving Medicare coverage, ask an accountant about this law. This Medicare deduction applies to people who are *on* Medicare, not to the Medicare tax all employees and self-employed individuals pay. Medicare tax is not health insurance, and is not deductible.

HEALTH INSURANCE FOR EMPLOYEES

Federal law requires employers with fifty or more full-time employees to provide health insurance for their employees.

Small employers are not required to purchase employee health insurance, and the truth is, for many small businesses, health insurance is prohibitively expensive. But providing employee health insurance, if you can afford it, will be a key selling point to attract and keep good workers. Health insurance is a major reason employees come, and stay. I often hear the story of some business that finds a good employee, trains the employee, and comes to depend on the employee, just to lose the person to another company that offers health benefits.

If you as an employer do pay for employee health insurance, premiums you pay for your employees, their spouses, and dependents are 100 percent deductible for you and not taxable to the employees. Employers with twenty-five or fewer full-time workers may also be eligible for a health coverage tax credit, to offset the cost of providing health insurance to your employees.

Instead of, or in addition to, health insurance for your employees, you can pay your employees' actual medical, dental, and eye care bills, and get a 100 percent deduction. Self-employed individuals cannot get a deduction for paying their own medical bills; they only have the deduction for medical insurance.

Although you can buy health insurance for your employees, you should not reimburse employees for health insurance they purchase for themselves. Reimbursements are considered taxable wages, and may be subject to an additional excise tax. Employers with fewer than fifty employees, however, can set up a program called a Health Reimbursement Arrangement (or HRA) that does reimburse employees for health insurance and medical bills, and that is tax deductible for the employer and tax-free to the employees.

Employee health insurance is deducted under "Employee Benefit Programs."

Spouse on payroll: If your spouse is an employee of your business, on the payroll with regular employee payroll deductions, your spouse *and* family—that is, you and your children—are eligible for full employee health benefits, and the cost is fully deductible as a business expense. You come under these "employee health insurance" rules, not the self-employed insurance rules. However, to get this deduction, all of your employees, if you have other employees, must be covered. Also, the IRS says that the spouse must be the primary insured on the policy, and premiums must be paid from the business bank account.

Putting your spouse on the payroll as a way to write off your own health insurance as a business deduction, and therefore lower your income and self-employment taxes, is a "loophole" in the law that is totally legal, but only if your spouse is doing real work in the business. The IRS sometimes disallows this deduction, claiming that the spouse is not really an employee doing real work, but only a tax maneuver to beat taxes you'd otherwise owe. I suggest talking to an accountant if this is in your plans.

Corporations: In a regular C corporation (not an S corporation), you and your family are eligible for tax-free employee health benefits, and your corporation is allowed a full deduction for the cost, but only if all of your employees are covered, not just yourself.

In an S corporation, health insurance for an owner-employee comes under the same rules as sole proprietors. Owner-employees of S corporations should purchase their own health insurance, separate from the business. An S corporation should not purchase health insurance for an owner-employee, because the IRS considers that insurance to be part of the owner-employee's wages, subject to all payroll taxes.

Nondeductible Expenses

Certain expenses are specifically disallowed by law and cannot be deducted, no way, no how:

1. Business expenses not meeting the ordinary, necessary, and "lavish" test.

2. Federal income tax and tax penalties.

3. State income taxes, except for C corporations, which can deduct state income taxes.

4. Fines or penalties for violation of the law. Even though you were parked while on business, you cannot deduct that parking ticket. Other business fines or penalties, if they don't involve breaking the law, are deductible.

5. Payments to yourself. The only way you may pay yourself a wage and deduct it as an expense is to incorporate.

6. Loan repayments. The loan was not income when received and is not an expense when paid. Interest on the loan is usually deductible.

7. Repaying an investor. Like a loan, an investment in a business is not income when received and is not an expense when paid.

8. Regular clothing. Uniforms, clothes with your company logo or advertisement, and clothes used exclusively for work that are unsuitable for street wear are deductible.

9. Regular meals at work; see "Meals" for exception).

10. Regular commuting expenses between your home and usual place of business.

11. Cost of land, until you sell it. Only the structure on the land may be depreciated.

12. Certain start-up expenses as explained above, under "Start-Up Expenses."

13. Club dues.

14. Purchase or lease of entertainment facilities or pleasure craft.

15. Charitable donations (except for corporations) and political donations. But see "Donations" for ways to deduct some of these donations.

16. Entertainment.

Self-Employment Tax

Self-employment tax, also known as SECA (Self-Employment Contributions Act), is combined Social Security and Medicare tax for business owners and self-employed individuals. Self-employment tax is based on your taxable profit from the business.

Sole proprietors, partners in partnerships, and active owners of limited liability companies are subject to self-employment tax (but see "Limited Liability Company" in the Growing Up chapter regarding self-employment tax on LLC members).

Self-employment tax is apart from and in addition to federal income tax. You may owe no income tax but still be liable for self-employment tax. Retirement deductions, deductions for health insurance, and the regular personal deductions and exemptions, which reduce income tax, cannot be used to reduce self-employment tax.

Self-employment tax often comes as quite a shock to new businesses. People, particularly in part-time and sideline businesses, are not making enough profit to worry about income taxes, but they never realize they may have a substantial self-employment tax bill.

Only "business income" is subject to self-employment tax. The difference between business and non-business income is explained in the Keeping Records chapter under "Defining Income."

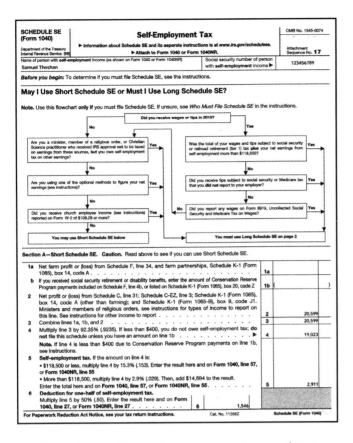

Special note: If your business profits are $400 or less, you do not have to pay any self-employment tax and can skip this entire chapter. If you net $401, you pay self-employment tax on the entire $401, not just the dollar over the $400 minimum (go back and round off those pennies). If you made $400 or less but want to pay self-employment tax, to increase your Social Security account, the IRS provides an optional method so you can pay into Social Security and Medicare. It is explained on the 1040-SE tax form.

Corporations: Self-employment tax is not imposed on corporations. If you own a small corporation, you are an employee of your business and pay regular Social Security and Medicare instead of self-employment tax.

FIGURING THE SELF-EMPLOYMENT TAX

The self-employment tax rate is 15.3 percent, combining 12.4 percent Social Security tax and 2.9 percent Medicare tax, on profits up to $128,400. On profits above $128,400, the tax rate is 2.9 percent. The maximum subject to the tax changes from year to year.

Your actual tax will be lower than these rates indicate, because of two deductions, one reducing the self-employment calculation, and a second reducing your taxable profit on your 1040 return.

The calculations are rather convoluted—you aren't surprised, are you?—but the tax forms lead you step by step through them (or just let your accountant figure it for you).

Self-employment tax is computed on your 1040 federal income tax return, using Form 1040-SE. If you have more than one unincorporated business, combine all profits and losses to figure self-employment tax. You file only one 1040-SE.

Spouses in business: If a married couple operates a business together, who pays self-employment tax depends on how the business is set up. If the business is a joint venture, a partnership, or an LLC, both spouses pay self-employment tax. Each spouse files his or her own Form 1040-SE. If the business is a sole proprietorship, only one spouse owns the business, and only one spouse pays self-employment tax. See "Married Couples" in the T.C.B.: Take Care of Business chapter.

Outside employment (you also hold a job): Self-employed people who are also holding jobs where Social Security and Medicare are withheld from their pay combine the two incomes, your job wages and your business profit, to arrive at the self-employment tax maximum. If the combined incomes are in excess of the Social Security $128,400 maximum, only a part of your business profit will be subject to self-employment tax. The 1040-SE tax form includes a calculation to determine how much of your profit is taxable.

For more information, see IRS Publication #553, "Information on Self-Employment Tax."

RETIREMENT DEDUCTIONS

The IRS allows you to invest a portion of your business profit in a retirement plan and pay no income tax on the money invested or the interest earned until you retire and withdraw the funds. There are several "tax-deferred" retirement plans, as the IRS calls them, available to self-employed individuals, business owners, and their employees. Some plans are like bank accounts, paying fixed interest. Some plans are investment arrangements, with possible risks. Some plans have setup and administration fees; some plans charge no fees at all.

Each plan has different contribution maximums (how much you can contribute every year), different income maximums, and different deadlines for making contributions.

You can choose one plan, or you may be able to set up multiple plans. Once a plan is set up, you are

	Maximum Contribution for Yourself	Minimum Contribution	50-or-Over Catch-up Contribution	Include employees?	Deadline
IRA	$5,500 (add'l $5,500 for spouse)	none	$1,000 (add'l $1,000 for spouse)	no	set up & contribute by tax return filing date (no extensions)
SEP (SEP-IRA)	25% or $55,000	none	none	yes	set up & contribute by tax return filing date (including any extensions)
SIMPLE	$25,000	none if no employees	$6,000	yes	set up by October 1, contribute by January 31
QUALIFIED 401k, Keogh	$55,000	varies	$6,000	yes	setup by last day of year, contribute by tax return filing date (including extensions)

not required to make additional contributions if you don't want to. You can skip a year, or several years, or not make any more contributions at all.

A caution about the plans described below: All of the plans except the IRA require that you include employees if you have employees, and pay a share of their contributions. If you have employees, you should investigate the requirements before starting a plan. Contributions you, as employer, make for your employees are tax deductible.

The maximum contributions listed below only apply to you, as the owner of your business. Contribution percentages and maximums for your employees are sometimes different. Contribution amounts change almost every year. Get advice from your accountant or your plan provider before setting up a plan.

Individual Retirement Arrangement (IRA)

The simplest plan is the IRA, short for Individual Retirement Arrangement, also known as a traditional IRA, original IRA, ordinary IRA, or regular IRA. Anyone can set up an IRA. There are no IRS fees or IRS forms to file, although many banks charge fees to set up and maintain IRA accounts. Employers are not required to include employees.

Traditional IRAs can take two different forms: (1) Individual Retirement Accounts, which are bank certificates of deposit (CDs): You deposit money, and it sits there and earns interest; or (2) Individual Retirement Annuities, which are investment accounts where the balance can go up or down depending on the type of investment.

One drawback to an IRA is that you cannot put a lot of money in it any one year. The maximum annual contribution is $5,500 ($11,000 if you have a non-working spouse) or your taxable earnings, whichever is less. This maximum amount changes from year to year, so you may be able to put more money into the IRA in future years. The maximum is reduced if you or your spouse has an outside job that includes a retirement plan. If you are fifty years old or older, the maximum annual contribution increases by $1,000 ($2,000 if your spouse is also fifty or over).

You can set up a new IRA any time during the year and right up to April 15 of the next year. Once the IRA is set up, each year you can decide if you want to add to the IRA or not. You have until April 15 of the following year to decide if you want to make additional contributions. You can change the contribution amount each year up to the maximum, or not contribute to the IRA at all. There are no minimum contribution requirements set by the IRS.

There is a different kind of IRA, called the Roth IRA (named after the senator who created it), where contributions are not tax deductible. You pay full tax on your business profit. But withdrawals from the Roth IRA, including the interest earned, are completely tax-free, just the reverse of the regular IRA. Roth IRAs have the same contribution requirements as traditional IRAs.

Simplified Employee Pension Plan (SEP)

Another easy-to-set-up IRS retirement plan is the SEP (also called a SEP-IRA). Although the plan is called an "employee" plan, you don't have to be an employee or have employees to open a SEP. Any self-employed person can set up a SEP. But if you do have employees, under a SEP you have to make contributions for employees who meet certain requirements. You, the employer, pay the full cost of the SEP plan for your employees. The contributions are not taxable to the employees.

Like an IRA, a SEP can be a deposit account or an investment annuity account. There are no administration fees or IRS forms to file. The maximum annual contribution is 25 percent of your net earnings, up to a maximum annual contribution of $55,000. This maximum changes from year to year. So, you can put a lot more money into a SEP each year than you can put into a traditional IRA.

You can set up or contribute to a SEP right up to the due date of your tax return: April 15 of the next year, or later if you file an extension. Like IRAs, SEPs have no minimum contribution requirements; you can change the contribution, or make no contribution at all, each year.

You can have both a SEP and an IRA.

SIMPLE Plan

SIMPLE stands for Savings Incentive Match Plan for Employees. Unfortunately, the rules are not all that simple. Like a SEP, the term *employee* includes self-employed individuals.

If you have no employees, you can set up a SIMPLE just for yourself and contribute up to $25,000 a year. The maximum contribution you can make depends on your income and how the plan is set up. If you are age fifty or older, you can contribute an additional $6,000 a year. There is no minimum annual contribution if you have no employees.

If you have employees, you, the employer, contribute to the plan on behalf of employees who meet the plan's requirements. Your employees can also contribute their own money if they choose to, but they are not required to do so. Whether your employees contribute or not, you the employer are required to contribute for them. How much the employer must contribute depends on how the plan is set up.

A SIMPLE has to be set up by October 1 of the current year. You must make contributions by January 31 of the new year.

Qualified Plans: 401(k) and Keogh

The term *qualified plans* actually refers to several different IRS-approved retirement plans, better known as 401(k) plans, Keogh plans, or HR10 plans. These plans also are known as defined benefit plans, defined contribution plans, money purchase plans, and profit-sharing plans.

Qualified plans are more complicated than other retirement plans—more paperwork, more forms to file, often more expensive to administer. Under a qualified plan, you can contribute up to $55,000 per year for yourself, plus an additional $6,000 per year if you are fifty years old or older. Computing the actual maximum contribution is a bit complicated, as it includes two separately computed contributions: an employer's and an employee's share. A self-employed individual is considered both employer and employee.

Under a qualified plan, if you have employees, you, the employer, contribute to the plan on behalf of employees who meet the plan's requirements. Employees can also make contributions for themselves. Some qualified plans have annual minimum contributions, some don't.

You must set up a qualified plan by year-end. You have until the due date of your tax return, including extensions, to make contributions.

More Details: All Retirement Plans

Withdrawals: Under all of the plans, you cannot withdraw money without penalty until age fifty-nine and a half. Some plans can be tapped penalty-free for medical bills, health insurance, buying a first home, or for college tuition.

Calculating income: For self-employed individuals, the income figure you use to calculate retirement contributions is not the full profit from your business. You reduce the profit by one-half of your self-employment tax. You also have to include your non-business income and losses in determining total income.

Start-up tax credit: You are allowed an annual tax credit of 50 percent of the cost of setting up and maintaining a retirement plan (administrative cost, not the cost of contributions to the plan) for the first three years, but only if you have at least one "non-highly compensated employee." If you are the only person in your retirement plan, you cannot take the credit. Maximum annual credit is $500.

Self-employment tax: Retirement plan contributions for yourself are not deductible for computing self-employment tax. You base self-employment tax on your business profit before the retirement contributions made for yourself.

State taxes: Not all states allow retirement deductions in calculating state income tax. You may still owe state income tax on your full profit.

Employers: If you want to set up a retirement plan just for yourself, without having to pay for your employees, many insurance companies offer non-qualifying plans. But under the non-qualifying plans (so called because they do not qualify for an income tax deduction), you pay regular income taxes on your entire business profit.

Corporations: A corporation cannot have an IRA or Keogh plan. SEPs, SIMPLEs, and 401(k) plans are available to all businesses.

Banks and insurance companies offer all of the above plans. The interest or return on investment will vary with different plans and contribution amounts. Be sure to ask if there are any fees or annual maintenance charges. For more information, see IRS Publication #590, "Individual Retirement Accounts," and Publication #560, "Retirement Plans for Small Business."

ESTIMATED TAX PAYMENTS

Once you are in business and filing tax returns, the IRS requires you to make quarterly prepayments of the current year's taxes if your federal tax for the current year, income and self-employment tax combined, is estimated to be $1,000 or more ($500 for corporations). The IRS wants your tax money just like the taxes withheld from employees' paychecks.

The four quarterly installments are due April 15, June 15, September 15, and the following January 15. You do not have to pay the fourth estimate if you file your tax return by January 31 and pay the balance due.

How do you estimate your taxes? You can base your estimate on your prior year's taxes, even if you were not in business then. Whatever your total tax came to last year, divide it by four and send the IRS four equal installments. If your total federal tax last year, income and self-employment tax combined, was less than $1,000, you are not required to make any estimated tax payments. If your income was over $150,000, or $75,000 for married couples filing separately (not filing a joint return), the estimate is 110 percent of last year's tax. If you base your estimates on the prior year's taxes, you must have been a U.S. citizen or resident for the entire previous year.

You have the option to estimate your taxes based on your current year's income. Four times a year, you figure your taxable income for that quarter and send in the correct tax. As you can imagine, this is not an easy task. Under this method you may be hit with an interest penalty if you underestimate by more than 10 percent.

When you compute your actual tax at year-end, any overpayment of estimated taxes will, at your option, either be refunded or applied to the following year's estimates.

If you pay low estimated tax or none at all, and if you are having a profitable year, be prepared when April 15 rolls around. You may have to come up with a lot of cash to pay this year's taxes and to pay next year's first quarterly estimate; both are due the same day. You may want to make voluntary estimated payments or set some money aside to cushion the blow.

Estimated taxes are filed on Form 1040-ES. If you have more than one business, you file one Schedule 1040-ES combining the taxes on all the businesses. C corporations (not S corporations) use Form 1120-W.

Working a day job: If you are holding a job where taxes are withheld by your employer, instead of filing a Schedule 1040-ES, you can have your withholding increased to cover the additional income and self-employment taxes. The IRS doesn't care whether it gets your money through withholding or through estimated payments. Obviously, this is something of a guessing game, not knowing how much extra to withhold. But like estimated taxes, any over-withholding will be refunded or, if you prefer, applied to the following year's taxes.

Form **1040-ES** Department of the Treasury Internal Revenue Service	**Estimated Tax**	**Payment Voucher 4**	OMB No. 1545-0074

File only if you are making a payment of estimated tax by check or money order. Mail this voucher with your check or money order payable to **"United States Treasury."** Write your social security number and **"2016 Form 1040-ES"** on your check or money order. Do not send cash. Enclose, but do not staple or attach, your payment with this voucher.

Calendar year—Due Jan. 17

Amount of estimated tax you are paying by check or money order.

Dollars	Cents
603	

Print or type

Your first name and initial Samuel	Your last name Thesham	Your social security number 123456789

If joint payment, complete for spouse

Spouse's first name and initial	Spouse's last name	Spouse's social security number

Address (number, street, and apt. no.)
P.O. Box 1240

City, state, and ZIP code. (If a foreign address, enter city, also complete spaces below.)
Willits, CA 95490

Foreign country name	Foreign province/county	Foreign postal code

For Privacy Act and Paperwork Reduction Act Notice, see instructions.　　　　　　Form 1040-ES

-9-

Farmers, fishermen, and fisherwomen who derive at least two-thirds of their total income from farming or fishing only have to make one estimated tax payment for the year, due January 15 of the new year. You do not have to pay the estimate if you file your tax return by March 1 and pay the balance due.

BARTER

"In the beginning, there was no money." But there always was the tax man, and barter does not escape his grasp. Barter transactions are taxable just like all other business transactions.

When you exchange or trade your business goods or services for someone else's goods or services, it is called *barter*. The "fair market value" of the goods or services you receive must be included in your regular business income and treated just like any other business income.

If the goods or services you receive are to be used in your business, you get a business write-off on your taxes, just as though you paid cash.

For example, let's say you are a cabinetmaker, and you build a custom cabinet for the person who owns the local office supply store. In exchange for the cabinet, you get $1,000 worth of "free" office equipment. You have taxable income of $1,000. If you use the equipment 100 percent for your business, you also have a $1,000 expense you can write off. If any of what you receive in trade is for personal, non-business use, the personal portion is not deductible. The owner of the office supply store also has $1,000 to report as business income. If the cabinet is used in the store, the store has a $1,000 business expense. If the cabinet is for the owner's home, the owner does not have a deductible expense.

If you provide services to your landlord for free or reduced rent—for example, a handyman doing maintenance, a painter, an artist creating decorations—the rent reduction is considered taxable wages.

If the exchange is valued at $600 or more, and if it includes services (not goods), the business receiving the service must report it to the IRS on Form 1099-MISC. This is the same law that applies to independent contractors; see "Hiring Help" in the Growing Up chapter.

If you are bartering for services, be careful that the person providing the service is not an employee in disguise, one who should be on the books with payroll deductions, workers' compensation insurance, and the rest. An employee who gets paid in goods or services, instead of cash, is still an employee. The "fair market value" of the goods or services the employee receives is considered wages, 100 percent taxable.

If you join a barter club, exchange, or network, the rules are basically the same. But you recognize the income at the time you receive the "barter credits," even if you haven't yet "spent" them. Barter organizations are required to report all transactions to the IRS.

If you trade in bitcoins or other cryptocurrencies (virtual currencies), the IRS considers this to be barter. If you are paid in bitcoins, the income you report is the market value of the coins at the time of the transaction. If you purchase anything with bitcoins, your deductible expense is the fair market value of the goods or services you are getting in exchange for the bitcoins. The IRS has announced that they plan to examine every bitcoin transaction, suspicious of black market operations and tax evasion. Tread carefully.

In most IRS audits of businesses, one of the first questions often is, "Do you engage in trade or barter?" A yes answer is a red flag to expand the scope of the audit.

NET OPERATING LOSSES (NOL)

If your business suffers a loss this year you will owe no income tax on the business, which I'm sure you know. You may not know that this loss will also offset other income, such as a salary from an outside job or your spouse's wages, to reduce this year's income tax.

You can also use this year's loss to offset income and reduce taxes in future years. If the current year's income (if you have income from other sources) is not sufficient to absorb the entire loss, you may carry the balance forward to apply to as many as twenty future years.

Net operating loss (NOL) is not simply the business loss shown on your tax return. It is a complicated combination of business and non-business income and deductions. NOL calculations are complex, and there's no way to simplify the procedure. Step-by-step instructions are in IRS Publication #536, "Net Operating Losses." Don't be put off by their complexity; the NOL deduction may save you a bundle in income taxes.

Farmers: If you have an NOL, you can, at your option, carry the loss back two years and obtain a refund of prior years' taxes.

Examining Your Loss

Saving on income taxes because your business lost money is a consolation prize of sorts, but you are still losing money. If you don't know why, it's time to stop and figure out why. You need to determine whether you can turn the business around or

whether you should pack it in and try something else. "Businesses always lose money the first year" is not a good answer, and isn't true. If you are puzzled, get help. Hire an accountant for an hour's worth of advice. It will be worth every penny.

Lost Income

If you don't get paid by a customer or client for products or services you provided, you have a loss for sure, but you cannot deduct that loss on your tax return. Lost income is not a tax-deductible expense. The income was never recorded on your income ledgers.

YEAR-END TAX STRATEGIES

Put a little Post It note on the front cover of this book to remind yourself to read this section somewhere around the first of December. If you act before January 1, you may be able to juggle your income and expenses to decrease your taxable profit, and your taxes, for the year just ending. Here are several year-end strategies:

Income: If you are on the cash basis (see "Cash Accounting versus Accrual" in the Keeping Records chapter), you can reduce this year's taxable income, and this year's taxes, by waiting until the new year to bill your customers, or by encouraging your customers to pay their bills after the new year. Cash-basis businesses do not report income until they receive it. Even though you earned the money in December, if you get paid in January the income is considered January's income, and the taxes on it are delayed a full year. On the other hand, if your tax bill is already about zero for the current year, you may want to try to get paid by December 31, so next year's income and taxes will be lower. This year to year shuffling of income does not apply to businesses using accrual accounting.

By the way, if you receive a check in December but don't deposit or cash it until January, it is still December income. As far as the IRS is concerned, you were paid when you got the check.

Paying bills: Cash-basis businesses can accelerate, or delay, making payments on bills you owe. Pay the bills by December 31 and get a deduction this year; or pay the bills after January 1, and get the deduction next year. But there are some quirky IRS rules about when an expense can be deducted:

Checks: Checks written and mailed or delivered by December 31 can be deducted the year written, even if cashed in the new year. Don't hold on to that check. It has to be sent off by December 31 to get the deduction this year. If you wait until January to mail or deliver the check, you can deduct the expense next year.

Credit cards: Any charges to a bank credit card (VISA, MasterCard, Discover, or American Express) are deductible the year incurred, even if the bill is not paid until next year. This rule, however, does not apply to charges made to store or gasoline company credit cards. Those charges are deducted when you pay the bill.

Debit cards: Payments by debit card are the same as payments by cash. The year you charge the card is the year you get the deduction.

Automatic payments: Bills paid automatically that are deducted from your bank account (not charged to a credit card) are written off the year your bank deducts the money from your account. If you get an automatic billing late in December but it's not processed by your bank until January, the expense cannot be deducted until the next year. If the automatic billing is to your credit card, you can write off the expense the year the card was charged, even if you paid the credit card bill the following year.

Business assets: Business assets purchased and placed in use can be written off the year of purchase (within limits; see "Business Assets"). A new computer, business equipment, office furniture, even a vehicle, can be purchased right up to December 31 and get the full deduction. If you are short on cash, you can finance your purchase, pay for it next year, and still get the full deduction this year. Or, if you don't need any more deductions this year, postpone your purchases until January.

Inventory: If you need to restock your shelves or if you are running low on parts, you can deduct the cost of inventory the year of purchase.

Supplies: Stock up on and pay for business and computer supplies, postage, stationery, and other consumables, and write off the entire expense in the current year.

Monthly bills: Pay your January monthly bills in December and take a deduction in the current year. Most monthly bills are deducted the month paid regardless of what year they apply to, but there are important exceptions. See "Prepaid Expenses."

Annual contracts: If you are planning to sign up for a service that lasts up to a year—a new insurance policy, cell phone contract, maintenance contract—start and pay for the service in December and write off the entire amount in December, even though most of the contract is for the next year. See "Prepaid Expenses."

Retirement plan: December 31 is the deadline for setting up a new Keogh or 401(k) plan (a qualified plan), although you do not have to make contributions to the plans until the next year.

Hire your kids for the holidays: If you need extra help in December, and kids are on school vacation, put them to work in the business. Generally, a child under the age of eighteen can earn up to $12,000 a year tax-free, and you, the parent-employer, get a full tax deduction. The rules are explained under "Family Employees" in the Growing Up chapter.

Employee bonuses: Give your hardworking employees a year-end bonus. The bonus is taxable to your employees as wages, but you get an income tax deduction, and you generate a lot of goodwill from the people you rely on. The bonus is deductible for you, and taxable to your employees, the year it is paid. Only C corporations can pay year-end bonuses in January and still get a deduction for the prior year.

Tax law changes: For the last few years, Congress has had the irritating habit of changing tax laws late in the year and making them retroactive for the entire year. If you are spending money on something that has a tax deduction dollar limitation, check the latest IRS updates on their website, or ask your accountant to see if those limitations were increased.

After-Year-End Strategies

After December 31, there are still things you can do to reduce taxes for the year just ended:

Business assets: If you are depreciating equipment, furniture, machinery, or other business assets, if any of these assets are no longer functioning, are worthless, obsolete, broken, or missing (*missing?*), you can write off the entire balance (the undepreciated cost) on your taxes for the year just ended. See "Depreciation." If you've already written off the assets, or if you took the first-year write-off, there is no further tax deduction.

Retirement accounts: You can open and contribute to an IRA or a SEP (or both) up until your tax return filing date: April 15 for the IRA, extended date for the SEP. You pay no income tax on the contributions until you withdraw the money. See "Retirement Deductions."

Bad debts (for accrual businesses only): Take a good look at your accounts receivable, what your customers or clients owe you. If any are uncollectible, you can write them off and take a bad-debts loss for the year just ended, but only if you recorded the income in your income ledger. If you don't record income until you receive it (cash method), you cannot take a bad-debts write-off. See "Bad Debts" above.

Examine expenses: One almost sure way to reduce your taxes is to reexamine every purchase, every expense you made during the year. Make sure you've taken all the business tax deductions you are entitled to. The IRS is never going to tell you about a deduction you forgot to take, and your tax accountant is not likely to take the time to ask you about every possible tax deduction you might have. It's entirely up to you. Well, you and me. My guidebook on tax deductions, *475 Tax Deductions for Businesses and Self-Employed Individuals*, lists hundreds of legitimate tax deductions and tax credits, many more than I could fit in this chapter of *Small Time Operator*.

TAX CREDITS

Tax credits are special tax incentives created by Congress to stimulate the economy or to encourage businesses to act in socially or environmentally responsible ways. Unlike regular business deductions that reduce your profit, tax credits directly reduce your income taxes, dollar for dollar. They can be a real gold mine.

Tax credits come and go, available one year and not the next. If you fail to take a tax credit you are entitled to, the IRS will not tell you.

Last year, there were tax credits for buying electric vehicles; producing alcohol fuel; using alternative fuels; off-road vehicle use; research and development; providing low-income housing; making your business more accessible to disabled people; producing electricity from renewable resources; hiring and keeping employees who meet certain eligibility requirements; payroll taxes paid on employee tips; employers who pay for employees' adoption expenses; providing health insurance to your employees; rehabilitating old buildings and historic structures; investing in certain "economically challenged" communities; paying foreign income taxes; and railroad track maintenance.

Tax credits do not reduce your business income or your self-employment tax. The credits are listed on your 1040 form, not on Schedule C. Some credits also appear on partnership or corporation returns.

IRS Publication #334, "Tax Guide for Small Business," lists the tax credits currently available.

TAX SOFTWARE

Tax preparation software can organize your income and expense records so they match tax return categories, compare tax options, and prepare your entire tax return.

But business taxes can be quite complicated, as you know. It would take a clever and sophisticated program, and one without bugs, to know just the right questions to ask. The software would have to be fully up to date for the latest changes to tax law, which come constantly. And like any other software, you need to learn how to use it. This may be a lot of work considering you will be using that tax software only once; next year, the laws will be different.

I have talked to several tax accountants about tax software, and every one of them thinks you'd be making a mistake to trust your business tax return to a computer program, one that may or may not include all the peculiarities of small business tax law and your particular business.

Now, I admit that accountants would lose a lucrative chunk of their income if people started using software instead of them, but their warnings are valid. A face-to-face discussion with a tax accountant is much more likely to turn up tax savings than typing answers to formula questions on your computer. An accountant can spot possible problems you might avoid, by rewording an answer to a question, or relabeling an expense, or maybe by not claiming some deduction that might be a red flag to the IRS.

An accountant can show you how you might do things differently next year, to reduce future tax bills. An accountant can answer your questions, without you having to filter them through some search function or FAQs.

Of course, I am an accountant . . .

FAILURE TO FILE A TAX RETURN

I would like to cover an area about which I have received a surprisingly large number of questions over the years: What if someone has been in business a few years and never filed a tax return? It's rarely a case of intentional dishonesty. A typical example is a craftsperson who starts out with a hobby. At Christmas, he sells a few hundred dollars' worth of merchandise, and he never thinks of his craft as a business. But now, two or three years have passed, and he realizes that $10,000 or $20,000 a year is going through his bank account, and he's never filed a tax return. Now what?

Contrary to what many people think, the Internal Revenue Service is not all-powerful nor all seeing. Their computers are not set up for Big Brother snooping—not yet, anyway. The IRS will not know you have earned money unless you or someone else reports it to them. For most Americans, this information comes to the IRS on a Form W-2, report of income of employees, or on a report of bank account interest.

A self-employed person is most likely to be known to the IRS via something called a Form 1099-MISC, report of income paid an individual other than an employee. If you sell your services to another business (not goods, just services) and that business paid you $600 or more during one year, they are required to file a Form 1099-MISC, notifying the IRS that you have received this money. Limited liability companies also receive 1099-MISC forms. If you are an independent sales agent and you purchase $5,000 or more in goods for resale, from one company in one year, that company will report the purchase to the IRS on a 1099-MISC form. If you accept credit and debit cards, your sales will be reported to the IRS on a 1099-K form. If you receive large payments (at least $20,000, and two hundred or more payments) from PayPal or a web seller like Amazon, those payments will be reported on a 1099-K form. If a 1099 is filed for you, the business that files the 1099 must send you a copy of the form.

If you receive a Form 1099, the IRS has your name. If the amounts paid exceed the minimum requirements for filing, you are likely to get a letter of inquiry or possibly even a tax bill.

Forms you yourself file might alert the IRS to your existence, such as employment reports, sales tax reports, even state tax returns.

If no one reports you, and if you file no reports or other documents, the IRS will probably not know of your existence. Probably. But you are breaking the law, and there is no statute of limitations on how many years later they can come after you.

The law says, and I recommend, that you file returns for all those prior years, and pay the back taxes, interest, and penalties. Some people will just go on their merry way and never file and never be found; we've all heard of someone with that kind of experience. Other delinquent folk may decide that this is the year to file their first return, and let the prior years lie, hopefully, unnoticed.

THE INTERNAL REVENUE SERVICE AND YOU

Small Time Operator is not a manual for beating the IRS at their own game, nor is it intended to be another "101 Ways to Reduce Your Taxes." Still, a general knowledge of the Internal Revenue Service and its inner workings may benefit you in your dealings with the agency, and may even add to your peace of mind.

Most people, including most small businesses, file their tax returns and never get audited. The IRS audits less than 2 percent of all small businesses. IRS agents have to earn their keep, and they are not going to be nickel-and-diming every little business that files a return. In almost all instances, returns selected for audit are those obviously out of line with the IRS's idea of the "norm."

The IRS does sometimes conduct random audits, and they are a nightmare if you are selected, but the audits are truly random, and there is no predicting who will be among the chosen few.

All tax returns, big and small, are automatically checked on IRS computers for mathematical errors: addition, multiplication, tax computation. If there is an arithmetical error, you will be notified of the error and any change in your taxes due to it. This is not an audit; and if you make an error, it does not increase your chances of being audited.

Tax returns are checked against other documents sent to the IRS, particularly W-2s, 1099 forms, and other "information returns." If your tax return does not include income that was reported to the IRS on a W-2 or 1099 form, you may get an inquiry, or even a tax bill, from the IRS. This will not usually result in an audit if the discrepancy is resolved and any additional taxes paid.

Factors that will increase the likelihood of an audit include:

1. A loss or very low profit year after year, several years in a row.

People get very nervous when talking to the IRS and don't know when to be quiet. When a simple yes or no will do, they go into a whole explanation of all kinds of things that the agent doesn't need to hear.

—Accountant Howard Rosenbloom

2. Unusual or unreasonable expenses. Large expenses not usually found in your type of business. Large deductions for travel away from home. If you are taking a deduction for a large, unusual expense or for an expense that may be suspect, such as travel, you might include a statement with your tax return explaining the deduction and include written documentation to prove the validity of the expense. This is not required or even suggested by the IRS, but it might help you avoid an audit if an IRS agent winds up looking at your return. Ask your accountant about this.

3. Claiming 100 percent use of a business auto.

4. Estimated numbers. The IRS is suspicious of round numbers; they sound made-up.

5. Whether you've been audited before. If you have been audited in the past and wound up owing more tax, your chances of being audited again are increased. On the other hand, if prior audits did not result in more tax, you probably will not get audited again.

6. Businesses that deal mostly in cash, such as coin laundromats, vending machine operators, arcades, and many taxicabs. The IRS believes that cash businesses have a higher degree of "noncompliance" (i.e., cheating) than other businesses. What you write in the "occupation" box and the business code number on your tax return may affect your chance of being audited.

7. If you were audited by your state. The IRS has an agreement with most states to exchange tax information. If your state tax return was audited, the state may notify the IRS about the results of the audit.

8. Taking a deduction for the corporate jet.

9. Telling the IRS that the income tax is unconstitutional.

Home businesses: A lot of people think that home-based businesses (those claiming a home-office deduction) are more likely to be audited. In my experience, this is not true. A home business is no more likely to be audited than any other small business, unless the home office deduction is large compared to the size and income of the business. Any unreasonable or out-of-line deduction could trigger an audit.

Business Loss and Hobby Losses

A loss on your tax return is by no means a sure cause for audit. It is not uncommon for new businesses to show a loss the first year or two, with high start-up costs and early, slow business.

A warning, however, to people who manage to show a business loss year after year: If you do not show a profit for at least three out of five consecutive years, the IRS, if it audits you, might rule that your business is not really a business, but a hobby. The IRS treats any income from a hobby as taxable income, but losses are not deductible. By contrast, a business loss is deductible. (If you breed, train, race, or show horses, the IRS hobby loss test is two out of seven years instead of three out of five.)

The Hobby Loss rule is not a firm rule. A business can deduct losses for several years in a row without ever being challenged by the IRS. In the event of an audit, the IRS will allow the ongoing losses if they are convinced that you are operating a real business and trying, though unsuccessfully, to make a profit. The key issue is intent. What are you really doing? Trying to earn some money, or just having fun? It will help if your business looks like a business—business licenses, income and expense records, bank account, business cards—and if you're devoting time to it in a businesslike manner.

Notice of an Audit

Your first notice of an audit will be a letter from the IRS informing you of the audit and the year or years to be examined. Now before you panic, keep in mind that the IRS often sends letters to taxpayers regarding errors they find on tax returns, correcting the errors, and sending a bill for additional taxes or a refund for overpayment. This is *not* an audit and does not increase the likelihood of an audit. Also, the IRS never calls taxpayers on the phone about audits or tax money owed. If you get a phone call from someone claiming to be an IRS agent, hang up. You're being scammed.

If you do get a real audit notice in the mail, it may ask you to come in person to a meeting with an agent or merely to send in written information. The IRS may want to see a bill or proof of payment to support a specific expense, or they may want to see your entire set of records. You may be asked to

---

People will do silly things to avoid taxes.
—J. C. Small, attorney, New Jersey Division of Taxation

"You're saying that as a professional writer, your expenses totaled $22,000 more than your income? What kind of way is that to make a living?"

supply copies of your prior years' tax returns. The auditor may want to visit your business. The auditor may visit your website or Facebook page looking for information that may indicate how much money you're making and possibly not reporting. If you're reporting business losses, maybe you don't want to put a photo of your new Ferrari on the internet.

When audited, you may be required to prove the accuracy of your income and expenses, supplying bank statements, invoices, or whatever else the IRS requests. Federal law requires you to keep adequate records to support your numbers, and the IRS has the legal right to examine those records. If you can't provide documentation for a deduction, the IRS can disallow it. The tax court will sometimes overrule the IRS and allow deductions without any records, but you really don't want to be in that situation.

If you are audited, it may be a costly decision to face the IRS without an accountant there to help. IRS agents are trained to ask leading questions in order to get information from you that may increase your tax bill or lead to an expanded audit. A good accountant knows what to expect and can help answer questions, honestly and legally, but in a way that may avoid unnecessary trouble. The accountant can possibly help narrow the scope of the audit. The accountant can arrange to meet the auditor at the IRS office or the accountant's office instead of your own business location.

The accountant, being a professional and used to dealing with IRS agents, can defuse any personal animosity. Business owners often get angry at IRS agents. And IRS agents, being human beings, are sometimes harder on people who are unable to control themselves. A little politeness can go a long way in helping an audit along.

Federal income tax laws and their legal interpretations fill entire bookshelves. Small business law by itself is full of special rules, exceptions to those rules, and tax court rulings overthrowing or restricting those rules. IRS agents are tax experts, but they do occasionally make mistakes. Honest mistakes, I'm sure. But if you don't know the law, you don't know if the IRS agent is right or wrong when he says that you cannot deduct some expense you thought you could. A good tax accountant, one experienced in small business, knows those rules inside and out. I have saved some of my tax clients lots of money by being at the audit, tax books in hand, showing an IRS agent that his ruling is incorrect.

If the audit goes against you, and you still feel you are in the right, the IRS provides all taxpayers an elaborate system of appeals, starting with informal meetings with agents and going right up to the Supreme Court.

IRS Penalties

Generally, no penalties are assessed where there is an honest mistake on a tax return. You will owe only the back taxes and interest, as long as you pay up when the IRS says to pay up.

There are a large variety of IRS penalties, some mild and some severe, for various offenses: Failure to file. Failure to pay. Negligence. "Intentional disregard of rules and regulations without intent to defraud." And "Willful attempt to evade or defeat taxes," which means fraud. Where fraud is involved, the IRS can impose both civil and criminal penalties. Civil penalties (fines) can be imposed in the normal course of an audit. Criminal penalties (large fines and jail) may only be imposed after full due process of law.

If you cannot afford to pay the taxes when your tax return is due, file the return on time anyway. The penalties will be less. Quite often, the IRS will waive penalties where failure to file a return or failure to pay the tax is due to "reasonable cause."

Except for special situations, the general statute of limitations, the length of time the IRS has to audit a return and assess back taxes, is three years from the time the return is filed. If you omit more than 25 percent of your income, the statute of limitations is increased to six years. If your return is "false or fraudulent" or if no return is filed, there is no time limit. Most IRS audits, however, are initiated within eighteen months of filing the return. If you haven't heard from them by then, you probably won't.

This chapter is full of vague terms: reasonable cause; without intent to defraud; intentional disregard of rules and regulations; willful attempt to evade; "unusual" this and "unreasonable" that. Many people make their living arguing over these and other godawful terms. As with so many other legal situations, the words often wind up meaning whatever the agent or the judge wants them to mean. This is not an area for amateurs. If you are caught up in an audit involving these issues, your philosophy and your finances will have to dictate your reactions. Good luck.

Amending Old Tax Returns

There may be gold in old income tax returns. Two facts few people know: (1) Most business income tax returns, especially small business returns, have errors no one, not even the IRS, discovered; and (2) You may amend prior years' tax returns and get refunds of overpaid taxes.

The IRS catches glaring and obvious errors on tax returns: mistakes in addition or tax computation, missing forms, entries on the wrong line, improper procedures. Beyond the obvious, unless you get audited—and less than 2 percent of small business tax returns are audited—your return will be accepted as is, errors and all.

How do you know if there is an error or omission on your tax return? If you prepared the return yourself, there's probably an error. The tax laws are so complex, even the experts don't know it all. Unless you studied the tax laws thoroughly, you probably missed something.

If you took your taxes to one of those tax chains or storefront tax operations, your return was probably prepared by someone with little experience and brief training. These people do not take the time to look into your business finances in search of tax savings. If the tax preparer took your numbers and asked few or no questions, chances are good your return is not all it could be.

The most common omissions and errors I've found on business tax returns are: Not taking tax credits you are entitled to. Failing to accrue expenses at year-end. Incorrectly computing depreciation. And overlooking legitimate business expenses that didn't get into your expense records or your business checkbook, such as out-of-pocket cash payments, business expenses paid out of your personal checking account, automobile expenses, home office expenses, purchases that are partly personal and partly business, bank service charges, and equipment and furniture used in your business but purchased prior to starting your business

If you find or suspect an error or omission, ask your accountant about it. If you prepared your own return or if it was prepared by someone of questionable competence, locate an experienced accountant (see "Professional Help" in the T.C.B.: Take Care of Business chapter), and ask the accountant to look over your return. Most accountants will give it at least a glance. Some will catch and correct an error. Others will want to redo the entire return; they're less likely to make a mistake if they are not working from someone else's mistake.

Tax returns are amended on Form 1040-X for sole proprietorships, 1120-X for regular corporations, 1120-S (marked "Amended") for S corporations, and 1065 (marked "Amended") for partnerships and LLCs. Refunds are fairly prompt.

Amended tax returns must be filed within three years from the date you filed your original return or within two years from the time you paid your tax, whichever is later. A return filed early is considered filed on the due date. So for 2017 tax returns filed and paid on time (April 15, 2018) or ahead of time, you have until April 15, 2021, to amend the return.

If your federal return was in error, your state return was probably also in error. States have similar procedures for amending returns. Some states require you to amend the state return if you amend your federal return.

An amended return is more likely to get reviewed by an IRS or state tax auditor. My experience, however, is that amended returns are not more likely to be audited than original returns. Still, if the refund is only a small amount, maybe you should just skip it. Why chance involving the IRS in your business if you're only getting a few bucks?

Information Returns

Certain business transactions must be reported to the IRS on special "information returns." These reports are not tax returns, and no taxes are paid with them. In most cases, you also give a copy of the information return to all parties involved in the transactions. Many, but not all, states require similar information returns to be filed with the state.

Below are the federal information returns currently required:

Outside services. Businesses paying $600 or more a year in fees, commissions, or prizes to a nonemployee, independent contractor, sole proprietor, or a limited liability company file Form 1099-MISC.

Independent sales agents. Businesses selling $5,000 or more a year of consumer products to an outside sales agent file Form 1099-MISC.

Rent payments. Businesses paying $600 or more a year in rent (for business premises, machinery, or equipment) file Form 1099-MISC.

Tips. Restaurants with more than ten employees earning tips file Form 8027.

Payments to lawyers. Any payment to a lawyer must be reported on Form 1099-MISC.

Interest payments. If you pay $600 or more in interest in any calendar year on a business debt, report the payment on Form 1099-INT.

Interest received. If your business receives $600 or more of mortgage interest from an individual in a calendar year, report the income to the IRS on Form 1098.

Real estate transactions. The person responsible for closing real estate transactions (usually the title company, but sometimes the broker) files Form 1099-S with the IRS.

Royalty payments. If you pay $10 or more in royalties to one person in a calendar year, report the payment to the IRS on Form 1099-MISC.

Dividend payments. Corporations paying $10 or more in dividends report each payment to the IRS on Form 1099-DIV.

Owners or operators of fishing boats. Report all payments to crew members on proceeds from sale of catch on Form 1099-MISC.

Fish resellers. If you buy more than $600 of fish from fishing boats, report the payments on Form 1099-MISC.

Lenders. If you lend money in connection with your business, and in full or partial satisfaction of the debt, you acquire an interest in property secured for the debt, file Form 1099-A.

Stockbrokers. Report sales of stocks, bonds, commodities, etc., on Form 1099-B.

Renters paying $600 or more a year file 1099-MISC.

Medical expenses. Businesses paying $600 directly to a physician file Form 1099-MISC.

Employers with fifty or more employees report health coverage for each employee on Form 1095-C.

Promoters of tax shelters must report all transactions to the IRS.

Large cash transactions. Businesses that receive $10,000 or more in cash (currency), money orders, traveler's or cashier's checks (but not personal or business checks) in a single transaction or in two or more related transactions, report it to the IRS on Form 8300.

Suspicious activity. Businesses that issue or redeem money orders or traveler's checks of $2,000 or more that seem to be "suspicious" (whatever that means) must report the transaction to the IRS within thirty days on Suspicious Activity Report Form TD-F-90-22.56. Welcome to the United States of America, Home of the Brave, Land of the Free.

FEDERAL EXCISE TAX

Most small businesses are not liable for federal excise taxes.

Excise taxes are imposed on manufacturers of trucks, truck trailers, truck parts, tires, inner tubes, fishing equipment, outboard motors, bows, arrows, firearms, ammunition, coal, gasoline and gasohol, lubricating oils, and cars that do not meet fuel economy standards; on businesses operating aircraft; on businesses using fuel in inland waterways; on retailers of heavy trucks and trailers; on retailers of diesel, gasoline substitutes, noncommercial aviation and marine fuels; on tanning salons and services (people tanning, not animal hides). The excise tax is payable quarterly on Form 720, "Quarterly Federal Excise Tax Return."

Excise taxes are also imposed on brewers; on wholesale and retail beer, wine, and liquor dealers; on manufacturers of stills; on tobacco; and on importers and dealers in firearms. These excise taxes are paid on Form 11.

A highway motor vehicle federal use tax is imposed on owners of large highway trucks, truck trailers, and buses. Form 2290 is filed annually. For more information, see IRS Publication #349, "Federal Highway Use Tax."

Businesses that are required to file excise tax returns must have an Employer Identification Number (EIN) even if you are not an employer. Log on to IRS.gov or fill out Form SS-4 to request a number.

Some states call their corporate income tax an excise tax, not to be confused with these federal excise taxes.

For more information on excise taxes, see IRS Publication #510, "Excise Taxes."

STATE AND LOCAL TAXES

A list of state and local taxes would be endless. If you're doing anything to try to make a living, it's taxable, often multiple times by multiple government agencies. You should make an effort to find out about your state and local tax laws on small businesses. Look on their sites, call government offices, ask other business owners, ask your accountant. You don't want to be caught by surprise or hit with some whopping penalty for failure to file a tax return you didn't know about.

Below is a list of some of the more common state and local taxes. With the exception of some income taxes, state and local taxes are tax deductible.

State Income Taxes

As of last year, every state had some form of income tax on resident unincorporated businesses except Alaska, Florida, Nevada, New Hampshire, South Dakota, Tennessee, Texas, Wyoming, and Washington, though New Hampshire has a "business profits tax," which is really an income tax. All states except Nevada, Washington, and Wyoming have an income tax or a franchise tax (a form of income tax) on corporations.

Most states compute state tax as a percentage of your federal income tax, or based on a percentage of the income shown on your federal return. A few states have income tax rules just different enough from the federal rules to require separate calculations.

State income taxes, like federal income taxes, are based on your net income (net profit). Total income less deductible expenses gives you net income.

Generally, states allow businesses to deduct the same expenses as the IRS allows, with a few important exceptions: Depreciation rules and charitable contribution rules are sometimes different. Some states do not make allowances for net operating loss carryforward or have different years allowed for carryforward. Self-employment tax is a federal tax only, although some states allow a deduction for it. Not all states allow the same nontaxable retirement contributions the IRS allows. Many states offer tax credits, reducing state income taxes; some of these credits are similar to federal credits, some are completely different.

Federal income taxes are deductible on state returns in many states. State income taxes are deductible on state returns in a few states. State income taxes are deductible on federal tax returns for C corporations only.

Most state income tax returns for calendar-year taxpayers are due April 15. Five states have later due dates: Delaware, April 30; Hawaii, April 20; Iowa, April 30; Louisiana, May 15; Virginia, May 1. Many states have extended due dates to file returns, three to six months, if the taxes are paid by the original due dates.

Corporations: The above due dates are for unincorporated businesses. Corporate due dates vary considerably from state to state. Many states require corporations to file state income tax returns a month earlier than the federal return.

State Gross Receipts Taxes

A gross receipts tax is a tax on total business receipts—sales, income—before any deductions for expenses. The tax is in addition to any income or sales tax.

Some states call their sales tax a gross receipts tax, but the tax referred to here is not a sales tax. Sales tax is collected from your customers. Gross receipts taxes are paid out of your own pocket. As of last year, the following states had a gross receipts or other unusual tax, on small businesses:

Alabama has a Business Privilege Tax, varying from 25¢ to $1.75 per $1,000 of business net worth, with a minimum tax of $100.

Alaska has a gross receipts tax on the fishing industry.

Delaware has a gross receipts tax called a Merchants and Manufacturers Tax. The amount is $75, plus a varying percentage (under 1 percent) of receipts in excess of $100,000 a month.

Michigan has a 0.8 percent gross receipts tax on business income.

Nevada has a Commerce Tax ranging from 0.051 to 0.331 percent of gross revenue.

New Hampshire has a Business Profits Tax, 7.9 percent of the profits on your federal tax return if your business grossed more than $50,000. New Hampshire also has a Business Enterprise Tax of 0.675 percent of the business's tax base, but only for businesses grossing $208,000 or more, or having a tax base (value) of $104,000 or more.

Ohio has a Commercial Activity Tax. Businesses with gross receipts from $150,000 to $1 million pay $150. Above $1 million sales, the tax increases.

South Dakota has a 2 percent Excise Tax on some building contractors, and a 4 percent Excise Tax on farm machinery.

Tennessee has a State Business Tax on a variety of businesses and at varying rates.

Texas has a Business Margin Tax varying from 0.375 to 0.75 percent.

Washington has a Business and Occupations gross receipts tax varying from 0.47 percent to 1.5 percent, depending on type of business. Washington also has an Enhanced Fish Tax, a gross receipts tax on the fishing industry.

West Virginia has a one-time Business Registration tax of $30. West Virginia also has a gross receipts tax on soft drinks.

Other State Taxes

Many, but not all, states tax:

1. Manufacturers, wholesalers, and retailers of alcoholic beverages, fuels, tobacco, motor vehicles, boats, and airplanes.

2. Mining, logging, forest land, and real estate dealings.

3. Admissions on theaters, amusement parks, clubs, music halls, horse racing, boxing, and other entertainment venues.

4. Recycling and disposal of petroleum products, air conditioner and refrigerator coolants, video monitors and televisions, tires, and other environmentally unfriendly trash.

5. Freight, delivery, transportation, and tour bus companies.

6. Chain stores, for businesses with more than one location.

7. Hotel and motel room rentals.

8. Grain handlers and processors.

9. Financial and investment businesses.

10. Car rental businesses.

11. Some states have state business licenses and annual fees, sometimes called a "business privilege tax."

Local Taxes

Counties (parishes in Louisiana) almost always impose property taxes, also called *ad valorem taxes*, on real estate.

He says we're free.

Some counties impose a "personal property" tax on business assets such as equipment, furniture, and tools, and it can be quite high if your assets are assessed at a high value. Examine this tax bill. Make sure retired or sold assets are not included, and that older assets are not overvalued.

Some counties impose an inventory tax, sometimes called a "floor" tax, which is a property tax on business inventory on hand at a given date, or based on an average inventory over the last twelve months.

Some large cities impose income taxes, gross receipts taxes, and/or sales taxes on businesses. These taxes are in addition to any similar state tax.

Many cities impose business licenses on all businesses. A few cities impose a flat "business tax" or "business registration fee" in addition to the regular business license. Your business may have to pay special sewage or disposal fees.

It is our Patriotic Duty to keep as much money out of the hands of our government as we can.

—Philosopher Walter Camp

The best thing Congress can do is go home for a couple of years.

—Will Rogers

Chapter Five

HOME-BASED BUSINESS

Once a month I venture into rush-hour traffic to remind myself of what I'm missing.
—Jeannette Scollard,
SCS Manufacturing

HOME, INC.: STARTING A HOME-BASED BUSINESS

I'd guess that on every city block and on every rural road in the United States, someone is operating a business out of a home.

Some of the largest and best known businesses in the United States were started in someone's home. Bill Hewlett and David Packard started their legendary company in Mr. Hewlett's garage. Walt Disney created Mickey and Donald and the Walt Disney Company at his kitchen table. William Harley and the Davidson brothers started their motorcycle business in a shed in the Davidson backyard. Steve Jobs started Apple Computer in his home; Bill Gates started Microsoft in his. Mrs. Fields started her cookie business at home. Jeff Bezos founded Amazon.com in his apartment in Seattle.

According to the U.S. Small Business Administration, 56 percent of all businesses in the United States are home based, and they generate $102 billion in annual revenue. The U.S. Department of the Census and the U.S. Bureau of Labor Statistics report that there are over ten million full-time home-based businesses in the United States, and an additional nine million part-time and sideline home businesses. Despite the huge growth of Hewlett Packard, Harley-Davidson, and many other famous former home businesses, 80 percent of all businesses that start in the home stay there.

The Low-Cost, Low-Stress Business Training Ground

People who start businesses are often portrayed as "risk takers." But the smart new business owner is really just the opposite, what I call a "risk minimizer." A home-based business is the easiest and least risky way to test your untested business ideas and build your business at your own speed.

You can start with a minimum investment, in your spare time. You can keep your job, you don't have to refinance your home, and you don't have to gamble your savings. Find out if the business will work, find out if you are cut out to run a business. Some people think they have the world's greatest idea, and maybe they do, but maybe they don't. Some people think they'll love being their own boss and find out they hate it.

When you start at home, your mistakes are less costly than if you were going at it full-time with lots of overhead, bills to pay, can't afford any mistakes, a real pressure cooker. Every new businessperson makes mistakes. And some of those mistakes are going to cost you money. You charged too little. You paid too much. You said the wrong thing to the wrong person, and lost a customer. You forgot an important detail when agreeing to a job, and lost your shirt.

If you start part-time, as cheaply as possible, out of your home, your disasters will always be small ones: A $200 mistake and a $20,000 mistake could be the same mistake. Your business can afford to make low-budget mistakes. The start-slow-and-learn-as-you-go home business eliminates most of the pressure. You can learn from your mistakes. You'll be able to learn your trade, and learn business in general, in a more relaxed, low-pressure environment.

Defining a Home Business

The term *home business* (or *home-based business*—I use the terms interchangeably) applies to anyone working for himself or herself, whose main business location is in the home or in a separate structure on the home property. Home business applies not just to businesses that buy and sell goods, but to home-based inventors, professionals, freelancers,

---

It's riskless. You can test it. If it tests no-go, you don't go.

—Doris Christopher, owner, The Pampered Chef

designers, consultants, internet entrepreneurs—anyone who is self-employed.

Home business also applies to self-employed individuals who earn their income away from home—such as contractors, tradespeople, musicians, caterers, sales reps—but do their business administrative work at a home office: scheduling, paying bills, posting their records, and any other business-related work. Self-employed on-demand (sharing economy, gig economy) workers who do their administrative work at home are also considered home-based businesses.

Just about everything in *Small Time Operator* applies to home businesses. But home businesses are also subject to government rules and restrictions and income tax laws that apply only to home-based businesses. And home businesses, just because they are in your home, have their own unique problems and rewards.

Types of Businesses

Some businesses are naturally suited to being operated out of a home, and others, of course, are not. Ideal home businesses are those where the location of the business is not a significant factor in the success of the business; businesses that require little physical space; and businesses that do not intrude on neighbors and the character of the neighborhood. So, retail stores, manufacturing operations, restaurants, auto repair shops, and businesses where a lot of customers come to the business premises are usually not suitable for operating out of the home. Also, most jurisdictions place restrictions on, or outright prohibit, the use of a home kitchen for preparing foods for public sale or consumption.

Ideal home businesses include:

1. Internet businesses.

2. Publishing.

3. Professionals, consultants, freelancers, designers, writers, computer programmers, paralegals, bookkeepers, and other office services.

4. Service businesses where you go to your customers instead of having them come to you, such as repairs, cleaning, sales agent, or contractor.

5. Crafts, as long as the workshop isn't too noisy or smelly, and assuming you deliver your goods to your customers as opposed to having a retail shop or showroom at home.

6. Inventors (don't blow up the garage).

The Good, the Bad, and the Family

When a business is in the home, constantly staring at you 24/7, business owners tend to put in many more hours than they would if they had to get in the car and drive to the office. After dinner, early in the morning, late at night. It's life for a lot of home business owners.

More than in any other endeavor, a home business demands that you find a balance, that you make time for your family and for yourself. Successful home business owners set regular business hours, and stick to them, most of the time, anyway. At 5 p.m., they turn off the phone, lock the door to the office, and "go home."

But the opposite is also true. For some people, the special advantage of a home business is that they can work when the inspiration hits. The middle of dinner or the middle of the night is not off limits. The family, if they have a family, understands it, or tolerates it, or maybe hates it, but the bottom line is that it is your business. It will only be successful if you run it the way you want.

Perception Is Reality

Home business was once thought to be the poor stepchild of the business world, a second-rate way to make a living. Part-time hobbyists, stay-at-home parents, laid-off executives. Why aren't you good enough to have an office downtown? Times and perceptions, fortunately, have changed. Many professionals and tradespeople work from their homes. Most internet entrepreneurs work from their homes.

The old stereotype is fading. But it is not completely gone. Everything you do to help create an image of professionalism will help. Design a professional website, stationery, business cards, brochures. Don't skimp. Create the image you want to convey.

If your customers (clients, students, patients) will be coming to your home, you have a lot of work to do to make the business look professional, to separate it from the living part of your home, to make the entire home and surroundings look clean and prosperous. Wash the windows. Mow the lawn.

Sweep the stairs. If you have pets, keep in mind that many people don't like animals. Many people are allergic to animal hair. The little things add up. People do judge you by your appearance. They judge your business the same way. Remember, you are your business. And now your home is also your business.

Privacy is extremely important to many people. Customers do not want to conduct business with your family sitting nearby. If it is possible to have a separate entrance, neither you nor your clients need to deal with your living area.

Safety First

Make sure your home business is safe for visitors. Business customers and clients will not be forgiving of a spill that makes them slip and fall, or an obstacle that makes them trip. Even if you don't get sued, you'll lose a customer for sure.

Keep walkways well lit. Check for icy paths, slippery steps, obstacles underfoot, and loose rugs. If there is an unexpected step up or step down, post a warning. If there are sliding glass doors, put some decal or decoration on the glass so someone doesn't walk right into it. Tie up the dog.

The Well-Hidden Home Business

Many home businesses might benefit by, if not out and out hiding the fact that the business is in the home, at least downplaying the fact. You also may not want strangers, salespeople, and the like coming to your home, bothering your family or the neighbors.

If you do not want people dropping by your home unannounced, make sure the telephone directory does not list your address. Don't publicize your street address. Use a post office (PO) box, or a "suite" number (also called a PMB or personal mailbox) at a commercial mailbox store. A PO box will also protect your mail from being stolen or blown away.

Unfortunately, this often backfires because a lot of people, particularly those who don't know you, are suspicious of businesses with PO box and PMB addresses. Is this a real business, or some scam or fly-by-night operation? It's too easy for you to close the box and disappear. Also be aware that a few states require businesses to put a street address on advertising, invoices, and order forms (a law few people know about and that is rarely enforced).

Many post offices let PO box holders use the post office's street address. The post office has a form to request this address option.

Finally, be sure to let the local UPS and FedEx drivers know where you live.

Bill Tann, internet consultant, New York City: "Home business owners should be open about the nature of their operations and not project any embarrassment or lack of confidence about being based at home. That should be a completely neutral factor provided the entrepreneur handles it correctly. Don't be apologetic. Don't be defensive. These days, a person's office is wherever his computer is, and there are very few limits to what can be done at home. But the essential message you must convey to clients, to suppliers, to bankers, to investors, is that you are every bit as serious, sophisticated, and growth-minded as you would be in any other location."

Deliveries and Shipments

United Parcel Service (UPS), FedEx, and other delivery services will make deliveries to your door. You don't have to be signed up with the company to get deliveries to a home business.

If you ship out via UPS or FedEx, you can sign up with the company, and they will come to your home for pickups. They will come five days a week to see if you have anything to go out. They bill you a flat-rate weekly charge plus the shipping charges for packages you ship. If you only ship once in a while, you can instead arrange for a pickup only when you request it, and pay a per-pickup charge instead of a weekly charge, plus the shipping charges for packages you ship. You can avoid pickup charges by taking packages to a FedEx or UPS office or drop-off box. Home businesses and businesses in some rural areas pay higher pickup charges and shipping charges than businesses in commercial locations. UPS and FedEx have different fee structures for pickups, and different surcharges for home businesses, but their shipping charges, which are based on weight and destination, are identical.

Trucks (common carrier shippers) will deliver freight to home businesses. If you are expecting a large or heavy shipment, you should discuss the delivery with the trucking company ahead of time. Most trucks can make street level deliveries; their doors are low to the ground or they have hydraulic lift gates. Some trucks, however, have high doors requiring unloading at freight docks or with forklifts. Some truck drivers will help unload freight, and some will expect you to do the unloading (sometimes a $20 bill works wonders). Some trucks will deliver only to the curb or as close as they can drive to your door, and they expect you to haul the stuff inside. Freight companies charge extra, sometimes quite a bit extra, for inside delivery. If the freight charge is coming COD, find out ahead of time if you will need cash or if the trucker will take a check.

Zoning

Home businesses are often subject to restrictive zoning laws. Zoning laws vary considerably from one location to another. Some communities outlaw home businesses entirely (though I still stand by the first sentence in the introduction to this chapter!). Some communities restrict the type of business that can be operated out of a home, the size of home businesses, the number of employees, number of visitors, amount of inventory on hand, number of vehicles, parking, signage, even the hours of operation. Some communities allow home businesses in the residence but not in a freestanding garage or shop on the property. Some communities, *hallelujah*, have no restrictions whatsoever.

For specific zoning regulations, contact city hall if you are in city limits, or county offices if you are outside city limits. Don't tell them who you are; just ask if there are zoning restrictions on home businesses. And don't rely on verbal information. Get a copy of the written law and read it. If certain types of home businesses are allowed, find out what types of businesses are and are not allowed. Try to define your business to meet the zoning requirements. Sometimes all you have to do is get the terminology right.

Also be aware that different areas of cities have different zoning classifications. There are different classifications of commercial zoning, permitting and prohibiting different types of business activity. You may live on a residential street that may have a commercial zoning, allowing some low-impact commercial activity. City hall will have a map of the city showing the zoning on every street.

Before you get totally bogged down in zoning prohibitions, you should consider the reasons for zoning laws. People do not want a lot of noise, odors, trash, traffic, parking problems, and strangers near their homes. They want quiet and peaceful residential neighborhoods. So they banish businesses, which often bring noise, traffic, and strangers, to other areas of the community.

If you plan to start a home business where you will be operating noisy machinery in the garage, where you'll be storing stuff outside, where people will be coming to your home, or where the sign in the window and the business appearance of your home detracts from the neighborhood image, you can expect complaints from your neighbors and problems with zoning authorities.

But if you have some small office business or quiet (and odorless) crafts business, and if few if any customers come to your door, you are not likely to disturb your neighbors, and you are not likely to get in trouble with the zoning authorities, even if you are technically breaking the law. Zoning officials don't go snooping around looking for violations; they almost always act only when they receive a complaint.

The first and foremost zoning law, in my opinion, is: Be considerate of your neighbors. Put yourself in their situation. How would you feel if a neighbor started a business like the one you plan to start? If it seems appropriate to you, talk to your neighbors and tell them of your plans. Find out, before you start your business, if there will be opposition or bad feelings.

Find ways to minimize the impact of your business on the neighborhood. If you will be having several people come for a conference, consider renting a small room in a local restaurant or hotel instead. If you receive or ship a lot of packages, consider using a mailbox store for pickup and drop-off of packages. Have a parking space in front of your home or on your driveway for visitors. Keep signs small and tasteful; a small plaque next to the door may be all you need. Consider renting storage space for your inventory.

If you are quiet, not troubling your neighbors, chances are you could operate a business undetected and unharassed just about anywhere. Most rules are ignored, aren't they? As one famous politician said, "Don't ask, don't tell."

What happens if you are operating a home business and are suddenly visited by an official of the zoning board, advising you that you are breaking the law? Ask if a complaint has been filed, and if so, why? Are you causing a genuine nuisance? Will the zoning people allow you to alter your practices to eliminate the nuisance? Can you file a petition or request a waiver, variance, or special use permit that will allow you to continue in business?

A public hearing is part of the variance application in most cities. If any neighbors show up to oppose the variance at that hearing, your chances are pretty much shot. So it is a good idea to get on friendly terms with your neighbors, and let them know just what you are doing before you apply for a variance. Your neighbors might help by writing letters or signing a petition in support of your business.

If worst comes to worst, and you are forced to shut down, can you have thirty or sixty or ninety days to relocate? I am not suggesting that you may have to move to run your business without zoning hassles, but you wouldn't be the first person who did. This is more likely to happen to someone who operates a retail shop or an intrusive workshop as opposed to a quiet office or service business.

The town of Yellow Springs, Ohio, enacted a zoning ordinance restricting home businesses, limiting the number of employees and the number of client visits per day, forbidding outdoor storage, and adding other regulations the local newspaper described as, "at best useless, at worst potentially harmful to the community." The editor added, "I wrote that hesitantly, because the people who created the law are smart people who intended to create nothing at all like this mess we have. But when you get into the details of defining just what is a home business that does not disturb a residential area, it becomes almost impossible to draw a fair line that will be applicable to all cases. The best defense of the law is that it won't be enforced. But of course it will be; not equally against all home businesses, but against some in some neighborhoods, when a neighbor demands it. Home businesses can exist, or not exist, according to their neighbors' preference, mood, personality, or whim."

Landlords, Condominiums, Co-ops, and Homeowners Associations

A bigger problem than zoning regulations are residence contracts. If you rent your home, live in a condo or co-op, or live in some type of restricted housing development, be sure the lease, ownership agreement, or real estate covenant does not prohibit a home business. Co-ops in particular often have strictly enforced restrictions on home businesses.

Setting Up Your Office

Just because corporate America defines an office as a claustrophobic cubicle doesn't mean you have to set up your own office as such. The luxury of a home office is that you can spread out wherever you want. And, often, the problem of a home office is that you can spread out wherever you want.

When home and home business overlap, chaos starts creeping in. It is too easy to mingle personal and businesses equipment, computers, files, and paperwork. The result is inaccurate business

Linda Blair Design, Scarsdale, N.Y.

records, inaccurate tax returns, and wasted time sorting out what's business and what's personal. Keep your business and your personal life as separate as possible.

If at all possible, have a separate room, or at least a separate area, desk, files, and shelves, dedicated to business and nothing else. The simple act of physical separation will make your office more organized, your business more manageable, your life more sane. Most studies have shown that people who mix residential space with work space tend to become disenchanted with working at home.

The more office equipment you have, the more electricity you'll be using. If you find you are overloading your home circuits, tripping circuit breakers, you may need an electrician to rewire the house. Or you may not need any rewiring. You may only need to reconfigure where equipment is plugged in. Different electrical outlets in the same room may be on different circuits, enabling you to break up the current draw. If you know where the circuit breakers are, shut off one breaker at a time, and see which wall outlets are wired to which circuit breakers. You can run your computer off one circuit, the electric heater off another, avoiding current overload.

The Business Telephone

Whether you use a landline or a cell phone or smartphone, how you answer the phone and how it's identified on caller ID displays can make a big difference in getting customers. Almost all conventional businesses (those that are not home-based) have a business number separate from the owner's personal phone. When you call the business, the phone is answered in a businesslike manner.

Many home-based businesses, particularly when getting started, do not get a separate business telephone number. But if you want your customers to take you seriously, a dedicated business phone, answered as though it was a business and not the kitchen phone or your personal smartphone, is the first major step. Answering a business call with "Hello" doesn't exactly sound professional. The customer is confused. "Is this, uh, is this a real business?" If you do not answer the phone, does your recording say, *"Hey, leave me a message"* or a prerecorded, *"The number you have reached . . ."*? If you were a new customer, would you leave a message? Or would you just hang up?

People with landlines can easily and inexpensively add a second line, but how many people want to walk around with two smartphones? Self-employed professionals and tradespeople who do business under their own names can easily solve the problem by answering with your name ("This is Hugo") or if you want to sound more professional, something like, "Good morning, this is Hugo Hackenbush." But if you are trying to start a business with a business name other than your own name, how you answer the phone and how you record messages will have a major impact on your success or failure.

Tax deductions for phones used by home-based businesses are covered below.

Insurance

Homeowner and home renter insurance policies probably don't cover your home-based business, and do not provide liability protection if someone visiting your home on business is injured. If a customer, supplier, delivery person, employee, contractor, or any business-related person is injured, you may wind up with a lawsuit and medical expenses. Your insurance carrier may not only refuse to pay the claim, the insurance company may terminate your coverage.

Don't keep your home business a secret from your insurance company. Talk to your insurance agent about your home business. If you use a separate building, such as a garage or barn, for an office or storage or other business use, mention this to your insurance agent. Some policies cover only the residence itself.

There are two types of home business insurance available to you: endorsements and in-home business policies.

Endorsements: If your business is a small office type of business, no employees, few if any customers coming to your office, and a low dollar value for equipment and inventory, you may be able to add an endorsement (also called a "rider") to your existing homeowner or home renter policy. The additional premium is usually low. Endorsements usually cover liability, damage to the building, and a small amount of coverage to business assets. For many home businesses, this endorsement may be all the insurance you'll ever need.

In-Home Business Policies: If your home business is a bigger operation, if you have employees or customers coming to your house, or if you have valuable equipment or inventory you want to insure, you probably will need what's called an in-home business policy. This is a separate policy from your regular homeowner policy. It offers coverage for businesses that exceeds the limits on homeowner endorsements. In-home policies often include liability coverage, damage to the building, coverage of business assets, and sometimes business interruption insurance, which will pay you for lost earnings if you are unable to operate your business because of damage to your home. These different types of insurance are covered in more detail under the "Insurance" section of the Getting Started chapter.

If your current home insurance company is not receptive to your needs, look elsewhere. Some insurance companies do not want to insure home businesses, but some insurers are eager to do so. Trade organizations and professional societies sometimes offer home business insurance.

Read your insurance policy. Don't just accept the insurance agent's word, verify it. If the language of the policy is confusing, or if it seems to contradict what the agent told you, take the policy to your agent and sit down and discuss it. Your home, your business, and your money are all at stake. Know what is covered.

Federal and State "Home-Work" Laws

Employees you hire to come to your home to work need to be covered by workers' compensation and all other employment laws, just like employees of any business.

Employees you hire who work from their own homes (not at the employer's home) may come under special "home-work" laws. The U.S. Fair Labor Standards Act and several states restrict some businesses from hiring employees who work from their own homes, and require the employer to be certified by the Department of Labor. Contact the U.S. Department of Labor and your state's department of labor for details. These home-work laws usually don't apply to people who own home-based businesses and work from home, but you should check with your state to be sure.

If you hire people who work from their own homes where you provide them with the materials to work on (typically seamstresses), these people come under a peculiar employment category called "statutory employees." Statutory employees are subject to regular employee Social Security and Medicare taxes and unemployment insurance, but otherwise are treated as outside contractors. Statutory employees do not pay self-employment tax or file schedule SE.

Michael Karna owns Karna Construction Company: "My business is run out of my home. For display, I completely remodeled my kitchen with every kind of cabinet, an island with a cooktop, an archway into the dining area, and a deck behind the kitchen. It has helped sell quite a few kitchens, plus we enjoy the luxury."

Income Tax Laws

When it comes to reporting and paying income taxes, the Internal Revenue Service treats home businesses just like every other business. Everything in the Taxes chapter of this book applies to home businesses. Home expenses that are part business and part personal should be prorated, and the business portion deducted.

There are, however, a few tax laws that apply only to home-based businesses.

COMMUTING EXPENSES
The IRS does not allow a travel deduction for commuting. Regular commuting costs, home to work and back, are not deductible. Home business owners do not commute, so this is not a problem, except for one fine point in the law.

If you work away from the home, such as a home-based contractor, or if you drive around town visiting clients, the IRS considers the trip from your home to your first job or first client of the day to be a commute, not deductible. The same goes for the trip home from your last call of the day. Any other local business travel is deductible.

There may be a way to avoid this loss of a deduction. If you go to your home office and do some work before you visit your first client, most accountants feel that you already did your commute (to your home office), and that your first client visit is deductible. Ditto for returning home after visiting your last client, if you return to your home office to work before quitting for the day. Pretty picky rules here, I admit. Part of the secret to success in business is (1) knowing the rules; and (2) knowing how to get around them.

TAX DEDUCTIONS FOR TELEPHONES

For home businesses, there are different tax-deduction rules for landline phones than for cell phones and smartphones. If your phone is a landline phone, you may not deduct the basic monthly rate for the first landline into the home. For tax purposes, it does not matter to the IRS how the phone is used or how it is listed, business or personal. The basic rate for the first landline phone into your home is not deductible even if it is listed as a business phone, even if it is used 100 percent for business. Expenses beyond the basic rate, such as business-related long distance calls, optional services, and any special business equipment, are deductible. Any additional landlines into the house after the first line, if used exclusively for business, are fully deductible, no matter how the lines are listed.

Cell phones and smartphones do not come under these restrictions. If you use your cell phone or smartphone 100 percent for business, you can deduct the entire cost. If you use the phone partly for business and partly for non-business use, you can deduct the business portion of the cost of the phone and all related charges. The cell phone rule also applies to a "cellular home phone," a regular telephone that's connected to your cell service, not to landline wires.

These contradictory tax rules exist because the limitation on "the first line in a residence" (which is the wording in the IRS tax code) was written before cell phones existed, when all phones were hooked up to a "line" (a wire). When people started using cell phones, the IRS ruled that cell phones were not a "line in a residence" and were exempt from the law.

MOVING EXPENSES

If you move to a new home, the portion of the moving expenses attributable to the business is fully deductible.

BUSINESS USE OF YOUR HOME: THE "HOME OFFICE" DEDUCTION

This is the biggest and most important home business tax law. This is one of the few tax laws that you really should understand thoroughly. A lot of money—your money—is at stake.

This law is commonly known as the home office deduction, but it is about any home business space—office, workshop, studio, warehouse, store, showroom—and the expenses directly related to the space, including rent or depreciation on the home, utilities, insurance, mortgage interest, property taxes, and home repairs. All references in *Small Time Operator* to the "home office deduction" or "office in the home" includes all business uses of the home, not just an office.

The term *home* includes a house, apartment, loft, condominium, trailer, mobile home, or boat (if you are living on it). The term also includes any separate structure that is part of your residence, such as a garage, shop, barn, or other building.

Failure to qualify for the home office deduction doesn't prohibit you from operating your business out of your home. It only means that one possibly large expense is not deductible on your federal income taxes. You can still deduct all legitimate business expenses other than those directly related to the business structure itself, including office furniture and equipment.

Partners and LLC members: You, as a partner or LLC member, are allowed a home office deduction on your personal 1040 tax return (on Schedule E), but only if the partnership or LLC agreement requires you to have a home office and required you to pay the costs. If your current partnership or LLC agreement does not include such a statement, amend the agreement to include this requirement. As an alternative, the partnership or LLC can reimburse your home office expenses. The business itself then gets to take the deduction. The IRS requires that you have an "accountable reimbursement plan," which is a written policy that the expenses are business related and the expenses are substantiated (you have receipts).

Corporations: If you own a corporation, the corporation can reimburse your home office expenses and get a tax deduction on the corporate tax return. Like partnerships, the IRS requires that you have an "accountable reimbursement plan," which is a written policy that the expenses are business related and substantiated (you have receipts). Unlike partnerships, you do not have the option to deduct the expense on your personal 1040 return. These are nit-picking fine-print laws, but if you do not follow them you cannot take the deduction.

One option to avoid is leasing your home office to your business. While this gives your business a legitimate deduction, it saddles you with taxable rental income and a possible loss of your home tax exemptions.

DEDUCTION RULES

To be eligible for the home office deduction, your business must meet two basic rules: (1) regular and exclusive use, and (2) principal place of business.

Rule One: Regular and Exclusive Use: To be eligible for the home office deduction, a part of your home must be used regularly and exclusively for business. It can be a separate room or even part of a room as long as it is used for the business and nothing else. No television in the room. No personal paperwork at the desk. (No games on the computer?) The business area can't double as a guest room, or kid's playroom, or anything else, even when you are not working.

If you are using part of a room for your business, block it off with a partition or a bookcase or file cabinet. This way you have a clean delineation of where the business space begins and ends. Should you ever be audited, you can much more easily defend you home office deduction.

One exception to the exclusive rule: If your home is your sole fixed location for a retail sales business and if you regularly store your inventory or your samples in your home, the expense of maintaining the storage area is deductible even if it isn't exclusive use of the space.

Rule Two: Principal Place of Business: In addition to the regular-and-exclusive-use rule, your home office must meet at least one of the following three requirements:

1. The office must be your principal place of business, defined by the IRS as "the most important, consequential, or influential location," with the main emphasis on where you meet with customers or clients. A second, but less important, guideline is where you spend the most time.

2. The office must be used regularly (not just occasionally) by customers, clients, or patients, or to generate sales.

3. The office must be the sole fixed location where you conduct substantial administrative or management activities for the business: where you do your paperwork, or your research, or ordering supplies, or scheduling appointments. You don't have to do all of your administrative or management work at home, but the great bulk of it must be done at home. If your business is also operated out of another location such as a store or shop, you are still eligible for a home office deduction, in addition to the cost of renting the store, if the home office meets the above requirements.

You can have a separate principal place of business for each trade or business you operate. And keep in mind: You only have to meet one of the three above requirements to qualify.

Part-time business: If you operate a business part-time on a regular basis, you can take the full home office expense deduction. You do not have to prorate the expenses. For example, if you work three days a week throughout the year, you can take the full deduction. The IRS does not define part-time nor does it define "regular basis," but the IRS does say that "incidental" or "occasional" business use does not qualify. I'm sure you can figure a way to set up your business work schedule to qualify for this deduction. This part-time rule does *not* apply to part-year or seasonal businesses. See below.

Part-year business: If you operate a business for only part of a year—if you operate a seasonal business or a pop-up business, or if you start or close the business during the year—you prorate the home office deduction for how many months of the year the business is in operation. Any month that you operate a business for fifteen or more days can be counted as a full month in making the proration. All other business expenses other than the home office deduction are fully deductible; they do not have to be prorated.

TAKING THE HOME OFFICE DEDUCTION

There are two options for taking a home office deduction: (1) You can take a standard flat-rate deduction; or (2) you can deduct actual expenses.

Deducting actual expenses involves keeping detailed records of expenses, making multiple calculations, filing Form 8829 "Expenses for Business Use of Your Home," and, if your home office is in a home that you own, possible tax problems when you sell the home.

The standard flat-rate deduction (the IRS calls it the "safe harbor method") is simple to figure, does not require Form 8829, and eliminates any tax complications when you sell your home. The flat-rate deduction is much easier to figure and requires much less paperwork than calculating actual expenses, but it probably will result in a lower deduction amount. You can calculate the home office deduction both ways and then decide which will give you the biggest deduction and the fewest hassles. Once you select a method, you are not stuck with it for future years. You can use one method one year, and the other method the next year if you want.

OPTION ONE: FLAT-RATE (SAFE HARBOR) DEDUCTION

The deduction is $5 per square foot of office space, up to a maximum of 300 square feet. So the maximum annual flat-rate deduction is $1,500. This flat-rate option is in lieu of deducting actual expenses for the space itself: rent or depreciation, insurance, property taxes, utilities, repairs, remodeling, maintenance. Office furniture and equipment, as well as all other normal business expenses other than those directly related to the office space, are deductible in addition to the flat rate.

The flat-rate deduction cannot exceed the net profit from the business. You can take the flat-rate deduction only up to the point your profit drops to zero. If your business is already showing a loss, you cannot take the deduction at all. Any unused part of the deduction cannot be applied to future years. The actual expense deduction (Option Two) can be carried forward to future years. This is covered below.

More than one business: If you have more than one business, the 300-square-foot maximum is for all businesses combined. If a spouse or housemate also has a business, that person is also entitled to a $5 deduction for up to 300 square feet, but not for the same portion of the home. If two people share the same office space, the combined deduction cannot be more than the $5 per square foot.

Property taxes and mortgage interest: If you take the flat-rate deduction, you can still deduct property taxes and mortgage interest on Schedule A of your personal 1040 return if you itemize deductions.

OPTION TWO: DEDUCTING ACTUAL EXPENSES

If you choose this option, deductible home office expenses include a percentage of your rent if you rent your home, or a percentage of the depreciation if you own your home, and an equal percentage of home utilities, garbage pickup, property tax, building maintenance and repairs, mortgage interest, and insurance. Home repairs, such as a new roof or furnace, are partly deductible.

You can determine the percentage of the home eligible for the home office deduction based on any reasonable allocation. Most people use either square footage or number of rooms in the house. The best way to figure percentage is to measure square footage. If 20 percent of the square footage is used exclusively for business, then 20 percent of the rent can be deducted, or 20 percent of the cost of the house (land excluded) can be depreciated, and 20 percent of home utilities, insurance, taxes, and maintenance can be deducted.

You can calculate business use of the home based on a room count, but unless all of the rooms are the same size, you will not get an accurate percentage. You may be cheating yourself, or you may be cheating the IRS, by saying one room in five equals a 20 percent deduction. Still, this number-of-rooms formula is used by many home businesses and is acceptable to the IRS.

If the business uses a larger percentage of the utilities, you can deduct the actual percentage used by the business. If, for example, the business space is 20 percent of the home but the business uses 40 percent of the utilities, you deduct 40 percent of the utilities and 20 percent of the other related expenses.

If your homeowner's insurance includes special coverage or additional premiums just for the business, the business coverage is 100 percent deductible as a business expense. The balance of the homeowner's insurance, the coverage that applies to the entire home, is prorated, based on the percentage of the home used for business.

You can take a 100 percent deduction for painting, decorating, cleaning, maintenance, and upgrades to the business area. If you install a security system, you can deduct or depreciate the full cost if the system is just for the business; you can deduct a percentage of the cost if the system is for the entire house.

Landscaping and lawn care: For years, the IRS has ruled that landscaping and lawn care are not deductible for home-based businesses, even if done solely to enhance the image of the business. The only exception to this rule has been for home-based landscapers, if they are using the landscaping to demonstrate or advertise their services. The tax courts have overruled the IRS on this issue several times, but the IRS has never changed the rule. You should check with your accountant.

Business loss: If your home business shows a loss, part of your home office expenses are not deductible this year. You may deduct all of your regular business expenses other than expenses for the office space itself, and you may deduct interest and property taxes on the office, regardless of profit or loss. But the remaining home office expenses may be deducted this year only up to the point that the net income (profit) from the business drops to zero. Any expenses you cannot deduct due to this limitation can be carried forward to the next year, and future years if the next year's income is not sufficient, and deducted then, again only up to the point where they do not create a loss next year. The carryforward does not apply to interest and property taxes on the home office, nor to any of your other business expenses. These expenses are deductible only the year incurred. This carry-forward applies only to Option Two. Businesses using Option One, the flat-rate method, cannot carry forward any of the flat-rate deduction to future years.

Tax trap for homeowners: If you are eligible for the home office deduction, you will run into tax complications when you sell your house. Any depreciation you were allowed must be "recaptured." This means that you add up all the depreciation during all the years you had a home office and pay tax on that depreciation when you sell the house. The tax you pay on the recaptured depreciation, however, is in most situations more than offset by the tax savings you got by taking the depreciation during the time you had the home office.

Another warning: If your home business is located in a separate structure on the same property—such as a detached garage, barn, even a structure specially built to house your business—when you sell your home, this structure is not eligible for the tax exemption homeowners get when they sell their homes. Any profit on the sale of the separate business structure is taxable. This quirk in the law applies only to separate structures, not to a home business located inside your main residence or in an attached garage.

These two warnings to homeowners only apply if you are deducting actual expenses. If you take the flat-rate "safe harbor" deduction, you don't have to calculate depreciation recapture or lower homeowner's tax exemptions.

If you own your home, talk to your tax accountant when you first start your home business. Or just take Option One and don't worry about it.

SPECIAL SITUATIONS

Child care and day care businesses: The home deduction is allowed only if your business is officially licensed or a license is pending (unless your business is exempt from state licensing rules) as a child care or day care business and your business cares for children, people age sixty-five or older, or people who are unable to care for themselves.

Child care and day care businesses are exempt from the exclusive use rule; you get a full deduction for rooms used in your business even if they are also used for non-business purposes. Only the space used for the child care activities can be deducted, and only for the days used. Any day your home is used for child care can be considered a full day of use; there is no need to prorate it for hours of use.

Lodging businesses: If you operate a separate hotel or inn on your property, it is not considered a home business. You do not have to meet the home office rules. If you operate a bed and breakfast, boardinghouse, or rooming house in your home, only the portion of the home used exclusively for the business can be deducted. Shared space (combined personal and lodging) and your private space cannot be deducted. However, you could have an office in your private space and get a deduction for the office in addition to the deduction for the lodging space, assuming the office meets all of the requirements.

More than one home: A home office deduction is allowed only for your "principal place of business," which can't be two different places. You can't run a business out of two homes and get two home office deductions.

If you move to a new home during the year, you can have two principal places of business for different parts of the year, but curiously, the IRS will not allow you to take the safe harbor flat-rate deduction (Option One) for both homes. The IRS will allow you to take Option Two, itemizing expenses, on both homes, part of the year on one home and part on the other.

You can operate two different businesses out of two different homes and get a home office deduction for each business. You now have two "principal places of business" independent of each other. However, taking a home office deduction for two businesses, though it may be legal, is definitely stepping into IRS "red flag" territory, pushing the limits of what you can deduct maybe far enough to invite an audit.

Keep in mind that this multi-home tax law lunacy applies only to the home office deduction, which the IRS has a perpetual obsession with. These rules do not apply to any business deductions other than the home office deduction.

Renting your home to your business: Some business owners rent their home office to their business and take a business deduction for the rent expense. This is not usually a good idea. While this gives your business a legitimate tax deduction, it saddles you with taxable rental income and a possible loss of your home tax exemption.

CLAIMING THE DEDUCTION

Sole proprietorships and joint ventures: A sole proprietor and married couples in a joint venture take the home office deduction on Schedule C. If you deduct actual expenses, also fill out Form 8829, "Expenses for Business Use of Your Home." If you take the flat-rate "safe harbor" deduction, you do not use Form 8829. Note that you do not report home office depreciation, utilities, property taxes, or other home office expenses on the expense categories on Schedule C normally used for these deductions. All home office expenses are reported on Form 8829.

Partnerships: If you are a partner in a partnership or an owner (member) of an LLC, the deduction goes on Schedule E of your personal 1040 tax return. It does not go on the partnership or LLC return unless the business is reimbursing you for the cost of the office, as explained above.

Corporations: If your business reimburses you for the cost of your home office (covered above), the deduction goes on the corporation tax return.

For more information, see IRS Publication #587, "Business Use of Your Home."

THE HOME OFFICE DEDUCTION AND IRS AUDITS

There is a widespread fear that taking a home office deduction will increase your chance of being audited by the IRS. This is a myth that's been repeated over and over. It is not true.

As I mentioned in the Taxes chapter, the home office deduction itself does not increase your chance of an audit. A *large* home office deduction coupled with low income will, yes, increase your chance of an audit, the IRS being suspicious that maybe this isn't really a business. But even then, your odds of being audited are less than 2 percent. If you are entitled to a home office deduction (and if you won't have problems with the tax trap explained above), I suggest you take the deduction. If the U.S. government in its wisdom is allowing a deduction, you in your wisdom should take it.

"THIS IS A BUSINESS"

People who work in an office, a store, a warehouse, or any out-of-the-home business location are working in an atmosphere that is totally business, totally a workplace. The only other people they are in

contact with during work hours are coworkers, customers, and suppliers. It is an atmosphere conducive to work: You go to work, get your work done, and then you go home.

People who run businesses out of their homes often do not have that clear-cut distinction of a work space versus a home space, and work hours versus personal hours. If you have a family, particularly if you have young children not yet in school, the distinction blurs even more. You may set up a separate office, put it in a spare room or the basement or garage, and you may say, "Ten to four is work time, period," but you will find again and again that others are not cooperating as much as you'd like. "Keep an eye on the kids for an hour, will you, honey, while I run to the store." Friends call or stop by to visit during work hours. People who would never expect you to take a break in the middle of the day if you are at the office will think nothing of it if you are working at home.

What's the solution? Have firm rules that your work space and your work hours are to be honored, and then be prepared to have those rules broken regularly. Ever try to explain rules to a three-year-old? Or to a tired spouse who needs a break from the kids?

There has been more than one home business that relocated to a separate business location just to get away from the family and the constant interruptions.

OUTGROWING THE HOME

The great majority of successful home businesses never leave home. The home business owners manage to balance growth, making a living, and keeping a physically small space.

But many home businesses eventually move out of the home. Resistance from customers and clients, who don't feel comfortable working with a home operation, is occasionally a reason. Zoning problems sometimes cannot be solved. Growing families sometimes cramp the space. The need to put a clear distinction between your business and your personal life can be a powerful motivator to move the business out of the home.

The main reason most home businesses move out of the home is because the business grew to a point where the home could no longer hold it. More products to store, more room to work, more employees. Success is forcing you in a new direction. "Forcing" is hopefully too strong a word. Hopefully, your success is happily leading you in that new direction.

If you are, in truth, being "forced" to move when you'd much rather stay home, give serious thought to how you can restructure your business so that it can stay within the confines of your home and still be successful. Do you really need to add new products? Do you need more clients? Can you outsource some of the clerical or repetitive work to another business, maybe someone working out of his or her home?

Before making a final decision whether or not to move out of the home, be sure you've figured all of the added expenses involved. Whether you bring in a single extra dollar or not, when you move the business out of the home, you will be paying additional expenses for moving costs, rent, permits, insurance, utilities, telephone, fixing up the new premises, and commuting expenses. Can your current income support those additional expenses? Or will you feel the pressure to have to bring in additional income that you may or may not be able to generate? You will have to deal with landlords, neighboring businesses, traffic and parking, neighborhood problems, civic responsibilities—the list sometimes seems endless. Are you sure you want to move out?

Remember, the goal is to work at home, not to feel like you live at work.

—Jacquelyn Lynn, *Business StartUps* magazine

Chapter Six

ONLINE OPERATIONS

The Internet is about velocity, how quickly business is transacted, how information access alters the lifestyle of consumers and their expectations of business.

—BILL GATES

THE ONLINE SMALL TIME OPERATOR

It's a rare business that doesn't have an online presence. Online businesses come under the same laws as all other businesses and have the same issues to deal with. Online businesses, like many other types of business, can start small and easy, learn as you go, and build from there.

This chapter has two main sections: websites, and selling online.

WEBSITES

According to the U.S. Small Business Administration, there are over forty million websites (also called domains or URLs, which stands for "uniform resource locator") owned by U.S. small businesses, self-employed individuals, independent professionals, and freelancers, many of them one-person and home-based operations.

Social media may have bypassed websites for promoting small businesses, but social media requires constant attention. Social media comes with restrictions, and anything you put on social media sites can be used by those sites for any purpose they like (see "Copyright on the Internet" below). There are still people who won't have anything to do with social media, but everyone will look for a website. And if you want to sell merchandise on the internet, you'll need to work from your own or someone else's website. What's more, it costs next to nothing to have a website. Web registrars offer domain registration and a small fill-in-the-blanks site starting at less than $15 a year. And for an additional fee, typically ranging from $5 to $12 a month, you can have a full-blown internet presence.

Business Success on the Internet

Brand-new businesses are started and operated 100 percent on the internet. No store, no shop, no public visibility, but genuine and successful businesses just the same, providing a product or a service, marketed and sold entirely on the internet.

Small local businesses are getting national and international customers from the web. Established "bricks and mortar" businesses (businesses with a physical location in the real world) use the internet to increase visibility and sales. Professionals, freelancers, independent contractors, and tradespeople create websites to communicate with old clients and attract new ones.

Color catalogs, often prohibitively expensive when printed on paper, cost almost nothing on the internet. You can change products, prices, and descriptions, and you can correct mistakes, instantly.

Business-to-business (b-to-b) auctions and marketplaces are a way to sell overstock, damaged goods, and outdated merchandise that you can no longer sell through your regular business channels.

eBay and similar consumer sales sites have converted thousands of flea market vendors into internet entrepreneurs. Instead of reaching a couple hundred people on a Sunday afternoon when you'd rather be at the beach, you reach thousands of people while you *are* at the beach.

The internet lets you have multiple businesses, and change businesses on a whim. You can be selling antique typewriters one week, and then switch, overnight, to guitars. Or do both at the same time. The internet is especially valuable to businesses that sell unusual products, old and rare items, and goods with limited interest. People looking for such

---

Know what your site is supposed to accomplish before you design the web pages. If you don't know what your site is for, your visitors certainly won't either. This may sound obvious, but you would be surprised how many commercial sites are out there that look like they have no clear purpose.

—James Dillehay, author,
The Basic Guide to Selling Crafts on the Internet

goods are usually determined to find them. These people will take the time to search the internet. If you are on the internet, there's a good chance they will find you.

If you have a specialized niche or esoteric market (such as a business that sells unusual collectibles, or that caters to a specialized group of hobbyists, to people who love a certain breed of animal, or to fans of a certain kind of music), you can easily make your presence known. By focusing on one unusual area, you can easily become the specialist, the expert, the place a small but loyal group of customers will return to, and tell others about.

Savvy businesses use the internet for market research. You can easily study the websites of competing businesses, see what they are offering, see what they are charging, see the newest trends, and pick up some good ideas to use on your own website.

If you are researching a new product you want to carry, or a new type of business you want to start, or a franchise you might want to invest in, or a company you might want to buy from or sell to, the internet can probably provide more background information than anywhere else. For import and export businesses, the internet is the quickest way to find overseas customers and suppliers. The U.S. Census Department provides a wealth of free demographic and economic information about communities all over the United States; the census is a marketer's dream come true. Log on to census.gov.

Acquiring a Website

To get your own website, start by choosing a domain name that no one else has claim to. Many businesses want to use their business name, a product name, a product category, or some other name that is easily identified with the business. But with millions of sites already on the internet, this may be a difficult task. You may have to get very creative to come up with a name no one else has thought of.

Log on to the internet and type in your business name .com and see if anyone already has it. Or go to the site of any web registrar, type in the domain name you would like, and you will get an immediate answer whether the name is available or not. Domain name registrars maintain a database of all domain names in use.

Registrars are internet businesses authorized to issue website addresses, and there are many of them. For a full list of registrars, log on to www .ICANN.org, the Internet Corporation for Assigned Names and Numbers. This is a nonprofit organization authorized to license the registrars and to oversee the internet. Or type "domain name" in a search engine.

If the website you want is available, don't hesitate: Register it immediately and lock in the site name before someone else grabs it. It only costs about $15 to register a website. The domain name will be yours for as long as you want, just by renewing the registration every year. Don't worry about how your site should look or if there are better or cheaper packages. Once you have the domain name you want, you can change registrars and hosts and packages at any time.

If the website name you want is already taken, try variations that you think might work. If your business is, for example, Bell Springs Publishing, and bellspringspublishing.com is already taken, try bellspringspublisher.com or bellspringsbooks.com or simply bellsprings.com. You can add dashes or underlined spaces in your domain name, such as bell-springs.com or bell_springs.com, but chances are no one will remember to put in the dash or the space. You cannot use blank spaces. You cannot use ampersands; when the bookstore Barnes & Noble went online, it became barnesandnoble.com. You can use capital letters, but the internet will ignore them. MyBusiness.com and mybusiness.com are the same domain name. You can glue several words together and have the awkward but possibly unique www.smithaddingmachinerepair.com.

You could also use a domain name that doesn't end in .com. The suffix at the end of all website addresses, after the dot, is called a top-level domain, and .com is but one of dozens available to you. Any business, in fact anyone, can choose from dozens of other top-level domains, including .org, .biz, .net, .info, .us, and more. You can see a complete list of top-level domains on the ICANN.org website. The problem with top-level domains other than .com is that people will not remember that your domain name ends in .org or something, type in .com anyway, and wind up at someone else's website.

The Internet has made shopping impersonal, to say the least. Customers really want to know there's someone on the other side of the browser. We try to respond personally to each customer. It's amazing how much people appreciate that.

—Richard Hooten, Americabilia.com

When you find an available domain name, make sure that the domain name is not trademarked by another company. The owner of the trademark has the legal right to take the domain name away from you. See "Choosing a Business Name" in the Getting Started chapter and "Trademarks" in the T.C.B.: Take Care of Business chapter.

Finally, keep in mind that the internet is global. You probably don't want your site name to mean "idiot" or "free sex" in Dutch.

Website Already Taken?

If all of your choices are taken, take a closer look at the sites. Do they look active? Or do they look like no one has paid any attention to them for a long time? You may be able to purchase a domain name from the person who already has the rights to that name. See if there is contact information on the website. If not, information about many domain names—who owns them and how to reach the person—is often locatable by doing a search on one of the many "who is" directories on the internet. Type in "whois" in a search engine.

Some registrars maintain a list of domain names being offered for sale by the name holders. And there is a lot of website turnover. People let their registrations lapse. The "who is" information includes the date the registration expires for each domain name. You can check back to see if the name has been renewed.

Another way to try to get a domain name you want: Some registrars let you put a hold on a domain name that's already taken. You reserve the domain name with your credit card. If it becomes available, the registrar will try to get the domain name for you. Putting a domain name on hold does not guarantee that you'll get the name, as there may be several people who have put the same name on hold. Your credit card will not be billed until you get the site. You can cancel the hold any time.

As you can see from the "who is" information above, who owns a domain name is public knowledge. When you get a domain name, your own name, address, phone number, and email are accessible to anyone who wants to look it up. You can pay an extra fee to have a "private" domain (unlisted). However, no one verifies the names, addresses, or phone numbers people use when they register websites; the information could be totally fake.

Multiple Websites

Some businesses set up separate websites for different products or different areas of interest. Specialized and niche sites often draw more viewers than general sites. People often have trouble focusing when they visit a website that covers a potpourri of businesses or subjects. You can easily have one business with multiple, and entirely different, websites.

Domain Renewals

You can renew your domain name as many times as you want. As long as you renew before the current registration expires, you retain rights to the domain name indefinitely.

Most registrars offer automatic renewals, automatically billing your credit card every year, if you choose that option. If you don't want automatic renewal, the registrar that handled your registration is supposed to notify you by email when your domain name renewal is due. If you fail to renew, there is usually a 30- to 60-day grace period, giving you the opportunity to reclaim your domain name, after which time the domain name goes back into the available list, up for grabs by anyone who wants it.

But do not rely on being notified. Know when your domain name is up for renewal, and renew the name by the deadline. Losing your domain name will be a first-class disaster. The responsibility is yours.

Website Hosting Services

Registering a domain name does not automatically give you a working website. You will need a web host, a business that puts your site on the internet. A web host is a business that has your website on its servers, along with hundreds or thousands of other websites, and has a hookup to the internet so anyone using the internet can access your site.

Actually, you don't have to have a web host. You can host your own site, instead of paying a web hosting service, if you have the necessary equipment and hookups. But few small businesses have the time or knowledge, or care to invest in the equipment and training needed, to host their own sites.

Many domain registrars offer web hosting and even include a small one-page website as part of their registration fee. You can get a simple, but often nice looking, fill-in-the-blanks design that you can have up and running in less than an hour. Some registrars offer custom design and full web hosting services. And there are many web hosting services that are not registrars. Once your domain name is registered, you can use any web host you want. Costs run from just a few dollars a month, and go up in price depending on the features and complexity of the site. Many hosting services advertise in business magazines and on the web, or you can ask for recommendations from people you know who already have websites.

Your website depends on your web host. Investigate web hosting services carefully. Compare packages and prices. Don't sign a long-term contract unless you are completely confident about your host's ability to deliver what's promised. Your website is yours, so if you do not like your hosting service, you can switch to another host without having to change your web address. Some important issues:

1. Be cautious if a web host registers your domain name for you, or if a web host offers you a free domain name. Some web hosting services register your domain name under their own name, and they control ownership. If you leave the web host, you may be shocked to learn that your domain name is not yours and that you cannot take it with you to a new web host. Be sure your domain name registration is under your name and is 100 percent yours.

2. Make sure the host is "transparent," invisible to your site's visitors. No ads, no links, no "hosted by" messages.

3. Pick a web host that looks like it has staying power, one with ample resources, not likely to close their doors without warning.

4. Ask about the web host's restrictions on your website activities. Can the host shut down your website if they do not like the content of your site, or if you attract too many visitors, or if you send or receive a lot of email? Will the host charge you more per month if your traffic increases?

5. Ask about downtime and technical problems. Does the host have a poor record of breakdowns? Is the host monitoring its systems twenty-four hours a day? Does the host have a backup generator if the power goes out? Is the host prepared in case of a technical emergency or a natural disaster?

6. Does the web host offer a secure server for credit card transactions and transmission of private data? Is the system flexible, with different options?

7. How is the host prepared to deal with hackers and other breaches of security? Does the host have procedures that keep unauthorized people from getting into your website or obtaining technical information about your site? Does the host have insurance or a bond to cover you should a security lapse cause you or your customers financial loss or other problems?

8. Is the host located in a state that is trying to demand sales tax collections from the host's customers? See "Sales Tax" in the Getting Started chapter.

9. If you want to transfer to another hosting service, or if your hosting service goes bankrupt, will you be able to gain access to your site?

10. Don't choose a host that allows adult sexual content or bulk spam. These hosts, and all of the websites serviced by these hosts, are often blacklisted by search engines.

11. Read the fine print in the contract (sometimes called a Terms of Service or Terms of Use agreement). Every word in the web host's contract is there to protect the host, to limit its liability. Be very careful if the contract states that you indemnify the host against any problems caused by your website. "Indemnify" means that you agree to pay the host's attorney fees and court costs if there is a lawsuit.

12. If you don't like your web host, you can usually cancel your agreement and find a new host, though you are not likely to get a refund.

Website Basics

Below are some of the business and legal basics of having a website. Most of it is Benjamin Franklin's ounce of prevention—a few pieces of advice to save you from possible problems down the line:

1. Register your domain name yourself. Don't go through a third party who may offer to register the site for you, and don't let a web designer register the site for you. You don't want to find out too late that someone else holds the rights to your domain name.

2. Avoid website names that are also the name, or include the name, or sound very similar to the name of a large corporation or organization or famous individual. Because sooner or later, they'll find your website and send their lawyers after you and demand that you change the name of your website. Large corporations and famous people have much more expansive trademark rights than most trademark owners, and they are often very aggressive in protecting their name. Their lawyers are bullies, and they can get nasty. Even if you have a legal right to your domain name, you most likely will not be able to afford the cost of defending yourself in a lawsuit.

3. Make your website your home page so that every time you log on to the internet, your website pops up. It's an automatic way to check that you site is up and online. I once had a website I hadn't looked at in a while, and I had no idea it was down until one of my customers took the trouble to call me on the phone and tell me she couldn't get to my website. Due to a glitch at the company that hosted my site, my website had been off the internet for over two weeks, and I had no idea. My now-former host apologized, but really it was my own fault for not taking care of business.

4. Most website registrations are for one or two years. Don't forget to renew your website before it expires. There are many rotten people around the world who grab up expired websites as soon as someone fails to renew them, and then will be happy to sell the site back to you for whatever they can extort out of you.

Website Design

Anyone who has spent time on the internet knows how many different designs there are for websites. Your options are limitless. And yet, how many business websites have you visited where you couldn't quite figure out how to navigate, how to find what you want, how to contact anyone? There are a lot of awful websites out there.

Entire books have been written, and entire college courses given, on website design. I suggest that you study popular business websites, particularly websites for your type of business. Note how these sites invite, or chase away, visitors. Note how the sites inspire customer confidence. Note how easy or difficult it is to navigate these sites, to get information, and to place orders.

There's a real skill to website design and if you don't possess it, it will be worth your time to hire someone who has that skill. Some important considerations when designing a website:

1. People always have and always will judge you by your appearance. A good paint job helps to sell a car, a good cover helps to sell a book, and a good looking website helps to sell a business. Your site should look good and look professional.

2. Don't force people to register on your site, get a password to enter the site, or give out personal information. If you require people to log into your website or to give personal information, you will lose most of your visitors.

3. Your website should download fast. People have little patience for slow loading websites. Many people have old computers and slow connections, and these will make a slow loading site even slower. Large graphics, animation, and other flashy software are a main cause of slow loading sites. A good website designer knows how to code graphics so they load fast.

4. All websites start off with "www," which stands for World Wide Web. For most websites, you do not need to type in the "www" to access the sites. However, some websites require that you type in the "www" to access the site. This is a flaw in the programming of the site, and can result in many lost visitors who didn't type in the "www" and think that your site doesn't exist.

5. Make your site easy to understand and easy to navigate. The best websites help people quickly find the information they want.

People have no tolerance for confusing, complicated sites. People like sites that are "intuitive"; that is, sites people can figure out without reading the instructions. A large percentage of visitors leave sites solely because the visitors cannot figure out how to use the sites.

6. Avoid color combinations and background designs that make reading difficult. Many people have trouble reading dark type on a dark background, light type on a light background, "drop out" lettering (a dark background with white or very light-colored words), and words typed on top of "busy" (illustrated) backgrounds.

7. Every page on your site should have a link to your home page. Quite often, someone using a search engine will find one of your pages but not your home page. Someone who is directed to the middle of your site by a search engine might get confused if your site does not make it clear on every page who you are, how to reach you, and how to find your home page.

8. Include contact information on every page of your website. Some people print out or download a page from your site and then can't remember who you are or how to contact you.

9. Keep web pages short if possible, and keep the text narrow. People do not like to scroll down too far, and they hate having to scroll back and forth, and back and forth, to read lines that are too long for their screen. Some printers cannot copy wide web pages, cutting off part of the right-hand side of the page.

10. Do not underestimate the importance of good grammar, correct spelling, proper sentence structure, and all that other stuff you didn't learn in high school. People who know good English when they see it will be critical, and possibly distrustful, of a website that uses poor English. Incorrect grammar makes sentences harder to read and harder to understand. Bad grammar often results in miscommunication. If you are not good at English composition, find someone to edit the content of your site. Even if you are an excellent writer, have someone proof your

work. It's easy to miss typos. A second set of eyes helps tremendously.

11. Check your site from other computers using other operating systems and other browsers, from laptops, from iPads, and from smartphones, to see if the site works for everybody trying to access it.

12. Ask friends to "test drive" your site, navigate the entire site, and look for flaws, problems, things that might confuse people.

13. Check your site regularly. Make sure your server has it up and running properly, and that no error messages have suddenly appeared.

14. If you want repeat visitors, change things on your site regularly, just as a retail store changes what's in the window. Let your fans know what's new. Create an email newsletter, or develop an "Ask The Expert" column, or set up a blog (one that you can control). Keep your site current; if you have a holiday theme, don't forget to take it down after the holiday.

15. Solicit feedback from visitors, and use that feedback to improve the site, making it easier to use, adding new features. Show your email address prominently on your site and encourage visitors to contact you. Make sure the visitor can simply click on your email address and automatically have a pre-addressed email dialog box, ready and waiting. Check your email regularly.

16. Don't be afraid to experiment with your site. If you are not getting any feedback from visitors, if you're not getting any sales, maybe your site needs rethinking. One great advantage that websites have over printed catalogs and retail stores is the ability to try a new design or a new offer, and see near-immediate results. What happens if you offer a 10 percent discount versus a 5 percent discount, or no discount at all? You can test your prices quickly, sometimes within a few hours, and keep revising your offers until you find out what works. Try offering free shipping, and see if sales increase; more and more online customers are expecting free shipping. What if you offer free gift wrapping? If you think that an offer of free gift wrap might

boost sales, you can test that idea for a few days, and measure the results before investing in a truckload of wrapping paper.

Before you promote your site to the world, test and fine-tune it until you like what you see. Once you are satisfied with the site, include the web address on advertisements, business cards, and everywhere else you promote your business.

Web Designers

There are web designers, amateurs and professionals, in every town in the country. You can hire an individual or a business. You can hire someone who advertises nationally, someone who you never meet in person. Or, as I much prefer, you can hire someone local, who you can meet and work with, face-to-face.

Get recommendations from other businesses. If you work with a local internet service provider (ISP), they will know, or even have, people who design sites. A local computer shop, or the local college computer instructor, can usually recommend web designers. Three important considerations:

1. Look at other websites the designer created. Do they look good? Do they load fast? Do they work well? Consider contacting the website owners to ask if they'd recommend the designer.

2. Do the major search engines find the designer's websites and give them prominent listings? A good web designer knows how to design a website so search engines find the site.

3. Will the designer create a site for you that you can maintain, change, and update yourself without the designer's ongoing assistance?

CONTRACTING WITH A WEB DESIGNER

All aspects of the design work should be discussed in detail, in advance. There are many variables when it comes to designing a website, hours spent that may not produce the results you want, work that may require fine-tuning or even starting all over. Don't be embarrassed to talk money; don't leave it to "We'll work it out later."

All of the details should be in writing, part of a written contract. If you leave the details to chance,

chance is you'll wish you hadn't. Some things your contract probably should cover:

1. What the designer will create, how big the site will be, what will be included in the site, how long the work will take.

2. Cost and payment terms. Do you pay the designer a flat fee for a complete job, finished to your satisfaction, and pay when the job is done? That by far would be your best deal, but the designer may not care for such a contract that leaves the designer vulnerable to not getting paid. Do you pay by the hour, no matter how many hours are spent, no matter what the results are? Do you set a maximum number of hours? Do you pay a deposit? Do you pay in installments? What if you do not like the work? What if you want to make changes after the work is completed? Do you set deadlines for completing the work? What if the deadlines are missed?

3. Does your contract include an agreement for ongoing help from the designer, or for making changes to the website after the site is designed and online? Will the designer teach you how to maintain and update your website yourself?

4. Your contract should state clearly that you own all of the rights to the contents of the site, the overall design of the site, the wording, and the illustrations. This is a critical clause in the contract. If you do not establish your ownership right with a signed contract, the designer of your site can sometimes claim legal ownership of the contents. Don't let this happen.

Many designers have their own contracts. Experienced designers have been through this before. The designer's contract probably covers all of the above issues, which may be a good thing. There will be no ambiguity. Hopefully.

For more information about contracts, see "Contracts" in the T.C.B.: Take Care of Business chapter.

Copyright on the Internet

Copyright laws are the same on the internet as they are everywhere else. Your website and any of your original work is protected by copyright law.

Copyright law, and how to obtain a copyright, is covered in the T.C.B.: Take Care of Business chapter.

But it is much harder to protect your copyright on the internet, where anything and everything is so easy to copy, duplicate, and alter. Many people who "borrow" material from a website do not fully realize that they are stealing. People think of the internet as a place where everything is free, including your hard work. Quite often, just reminding your visitors that everything on your website is copyrighted, and that copying is not permitted, will stop many of them from taking anything.

If you find that someone has taken any of your work or any part of your website and put it on their own website, you can send a "cease and desist" letter or email, notifying the infringer that such use is illegal, demand that the material be removed from the infringer's website, and suggest that failure to comply can result in legal action. Quite often such a letter is all you need to end the problem.

The tone of the letter can have quite an effect on the infringer's response. Being polite but firm is often more successful than being belligerent, rude, or accusatory. A cease and desist letter or email does not commit you in any way to legal action; it can be a bluff. But be sure to keep a copy of the letter and any response, should you decide in the future to talk to a lawyer.

Technological Copyright Protection

Posting a copyright notice and reminding people not to copy your website will stop many people from downloading, printing, and reproducing your work. But there are people who don't care and who will help themselves to whatever they want from the internet.

You can purchase software or subscribe to an internet service that will help protect the contents of your website from unauthorized copying and downloading. Digital rights management, digital object identifiers, password access, encryption, digital watermarks, and lock-down technology are different terms for different ways to limit access and use of your site and its contents.

If you put photographs or illustrations on your website, you can easily put a copyright notice that includes your domain name directly on the photo

---

The Internet is one giant copying machine.

—PC Magazine

or illustration. If someone borrows your work, the copyright notice will stay with the photo. People who view your work on someone else's website, and like what they see, can use the information from the copyright notice to find your website. In a way, it's a form of free advertising.

No technology will stop a determined hacker. But just as most thieves can be deterred simply by locking a door, most web pirates can be thwarted with simple protection methods. There's plenty of easy pickings on the web, no need for some reprobate to spend a lot of time trying to decode your site.

Social Media and Video-Sharing Sites

When you post any of your work on a social media site such as Facebook or a video-sharing site such as YouTube, it's an entirely different legal situation. The agreement that you "accepted" when you first signed up usually includes a clause that allows the website to use your work however they want, for as long as they want, with no compensation to you. The sites can sell or license your photos or videos to advertisers, or use them for their own promotion, or just about anything else. You still own the copyright to your work, and you can do anything you want permitted by copyright law, but you no longer have exclusive use and control of your work. Before uploading any of your work to any website other than your own, I suggest you actually read what rights you are giving away, what rights the website has instantly acquired for free, before accepting their agreement.

Links

Links from other websites will bring more visitors to your site. A link is like a recommendation, like word of mouth publicity, and usually costs nothing.

Let me give you a real-life example. My own publishing company, Bell Springs Publishing, publishes a pinball machine repair book, which appeals to a small but eager group of people. Bell Springs set up a separate website just for that one book (aboutpinball.com). We then went surfing the internet, using search engines, and found several hundred websites about pinball. Some were businesses, some were pinball organizations, many were individuals with websites dedicated to their hobby. We emailed every site we found, requesting a link. Many of the sites happily agreed. The links brought many additional visitors to the aboutpinball.com website.

Links have extra benefits. Search engines often find a link to a website rather than the website itself. It is effortless for a web surfer, led to a link, to click on the link and get rerouted to your site. Links from other sites also can boost your search engine rankings.

If your own website includes links to other sites, be sure that the other sites want to be listed on your site. Some sites do not want to be linked to others. Some sites may have libelous, objectionable, or illegal material on them, which can cause you legal problems, and angry visitors, if you add the offending site as a link on your site. What's more, do you really want to add a link to some other website, and send your visitors away?

Email

If you want your business email to look professional, be sure the service you use does not tack on an ad. Some free email services put an advertisement on every email. Prospective customers will be wondering if this is a real business.

Email is a double-edged sword. Because email is informal by nature, people type things in email that they'd never write in a letter, let alone say to someone's face. Once an email is sent, there's no retrieving it. It's as good as cast in stone. Email, being so spontaneous and often not well thought out, has gotten some people in legal hot water. Lawyers often talk about "smoking gun" documents in legal cases. Email has become the #1 source of damaging evidence in many legal disputes.

Lastly, check your spelling. Most software includes a spell checker.

Email from a Website

I like websites that let visitors send you an email directly from your site. The visitor does not have to log off the site or type in your email address, to send you an email.

Many websites use an email address that includes the domain name of the website. For example, if your domain name is www.buystuff.com, your email can be sent to you@buystuff.com, or catalog@buystuff.com, newsletter@buystuff.com, or any-name-you-want@buystuff.com. You can have multiple email names @buystuff.com.

An email address through your own website has a professional appearance, and makes it easy for customers to remember your email address. An email address through your website eliminates the problem of losing your email address if you switch ISPs. The website can direct email from the site to any ISP you choose.

When choosing email addresses, be aware that spammers have "harvesting" software that automatically targets common addresses like "info@" and "webmaster@." Better choices would be your actual name, or something not used by every other website out there.

SELLING ONLINE

There are two ways to sell merchandise online: directly from your own website, or sending your customers to another website that sells your merchandise.

Selling Through Others' Websites

The easiest way to sell merchandise, which does not require you to set up a shopping cart or sign up as a credit card merchant, is to link your website to a different site that has your merchandise for sale. If, for example, Amazon.com sells your merchandise, or if you sign up as an Amazon merchant to sell your products on Amazon, you can add a link on your website that will send your site visitors to the page on Amazon that has your merchandise for sale.

You don't need to sign up with the site you link to unless you want to earn a few extra bucks as an "affiliate," an option offered by some large internet sellers where they pay you a percentage (sometimes called an "advertising fee") every time someone follows a link from your website to theirs and purchases something.

If your merchandise is offered for sale on several websites, you can list all of the links, and give your site's visitors the option of picking which site they want to buy from. Amazon.com may rule the world, but there still are other businesses out there, and it's nice to share the wealth a little.

Any time you have a sales link on your website, you should test it regularly, at least once a month. Go to your own website, click on the link, and make sure it still works. Links do occasionally break down and need to be removed and then reestablished. Also check the links to be sure your merchandise is still being offered for sale.

Selling from Your Own Website

There are two common ways that you can sell merchandise from your own website: using an online payment service such as PayPal or Google Wallet, or accepting credit and debit cards.

ONLINE PAYMENT SERVICE

The easiest way to sell online from your own website is to go through an online payment service, an online business that collects money from buyers and remits the money to sellers. But online payment only works if your customers are comfortable with online payment and know and trust the business that is providing the service.

There are several online businesses offering payment services, but most are not well known. One service dominates the online payment world: PayPal, the largest and best known online payment service. PayPal is located in the United States, which is important to people who do not trust overseas operations.

Online payment works best if you are only selling one item and if you charge a flat price for the merchandise, a price that includes shipping and any taxes. If you have multiple items, or if you have different prices for people who have to pay sales tax, or for people who are ordering from overseas where the shipping is very expensive, people will have to compute their total cost themselves, which will discourage purchases. And they'll make mistakes.

A problem with PayPal is that, despite the fact that PayPal claims to have 100 million users, many people do not have PayPal accounts. They don't want to open an account, don't want to deposit money in PayPal, and don't want to give PayPal their banking information. PayPal does allow people to pay with a credit card instead of opening an account, but a lot of people don't know about that option, and PayPal seems to go out of its way to downplay it. Some people think that PayPal charges buyers a fee to use PayPal, which PayPal does not do.

Another problem with PayPal is that some people have a perception that PayPal is not professional or businesslike, that a "real business" would have its own credit card processing and would not be selling through PayPal; the buyers are therefore hesitant to do business through PayPal.

ACCEPTING CREDIT AND DEBIT CARDS ONLINE

If you want to sell merchandise directly to your online customers without turning the transaction over to a payment service like PayPal or waiting for someone to mail you a check, you will need to set up a mechanism to accept credit and debit cards on your website. There is a section in the T.C.B.: Take Care of Business chapter, "Accepting Credit and Debit Cards," that explains how to become a credit card merchant. This chapter explains how the cards can be processed through your website.

SHOPPING CARTS

Before you can process a credit card, you have to get the order and collect the purchaser's information. The most common way to take online orders is through a shopping cart. This of course isn't a cart at all, but software that collects a buyer's information and transmits it to the seller.

Some shopping carts are also online card processors, charging the buyer's credit or debit card, depositing the money to the seller's account, and deducting the transaction fees. Most small businesses' shopping carts, however, do not process credit cards. The shopping cart only collects the information from the buyer and forwards the information to the seller. The cart is nothing more than an electronic order form. No actual transaction has occurred; no credit or debit card has been billed. After the seller gets the order from the shopping cart, the seller submits the purchase information to the seller's card processor (the seller's bank or online service), which does the actual billing, and then the seller ships the merchandise.

There are several websites offering free or inexpensive shopping carts. Web hosts offer shopping carts as part of their web packages. Most shopping carts are quick and easy to set up. While all shopping carts are similar, there are subtle but sometimes significant differences between the carts. Some allow more flexibility and customization than others. Some are more user friendly than others.

Internet buyers are quick to abandon a shopping cart that confuses them, that makes them work too hard to use the cart, that requires them to register, or that asks unnecessary personal questions. Buyers also abandon shopping carts when they can't find out, before placing an order, what the shipping and handling will cost.

A good shopping cart will include an automatic follow-up email sent to the purchaser, confirming the order, letting the purchaser know when the goods will be shipped, and giving the purchaser a way to contact the seller if something is wrong.

After you sign up for a shopping cart, test it out yourself. Make a small purchase, just $1 is enough, and see how easy or difficult the cart is to use, and see how the cart processes the order. If you don't like how the cart works, do what your customers will probably do: dump it. Try a different cart.

Simple stand-alone shopping carts are okay if you are not processing a lot of orders every day. But if you are constantly filling orders, you will get pretty tired pretty quickly of all the time it takes to process orders. Online credit card processors and payment services and some web hosts offer complete packages that combine all of the steps and streamline order processing. Credit card processing is covered in the T.C.B.: Take Care of Business chapter.

SECURE SERVERS

Most shopping carts use "secure servers" to shield personal information and credit card numbers. A secure server scrambles ("encrypts") the information into an unreadable code so it cannot be understood until it is unscrambled. Encrypted information keeps thieves and hackers and unauthorized people from understanding the information should they be able to access it. Many internet shoppers look for a statement, or for the little padlock logo or a domain address that starts with https instead of http (the "s" indicating the site is "secure") that tells them they are on a secure server. These shoppers are much more likely to order from you if you have a secure server.

Still, secure servers are not secure if someone obtains user names and passwords to steal shopping cart information. Information stored on a shopping cart after the order is placed is not encrypted; it's there for anyone with the correct password to read, even on secure sites. Shopping carts often store sales information for a period of time or for a certain number of transactions before deleting the information. I suggest you take your own precautions. After you fill an order, delete the information from the shopping cart. Don't leave credit card numbers and buyers' personal information anywhere on the internet or on stored emails.

Even with every precaution you can take, how secure "secure" really is depends on a lot of factors including the security measures programmed into websites, the systems set up by your web server, and the determination of a potential thief. Truth is, nothing on the internet is 100 percent secure. I suggest that you do not make any claims about internet security.

Some states have state laws regarding website security, and laws protecting online shoppers located in those states. Some states require website owners to notify in-state customers if the websites have been hacked and customers' personal data possibly seen or stolen.

Internet Transactions without Becoming a Credit Card Merchant

Businesses that accept PayPal or Google Wallet or a similar online payment service (also known as peer-to-peer money transfers) do not need to be a credit card merchant. These are two completely separate payment options. Businesses can easily have both.

Businesses that set up shops or offer products through third-party marketplaces such as eBay, Amazon.com, or Etsy do not need to be credit card merchants. You are not making the sale directly; your customers are buying from a third party, not from you.

"Google Yourself"

Every once in a while, at least two or three times a year, do an online search of your business. Do it on all the major search engines, as some search engines find websites that others miss. See what information, and misinformation, is out there. I recently checked on a business I own and found it listed under three different addresses, two of which I never heard of. I found a Google map showing my business on a street that doesn't exist. I found a Facebook page a former employee set up five years ago that is long out of date. It may take some effort, and repeat requests, to get incorrect or out-of-date information corrected or removed, but it's important to take care of it.

And then, of course, you will probably find someone, usually someone anonymous, criticizing you or saying something false about your business or your product. If the statements are blatantly false, and if you can prove them to be false, contact the website that posted the statements, make your case, and request that the comments be removed.

If there is a way to answer a criticism, consider if an answer will help your business or just make you look worse. I suggest that you don't attack your attacker. You'll never win support that way.

Protect Your Business

The more your business relies on technology, on the internet, on anything not directly within your control, the more you risk that some technological glitch, some programming error, some power outage can shut you down or do damage to your business operations, your records, your transactions, and your relationships with your customers and suppliers.

I won't get into the usual nightmare list of possible disasters. I simply suggest that you sit down, right now while everything is working properly, and make contingency plans to protect yourself if the tech world you depend on causes you a problem or two.

You should have backup data for all of your business records and on everything on your website, data that is not on the internet and not on your hard drive, data you can get your hands on if the power fails, if the computer blows up, if your web host or your internet service provider shuts down and vanishes. And you should keep your backup data up to date. Backing up your files is extra work, and it's a nuisance, but sooner or later you will lose something in the computer or on the internet. Your backup is your insurance, and you write your own insurance policy on this one. It's up to you.

Limit access to your computer. If employees or others will be using your computer, establish passwords that let people only into the areas you want them to be able to access. Change the passwords if an employee quits or is fired. Lock the door when you are not around.

Don't leave your internet connection on all the time. A sitting, internet-connected computer gives hackers lots of time to try to break in.

Do not store your customers' personal information on your website. Once a transaction is complete, move the information offline. This way, should anyone gain unauthorized access to your site, there will be no credit card numbers and other private customer information to steal.

Protect Your Privacy

The internet is a very un-private place. Anyone can see your website and Facebook page, and many people could wind up reading what you thought was private email. Information you give to others over the internet, even confidential information, can find its way to websites, other businesses, individuals, and—uh oh—government agencies.

Internal Revenue Service auditors sometimes look at websites and Facebook pages of businesses they are auditing. The auditors get an idea of what the company does, how big it is. Auditors look for information on the site that might have a bearing on what the company reported on its tax return. Isn't this a great way to end the chapter?

Aaron Brown, cofounder, CRaider.com, New York City: "The internet is smart and flexible, while big companies are mostly pretty stupid. While business is trying to take over the internet, the internet will take over business."

Mark Monaco, partner, DiBruno Brothers Gourmet Foods, Philadelphia: "We took an intimate, personal retailer and made it work across four time zones."

Robert D. Hof, *BusinessWeek:* "If you click past the famous brand names, you'll find thousands of small businesses you never heard of, quietly making a go of it online, providing welcome relief from the big brands. The small businesses thrive because they're focused on narrow niches they know really well."

Eric Rydholm, Motley Fool Corporation: "To succeed online you need to build a cult, because you can sell a lot of stuff to a cult."

Chapter Seven

THE ON-DEMAND ECONOMY

In surveys by the company, customers reported that the food ordered on a smartphone tasted better.
—Darren Tristano, Technomic Research

IT ALL STARTED WITH UBER

Uber has not only revolutionized the transportation industry, but its shared-economy business model has caused a ripple effect that is bringing a strong sense of positivity among customers and independent contractors alike. Every business model may soon look like Uber's.

—*Inc.* magazine

It's called the on-demand economy, the sharing economy, the gig economy, and it all started with Uber. Some guy, angry that he couldn't find a taxi when he needed one, got the idea for a mobile app that would connect people who needed a ride with people who had a car and were willing to provide a ride. Uber wasn't a taxi company because they didn't have any permits or licenses to operate taxis; they didn't have any drivers on the payroll; they didn't even own any vehicles. Uber liked to describe itself as a ride-sharing service. Which, of course, it wasn't. Nobody was sharing anything. It was a business idea, and the idea caught on, big time. Uber's "ride sharing" launched the term "sharing economy" to describe this new kind of business model, which rapidly grew from offering rides to offering every kind of service.

The term *gig* was first used by jazz musicians back in the Roaring Twenties, nearly a hundred years ago, to describe a musical engagement. "Gig" has been used by musicians ever since, but the term has grown to encompass all kinds of temporary employment. Gig originally meant, and still means today, that the job was a one-shot, with no guarantee of any future work. Musicians have always lived in a gig economy. Now all kinds of occupations are headed there. Whether it's providing a ride, arranging a meal, fixing a leaking sink, or any other service offered through an app, gig workers are on their own, just as they have been since the beginning of economic time: the services they provide, the expenses they incur,

the pay they get, the records they keep, the tax returns they file.

Today's on-demand economy uses new and constantly evolving smartphone and internet technology to speed, streamline, and bring ever-growing efficiency to conducting business. It's an electronic middleman, taking a cut to connect independent service providers with customers. The on-demand businesses basically reinvented the yellow pages for the smartphone, making it easy, and even fun, for people to quickly find the help they need.

But the on-demand businesses have become successful, at times extraordinarily successful, because they've found a way, a loophole in the law, to eliminating the #1 biggest expense most businesses face: employees, and all of the costs and paperwork and employment laws associated with hiring employees.

On-demand businesses hire people who are not legally employees, who are contract workers—the IRS calls them "independent contractors"—which lets the on-demand businesses operate without paying any of the costs required of regular employers: payroll taxes, workers' compensation insurance, unemployment taxes, and health insurance coverage. No vacation pay, no holiday pay, no overtime pay, no sick leave. The on-demand companies do not have to comply with minimum wage laws, employment safety laws, discrimination laws, or termination laws. The on-demand companies refer to themselves as "disruptors." They've "disrupted" a legal system that was put in place to protect employees and to protect consumers.

Whether you love the disrupters or hate them or just don't care, the bottom line is that if you are a gig worker, you are self-employed. You are, no matter what you or anyone else calls you, in business for yourself. Some gig workers are quite angry about it, viewing it as getting cheated out of the benefits and protections they'd have as employees.

The shrewd workers, the ones with real vision, approach the on-demand world for what it can be:

a way to take advantage of all the perks, the freedoms, and the generous tax deductions that self-employed people have, and employees don't. It is a golden opportunity to direct your own future, to launch your own business, to Be Your Own Boss.

Some Terminology

The on-demand businesses also call themselves sharing businesses, ride-hailing businesses (for the Ubers and Lyfts), marketplaces, app-enabled, and platforms. Some of the businesses refer to themselves simply as apps. The businesses often refer to the contractors they hire as workers. (Uber calls them partners.) The workers, who are really self-employed individuals, are never called "employees," because that's a word, and a legal relationship, that the on-demand companies want to avoid. Their entire business model is based on not having employees.

1099 Workers

The term "1099" refers to the 1099-MISC tax form that companies are required to send to the IRS for any individuals (other than employees on a payroll) who receive $600 or more in a calendar year. I mention this elsewhere in the book, but it's worth repeating: There is no such thing as "1099 income" or a "1099 worker."

Any company that pays an on-demand worker $600 or more a year is required to report the amount paid on Form 1099-MISC, sending a copy to the worker and to the IRS. But workers are not responsible for 1099s. As an on-demand worker you are not required to have a 1099 form, do not have to request a 1099 form if you don't get one, and do not attach the 1099 form to your tax return. It does not matter to you whether you receive a 1099 form or not. But the income is taxable. It is part of, or maybe all of, your self-employment income.

Your Legal Status and Your Income Taxes

On-demand workers come under the same income tax laws as self-employed individuals and most one-person business owners. Legally, you are a sole

---

I value my freedom as an independent contractor too much, and I don't want Uber to tell me when or where I have to drive.

—Carlos Olivia, Los Angeles

proprietor. You file a sole proprietorship tax form, Schedule C, "Profit or Loss from Business," that attaches to your 1040 income tax return. You report your income from your gigs on Schedule C, you deduct the expenses related to the gigs, and you pay income tax on the profit: total income *less* deductible expenses *equals* taxable profit.

You also have to pay self-employment tax, which is a combined Social Security and Medicare tax. Employees on a regular payroll have Social Security and Medicare taxes deducted from their paychecks, and their employers contribute an equal share for the employees. But you are not on a payroll, there are no tax deductions withheld from your pay, and there are no contributions from the company hiring you. You pay all of it, both the employee share and the employer share.

You are responsible for your own insurance, your own health coverage, and your own retirement savings. You are on your own if you are not working; you cannot collect unemployment insurance.

The tax deductions you are entitled to, the taxes you pay, the forms you file, and the records you keep to enable you to figure your taxes, are all covered in this book. Everything in this book applies to on-demand workers.

One important tax law that on-demand workers should know about is the home office deduction. Home-based, self-employed individuals can get a tax deduction for having an office in their home, which can reduce your taxes significantly. You don't have to actually be doing your work in your home to get the deduction. You can be working in a client's home, or driving your car, or whatever else a platform contracts you to do, and still get the home office deduction. You do have to comply with certain IRS requirements to deduct the home office, but they are easy to meet. Read the Home-Based Business chapter.

Your Rights

One of the great benefits of being self-employed is that you really are your own boss. You are not obligated to work a certain amount of hours or days, or work when a platform wants you to work, or take every job offered to you. A platform cannot require you to work exclusively for them, or prohibit you from taking jobs with other platforms or working on your own. Many on-demand workers are already self-employed, picking up extra work through the platforms.

If you are providing a service for a platform's customer, you have no legal obligation to book repeat customers through the platform. Many workers use the platforms solely to find first-time customers for themselves. The contractors then deal directly with the customer, and eliminate the middleman. The platforms refer to this as "leakage," and there is nothing they can legally do to stop it.

Of course, the platforms have the same legal rights that you do. They are not obligated to continue to do business with you. They are not obligated to guarantee you work, or pay you a minimum fee. Doing business as a worker for an on-demand platform is very much a two-way street.

How On-Demand Businesses Work

Different on-demand platforms operate in many different ways. Some are rigidly structured, particularly the ride-hailing companies such as Uber and Lyft. They try to control everything. They set the fees, and change them whenever they want.

Many on-demand companies are not much more than a referral service, getting a fee for connecting you to customers. Some of these companies charge a fixed rate to the customers and pay a fixed rate to their contractors. Some on-demand platforms let you set your own rates, which sometimes can lead to bidding wars, hungry workers cutting prices to beat out other workers for the job. A few platforms simply post jobs offered and charge an up-front fee for the worker to contact the buyer, with no guarantee of work: The customer and contractor decide if they want to work together and what the contractor will charge.

The fees on-demand platforms charge vary from company to company, and typically range from 10 percent to 30 percent of the contractor's earnings. There is no standard fee structure. Even within one company, the fees the platforms charge their contractors vary depending on the extent of the job, or urgency, or maybe the company has introductory offers, or different fees for repeat customers.

Except for platforms that only provide leads, almost all of the on-demand companies handle all of the administration and paperwork. The platforms find the customers, do the scheduling, bill the customers, collect the money, and pay the contractors. Some platforms have insurance that covers customers if there is damage or a claim involving a service you provided. Some platforms have free or low-cost insurance for the contractors.

Some platforms provide recordkeeping and tax help. These are genuine services that many contractors are happy not to do themselves and for which they are very willing to give up a percentage of their pay.

Lodging Apps

HOUSE, APARTMENT, AND ROOM RENTALS
One of the biggest gig-economy sectors is short-term rentals of living spaces: renting out part or all of your home or your apartment for a night, or a week, to travelers and tourists. Companies like Airbnb and HomeAway are connecting people who need lodging with people who are offering lodging. These gig-economy lodging services are doing the same thing that ride companies like Uber are doing: connecting people who need something with people who are offering it.

LANDLORDS
Before you decide to rent out space in your home or apartment, check the rental or lease agreement to see if the landlord prohibits temporary rentals or any kind of subletting. Landlords have a vested interest in protecting their property, and they may be quite hostile to having people they don't know occupying their buildings. But if there is nothing in the rental agreement prohibiting tenants from offering temporary rentals, then tenants have no legal requirement to inform landlords or get permission, and I doubt any tenants do.

INSURANCE
Standard homeowner and home-renter insurance policies do not usually cover short-term rental situations. If someone renting a room in your house for the night causes damage to the home, your insurance company may refuse to cover the damage. If a renter is injured on your property and your insurance does not cover the renter, you could find yourself in an expensive lawsuit. Ask your insurance company if you are covered, and if so, read the policy to see how much coverage you have. If you are not covered, many insurance companies are offering supplemental coverage for occasional home-sharing rentals. Some companies offer by-the-day policies that you pay only when a room is rented. Airbnb and other platforms also offer by-the-day insurance coverage. Again, carefully read whatever insurance policy, or multiple policies, that you purchase to be sure you are fully covered. Insurance companies are

merciless whenever there is a claim that they think they can get out of paying.

LOCAL REGULATIONS

Some cities have laws, or are rapidly passing new laws, regulating temporary lodging in people's homes. Neighbors—whose lives have been disrupted by travelers checking in and out, and in and out, of the house next door or the apartment above them, partying at all hours, turning residential neighborhoods into Hotel Row—have been complaining, and demanding laws that minimize or even outlaw "transient occupancy." If you plan to offer temporary lodging in your home, check with your city or county to find out if there are any laws or restrictions on your plans. Some cities require short-term rental hosts to register with the city. Some cities limit the number of days a home can be rented.

OCCUPANCY TAXES

Most states tax temporary lodging such as hotels, motels, and bed-and-breakfasts. Sometimes the tax is part of the sales tax; sometimes it's a separate tax, usually called a hotel, tourist, lodging, or occupancy tax.

Temporary lodging in people's homes and apartments is usually exempt from occupancy taxes, but only if the lodging is occasional. If you are renting to travelers on a regular basis, if this really is a little rental business, most states say that the rental income is subject to the occupancy tax. That's where Airbnb and similar operations get murky, especially for people who are earning a nice income from their rentals. At what point does "occasional" (no tax) become "regular" (subject to occupancy tax)? And how is a state or city government going to make that determination and enforce it?

Unless you are actually in the business of renting rooms to travelers, in my opinion you have a legitimate argument, should any government agency inquire, that your rental income is "occasional" and not subject to occupancy tax. However, as Airbnb-type rentals get bigger, these laws are likely to change, and more taxes are likely to be required. Already, Airbnb is now collecting occupancy taxes directly from all renters in several cities, and remitting the tax to the city. If you live in one of those cities, for rentals through Airbnb, you do not have to pay any occupancy taxes.

TAX ON FURNISHINGS

Some states have a tax on business assets, a flat tax on everything the business owns: equipment, furniture, supplies. It's called a personal property tax. "Personal property" is a legal term for property other than real estate.

In states that have this tax, some cities are sending personal property tax forms to people who are registered with Airbnb and other rental platforms. The forms require you to list all of the property used by your renters—beds, dressers, lamps, linens and towels, even pictures on the walls—and will tax you on them. The tax is usually low, about 1 percent of the current value of the assets, but it's a tax you have to pay if the city finds you and sends the forms. And there is no proration. Even if you have only one rental a year, the assets are taxed.

INCOME TAXES ON RENTAL INCOME

Renting out part or all of your home or apartment comes under different income tax laws than on-demand work providing a service. A service you provide—driving a vehicle, making repairs, cleaning homes—is business income, self-employment income. Rental income, for IRS income tax purposes, is not business income. People who rent out a room are not considered to be self-employed. This is a most important distinction, because business income (self-employment income) is subject to self-employment tax, and non-business income, including rental income, is exempt from self-employment tax. Self-employment tax is combined Social Security and Medicare tax, and it is approximately 15 percent of your net profit, which can be a sizable chunk of money.

Rental income, even though it is not "business" income, is taxable. You report rental income and expenses to the IRS and pay income tax on the profit, though with one exception, a special gift from the IRS: If you rent your home or apartment, or part of it, for less than fifteen days in a calendar year, you do not have to report any of the rental income. It is tax-free income. Again, this tax break applies only to rental of your residence, not to rental of property you do not live in.

If you rent out your home for fifteen days or more a year, you report the entire rental income for the year, not just the income in excess of the first fourteen days. You report all rent money received during the calendar year, regardless of what period the rent is for. If you receive advance rental payments covering the next year, you report the income the year you receive it, not the year it applies to.

Normally, the IRS will only know what you report to them. However, Airbnb will notify the IRS, on Form 1099-K, about any payees who had over two hundred reservations *and* received more than $20,000 a year in payments.

Rental income and expenses are reported to the IRS on Schedule E, "Supplemental Income and Loss," which attaches to your 1040 tax return.

The rental income tax law does not apply to people who are in the business of renting temporary guest lodging. Owners of hotels, motels, and bed-and-breakfasts are considered self-employed. Their income is reported on the business tax form Schedule C, and the income is subject to self-employment tax.

DEDUCTING EXPENSES

Expenses related to rental income are deductible in figuring the taxable income on rentals: total rental income *less* deductible expenses *equals* taxable income.

Some expenses can be deducted when paid, and some expenses must be depreciated (spread out over several years). Generally, everything can be deducted currently except the cost of the building (if you own the building) and major repairs and renovations to the building, which must be depreciated over twenty-seven and a half years (with some exceptions). Expenses that can be deducted currently include rent if you are renting the residence (that is, rent you pay your landlord), mortgage interest and property taxes if you own the building, insurance, utilities, maintenance, cleaning, and most other routine costs associated with the building. If you hire maids or janitors, the cost of cleaning the rented area is deductible.

For people renting out their home or apartment occasionally, the expenses have to be prorated between personal (your own use of your residence) and rental (the percentage of the home being rented and the number of days of rental use). If you rent out your entire residence, you would deduct ¹⁄₃₆₅th of the expenses for every day your residence is rented (365 days in the year). If you rent out one bedroom of, say, a four-bedroom home, you would deduct ¼ of the expenses, which by the day is not much of a deduction: ¼ of ¹⁄₃₆₅th of the expenses for every day your residence is rented. Still, it can add up, and every dollar you can legitimately deduct is a dollar less income you have to pay taxes on.

If you feed your guests or provide other amenities, those costs are also deductible. But look out here: Pretty soon your operation starts to look like a bed-and-breakfast, a real business subject to all of the state and local regulations and taxes you're trying to avoid.

"It All Started With Uber" . . . And It All May End with Uber

The on-demand business model is still evolving. The platforms have been making up the rules as they go, and they are beginning to discover that they can't always do whatever they want. The platforms are encountering resistance from established businesses that have been "disrupted" and from the workers themselves. Some platforms are discovering that the on-demand model, hiring independent workers that the platforms have little or no control over, is causing the platforms more trouble than they expected. That's why businesses hire employees in the first place, to have control over how their business is run.

And the platforms are going to consolidate. There are just so many apps that people will pour into their smartphones, and there are just so many ride-hailing or apartment-cleaning services that can compete for the same workers and the same customers. The slower and underfunded platforms are going to disappear.

Most important, the platforms are finding out that there are laws they're not going to be able to get around forever. The legal definition of independent contractor, and who is or isn't an employee, is in a state of flux, and the rules are likely to change. This is partly the result of a growing number of lawsuits being brought by Uber drivers and other on-demand economy workers, arguing that the drivers and workers should be reclassified as employees.

California is the first state to rewrite the definition of independent contractor. The California Supreme Court recently ruled that workers are employees, not independent contractors, if their jobs are "central to a company's mission." The court ruled that independent contractors are people who work "outside the usual course of the hiring company's business." Uber can hire an independent electrician to rewire the office, because Uber is not in the electrician business. But Uber's drivers, who are without a doubt "central to the company's mission," will now (at least in California) have to be employees.

But for now, for most of the country and most of the on-demand business models, the workers are really in charge: You call your own shots. You are free to take jobs or not take jobs, to even try out a new occupation to see how you like it.

Taking on-demand jobs is an easy introduction to self-employment, to find out if you like working for yourself, if this might be something to build into a real business.

Chapter Eight
T.C.B.: TAKE CARE OF BUSINESS

"Mercy!" Scrooge said. "Dreadful apparition, why do you trouble me?"

The same face; the very same. Marley in his pigtail, usual waistcoat, tights and boots. The chain he drew was clasped about his middle. It was long, and wound about him like a tail; and it was made of cash boxes, keys, padlocks, ledgers, deeds, and heavy purses wrought with steel. His body was transparent; so that Scrooge, observing him, and looking through his waistcoat, could see the two buttons on his coat behind.

"You are fettered," said Scrooge, trembling. "Tell me why?"

"I wear the chain I forged in life," replied the Ghost. "I made it link by link and yard by yard. I girded it of my own free will, and of my own free will I wore it. Is its pattern strange to you?"

Scrooge trembled more and more. "But you were always a good man of business, Jacob," faltered Scrooge.

"Business!" cried the Ghost, wringing his hands again. "Mankind was my business. The common welfare was my business; charity, mercy, forbearance, and benevolence, were all my business. The dealing of my trade were but a drop of water in the comprehensive ocean of my business."

—EXCERPTED FROM *A CHRISTMAS CAROL* BY CHARLES DICKENS

HOW TO BALANCE A BANK ACCOUNT

There are not a lot of absolutely essential, must-do things in business, but balancing your bank account every month is definitely one. Your bank account is the lifeblood of the business, and you need to know how healthy and accurate it is. "Balancing" a bank account means reconciling the amount of money the bank shows on its statement to the amount of money you show in your checkbook or banking records.

By balancing your account (or reconciling the account, which means the same thing), you verify that you actually have the money in the bank that you think you have, that you didn't make some adding or subtracting or posting error, that bank charges are correct and posted to your records, and, very important, that there were no withdrawals that you didn't know about: someone or some stealth software that gained access to your account and stole your money.

If you are using an independent bookkeeper or a bookkeeping service to keep your financial records, I still think it is important to balance your own bank account, or at the very least, to examine every entry on the bank statement before giving it to the bookkeeper to balance. It's your money, and you really need to know that it is still there.

Balancing a bank account is the same process no matter how you keep your records. Some businesses keep bank records in a checkbook (check register), which is just a handwritten record of deposits and withdrawals. Many businesses use a spreadsheet or accounting software. Most accounting software walks you through the reconciliation steps, but it isn't automatic; you still need to know what needs to be reconciled.

Whatever recordkeeping system you use, you will not be able to balance your bank account unless you have a complete, up-to-date record of your banking activity: all deposits, all checks written, all debit card charges, all electronic transactions, and any cash withdrawals. If you don't have these records, it's time to go back and read the Keeping Records chapter. Otherwise, we've got the cart before the horse.

Balance the bank account as soon as the monthly bank statement arrives. Every day you delay, you've added more entries to your records, meaning more reconciling items, more time spent balancing the account, more chances for errors, and more risk of loss if there is a real problem.

The Bank Statement Balance

Balancing a bank account starts with the balance shown on your bank statement: the amount of money the bank says you have in your account at the end of the month. That amount will rarely agree with the balance in your records at the end of the month. But you know that. What you may not know, if you've never balanced a bank account, is that the difference is almost always easy to locate and reconcile. The difference is usually due to one or more of the following:

1. Checks you have written that have not yet cleared the bank, commonly referred to as "outstanding checks."

2. Debit card charges you have not posted to your records.

3. Electronic transactions (deposits, withdrawals, and automated payments) that you have not posted to your records.

4. Deposits you made at the end of the month that the bank did not receive until the first of the next month, known as "deposits in transit."

5. If you are a credit card merchant, credit card transaction fees you did not record.

6. Transactions that you authorized and recorded but have not yet reached your bank, such as billing a customer's credit card on the last day of the month.

7. Any returned (bounced) checks that you still show as deposits.

8. Interest earned or bank service charges you have not recorded in your records.

9. Someone's error—usually yours.

Updating Your Records

The first step in reconciling a bank account is to update your records to include transactions that appear on your bank statement that you have not recorded:

1. Unrecorded debit card payments or automatic payments.

2. Bank fees, check printing charges, ATM charges, and other bank service charges. If you get a bank charge you don't think is proper, call the bank and talk to them about it. Very often, the bank will cancel the charge. They would rather keep your business and your goodwill than get a $5 fee out of you.

3. If you are a credit card merchant, record any credit card fees your credit card processor charges you to process your customers' purchases. Many credit card providers show these fees as a separate deduction from your bank account, directly below the deposit made for the sale. Some credit card processors, however, do not show their fees separately. These processors deduct their fees from the amount of the sale, depositing an amount that is less than what you billed the customer. If you recorded the full amount of the sale, you now need to adjust your records to account for the fees. Record the difference (the difference between what you recorded as a sale and what the processor deposited) as an expense. You could, if you prefer, just reduce your income record to agree with the deposit. The net income is the same whichever way you record the transaction. But by netting the fees against the income instead of recording them separately, you don't have a record of your actual sales, because they've been reduced by the amount of the fees.

Neither the IRS nor your bank will care, as the taxable income is the same, but you may want to have that information: How much did you actually sell, and how much did you pay in fees?

4. If you receive electronic payments, such as through PayPal, record these the same way you record credit card income.

5. If your bank account earns interest, record the interest.

Reconcile

Once you have updated your bank account records, it's time to do the reconciliation. Some businesses reconcile using pencil and paper, and some businesses use software. The procedures are the same. If you follow these procedures, reconciling (balancing) your bank account will take only a few minutes each month. Hopefully.

1. The first step is to determine which checks you wrote have cleared the bank. (If you don't write checks, you can skip this step, and steps 2 and 3.) Match each check listed on the bank statement with your record of checks written. Mark or highlight the checks that cleared the bank. Compare the check amount on the bank statement with the amount you entered in your check record. Too many speedy check writers will write a check for $15.16 and post it in the check record as $16.15. It is known as "transposition" and is an occupational disease of even the best bookkeepers. There will most likely be checks you have written that have not cleared the bank yet. These "outstanding" checks are part of your reconciliation.

2. Some financial institutions and large corporations are using electronic check processing, also called check conversion, electronic checks, or e-checks. You write a regular check as you normally do, but the bank does not show the payment with their list of your other checks. The "converted" check will appear on your bank statement as a miscellaneous withdrawal or some similar heading, showing the check number, payee, and amount. You do not need to record the check any differently than you normally do, you

just have to look for it in a different place on the bank statement. Compare the amount shown on the bank statement with the amount you recorded in your check record, and mark or highlight the checks just like in step 1 above.

3. Add up the checks you have written that have not cleared the bank, the ones without a check mark next to them. These are your outstanding checks. Subtract this amount from the bank statement balance.

4. Match the deposits on your bank record with the deposits shown on the bank statement. If there are any late-month deposits you made that didn't get to the bank until the first of the next month, add these deposits (the "deposits in transit") to your bank statement balance.

Unlike checks, which can take days or even weeks to clear the bank, deposits should clear the bank immediately. Electronic deposits usually take two business days; mailed deposits take two to three days. Credit card deposits take one to two business days, or longer, if you have a delayed deposit agreement with your credit card processor. Any real lag in a bank recording of deposits may mean a lost deposit. Contact the bank at once.

The final figure you come up with—the bank statement balance reduced by the outstanding checks, and increased by any deposits in transit—should equal the balance on your bank records. It doesn't? Darn. Let's try to isolate the problem.

Did you record all of the transactions that appeared on the bank statement? When you checked off the canceled checks and the deposits, did the amounts all agree? Are you sure? If your bank statement includes photocopies of the checks, at the bottom right-hand corner of each canceled check you'll see a computer-generated number. This is the amount the bank actually paid out. You may find your error here. It may be different than the amount posted to your records.

What else? Examine the bank statement: The beginning balance should be the same as last month's ending balance. Was there a reconciling item on last month's statement you forgot to post to your records? Did you balance last month's bank statement? (I'm still trying.)

Does your software calculate your balances, or do you add and subtract them by hand? If you manually record the balances, the error is 99 percent certain to be in your running bank record balance. Sometime during the month, you wrote a check or made a debit card purchase and recorded the correct amount, but subtracted it incorrectly from the balance. Or added a deposit incorrectly. Go back and re-figure the balance, withdrawal by withdrawal and deposit by deposit.

I think that it is impossible to go through all these procedures and not locate the error. But if you've done the impossible, I suggest one more thing. Put it all away for a few days and forget it. Later, when you're in a better mood, repeat these procedures, from scratch. Don't look at your old calculations; if they are wrong, they will throw you off.

The one solution I failed to mention is the easiest: forget it. Assume you've made a mistake somewhere, correct your balance to agree with the reconciliation, and forget it. Especially if it's only a few dollars. But that's just not my nature, so . . .

Protecting Your Bank Account

A thief can get your bank account number (it's on every check you write), break into your bank's database, and withdraw money from your account. Thieves can accomplish this whether you do online banking or not. And you may not know anything about it until the monthly bank statement comes in.

Legally, businesses have only twenty-four hours to report unauthorized withdrawals and not be liable for the loss (individuals legally have at least thirty days to report). Some banks offer businesses a longer time period to report losses and will cover part or all of your losses. If your bank does guarantee the safety of your account, get that guarantee in writing and read it, especially the fine print. And then make sure your bank notifies you if they change the policy.

Banks advise businesses to check their bank activity and balance every day. Many business owners do, but most don't. Whatever cautions you do or don't take, examine your monthly bank statement as soon as you get it and report any unauthorized activity. Be especially alert to any very small deposits (pennies) you didn't make. Penny deposits mean that some crook is testing your bank account to see if it is active.

Some banks will, at a written request from you, automatically block all electronic withdrawals, all electronic deposits, or both. This will stop any hacker from taking money from your bank account. But this will not be possible if you authorize any automatic payments or if you are a credit card merchant processing payments through your bank account. There may also be a problem with checks you write that payees convert to electronic withdrawals, a process used by some large corporations.

This is not a theoretical "not likely to happen" scenario. It happened to a client of mine, a fraudulent withdrawal of thousands of dollars. My client was fortunate that the manager of the client's bank noticed the large withdrawal and was able to stop the transaction. One good reason to do business with a small, locally owned bank. Other businesses have not been so lucky. There are horror stories of businesses that had their bank accounts cleaned out, no cooperation from their bank, and no legal recourse.

Businesses that do online banking are even more vulnerable because the business's own computer can be hacked. A thief gets your user name and password and steals your money. Last year, a business in Michigan was hacked and had over $500,000 stolen from its bank account. The business computer was not protected well enough. The business's bank refused to make good on the loss. The fraud department at the bank told the business (and this is a direct quote), "What's wrong with you? How could you let this happen?"

If you don't do any online banking, make sure you don't have a user name or password that if stolen can be used to move money out of your account. If you do online banking, consider setting up a separate bank account that is not online and keep the bulk of your funds in the separate account.

If your account is compromised once, it will most likely be compromised again. You should immediately close the account and open a new one. It's a huge hassle and possibly a big expense (new checks, deposit slips, etc.), but it's the only way to stop the theft.

BALANCE SHEETS

A balance sheet, also known as a "statement of assets and liabilities" or "net worth statement," is a listing of your assets, liabilities, and net worth (equity) at any given point in time.

Most lenders and investors will ask to see a balance sheet when considering business loans.

Bear Soft Pretzel Co.
as of December 31

Assets

Current Assets		
Cash		$375
Accounts Receivable	$140	
Less allowance for bad debts	($20)	
		$120
Prepaid insurance		$150
Inventory (at lower of cost or market)		
Pretzels--hot	$25	
Pretzels--stale	$1	
Flour, sugar, salt	$75	
		$101
Other Assets		
Equipment, at cost	$2,300	
Less accumulated depreciation	($450)	
		$1,850
Total Assets		$2,596

Liabilities

Current Liabilities		
Accounts Payable		$120
Loan payable, portion due within one year		$250
Long-Term Liabilities		
Balance of loan payments		$750
Total Liabilities		$1,120
NET WORTH (owner's equity)		$1,476
		$2,596

Large, publicly held corporations are required to prepare audited balance sheets. Balance sheets are required on partnership tax returns if total income is $250,000 or more, or total assets are $1 million or more. Balance sheets are required on corporation tax returns if total income or total assets are $250,000 or more. Balance sheets are not required for Schedule C or Schedule C-EZ sole proprietorship tax returns.

Balance sheets are made up of three sections: (1) assets: property you own; (2) liabilities: money you owe; and (3) equity: the net worth of your business, the difference between the assets and the liabilities.

Assets

Assets are broken down into two categories:

Current Assets: Cash and assets that will be used or sold within a year. Current assets usually include accounts receivable (money your customers owe you), less an allowance for bad debts; notes and loans receivable (money owed to you other than regular credit accounts) due within one year; inventory, valued at cost or market, whichever is less; prepaid expenses beyond a year, such as next year's insurance. Current year's prepaid expenses are not included.

Other Assets: Cost of fixed assets such as equipment, vehicles, furniture, and buildings less the accumulated depreciation (or the approximate current value of the assets); cost of land; intangible assets such as patents; notes and loans receivable that will not be collected within one year.

Long-term notes and loans receivable that are payable to you in installments over several years should be split between "current assets" and "other assets." The amount coming due within one year should be shown as current; the balance should be listed under other assets.

Liabilities

Liabilities are divided into similar categories:

Current Liabilities: Accounts payable (your unpaid bills: money you owe your suppliers); loans payable due within one year; unpaid taxes; unpaid wages.

Long-Term Liabilities: Any loans or other liabilities due after one year. Loans payable in installments over several years should be split between "current" for the amount due within twelve months and "long-term" for the balance.

You should include under liabilities any "contingent" liabilities you know about. Contingent liabilities are crystal ball suppositions about the future: liabilities that may or may not materialize. If the IRS is auditing you or you are being sued, for example, and there is a possibility you will owe money, some dollar estimate of the liability should be included on the balance sheet. Contingent liability estimates should be clearly labeled as such and should be explained fully.

Some small businesses prepare balance sheets every month. Many small businesses never prepare balance sheets. The more complicated and diverse your business, the more likely a balance sheet will help you keep track of your assets and liabilities.

Most accounting software includes a balance sheet. You don't have to do anything except type in a date. If you do have the software, it is a good idea to print out a balance sheet at least once or twice a year and just give it a look, see if what it says you have (cash, assets) agrees with what you think you have.

PROFESSIONAL HELP

Accountants

This book should help you with most aspects of beginning and operating a small business without the need of an accountant. But the time may come when your finances are getting a bit too complicated, or you may need help incorporating or setting up an LLC. Anyone buying a going business or a franchise should get an accountant's help. And then there's income taxes. It's a rare business owner who has the time and inclination to study and understand tax laws.

How do you find a good accountant? Locating a good accountant is like trying to find a doctor or a reliable car mechanic: You have to ask around. The best people to ask are other business owners. It is essential to find an accountant with small business experience. It is not important what kind of small businesses the accountant works with, because small business tax law is pretty much the same whether it's a store or a freelancer or a professional or a home business.

If you do not know an accountant and can't get a reliable recommendation, here are a few suggestions and warnings to help in your search.

Do not pick a name at random from an internet listing or the phone book. There is no way to know what kind of person you will get or how qualified he or she may be.

Stay away from the storefront tax operations, the ones that open shop every January and promptly disappear April 15. Most of the people who work for these franchises have little experience, brief training, and are usually familiar only with Mr. and Mrs. Nine-to-Five and their typical tax problems. These part-time accountants are not trained to handle complex problems nor do they take the time to delve into your business finances to look for tax savings.

Choose an experienced tax accountant, and expect to pay professional prices. It is not necessary to hire a certified public accountant. CPAs are certainly qualified, but many excellent tax accountants are not CPAs. There are also Public Accountants (PAs) licensed in some states; Enrolled Agents (EAs) licensed by the federal government (despite the ominous name, EAs are not IRS agents, although some of them used to work for the IRS);

It is more vital than ever that you assume greater responsibility for your financial future. You ought not to rely exclusively on paid advisors. You should be knowledgeable enough to raise good questions and evaluate answers when you deal with a professional. The informed client gets the best advice.

—Tax attorney Julian Block

and individuals who have no official license but who may be excellent tax accountants. Judge the accountant by his or her experience, how many small business clients he or she has, and whether you like the accountant or not.

Talk to the accountant personally before you commit yourself. Does the accountant seem familiar with your situation and your problems? Most important, does the accountant make sense to you? Beware of anyone who talks arcane business jargon or IRS code sections. You need an accountant to answer questions, in words you understand.

Ask the accountant if he prepares your tax return himself or if he outsources or subcontracts the preparation to someone else. Some accountants send their clients' tax returns off to mass-production tax processing centers, sometimes outside the United States. Do you want someone you don't know, or someone in another country, preparing your taxes?

It's important to understand what an accountant can do for you and, just as important, what the accountant cannot and will not do for you.

A good accountant will prepare your tax return faster than you thought humanly possible, and will know all of the tax options you have and help you make the best choice. A good accountant will show you ways you might reduce taxes by restructuring your business, changing your recordkeeping, timing certain purchases and payments, or making other changes that will help you better deal with taxes. This is the accountant's area of expertise, and you should make the most of it—you're paying for it.

Tax professionals are legally accountable for the work they do and the advice they give. They will not tell you how to break the law, and they don't want to hear about any illegal tax maneuvers. There is no legal confidentiality between you and your accountant. The accountant can report illegal activities to the IRS. Certainly you can and should ask honest questions—Is this legal? Is this deductible? Must this be reported?—but expect honest answers. Don't put the accountant in a situation the accountant shouldn't be in; you may be causing trouble for yourself and for the accountant.

These warnings don't mean that you and your accountant shouldn't explore questionable areas of the law if you are so willing, and if the accountant feels you have legal ground to stand on. Some tax laws are straightforward; but many are ambiguous, subject to interpretation, honest disagreement, what we call "gray areas" of the law. Some laws are so new and convoluted, no one is quite sure how to interpret them. The best tax accountants know, from experience and from studying tax manuals and court decisions, how to handle those gray areas.

Finally, avoid an accountant who takes your numbers, plugs them into a computer program, and hands you a return and a bill. Even if you don't know any questions to ask, your accountant should ask at least a few questions and put some personal thought into your return.

If an accountant prepares your entire 1040 tax return, only the business portion (Schedule C and related schedules) can be deducted as a business expense. Partnership and corporation returns are fully deductible.

Bookkeepers

Accountants are not bookkeepers, and at the rates they charge, you don't want them to have to do any of your bookkeeping. Don't show up with a shoebox full of receipts. Don't show up with incomplete records that need to be worked on. If you can't get your records right, if you hate posting that three-month backlog of invoices, hire a bookkeeper. Bookkeepers not only charge a lot less than tax accountants, bookkeeping is what they do every day. To locate a bookkeeper, get a recommendation from your accountant or from other business owners.

Some accountants do offer bookkeeping services, have bookkeepers who work with them, at a much lower cost than their tax services.

Attorneys

Most small businesses don't need an attorney. Your accountant can handle any tax matter and can probably provide all the help you need in drafting most business agreements. You may need an attorney's help filing legal papers, incorporating or setting up an LLC, but I suggest you check with an accountant first. The accountant will know what requires an attorney's signature and what doesn't.

If you are being sued or are suing someone, this is beyond the accountant's domain. But your accountant can probably recommend an attorney who specializes in business litigation.

ACCEPTING CREDIT AND DEBIT CARDS

It is easy and quick for a business or a self-employed individual to become a credit card/debit card merchant, to be able to accept credit card and debit card payments from your customers or clients.

Credit and debit cards are handled the same way, through the same account. As far as you, the seller, are concerned, you don't have to know if a card is a credit or debit card, and you don't have to get a PIN number from buyers. Throughout this chapter, all references to credit cards include debit cards.

To become a credit card merchant, also known as obtaining "merchant status," you do not apply directly to the credit card companies (VISA, MasterCard, Discover, and American Express). You go through a bank or an internet credit card processor (provider). Credit card processing is also offered by some trade and business associations and by membership businesses like Costco. Credit card processors are also known as independent sales organizations (ISOs) or merchant service providers (MSPs). The terms all mean the same thing.

Businesses wanting to accept credit cards have several options to choose from, and every one is different. But they all cost money, typically 2 percent to 4 percent of the sale. That percentage applies to the entire amount of a sale, including sales tax, any shipping or service charges, and tips if customers add them to the credit card bill.

So the first step in deciding about becoming a credit/debit card merchant is to consider: (1) Will your business lose sales if you don't accept cards? and (2) can you afford—are you willing to pay—2 percent to 4 percent of your income to accept cards? The answer to both questions depends a lot on the kind of business you operate.

Retail: Almost all retail stores accept cards. It's just about impossible to survive in a retail business if your customers can't pay with a card. There are exceptions, quirky one-of-a-kind shops that are cash only, but they are rare indeed.

Restaurants: Most restaurants accept cards. But unlike retail stores, there are still many holdouts, restaurants that will only accept cash and, in small towns where everybody knows everybody, checks. Still, it would have to be a very popular restaurant to be able to refuse cards and still keep customers. Out-of-towners and people driving through often don't have enough cash with them and don't feel like trying to find an ATM.

Manufacturers and wholesalers: Businesses selling to other businesses, businesses with regular repeat customers and large-dollar sales, usually do not accept cards. The customers are accustomed to paying by check, and that 2 percent to 4 percent can add up to a lot of lost money for every sale.

Professionals: Many accountants, attorneys, doctors, dentists, and similar professionals accept cards, but many don't. The bills often are high, so the cost of accepting cards can be significant. Also, clients choose professionals based on other factors than how the bill is paid. No one is going to switch accountants or doctors because they won't take a credit card.

Tradespeople: Like professionals, many contractors, electricians, plumbers, and other tradespeople do not accept cards. People with commercial shops, especially repair shops, usually accept cards.

Craftspeople: Just about every craftsperson I know accepts credit and debit cards. Many crafts sales are impulse buys, and if the seller can't take a card, the buyer is just going to walk.

Online businesses: Most online businesses that are selling directly to customers, as opposed to sending the customers to Amazon.com or some other sales site, take cards. Some small online businesses don't take cards but take PayPal. An online merchant can easily accept cards and PayPal payments if the merchant wants to. PayPal and similar online payment services are covered later in this chapter.

International sales: Credit cards are an easy way to handle international sales. You process international sales in U.S. dollars, and you get paid the same amount as though it was a U.S. transaction. No currency conversions to worry about.

How Credit Cards Are Processed

Credit card transactions are processed through a telephone landline or over the internet. Many banks offer both options, but internet processors only work through the internet. Other providers offer one or both options.

Some merchants prefer a landline connection because they find it more secure, or they are uncomfortable with internet transactions, or in some rural areas, there may not be fast or reliable internet service.

With a landline connection, a merchant buys or leases a credit card terminal, also known as a payment terminal or point-of-sale terminal, a device that takes credit card information and transmits it to your credit card processor. The terminal can share the line with a telephone, though you cannot use both at the same time, or you can install a second phone line just for the terminal. When you make a sale, you swipe or insert the customer's card and fill in the amount of the purchase. If you don't have the customer's card, you key in (hand enter) the card number and expiration date and the amount of the purchase. The terminal dials the bank's credit card processing service, verifies if the card is valid, processes the purchase, prints a receipt, and deposits the money in your account. It takes a few seconds, and it's done.

Internet credit card processing can be accomplished in several ways:

1. You can process cards using any computer or device that has an internet connection. Some processors refer to this as a "virtual terminal." Log on to the bank or card processor's website and enter the transaction. Most desktop computers, however, do not have an input to allow a card to be swiped, so the computer can only be used for hand-entered transactions.

2. You can use what's called "mobile" card processing: a smartphone or tablet (iPad). Banks and credit card processors offer their "mobile" merchants a free mag-stripe reader, a small square device that attaches to your smartphone or tablet and lets you swipe a credit card. If you are processing a telephone or internet order where you don't have the card, you can hand enter card information. For smartphones and tablets, you will have to download an app to enable the processing.

3. You can purchase or lease a stand-alone terminal, sometimes called a point-of-sale stand, sort of an internet-connected cash register (without the cash drawer) that works with an iPad or similar tablet. "Point-of-sale" is a card-processing term that means your

customer is there in person with a card (also called a "card-present transaction"). The point-of-sale process can be configured to accept payment apps, one-touch payment systems, "digital wallets," and similar tap-and-go payments, usually for additional fees. The point-of-sale system can be expanded to include a barcode scanner, printer, and even accounting software.

You are not limited to one of these options. Your credit card account can be accessed through any of them.

Costs

It doesn't cost anything to apply for a merchant account; at least it shouldn't. If a card provider wants money up front to "process" or "evaluate" your application, take your business somewhere else. Once you're signed up with a provider, you may have to buy or lease a terminal to process the credit cards; that is, if you need a terminal, which many businesses don't.

Every internet provider has a different fee structure. All providers charge a percentage of the sale, typically about 2.5 percent for swiped cards and 3.5 percent for keyed-in (hand entered) cards. Some providers charge a higher percentage to process international transactions. There is also a per-transaction charge, usually 15¢ to 25¢ for every sale processed. There are no other fees, no monthly charges, and no minimum usage requirements. Some providers, however, offer an optional package: For a monthly fee, usually about $20 a month, the percentages they charge are about a half-percent lower. Some providers also offer a flat-fee option covering all transactions, with no percentage deducted from each sale, for about $300 a month.

Bank fee structures are very different from those of internet providers. The percentages banks charge are often lower, sometimes a good deal lower, than what internet processors charge. But banks have monthly or quarterly service charges, and annual "compliance fees" that internet providers do not charge. For a small business, those bank fees can really add up. Businesses with a low volume of credit card sales will probably find internet services to be less costly than banks. Businesses with a large volume of credit card sales, however, will pay less by using a bank, because the lower percentages charged by banks will more than offset the monthly and annual fees.

If you terminate an account with a provider, there are usually no termination fees, but you should verify this before setting up an account.

Cost of a Terminal

If you need a credit card terminal, which almost all retail stores and restaurants need to process cards and print receipts, it is probably less expensive to purchase a terminal than to lease one. But some credit card processors make a lot of their profit from leasing terminals and often refuse to sell them outright. Processors are quick to point out that a leased terminal is automatically updated for new software or replaced for free if new hardware is required. If you are buying a terminal, do not buy a used terminal or one from a third party unless you know it will work with your provider. Different terminals are usually not compatible with different providers and different generations of software.

Getting Paid

An important consideration when comparing credit card processors is how and when you get paid. Card processors can deposit your sales into your bank account, and deduct their fees from your bank account, if you have a bank account and want to give the processor your bank account information; or the processor can put the money in a PayPal or similar electronic account; or, usually for an extra fee, mail you a check.

Find out how long it takes to get your money once a sale is made. Some processors deposit your money immediately, but some may have a one-day or two-day delay.

Some processors pay you the full amount of the sale, and deduct their fee separately, but some processors deduct their fee before sending you your money. Personally, I greatly prefer the two-step process, receiving the full amount of the sale and paying the fee separately. It makes it much easier to compare the sale with the money received: They will be the same amount of money. I can get confused when, say, I make a $25.00 sale but receive $24.15 (or whatever the amount is after deducting the fees). I much prefer to receive the full $25.00 and be charged a separate card processing fee.

One important thing to find out before you sign with an online processor is how a sale will appear on your customer's credit or debit card statement. The sale should say it was made by your business name, and not by Trust Us Credit Card Service or some other name that the buyer never heard of and thinks is a fraudulent transaction.

Finally, a question I'm always asking: Can you trust a credit card processor you never heard of? Well, I wouldn't. I suggest picking a service with a well-known name. Do some online snooping to see if there are a lot of complaints: Type the name of the processor in a search engine and see what shows up. But keep in mind that, the internet being what it is, there will be some complaints about *every* business. After you sign up, make a small transaction (use your own credit card and spend $1) and see how well it was handled. See how long it takes to get your money. Check your bank account every day for a week or so to be sure nothing "unusual" occurred.

Refunds

If you refund a customer's money, crediting the customer's card, the processors will take the money back out of your bank account. Most processors will refund the fee they charged you for the original transaction, but some don't. Most processors limit the amount of time after a purchase that they will process a refund, usually 60 to 120 days. Don't confuse refunds with chargebacks, which are an entirely different situation. You initiate refunds. The processors initiate chargebacks.

Chargebacks

A chargeback is when your credit card processor takes back money already distributed to you from a prior transaction because of a customer complaint. A chargeback occurs when your customer disputes the credit card bill, for any reason at all: The customer claims he never received the merchandise, or the merchandise was damaged or different than what was ordered, or the customer was overcharged or didn't even place the order.

If you are not able to resolve the problem with the customer, replacing the merchandise or crediting back the customer's card, the credit card processor will refund the money to the customer and deduct the money from your account. You really have no recourse when a customer refuses to pay a bill. Most credit card processors charge a fee, sometimes a substantial fee, for chargebacks. Most processors will cancel merchants who have an excessive number of chargebacks.

Chargebacks are not the same as fraud. Fraud involves stolen or bogus card numbers.

Fraud

If you fill an order that was placed using a fraudulent or stolen card, you may or may not be responsible for the loss, depending on your card processor's policies. Before signing up with a card processor, find out their policy regarding fraud.

Many processors, particularly banks, will cover fraud losses for in-person transactions. For orders taken online or over the phone, most credit card processors will not cover fraud losses. Even if your credit card terminal accepts the sale and gives you an approval, there is no guarantee that you won't get charged if the card was stolen or fraudulent.

Credit card fraud is a significant problem for some internet merchants. The ease with which people can hide their identities and use fraudulent credit card numbers is much greater on the internet than for in-person dealings. The internet invites all kinds of scam artists to try their luck. Businesses selling high-ticket items such as computers, cameras, and expensive jewelry, and businesses selling products people might be tempted to steal are more likely to be targeted than businesses selling less expensive or less "flashy" items: books, office supplies, stuff that does not attract thieves too much.

Possible indications of fraudulent orders:

1. Unusual orders, large-dollar orders, and orders for a lot of items. Most people order one item or only a few items. Someone who orders one of everything may be suspicious.

2. Orders from foreign countries.

3. Orders with different "bill to" and "ship to" addresses.

4. Orders requesting overnight or expedited delivery. A thief won't care how much it costs to ship, since he doesn't plan to pay for it anyway.

5. Orders from unconcerned customers, such as not caring about color or size.

6. Orders that do not include the customer's phone number.

7. Orders for "your product," obviously not caring about what it is you are selling.

If you have a reason to be suspicious of an order, you can contact your credit card company to verify a card owner's name and address. You can call the customer on the phone to "confirm" the order. Not many thieves will give you a valid telephone number. But use the confirmation as a last resort. Many people, people placing legitimate orders, may not want you calling their home or office. What if the order is a gift for someone in the family? (What if the order is a gift for someone *not* in the family?)

Applying for Merchant Status: Banks

Banks are very choosy about who they will set up as credit card merchants. Visible public operations such as retail stores usually have no trouble getting merchant status, but home businesses and internet businesses are often turned down, especially new businesses. If you've been in business a few years or if you have an established account with the bank, you are much more likely to be approved. Keep in mind that the bank, not the credit card company, decides who gets merchant status. So if one bank turns you down, try another (and another).

Most banks require their credit card merchants to have an account at that bank. If you do business at another bank, you may have to open a second account and then transfer money from one account to the other.

Applying for Merchant Status: Online Credit Card Processors

Online processors are less picky than banks. Most businesses, even brand-new businesses, are usually accepted by online processors. But not always. Some processors will run a credit check on you. People with bad credit are likely to be rejected. Even if you have good credit, some processors will decide, for reasons known only to them, not to accept your application.

Most online processors handle all credit and debit card sales regardless of how you made the sale: online, in person, telephone, mail order. Some online processors, however, only handle sales that are made online; that is, your customers made their purchases online. I suggest that you don't sign up with a processor that limits your sales to online orders only.

Some of the best known processors are Square, Intuit Go Payment (Intuit owns QuickBooks), PayPal (this is in addition to PayPal's better known money transfer service), and Stripe.

Whatever you decide, you are not stuck with it if you don't like how it's working out. You can switch processors. You can add or cancel card processing any time.

Your Customers

Most businesses charge the same prices to both cash and credit card customers. Some businesses, however, add a surcharge (or a "convenience fee" or "checkout fee," as some businesses like to call it) for credit card purchases—which, by the way, irritates some credit card customers, possibly enough to lose their business. American Express specifically forbids merchants from adding a surcharge. Federal law prohibits a surcharge on debit card transactions.

You can instead offer a discount for cash purchases—which, unlike surcharges, doesn't irritate anybody. There are no laws or credit card issuer requirements prohibiting cash discounts. Or you can have, as many gas stations do, two prices: one for cards, one for cash. You can set minimum-dollar purchase requirements for card sales. You can accept some types of cards and not others, which some merchants do because banks often charge different percentages for different types of cards. American Express in particular apparently takes a bigger cut than other cards, so many merchants do not take AmEx cards.

Some businesses have different prices for online customers than for in-person or telephone customers, or have special deals just for customers who go to their website. Personally, I dislike that kind of merchandising. I don't like businesses that want to charge me more because I order over the phone. Still, there's nothing illegal about it.

For more information about selling online, see the Online Operations chapter.

Collecting Personal Information

Many states have laws that specify what kind of information merchants can and cannot ask for or write down when a consumer pays with a credit card. Asking for addresses, phone numbers, and even zip codes is often prohibited when making in-person credit card sales. Asking to see a credit card

when taking a customer's check is often prohibited. Look up your state laws. Customers can get quite upset if you ask for too much information.

IRS Reporting

If you accept credit and debit card payments, the card processor will report your total sales for the year to the IRS. The processor will send you a Form 1099-K, "Payment Card and Third Party Network Transactions," no later than January 31 of the new year.

If you collect money through PayPal or other money-transfer service, or if you make sales through internet sales outlets such as Amazon.com, this income will also be reported to the IRS on Form 1099-K, but only if you make over two hundred sales a year *and* if the total sales exceed $20,000 a year. This threshold minimum does not apply to credit/debit card processors; they will report all sales.

Lara Stonebraker, owner, Cunningham's Coffee, a retail coffee store: "We thought about having accounts for people in the neighborhood but decided that we did not want to mess with it. It would take a lot of book work, keeping track of accounts and what they owe. But we do have MasterCard and VISA. People just don't carry the cash around anymore. I think people are more willing to spend money if they can charge it. They feel they won't be billed for a long time."

Nick Mein, owner of Wallpapers Plus, a neighborhood retail store: "I don't think the credit cards are worth it. We must have had $600 of credit sales at the very most. And they take 3 percent, which is a lot for a mini-merchant like me. Besides, everybody has a checking account. I'd rather take checks than VISA. In my business it's easy for me to take checks because the kind of people who buy our stuff are usually responsible. We've never had a bounced check."

MARRIED COUPLES

Married couples who own and operate a business together have several options for setting up the business. They can create a joint venture, a partnership, a corporation, a limited liability company, or a sole proprietorship. Each of these legal forms requires different paperwork, and each can result in differences in income taxes, Social Security, Medicare, and fringe benefits. It's basically up to the couple to decide how they want to structure their business.

In discussing the legal options and tax rules for married couples, the IRS considers any couple legally married in any state to be eligible for all of the options and benefits described in this chapter.

Joint Venture

The easiest, simplest way for both spouses to own a business together and share in all of the benefits of the business is to set up what the IRS calls a "joint venture." The couple splits the income and the expenses between them and files two Schedule Cs, "Profit or Loss from Business" (the same form used for sole proprietors), one for each spouse. There is no tax return or tax form called "joint venture," just the two Schedule Cs, which are included on the couple's joint 1040 tax return.

If both spouses are equally involved in the business, a determination the spouses themselves make, the income and expenses would be split 50-50. The amounts on each Schedule C would be identical. If the spouses decided that they did not equally share in the business, they can use a different division of income and expenses based on their individual involvement. For keeping records and calculating taxes, it certainly would be faster, easier, and simpler to decide that the business is a 50-50

MAY I HELP YOU, SIR?

venture. You could prepare one Schedule C, with half the income and half the expenses, and just photocopy it.

The laws for joint ventures are identical to the laws for sole proprietorships.

Partnership

The couple can set up a general partnership. The couple can be equal 50-50 partners or use a different division of income and expense. The spouses file a partnership tax return (Form 1065) and report their individual incomes from the partnership on their joint 1040 tax return.

The ownership, operation, and taxes for a spousal partnership are exactly the same as for the joint venture described above. A partnership, however, requires the extra tax return (the 1065 partnership return) and will have to be much more careful how money is put into the business and how expenses are paid. You should read about partnerships in the Growing Up chapter before deciding to start one. A joint venture accomplishes the same goals as a partnership but is much easier to set up and administer.

Sole Proprietorship

The couple could decide that only one of them, either spouse, is earning all of the income and is the sole owner of the business. The other spouse is not officially included in the business, not officially earning any money. No paperwork is required. Any payment either spouse gets is just money withdrawn from the business, like any sole proprietorship. (If this does not make sense to you, read about sole proprietorships in the Getting Started chapter.)

The spouse with the income (the spouse that officially owns the business) would file a Schedule C tax return, and the income would be included on the couple's 1040 tax return. The income taxes the couple pays, assuming the couple files a joint return, is the same they would pay as a joint venture or a partnership. The self-employment tax, however, would apply only to one spouse, the one who officially owns the business, and only that spouse would get Social Security credit (this is covered more below).

This "unofficial" status of one spouse is for tax purposes only. Both spouses could actually work in the business; both spouses could write checks if both spouses' names were on the checking account; both spouses could make tax-deductible business purchases. However, the "nonworking" spouse would not be able to write off any deductions for travel should he or she accompany the spouse who officially owns the business.

Despite the drawbacks and potential problems, many businesses owned by married couples are structured as sole proprietorships, usually because one of the spouses started the business alone or started the business before the couple married, and the other spouse joined after the business was established. If the couple wanted to convert the business from a one-spouse ownership to both spouses, the couple could easily turn it into a joint venture simply by splitting the income on their next tax return. It would basically be the same business. If the spouses wanted to convert the business to a general partnership, however, or a corporation or LLC, the result would be an entirely new business, requiring new licenses, new IRS and state ID numbers, new bank account, new tax procedures, and a world of new rules and regulations.

Limited Liability Company

If both spouses own an LLC, the spouses are taxed as partners. The LLC files a partnership tax return. If only one spouse owns the LLC, the owner-spouse is taxed as a sole proprietor and files a Schedule C tax return. The same married-couple issues that apply to partnerships and sole proprietorships apply to LLCs.

Corporation

A couple who set up a corporation would both be stockholders of the business, and on the payroll as employees. In states that allow one-person corporations, one spouse could own the corporation and could hire (or not hire) the other spouse as an employee. This, like setting up any corporation, is definitely an area to discuss with an accountant.

Income Tax and Self-Employment Tax

The income taxes on the profits of a joint venture, partnership, sole proprietorship, or LLC are exactly the same, no matter who owns the business, one spouse or both. The couple combines their incomes, and pays one income tax on the total business profit.

The income taxes from a small corporation will be similar.

Self-employment tax, however, is figured differently than income tax. Only the spouse who officially owns the business is subject to self-employment tax. If the couple owns the business as a joint venture or a partnership or an LLC, each spouse is a business owner and each spouse pays self-employment tax on his or her share of the profit. If the business is owned 50-50, each spouse pays self-employment tax on 50 percent of the profits. And each spouse separately earns Social Security benefits based on that spouse's share of the profit.

If the business is structured as a sole proprietorship, with only one spouse officially owning the business, only that spouse will pay self-employment tax, and only that spouse will get full Social Security benefits. I'm sure you can see the problems this might cause for the non-owning spouse, but it gets more interesting if the business is earning a profit in excess of $128,400 (see below).

If the business is a corporation, the owner or owners are employees of the business. Whoever is an employee of the business will pay Social Security tax and earn Social Security benefits. Whoever is not an employee of the business will not be paying into Social Security and will not be building up his or her Social Security fund.

Outside employment: A similar Social Security situation exists if one spouse has a high-paying outside job and is also the sole proprietor and the only official person in the business. The business profit subject to self-employment tax will be reduced by the amount of outside income (explained under "Self-Employment Tax" in the Taxes chapter), reducing the self-employment tax substantially.

Social Security Retirement

If one spouse is getting Social Security retirement, the payments are reduced if the recipient is also earning income above a certain amount (which is set by the Social Security Administration every year). If the other spouse was the sole owner of the business, the spouse receiving Social Security would not be penalized.

Businesses Making More Than $128,400

If the annual profit from your business is over $128,400, things change. (If the annual profit from your business is over $128,400, congratulations, you should be writing this book!) The Social Security portion of the self-employment tax, which is 12.4 percent, applies to income up to $128,400 (the current maximum, which increases every year). Above income of $128,400, you no longer pay the Social Security portion of the tax. Only the Medicare portion, which is a much lower 2.9 percent tax, continues above $128,400. There is no maximum earnings level subject to the 2.9 percent Medicare tax.

If one spouse is a sole proprietor and the other spouse is not officially part of the business, the first $128,400 of profit from the business is subject to the Social Security tax. However, if both spouses are officially part of the business, each spouse pays Social Security tax on each spouse's share of the business profit, up to $128,400 maximum income *per spouse*. Together, the spouses could pay as much as twice the maximum a one-owner business would pay.

Another Option: Spouse Hiring Spouse

A spouse could set up a sole proprietorship and hire his or her spouse as an employee. The employee-spouse would be on the payroll like any employee, with a wage, payroll deductions (including Social Security), W-2 statements, and all the rules and regulations that go along with hiring employees. It is an expensive and complicated way to have both spouses participate in the business, but it does have one tax benefit: Because one spouse is an official employee of the business, both spouses and their dependents are eligible for employer-paid health insurance, which is fully deductible as a business expense. This is explained under "Health Insurance" in the Taxes chapter. This tax benefit, however, is probably not worth the extra work and additional costs of hiring the spouse as an employee. This is something to discuss with an experienced tax accountant (or better yet, something to simply not pursue).

How about one spouse hiring the other as an outside contractor? What you've created are two separate businesses, two sole proprietorships. Unless the spouses want to own two separate businesses—and there is nothing wrong with that (see below)—it would be simpler and easier to set up a joint venture.

Two Separate Businesses

If married spouses each operate a business, where two complete and separate businesses exist, each spouse is a sole proprietor, each with his and her own set of records, permits and licenses, and Schedule C tax returns. If the couple files a joint tax return, the profit or loss from the two businesses are combined for figuring income tax. Each spouse pays self-employment tax on the profits from that spouse's business.

If the two businesses share any assets, share an office or other business space, or share any business expenses, the expenses should be divided between the two businesses, 50-50 if owned equally by both. It is not important which business actually writes the check or which has the equipment or lease or invoice in its name. Just be sure that each business keeps a record of its share of the expenses.

More Considerations

How a married couple's business is legally structured can have legal consequences well beyond IRS rules and tax returns. In some states (community property states), income earned by one spouse belongs equally to the nonworking spouse. Other states have different rules. People concerned about which spouse has legal rights to the earnings and assets of a couple's business should talk to an attorney. State laws vary on this important issue.

Just as important, the structure of the business can affect the feelings the couple have toward each other, how well they work together, and, alas, how difficult and how fair a divorce might turn out. This could be a particular problem if one spouse is not on the payroll or officially part of the business. What's more, if the unpaid spouse had to look for another job, it could be difficult to establish a work history or job- or credit-worthiness.

One very astute woman pointed out to me, "An unpaid worker is generally an unappreciated worker, causing resentment and possibly a great deal of difficulty in a marriage. Tax savings should not be the number one priority in a husband-wife business arrangement. Mutual respect, sense of responsibility, appreciation, and cooperation are far more important than saving tax dollars."

Unemployment Taxes, Workers' Compensation Insurance, and Retirement Plans

Regardless of whether the business is a joint venture, partnership, LLC, or sole proprietorship, neither spouse is subject to federal unemployment taxes and neither is eligible for federal unemployment benefits. Most states exempt spouses in business from state unemployment insurance and from workers' compensation insurance. Both spouses can participate in tax-deferred retirement plans.

Corporations come under different rules (as usual).

A Northern California business that provides consulting services is owned and operated by a husband and wife, but the business is in the wife's name only. When I inquired why they structured it that way, the wife answered, "Many of our clients are women who prefer to patronize businesses owned by women. It brings us more work."

MULTIPLE BUSINESSES

At one time, I owned three different businesses, all at the same time. It is not unusual for one person to have multiple income streams, to own and operate more than one business at a time. How you set up the businesses, the recordkeeping, licenses, and permits, and file tax returns depends on how you structure your businesses.

Sole Proprietorships

If your businesses are sole proprietorships, you have two options: (1) You can set up completely separate businesses, separate records, separate permits and licenses, and separate tax returns; or (2) you could combine the businesses into one business, with one set of records, one license, and one tax return.

If you have only one business, you need only one business license, one DBA, one insurance policy, one bank account, one payroll, and only one form—and one fee—for whatever government agencies are making demands on you. If you have more than one sole proprietorship, you may have to get two or more of everything.

The IRS requires you to fill out a separate Schedule C tax return for each sole proprietorship you

own. But the IRS lets you decide whether your ventures are separate businesses, or just parts of one business requiring only one Schedule C.

Your income and self-employment taxes will be exactly the same whether you have one or multiple sole proprietorships. The time and expense of filling out more than one tax return might be significant, especially if you hire an accountant, who will charge you for two Schedule C forms instead of just one.

If you have more than one business, the IRS requires that you keep separate records for each business. If you have only one business with several different "parts" or "divisions," you need to keep only one set of records.

If you want, you can easily separate the different parts of your business, using different columns in a ledger or different software categories, to separately account for each business-within-the-business; or you can lump them all together.

Although it is easier and less expensive to combine businesses, separating the businesses might be the most reliable way to really know how each business is doing. With completely separate records, you can be much more objective about the success of each business. If you ever want to sell one of the businesses, you will have separate records to show a buyer. If you want to get a loan on one of the businesses, particularly the one that is more profitable, the records for that particular business will paint a better picture.

If you do set up separate businesses or separate records for different parts of your business, shared expenses that apply to both businesses (such as office space, computer, telephone, employees working for both businesses) should be prorated between the businesses: 50-50, or any other split that reasonably approximates usage.

Whatever you decide, you can always change the business arrangement later. You can set up one business and then split it into two; you can set up two businesses and later combine them. You will not be able to backtrack, but you can make changes going forward.

Partnerships, Corporations, and LLCs

If any of your businesses are partnerships, corporations, or limited liability companies, each business must be accounted for separately, each with its own records, bank accounts, licenses, and tax returns, even if they are owned by the same person. That's not only the law, but also a protection for the owners of the businesses should legal or tax problems occur.

You can have multiple divisions within one partnership, corporation, or LLC, in much the same way you would set up multiple divisions within one sole proprietorship.

IMPORTING AND EXPORTING

Importing and exporting involve an entire world of international laws, special tax incentives, international trade procedures, licenses, duties and tariffs, and various "middlemen" such as agents, brokers, and freight forwarders that domestic businesses never encounter. You should be familiar with U.S. Customs and U.S. Commerce Department laws. You need to learn about standard payment terms, currency conversion, stability of foreign currencies, shipping terminology, and shipping methods.

Importing

Most of the people who get started in small-time importing are travelers on a trip or vacation overseas. They discover some handcraft or clothing that's attractive and inexpensive, or some clever invention or electronic marvel. They see some business potential in the products, and start figuring out how to bring the products back to the United States. And "figuring out" is something you really should do carefully.

CUSTOMS, DUTIES, AND QUOTAS

You can't just buy a few cases of whatever sparked your imagination and expect to bring it back to the United States without going through a maze of rules, customs, and duties. It is critically important that you have your paperwork in order. If your paperwork isn't done properly, Customs (U.S. Customs and Border Protection, or CBP) can confiscate and even destroy your merchandise. CBP has a book thicker than the New York City telephone directory, listing quotas and duties on hundreds of different products from dozens of different countries.

Some imports are subject to quotas: so many pairs of men's shoes from Honduras per year, for example. Many countries have formal agreements with the United States, called "quota visas," limiting the quantities of each item they are allowed to export to the United States.

Many imports are subject to duties, which are taxes you, the importer, must pay before CBP will release your goods to you. Duties vary, from insignificant amounts on handcrafts and electronics, and up to as much as 90 percent, 100 percent, and even 110 percent of your cost on some restricted items from restricted countries.

Politics, and things like "most favored nation" status, play a major role in determining how easy and how expensive it is to import different goods from different countries. Strong U.S. industries like tire manufacturers fight imports, so the duties on tires are much higher than those on, say, handcrafted items and other goods that are not made in the United States by large, influential corporations.

Certain types of goods—chemicals, products made from animals, agricultural and food products, products made with toxic materials (such as lead-based paints), goods made using child or indentured labor—are often restricted or prohibited.

If you want to know what tariffs are imposed on a product you want to import, the U.S. Customs office has a list of thousands of products, categorized by a four- or six-digit code number, under what's called the Harmonized System: Many countries use the same code numbers, in *harmony* with each other, so to speak. And those code numbers get very specific.

For example, do you want to import conveyor belts? Well, are they vulcanized-rubber belts, metal-reinforced belts, textile-reinforced belts, or plastic-reinforced belts? There are four entire pages of categories just for conveyor belts. The distinctions may seem ridiculous until you find out that metal-reinforced belts have a 25 percent tariff, but plastic-reinforced belts have a 74 percent tariff.

Goods are categorized differently if they're assembled or unassembled; if they're painted or unpainted; if they are shipped in durable or flimsy packaging; if an imported cup has a steel handle or a plastic handle; if an imported mirror is framed or unframed; if . . . well, I'll quit here. The bottom line is, it pays to do your homework.

SHIPPING

Beyond Customs regulations, the most important consideration is shipping. How will you get your merchandise into the United States? Will you bring it back with you on the plane? Will you ship it air cargo? Can you send it by sea mail, where the post office delivers it and collects duties when it arrives? How cooperative and reliable are the shippers and postal agencies in the exporting country? A friend of mine, an experienced importer who regularly travels overseas, always says that the first step is to ask, "How can I ship it?"

You can get more help from CBP (the federal agency that handles customs), or from a licensed custom house broker. Customs brokers are in business to prepare and expedite your paperwork and to help get your merchandise through Customs. You can locate them in the yellow pages of any major port city, on the internet, or through a trade organization.

FINDING GOODS TO IMPORT

If you don't like to travel, you can often find goods to import by going to trade shows and gift shows. Most industries have large annual or semiannual shows where manufacturers and distributors, including those from foreign countries, exhibit their wares. Sometimes you can close a deal and arrange all the details of shipping right at the show.

Be sure to examine actual goods before you order. I've heard of importers being very unhappy with merchandise ordered from specifications and illustrations.

IT'S AN UNPREDICTABLE BUSINESS

No matter how many precautions you take, no matter how careful you are to follow rules and procedures, whenever you are importing goods, anything might go wrong. Shipping charges can go up, import duties can change, or goods can be delayed, rejected by Customs, or not even be what you ordered. And often you have no recourse. You kind of take your chances when you import goods.

One reason many people are attracted to importing is because goods manufactured overseas are so inexpensive compared to U.S. made goods. Part of the reason some products are so cheap is because workers in some parts of the world are paid criminally low wages and required to work long hours in dangerous and unhealthy workplaces.

So, don't hesitate to look for a great deal, but as Jiminy Cricket said, "Always let your conscience be your guide."

Exporting

Many small businesses have overseas retail customers, small orders paid by credit card or electronic payment services like PayPal. Credit card processors and electronic payment services offer currency conversions, where you bill your customers in U.S.

dollars and the processor converts the dollars to the customer's currency. The customers pay in their country's currency (unless they have the ability to pay in U.S. dollars) and you get paid in U.S. dollars. The fees your payment processor charges you will probably be higher than the fees for U.S. transactions.

This type of transaction, of course, requires that your customers prepay for their purchases, something retail customers expect, but which may or may not be acceptable to wholesale customers.

Goods shipped out of the country by FedEx and UPS and by the U.S. Postal Service require a Customs Declaration, a form you fill out and attach to the parcel. Short form CN-22 (USPS Form #2976) is for goods valued at $400 or less. Long form CP-72 (USPS Form #2976-A) is for goods valued over $400. The post office also has prohibitions on certain goods. You cannot ship lithium batteries, medical devices, medicine, drugs, or cigars (Cigars? Why cigars?).

If you are shipping by FedEx or UPS, those shippers have their own additional requirements depending on the country you are shipping to.

EXPORT LICENSES

Most goods can be shipped out of the country with nothing more than the customs declaration; no special licenses required. Some "strategic" goods (usually those with military uses), and goods shipped to certain "restricted" countries, however, may require you to prepare a Shippers Export Declaration (SED). More information is available from the U.S. Bureau of Export Administration (BXA).

EXPORT BUSINESSES

If you do a lot of exporting, if that is a main source of your income, there is a world of rules and procedures you need to know about.

Exporting often requires travel to foreign countries and a knowledge of other cultures and foreign regulations. If you will be taking product samples or promotional materials out of the United States, check the duty requirements before you depart.

Trade between countries is a net positive. People don't kill their customers.

—Management consultant Randy Kirihara, Bloomington, Minnesota

LETTERS OF CREDIT

Charging an international customer's credit card or PayPal account is fast and easy. But if your business involves accounts with overseas buyers, and if an overseas buyer decides not to pay you, it may be difficult for you to collect what's owed you. Many exporters require an "irrevocable letter of credit," where the overseas buyer's bank guarantees payment.

A letter of credit is like a contract. The wording should be precise, particularly the details of what's being shipped, the time deadlines, and the point where ownership passes hands. If the letter of credit specifies an exact weight or an exact count, or specifies a firm shipping date or a firm delivery date, an exporter could lose everything if he is off by a pound or a day. If the letter of credit states that payment is due when the goods are safely in the customer's warehouse rather than when the ship leaves port, the exporter may never get paid if the ship sinks, if the foreign customs inspector rejects the shipment, or if the customer claims the goods are damaged or are not what was ordered. To be safe, many exporters obtain export or marine (cargo) insurance, which can be purchased for individual shipments.

You can avoid all of these international headaches by going through intermediaries, freight forwarders, export brokers, or others who will either arrange the paperwork for you or buy your products and then export them themselves. You can locate these people by asking other exporters or through a trade organization.

EXPORT HELP

The U.S. government encourages exporting, so there is also a lot of help. Contact one of the Small Business Administration's U.S. Export Assistance Centers. They offer not just advice, but through the Export/Import Bank, located at the same offices, banking and insurance assistance. To find the nearest office, call (800) U-ASK-SBA, or log on to SBA.gov and EXIM.gov.

The Commerce Department's Export Counseling Division can help you find overseas buyers, explain shipping options, and even help you get paid. The telephone at their main office in Washington, DC, is (202) 482-4811, or log on to bis.doc.gov. The Commerce Department and the SBA sponsor seminars, trade shows, and overseas trade missions where you actually visit potential overseas customers. For more information, call (800) USA-TRADE or log on to DOC.gov.

Also talk to FedEx or UPS. They are eager to help their business customers with exporting.

BUYING A BUSINESS

Buying a going business is certainly a fast way to jump right into the deep water. But such a purchase will require careful research. You should take your time considering this major commitment. (This section is not about franchises or business opportunities. They are covered below.)

Why buy a business someone else started? When you start your own business, it can be a year or more before it produces enough income to pay yourself a wage. When you buy a going business, you have an immediate income stream.

Another reason for buying a business is that someone else has done all the hard work: identified a need, set up the business, found the customers, worked through all the problems, and proved that it can be successful. Anything that can go wrong probably already has.

A third reason for buying is availability of financing. Investors and bankers are much more receptive to an "acquisition." A proven business is much less risky than a brand-new, untested one. Quite often, the assets of the business you are buying can be used as collateral on a loan. Sellers often help with financing as well.

Finding a Business for Sale

How do you find out what businesses are for sale? There may be a For Sale sign on the business or an ad in a newspaper or trade journal or on the internet. Hundreds of businesses are listed on Craigslist every day. But most likely, you will have to ask around. Bankers, accountants, local businesspeople, the chamber of commerce, and people active in community affairs are likely to know who has a business for sale.

I know of businesses that sold just because someone walked in and asked the owner if he or she had any interest in selling.

Real estate agents and professional business brokers will know about businesses for sale. But when an agent or broker helps put a deal together, they collect their fee, usually a percentage of the sale

---

It's easy to find a lousy firm you can afford.

—Larry Hammons, Rational Technology, Inc.

price, which will increase the price of the business. Keep in mind that brokers and agents are working for the seller and get paid only if the deal goes through. Don't rely on them for advice or anything other than just locating the business.

Find out who owns the business. If the business is a sole proprietorship, there is one owner, and that is who you want to deal with. If the business is a partnership, corporation, or LLC, be sure that the person you are dealing with has written authority from all owners to negotiate and close a deal. Don't waste your time with a partner who's eager to sell, only to find out later that the other partners have no intention of selling the business.

Is This the Right Business for You?

If the business you want to buy is successful, busy, rolling down the track like a fast freight, are you—the new owner, manager, clerk, employer, bookkeeper, and troubleshooter—ready to handle such an enterprise? Do you have the experience and the knowledge to jump right on and keep the business rolling smoothly? Or will your on-the-job training cause disruptions in the operation, possibly displeasing customers enough to lose them?

If the business depends on the owner's personality, or on the owner's training and experience—such as a repair shop or service business—taking over that business and keeping the customers might be difficult. Customers get used to certain businesses. Many customers are there because they like and trust the person who owns the business. And now, here you are, a new owner who they don't know. They've come to expect a certain level of competence, service, and convenience from a business they frequent. They expect certain merchandise to always be in stock—the former owner always had it in stock—or they expect a service to be performed within a time period they are accustomed to. If you can't get in sync with the way the business is already running, if you can't get a personal relationship with the customers almost immediately, the customers may have little patience for you.

Quite often, the buyer of a business will train with the seller, the two working in the business together for a period of time, so that the transition is smooth. Discuss this during negotiations with the seller, and whatever decision is made, include it in the written purchase agreement.

Is This Business Worth Buying?

Why does the owner want to sell? Is the owner moving away? Is he or she simply tired out? A lot of business owners, particularly in retail businesses, wear themselves out after five or ten years, working every day. They just want to quit, take a rest, do something else. Is the owner old or ill, and wants or needs to retire? Is a divorce forcing the sale? Is the owner in some sort of trouble and needs the cash? Make sure the trouble is not directly related to the business, and be sure to get legal help with this.

Is the business starting to fail? Does the owner know about some troubling future prospects for the business—problems with the neighborhood, or a corporate chain store about to move in, or some other upcoming development that will be detrimental to the business—and wants to bail out? What is the competition like? Is it growing? Are the competitors doing better than this store? Can you determine why? Is this type of business growing, or possibly a fad or trend on the wane?

HOW PROFITABLE IS THE BUSINESS?

Ask to see the records and tax returns for the last few years. Tax returns are an excellent source of information since no one tends to overstate income or profit on a tax return. Many sellers, however, are not likely to show you financial information until they get to know you a little better, until they get a feel that you are serious about this particular business. They don't want to see their figures and tax returns floating around the countryside (or the internet). It may help you to first open up to the seller, let the seller know about your own background, your financial condition, how serious you are.

When the seller finally does show you the records and tax returns, be sure you know how to interpret them. If you don't understand the numbers, hire an accountant to help you. Do the numbers make sense? Income shown on bank statements, sales tax reports, financial records, and tax returns should have some correlation. Don't pay an inflated price for revenues the owner claims he has been hiding from the tax man.

Are the profits on the increase, or on the decline? Is there enough income to provide you a wage and to eventually pay off the cost of buying the business? Don't forget that the profit from a sole proprietorship or partnership will not include any salary for the owner. The profit is his or her salary. If it's a corporation, how much of a salary is the owner taking? If the business has a hired manager or employees who won't be needed if you buy the business, eliminating their salaries may improve the profit figure significantly.

If the business expenses include travel for the owner, fringe benefits, or other legally deductible but unnecessary luxuries, eliminating these from your expenses will paint a more accurate, and attractive, profit figure. Be sure to figure in income and self-employment taxes. Taxes will reduce the profit considerably.

Equally important to profit is cash flow. Be sure the business has enough cash regularly coming in to pay the bills and to pay yourself a salary. Cash-starved companies fail quickly.

LOCATION AND LEASE

Is the business in a good location? Just because this business currently exists in this location doesn't guarantee that things aren't changing in the neighborhood. Read "Business Location" in the Getting Started chapter. Everything in that section applies here.

If you will be leasing the building, how many years are left on the lease? Can you assume the lease? To buy a business with no lease or a short-term lease means that the landlord can, on a whim, evict you, triple the rent, lord knows what. Find out if there are any city plans for rezoning that may affect your location.

ASSETS

What is the condition of the assets? Does the building need repair or remodeling? Is the equipment in good shape, or will it need to be repaired or replaced soon? Is the computer system functioning smoothly? Will you have to sink a lot of money into the business to fix it up the way you want, or possibly to meet a building or health code requirement? Building inspectors sometimes tend to leave old businesses alone but suddenly notice all sorts of code violations when a new owner takes over.

SUPPLIERS

How reliable are the suppliers? Are any closing their doors, moving away, or making other major changes? If you will be dependent on the same suppliers, talk to them and make sure they'll do business with you.

CUSTOMERS

Who are the major customers? Does the business depend on a handful of customers or a major contract with one customer? If so, contact the customers to ascertain if they plan to stay with you.

PRIOR OBLIGATIONS

Will you inherit obligations or problems? Are there outstanding guarantees or warranties to customers that you will have to honor? Contracts with customers or suppliers that you will be required to fulfill? Lawsuits or threats of lawsuits? Obligations to current or former employees? Contamination problems you might inherit?

The present owner of the business can probably answer all of the above questions, though you shouldn't expect unbiased answers. If you spend some time and study things closely, you will most likely find your own answers to the questions.

Observe the store, the customers, how much business is being conducted. Does what you see relate to the sales figures in the records? Walk around the neighborhood, see for yourself if there is any nearby competition, and how well they are doing. Talk to other business owners in the area, particularly close neighbors. Tell them your plans and ask their opinions. I guarantee you will get an earful of valuable information.

Customers and suppliers are another vital source of information. Try to locate former customers and suppliers. I'm sure they can tell you a lot about the business. So can the employees; if appropriate, talk to them.

Look up the business on the internet. See what people are saying about it, but keep in mind that anyone can post anything to the internet. One disgruntled customer—or a cutthroat competitor, or an angry ex-brother-in-law—can make a perfectly good business sound awful.

You should become Sherlock Holmes with the owner's figures. If this is a sales business, check month-to-month purchases as an indicator of how fast the inventory sells (called "turnover"). It may indicate if the business has seasonal cycles: slow at one time of year, busy at others.

Check the inventory carefully. It may be much larger or smaller than the owner tells you, and it may be damaged or obsolete or simply unsalable. How much dust is on it?

Be suspicious of any recent legal fees or any unusual, large transactions. What were they for? If you see loan or interest payments, ask about them.

If you won't be assuming a loan, you won't be making those payments.

HOW MUCH SHOULD YOU PAY?

Finally, you come to the most difficult question of all. Despite what the seller may tell you or what the textbooks say, there are few real guidelines and no reliable formulas when it comes to such a large, unique, emotion-laden transaction as the purchase of a business. The bottom line, always, is that a business is worth no more than what a buyer will pay. The seller may have to sell this business, but you do not have to buy it. It is up to you to determine what you are willing to pay for it, and then find out if the seller will accept your offer.

You should realize that the seller has probably never sold a business before, certainly not this particular business. He probably knows what the business is worth, but he really has no idea what he can expect to get for it. A business is not like a used car, or even a house, when it comes to figuring out what price it will fetch. Comparisons are difficult, and prospective buyers are usually few. So, the seller is in the dark himself when setting a price. Often, the asking price is no indication at all of what the business will actually sell for. Businesses often sell for half or less than the asking price.

The actual value of the inventory and equipment—what the present owner can sell it for if the business is closed and liquidated—is usually the bottom-dollar value of a business. A surprising number of businesses actually sell for close to this amount. So, first determine this value. The seller's original cost is a guideline, but consider age, wear, damage, and obsolescence.

Then, you can be sure the seller will want, on top of the value of the assets, additional money because the business is successful, established, earning a profit. Some people call this intangible value "goodwill," and they attempt to put a price on it, some dollar figure they pull out of the air, which is probably why this is also called, in business jargon, "blue sky." Often, the seller will ask for the equivalent of one or two years' profits. Again, throw out the formulas. It is entirely up to you, the buyer, to decide if you want and can afford to pay for some or all of this "blue sky."

Many small businesses are bought on the installment basis, with the seller extending most of the credit. It is usually to your advantage to have the seller help finance the business, as he or she is much more likely to want to help you be successful. Most sellers, however, would greatly prefer to get the cash and be done with it, and are usually willing to reduce the price considerably if you can finance the purchase yourself.

Keep in mind that the purchase price of the business is just a start. You will still need money for working capital (day-to-day expenditures, overhead, and new inventory) and possibly for repairs, remodeling, or sprucing up.

When you consider buying a going business, consider how much it would cost to set up, from scratch, a new, similar business at a different location. Why buy someone else's expensive business if you can start your own a lot cheaper?

PURCHASE CONTRACT

Once the buyer and the seller agree on the purchase price and payment terms, you will probably need an experienced accountant's help to draft the purchase agreement. Everything should be in writing. The precise legal wording can affect how the sale is taxed, how the assets are valued for tax purposes, and how much of the purchase price will be deductible.

You, the buyer, should be careful that you will not inherit old business debts, liabilities, lawsuits, or other problems you should not be responsible for. Make absolutely sure all creditors are notified that the business is being sold, and that old liabilities will not be the responsibility of the new owner.

This is particularly important if you are buying a corporation. If you buy the corporation's stock, you are the new owner of an old business, a business that may have old legal and contractual obligations that you may be stuck with. Often it is better to purchase the assets, the lease, the business name, and whatever else goes along with the deal, from the old corporation rather than buying the corporation itself. A buyer often gets a better tax break by buying assets instead of the business.

Many states have what's called a Bulk Sales Act or Bulk Transfer Act, which protects creditors of a business that is being sold. The act usually requires that all creditors be notified before the sale is completed, so the creditors can file claims for any unpaid bills or other obligations. The business sale is usually done through an escrow, much like buying a home. The escrow company contacts all of the creditors, and determines that all obligations of the seller are met, before disbursing the money and handing the buyer the keys.

Ask the seller to sign a statement that the business is not involved in any lawsuits or enforcement actions (called a "representations and warranties" clause). You will also want a non-compete clause, so the former owner doesn't turn right around and open a competing business down the street.

Both the buyer and the seller of a business must fill out IRS Form 8594, "Asset Acquisition Statement," with their tax returns. The forms, which specify how much money was paid for different assets, should be identical.

TAX DEDUCTIONS

The costs of investigating and buying a business come under a variety of IRS rules. Costs incurred before you pick a specific business you want to buy, such as travel and general research, are usually not deductible at all.

When you do buy the business, some of the cost is deductible, some of the cost is depreciated or amortized over several years, and some of the cost may not be deductible at all. A lot depends on how the business is structured legally (corporation, partnership, limited liability company, or sole proprietorship) and what the purchase agreement says.

For most business purchases, you are not actually buying a "business," you are buying a collection of assets that comprise a business: equipment, furniture and fixtures, inventory, supplies, possibly a building, possibly the accounts receivable, possibly the debts and liabilities. And you may be paying for "goodwill," money you are paying above the actual value of the assets. Each component of the business (assets, inventory, and goodwill) is valued separately, and each component comes under different tax-deduction rules. A lot of tax money is at stake here. You should talk to an experienced tax accountant before signing any agreement.

If you do not finally buy the business, the money you spent may qualify as a tax-deductible capital loss. This also will probably require help from an accountant.

FRANCHISE BUSINESSES

A franchise (sometimes known as "formula retail") is an individually owned business operated as though it was part of a large chain. Midas Muffler, McDonald's, and H&R Block are examples of well-known national franchises. Under a franchise, services and products are standardized. Trademarks, advertising, and store appearance are uniform.

With a franchise, your own freedom and initiative are limited. You lose a lot of autonomy, a lot of the feeling of being your own boss. The name on the store is not yours. But a well-known franchise gives you instant recognition. The goods and services are proven and trusted. Or, as an old Holiday Inn ad boasted, "No surprises here."

How Franchises Work

Most franchises work this way: For a fee, the corporation that grants the franchise (the franchisor) gives you (the franchisee) the right to use the franchisor's name and trademarks, and to sell its products or services. The franchisor provides, and requires you to follow, a marketing plan. The franchise agreement may require you to purchase your supplies or equipment from the franchisor, at their prices, even if you can get better prices from local suppliers. You may have to pay the franchisor a percentage of your gross sales (a percentage of your total sales before deducting any expenses), whether you are making a profit or not. You may have to pay part of the franchisor's advertising. There may be marketing fees, training costs, national office overhead charges, and charges for contract renewals. Franchisors can dictate what prices you charge.

There are hundreds of franchise companies, some well-known but some completely unknown, some with a good, profitable history, and some struggling like any other business.

Many franchisors offer a complete ready-to-run business, what they call a "turnkey" operation (all you have to do is turn the key in the door) that includes training and management support. But don't let the ready-to-run concept fool you. A franchise is not a "paint by numbers" business. It will be just as difficult and just as much work to run as a non-franchised business.

Franchisors help with financing. Franchisors have their own loan sources; a few even own their own finance companies. But be warned: A franchisor will

People confuse being a franchise owner with being an entrepreneur. And frankly, we've taken a lot of the fun out of being an entrepreneur.

—Don Dozier, American Fastsigns (franchisor)

If you're the kind of person who likes to do things your way, then Breadsmith, or any franchise, for that matter, isn't for you.

—Dan Sterling, founder, Breadsmith (franchisor)

require you to put up a chunk of your own money, and they may want a second mortgage on your home to guarantee the loan. Just because it's a franchise, even a well-known franchise, there is no guarantee that you will be successful. If you can't make your payments, the franchisor will not hesitate to foreclose and resell the franchise to someone else.

Investigating a Franchise

Investigate the franchise, thoroughly. This may be a lot of work, but you are making a large investment, and you'll be signing legal contracts. Now, before you sign anything or pay for anything or commit your future to anything, is the time to learn all you can about this venture.

The Federal Trade Commission requires franchisors to give prospective franchisees a copy of what's called a Uniform Franchise Offering Circular. This UFOC includes information on potential earnings, though these numbers are sometimes exaggerated and should not be trusted; the costs; the company's history and financial standing; and the terms of the agreement. The franchisor must give you a copy of the UFOC at least ten business days before you sign any contract. But you should get and study the UFOC long before those last ten days, before you've got so much time and money invested in researching this franchise. (Gasoline companies, auto manufacturers, and some franchises offered to experienced businesspeople are exempt from this law.)

When you investigate a specific franchise, try to get a complete list of all of their franchisees, and contact as many as you can. Find out how they are doing and what they think of the franchise. Ask each franchisee, "If you had to do it over again, would you invest in this franchise?"

Are there any lawsuits against the franchise? The Federal Trade Commission can tell you if any complaints have been filed against the franchisor. Contact the people who are suing the company and get their side of the story. Ask the franchisor for a list of former franchisees, call them up, and find out what happened to them. Also check with the Better Business Bureau. But keep an open mind. There are two sides to every story, and angry people aren't always reliable.

Find out if that particular franchise has a franchisee trade association, and contact them. Type the franchise name in a search engine and see what complaints, problems, or other troubles show up, but remember, anyone can put anything on the internet. If you are concerned by what you learn, show the information to the franchisor and get their side of the story.

Be particularly wary of franchises that are stagnant or shrinking, those with a high turnover of franchisees, and those with a small net worth. These signs may indicate trouble.

Franchise Agreement

The franchise agreement is a binding, legal contract. Once you sign it, you are committed to it. The agreement gives you certain legal rights, but keep in mind that the agreement was written by the franchisor, whose first goal is to look out for their own interests.

Study the terms of the franchise agreement. If you do not understand the wording, get help from a competent person who can explain the terminology. Get clarification, in writing, from the franchisor.

Some franchise agreements are negotiable. If you don't like the terms, percentages, restrictions, anything, propose changes. Some important issues that many franchisees face:

1. Will you have any flexibility, any of your own input, in operating your franchise? Or will you have to exactly follow the franchisor's formula?

2. Will you have territorial rights, and for how long? Territory (called "encroachment" in the contracts) is a major issue with retail franchises, and one of the most common rifts between franchisors and franchisees: How many Subway, or Burger King, or Jiffy Lube franchises are in your town, or within so many miles of each other?

3. Can the franchisor sell directly to consumers in your area, or on the internet, or inside a nearby Walmart, competing directly with you?

4. Will you be allowed to sell or advertise on the internet? Some franchisors restrict what you can do on the internet, even down to domain names you can or cannot use.

5. How much of the company's advertising money will be spent in your area?

6. Is the agreement binding for the life of your business, or can the franchisor revise it, possibly to your detriment, in a year, or five, or ten? Will you be required to meet sales quotas? And what happens if you don't?

7. Can the franchisor cancel your franchise, and essentially put you out of business, if the franchisor chooses to do so? If you are terminated, will you get any of your investment back?

8. Can you sell your franchise to someone else if you want out of it? Does the franchisor have restrictions on who you can sell the franchise to? Will the franchisor help you find a buyer? If you leave the franchise, can you start a similar (competing) business of your own?

All of these issues are exceptionally important. Large franchisors have aggressive attorneys and will not hesitate to sue you if you try to go against any of their contract provisions.

Do Your Homework

Just like starting any business, do your own market research. Even if you are convinced you are buying into a franchise that is well structured and well managed, make sure there is a local market—customers—for the product. Even famous franchises have stores and franchisees (individual store owners) that fail.

Once you've done all the investigating you can do on your own, have a lawyer or an accountant review the agreement with you and explain to you exactly what you're getting into.

Give serious thought to whether a franchise is the best route for you to start a business. Certainly, a restaurant on the interstate called Subway will do better than one called Ralph's Diner. A Best Western will be more inviting than Ralph's Motel. But if you're starting a local business, will your print shop, cleaning service, real estate office, or even hamburger stand be more attractive as a franchise instead of as a locally owned, independent business? How important is a famous name and slick national advertising? People will quickly get to know you and your business either way, and it will succeed or fail depending on your service and quality and prices. Why pay the fees and tie yourself to a franchise if it offers no discernible benefits?

There are many directories, magazines, and internet sites that list details about hundreds of franchises. Also contact the Federal Trade Commission, Washington, DC 20580, or log on to FTC.gov.

"BUSINESS OPPORTUNITIES"

Like a franchise, a "business opportunity" is someone else's idea, system, or distributorship to set you up in your own business. Unlike a franchise, a business opportunity is not a retail store or a famous name. There is no protected territory, no national advertising, little or no management support. But a business opportunity costs much less than a franchise, allows you to run your business any way you please, and does not collect royalties or ongoing fees. You can customize the business opportunity any way you please, or take parts of it to create a different business model. You can redesign it, sell it, or drop it completely. There are no contracts that you have to try to get out of.

Business opportunities are often some sort of business "kit," such as a cleaning or repair system, vending machines, sales carts, customized novelty items. There is usually a one-time purchase of equipment and instructions, and then a catalog of wholesale inventory or supplies.

Some business opportunities set you up to market a prepaid service plan, such as a prepaid legal service, where you yourself don't provide the service, you just sign up clients and get a cut of the fee.

A few business opportunity programs are regulated by the Federal Trade Commission's franchise rules, but most business opportunities have no federal oversight. About half of the states have some regulations on business opportunity sellers. Ask the company what states they're registered in, and ask to see any disclosure statements. Research the business opportunity as you would research a franchise.

If the opportunity company goes out of business, will you be able to locate other suppliers to provide the supplies, inventory, and equipment you need to keep your business alive?

Some business opportunities are legitimate and practical, and some are not. Use your good common sense, and do your market research.

Make $1,000 a week, at home, in your spare time, stuffing envelopes!

—Magazine advertisement

Multilevel Marketing

A common and popular business opportunity model is the multilevel business, also known as direct selling or network marketing (not to be confused with the term "networking," which refers to going to parties and events in search of new business connections). Multilevel marketing (MLM) is a form of business where you buy a bulk purchase of vitamins, or cosmetics, or, most often, some type of personal care product, and then try to talk your friends and relatives into buying these products from you. You are also encouraged to sign up other "networkers" to buy the products from you, and resell the products to their friends. That's where the term multilevel comes from: There are several "levels" of distribution. Multilevel businesses appeal to people who want to work from home, who don't want to work full-time, or who are just looking for a little sideline income, and who don't want to spend a lot of money and effort starting a business. Some people find multilevel businesses successful and fun, and some people fail and give up quickly. Successful multilevel small-time operators tend to be outgoing, know a lot of people, and are knowledgeable and passionate (or seem to be) about the products they're selling.

If you are considering signing up with an MLM company, do some research. Many of these businesses are excellent opportunities, but some are not well run, and a few are downright fraudulent. Beware of pyramid schemes, where the main focus of the business is recruiting new sellers (people lower on the pyramid), who in turn recruit more sellers (people even lower on the pyramid), until somewhere down the line, the whole thing collapses because the products are not being bought by enough actual users. The sellers who bought in late in the game, the ones at the bottom of the pyramid, wind up with no more recruits—and a storage room full of unsold goods.

Be cautious when dealing with new MLM companies and companies that require a substantial initial purchase, several hundred dollars or more. Many established, legitimate MLM companies offer "beginner kits" with a minimum investment of $100 or less. Be especially wary of a company that compensates you based on how much inventory you sell to new recruits, instead of how much is actually sold to the final users. And, as in the classic (and usually ignored) advice to gamblers, don't risk more than you can afford to lose.

Tax Deductions

Tax deductions for buying a franchise or a prepackaged business opportunity depend on what you are actually purchasing. A one-time fee to become a franchisee or distributor is considered an intangible asset, and is amortized over fifteen years. Ongoing (annual) franchise or distributor fees can be written off when paid.

FREELANCERS

Freelancers—professionals, consultants, artists, musicians, writers, photographers, designers, and similar self-employed individuals—are in business for themselves, like all other businesspeople, no matter how reluctant they are to deal with it.

Freelancers are sole proprietors unless they incorporate or form a partnership or LLC. Freelancers are responsible for their own business records, licenses, tax returns, and everything else covered in this book.

Freelancers should read "Hiring Independent Contractors" in the Growing Up chapter. Most freelancers fall into this category. Many on-demand economy workers are freelancers.

Royalties

If royalties from creative effort, such as writing or songwriting, are a regular and ongoing source of income for you, they are considered self-employment income, handled the same as any other business income with regular business deductions. These royalties are reported on Schedule C (if you are a sole proprietor), and subject to regular business taxes including self-employment tax. This also applies to licensing fees, assignment of copyrights, or any other similar income.

If royalty income is only occasional or a one-shot, it is not considered self-employment income. It is reported as "supplemental income" on Schedule E, "Supplemental Income and Loss," on your 1040 tax return. The income is subject to income tax but not to self-employment tax.

Advances

Freelancers sometimes get cash advances, deposits on work to be performed, or advances on royalties. How are these handled? If you use cash accounting, as almost all freelancers do, advances and deposits you receive are considered taxable income when you receive the money, even though it may be for work to be done in the future. If you refund all or part of an advance or a deposit at a later date, you reduce your income at that time, similar to making a sales return. You don't have to go back and correct the income records; just record the refund on the date you make the refund.

If you are using accrual accounting, the record-keeping and the taxes can get complicated. Accrual accounting recognizes income when it is earned, not when cash changes hands. You don't report income on your tax return if you haven't done the work. You report part of the income if you've done part of the work. This is one of many reasons why most small businesses use the cash method of accounting instead of accrual. By the way, if a writer's advance on royalties is not refundable, you keep it whether the book sells or not; for tax purposes, it is not considered an advance. It is current earned income, currently taxable, even for accrual accounting.

Reimbursed Expenses

If you have expenses that you add to your billings, the total amount you bill your customer should be included in your income. The actual expenses that you pay are recorded in your expense record and deducted on your tax return, so the net effect for taxes is zero.

CONSIGNMENT

Consigned inventory is merchandise a business or an individual places with another business for the other business to try to sell. A dressmaker may consign inventory to a dress shop. The person consigning the goods (the dressmaker) has not made a sale and does not get paid until the business that has taken the goods in on consignment (the dress shop) sells the goods.

For tax purposes, the consignor (in our example, the dressmaker) has not sold the dress. There is no income to report. The consignee (the dress shop) has not purchased the dress from the dressmaker until it sells the dress to its customer.

Consignors (in this example, the dressmaker) should be warned that these consignment laws—who owns the merchandise—are income tax laws only. They may not hold up in bankruptcy court. If the dress shop files for bankruptcy before it sells the dress, the court can seize and sell consigned inventory to pay off the creditors of the dress shop, even though the shop doesn't legally own the goods. The dressmaker will have to stand in line with all the other creditors hoping to get paid.

The dressmaker may be able to protect himself or herself by filing a UCC #1 form (UCC stands for Uniform Commercial Code) with the county or state where the dress shop is located. This is a legal notice that the goods belong to the dressmaker and not to the dress shop. Note that Form UCC #1 is filed in the government jurisdiction where the consigned goods are located, not where the consignor is located. The UCC #1 will usually hold up in bankruptcy court, enabling the consignor to get the unsold merchandise back—though sometimes not: Bankruptcy judges can be very difficult when they want to be. Several hundred copies of this very book you're reading were seized by the bankruptcy court when one of the book's distributors filed for bankruptcy a few years ago. The judge refused to honor the UCC #1 filing.

If consigned goods have been sold by the business that took the goods on consignment (in our example, the dress shop), but the shop filed for bankruptcy before paying the dressmaker, the courts hold that this was a sale: the dress shop legally purchased the dress from the dressmaker when the shop sold the dress to a customer. The dressmaker is just another creditor who probably will never see any money. The UCC #1 filing will not help in this situation.

PRICING

There is no simple, "one size fits all" answer to the question every new business owner asks: How to price a product or service? There is no magic formula, no industry standard, and no single markup percentage that works for everybody.

Cost Factors

For sales and manufacturing businesses, the first consideration when setting a price is what your inventory costs you: the products you sell, and the parts and materials that go into products you make or repair. These are your "direct costs" of doing business, also called "variable costs," because they vary with your sales volume.

An important but often overlooked factor is your overhead, also known as "fixed costs," the dozens of large and small expenses you pay whether you

HONEST FRED'S
VARIETY HARDWARE

SAVE $49.75.
DON'T BUY
THIS LAMP.

SAVE $29.80.
DON'T BUY THIS
ELECTRIC IRON

SAVE $249.20!
DON'T BUY
THIS TV.

SAVE $62.50
DON'T BUY THIS
SUITCASE.

Tuli Kupferberg

are generating income or not, such as rent, utilities, phone, insurance, maintenance, office supplies, permits, and advertising. These costs cannot be tied directly to a product or service, but you need to factor them into your pricing.

Taxes—federal income, state income, and self-employment—should be figured into your pricing. These taxes depend, of course, on how much of a profit you earn, making them difficult to calculate in advance, but they are significant costs, anywhere from 15 percent to 40 percent of your profit.

So, the first step in pricing is to know your true operating costs. If you cannot recoup these costs from sales, you are in a situation commonly known as "going broke." Sounds pretty basic, right? You'd be amazed how many new businesses lose money because they never consider all the obvious and not so obvious expenses.

PROFIT FACTORS

How much do you mark up a product or charge for your services to bring in enough income, above and beyond your costs, to pay you for the time you put into the business, to pay you a wage, to make it all worth doing? There are no standard answers. Only you know the answers to these questions.

HOW MUCH CAN YOU CHARGE?

What are your customers or clients willing and able to pay? What are other businesses charging for similar goods and services? And what are they offering for that price?

You may or may not be able to charge more than what other businesses are charging. Factors such as how good your product or service is, how reliable you are, how important you personally are to your customers (such as being a highly regarded auto mechanic), or some other important consideration—being a business your customers personally know and trust—may allow you to charge more than the business down the street or on the internet.

If you sell to wholesalers or retailers, they have to get a good enough price from you to be able to mark up the goods themselves, typically another 30 to 60 percent, depending on the type and price of the product.

If you are selling a product on the internet that is also available from other businesses, you will not only need to set a price that matches or beats other internet prices, you will have to have something mighty persuasive to get customers, particularly customers you have not previously done business with, to buy from you.

You also don't want to make the mistake of underpricing yourself. You can actually charge too little for a product or service, and make people suspicious that you have a cheap (that is, lousy) product, or that you are not experienced enough to charge a fair price for your services. You are setting your own precedent. People judge your worth by what you charge. In the business world, it's called "perceived value." Price is a big part of this perception. The price of a product tells consumers what to expect in terms of quality and value. Things that sell for cheap *are* cheap. Things that sell for a higher price *are* worth more. We all know that's not really true, but it is how consumers evaluate things they buy and how they evaluate people they hire.

For many small businesses, the secret to success is not charging the lowest prices they can, but instead charging a higher price and offering something extra: a better service, a friendlier or more elegant atmosphere, whatever it takes. Face it: You can't compete with Walmart or Amazon. The secret is, don't even try. Consumers are willing to pay more—in fact, they *expect* to pay more—for quality and value. Ask yourself how much you'd pay for the same product or service.

People selling services (selling their time) might charge by the hour or by the job. If you are a fast worker, and you have a good idea how long a job will take, charging by the job might earn you quite a bit more. It takes the pressure off your customers, who know in advance exactly how much it will cost, don't have to worry if you're taking an extra-long lunch hour, or feel the need to secretly keep track of your time.

If some of these factors seem difficult or downright impossible to calculate, don't be discouraged. That's the way it is for most new businesses. You don't know many of your costs when you are getting started, and you certainly have no idea of the volume of sales or number of hours you'll be working. It is yet one more reason to try to start a new business on a small, part-time basis and to learn as you go.

Pricing is an inexact science. Some businesspeople work hard at the numbers, keep track of the hours, and try to arrive at a logical formula that works all the time. Retail stores often decide on a flat markup for every item, or for every item in a certain category (sometimes called "cost plus pricing"). Some people simply charge what everybody else is charging, and hope it will be profitable. Some tradespeople, craftspeople, and even some professionals "eyeball" their client's appearance, their car, their clothes, or feel out how price conscious the client is, before quoting a price or an hourly rate: the old sliding scale. Don't be afraid to experiment; that's about all you can do anyway.

Different pricing for different customers, however, may backfire on you. If someone paid you $20 an hour and later learns someone else got you down to $15 an hour, you will have one angry customer on your hands. But you can offer first-time discounts, off-season discounts, repeat-business discounts, limited-time-offer discounts.

And what about friends who want a "deal"? Some people let their friends know that this is their living, their survival, and already offer the best price they can. Some people automatically give their friends 10 percent or 20 percent off; some people just offer their service for free; after all, they *are* your friends.

Federal Laws on Pricing

The federal Robinson-Patman Act, also known as the Anti-Price Discrimination Act, prohibits companies that sell wholesale goods from discriminating between customers by offering price discounts or other special terms to one customer but not to another.

This law applies only to wholesale goods: parts and finished products sold to other businesses for resale. It does not apply to retail goods, and it does not apply to any services such as consulting, repair work, and contracting. And, to tell the truth, it is not often enforced. But if you are buying wholesale goods from a wholesaler who is offering the same goods in the same quantities at a lower price to another of its customers (that is, if you have any way of determining that), you could probably get your cost lowered by discussing the situation with your supplier.

The Sherman Antitrust Act forbids competing companies from entering into contracts or other agreements, written or verbal, "in restraint of trade." That means it is illegal to make deals with your competitors about what price you'll charge. This law doesn't prevent you from raising or lowering your prices to match or beat a competitor's price. You can do that any time you want; you just can't consult with the competitor about it.

Sam Leandro, business owner: "The price of a product tells consumers what to expect in terms of quality and value before they even buy it. Consumers are willing to pay more for quality and value. Not only willing, they expect to pay more."

Glenn Kabler, business owner: "I just don't understand why, if I pay $1 for something and try to sell it for $2, people turn away. If I sell it for $5, I get bombarded with business."

Grady Harper, watercolor artist: "One of my large paintings just never would sell even though it seemed to be the main attraction in my exhibit at all of the shows. After reading a pricing article, I decided to follow the number-one suggestion concerning top pricing secrets. I increased the price from $325 to $750. It was purchased after being on display only a few hours."

Dean Ritz, consultant, Washington, DC: "I raised the price with each job until someone balked. Then I knew I had reached the appropriate level."

Sanat Sivdas, yoga teacher, Key West, Florida: "In this country, yoga classes that charge a lot attract more pupils than classes that are free. In this culture, it seems, price equals overall value. It's taken me three hard years of offering free yoga classes to realize this. I'm moving to India."

TRADEMARKS, PATENTS, AND COPYRIGHTS

Trademarks, patents, and copyrights are known as *intangible property* or *intellectual property*. You cannot see or touch them, but they exist, and they are quite valuable.

The IRS calls patents, trademarks, and copyrights "Section 197 Intangibles." Their costs cannot be written off the year incurred. They are written off over a period of years (except for trademarks purchased or licensed from another business). See "Depreciation" in the Taxes chapter.

Trademarks

A trademark is like a brand name. When a business owns a trademarked name, no other business can use that same name or a similar name for a similar product. For example, Fender Musical Instruments owns a trademark for a guitar called Telecaster; no other company can use the name Telecaster for anything related to musical instruments. The Anheuser-Busch Company owns a trademark for a beer called Budweiser; no other company can use the name Budweiser for a beverage.

A trademark can also be a slogan or expression; a symbol, shape, design, or logo; a color or combination of colors; a unique sound; or some combination of these. Apple Computer's famous apple logo, with the bite out of it, is a trademark. All the silly slogans corporations use in their advertising are trademarks.

There is an important distinction between a design or logo that identifies your products or services, which can be trademarked, and original artwork, such as a poster or T-shirt design, which can be copyrighted but cannot be trademarked. These are two different procedures with two different sets of laws.

The same trademark can be used by two companies selling unrelated products or services. However, large corporations that own famous name trademarks, McDonald's, for example, can often stop all other businesses from using the same or similar trademarks. Even if some other McDonald's couldn't possibly be mistaken for the McDonald's fast-food chain, McDonald's can invoke "famous trademark" protection (also known as "trademark dilution") to force other companies from using anything remotely resembling the word *McDonald's*.

Trademark rights are only for the trademark itself. A trademark does not prevent others from making or selling the same or similar goods.

Another term, *trade dress*, refers to a product's appearance or packaging—how it's "dressed up." It is basically no different than a trademark. A third term, *service mark*, applies to services instead of goods, but the rules are the same. All references in this chapter to trademarks include trade dress and service marks.

WHAT CANNOT BE USED AS A TRADEMARK

You cannot have a trademark that is so similar to another trademark that it could confuse people. You cannot have a trademark that is misleading, as to who you are or what you are selling. You cannot get a trademark for a geographical name, such as *Northwest*. You cannot trademark expressions already in common use, such as *"Have a nice day."*

The Trademark Office will not issue a trademark for words that are "immoral, scandalous, or disparaging." (No, I don't know who decides what words are immoral, scandalous, or disparaging.)

You cannot trademark your own surname, unless your name happens to be William Harley, or H. J. Heinz, or Leo Fender, or somebody else whose products have become closely associated with their names.

You cannot trademark words that describe your product. A window manufacturer cannot trademark the word *windows*, but, obviously, a software company can trademark "Windows."

INTERNET DOMAIN NAMES

Trademark law extends to the internet. Conflicts occur when someone owns a domain name (a website address) and someone else owns the trademark to that same name. Owners of registered trademarks can usually stop someone else from using the trademark as a domain name. But if the trademark is not officially registered, or if the trademark was registered after the domain name was claimed by someone else, or if the other party is outside the United States, internet policy gets unpredictable.

The owner of a trademark may or may not be able to force someone to abandon their domain name.

Trademark owners, aware of this domain name problem, try to acquire ownership of all domain names that are the same as or similar to their trademark name.

You cannot trademark a domain name that is your company name, unless the company name is identified with your product or service. You cannot trademark a generic or descriptive domain name, such as aboutpinball.com (a website that sells pinball books), but a domain name with a unique expression probably can be trademarked. The website LouisianaTreasure.com, which sells books about New Orleans music, is a registered trademark. Sometimes a website is so well branded that its name is synonymous with its products or service. Thus, companies such as eBay, Google, and Amazon .com can easily trademark their domain names. The overall design of your website can sometimes be trademarked under the trade dress laws, but most website layouts cannot be trademarked. Websites are protected by copyright, however (covered below).

ACQUIRING A TRADEMARK

You acquire a basic trademark right, though with limited legal protection, simply by creating and using your trademark. You acquire stronger and more easily defended legal rights to a trademark by registering with the U.S. Patent and Trademark Office, or your state trademark office.

Federal trademark registration gives you protection throughout the United States and in fifty other countries that have signed the International Trademark Treaty. You must be doing business across state lines (interstate commerce) to get a federal trademark.

For businesses not involved in interstate commerce, state trademark registration gives you legal protection within your state but no protection outside your own state. You cannot get a state trademark if someone else has a federal trademark. Not all states offer state trademark registration. If you have a federal trademark, there is no reason to get a state trademark as well.

Trademark rights depend on two important issues:

1. *First use.* The first business to use a name (or slogan or logo or whatever else you want to trademark) owns the rights to that trademark. When you first start using your trademark, note the date. Keep a copy of an ad or a contract or some other documentation to prove the date you first used the name.

2. *Confusion.* Trademark rights are meant to eliminate confusion, by not allowing different businesses to have identical or similar names that confuse buyers as to which business they're doing business with. Businesses with the same trademark can coexist if there is no chance that people will be confused which business is which.

REGISTERING A FEDERAL TRADEMARK

If you are not already using a trademark, you can file an Intent to Use application with the U.S. Patent and Trademark Office, which is good for six months and can be renewed every six months for up to three years. This protects your trademark until you actually use it. The original application costs $100. Each renewal costs $150.

Once you are actually using a trademark, you apply for regular trademark registration. The fee varies from $275 to $375 and can take up to a year to process. This fee is in addition to any fees you paid with the Intent to Use application.

After you apply for a trademark, the Trademark Office will conduct a trademark search to see if anyone else owns the trademark. If the trademark is already owned, you forfeit your application fee. You can avoid this problem by doing your own trademark search. The Trademark Office has a complete list of federal trademarks on their website, USPTO .gov, that you can search. Or you can use an online service offering trademark searches, or hire a lawyer or trademark search company to do the search for you.

The initial trademark registration remains in force for ten years, but you must file a Declaration of Use statement between the fifth and sixth years. The trademark may then be renewed every ten years, for as long as you like.

The familiar ® symbol means that a trademark or service mark is officially registered with the U.S. Trademark Office, and full legal protection has been secured. The equally familiar TM symbol (or SM for service mark) is a notice that you are claiming ownership of a trademark but have not registered it. The TM or SM symbol can be used even if no federal trademark application is pending, even if you never plan to register it. Using these symbols, however, does not provide the full legal protection accorded a registered ® trademark.

As you may realize after reading these rules, what can or cannot be trademarked is, at times, subjective, open to interpretation. With careful research, a well-worded application, and a little help from a friendly trademark examiner, you might be able to get the trademark you want. For more information, contact the U.S. Patent and Trademark Office, toll-free (800) 786-9199, or log on to USPTO .gov.

PROTECTING YOUR TRADEMARK

Once you have a trademark, you should continually remind the public, in your promotions, on your website, and wherever else you mention your business, that your name is a registered trademark. Use the ® trademark symbol. If you don't use your trademark for two or more years, it is considered abandoned. Anyone can claim the trademark. Use it or lose it.

Trademark law requires you to police your trademark. If you find anyone using your trademark, object immediately. If you ignore the unauthorized use, or wait too long to complain, you could lose your trademark rights.

By the way, businesses that purchase trademarked goods to sell in their stores or websites, such as a clothing store selling Levi's jeans, sometimes are not allowed to mention the trademarked name or use the logo in advertisements, as ridiculous as that sounds. Before you invest in an expensive ad promoting some manufacturer's product, you may want to find out if they will object. It is their trademark, after all.

Now that you know all the work and money involved in getting a trademark, do you really need one? If yours is a small local sales or service business, and you plan to stay small and local, I don't think you need to protect your identity with a trademark. If, however, you are creating a product that will get widespread distribution and get to be well known, at some point a trademark will be a good investment.

Whether you have a trademark or not, the best way to keep other businesses from picking your same name is to make your name well known and easy to find. Promote your web presence. Get listed in directories. Get publicity. People don't maliciously steal names; they just don't know you're there.

TRADE NAMES

There is a distinction between a trademark, which identifies your products, and a trade name, which identifies your company. For example, a company called General Motors (a trade name) sells a product called Cadillac (a trademark). Sometimes the trademark and the trade name are the same. A company called Ford (a trade name) sells a product called Ford (a trademark). A trade name cannot be federally registered, although it does have some legal protection. Sometimes, however, the name of the company is so identified with its products or services (such as Honda and Google) that the name is easily trademarked, even though it isn't the actual name of the product. An artistic rendition of a trade name, or a logo that includes the trade name, can often be trademarked.

COPYRIGHT VERSUS TRADEMARK

Trademarks are very different than copyrights. A copyright protects writing and illustrations, but does not protect names. You cannot copyright a business or brand name. You can copyright your logo, and it's a good idea to do so, but the copyright will not prevent another business from designing their own logo with the same brand name. Copyrights are covered below.

Patents

Patents apply to physical products such as inventions, to improvements on old inventions, to some processes for creating something, to some industrial designs, and to new plant varieties. Some software can be patented. New methods of doing business can sometimes be patented.

A patent prohibits others from making, using, or selling your creation without your permission. A patent is an official legal notice that this is yours, you invented it, and you and only you have the right to market it, sell it, and license it. Most patents are good only within the United States.

A patent does not guarantee enforcement of your rights. The patent owner, not the government, is responsible for protecting a patent, through legal channels (i.e., expensive lawyers).

Many small, independent inventors obtain patents, and many are successful. But a patent is no guarantee of success. How useful your invention is, how commercial it is, how easy or difficult it will be to produce, and how well you are able to market your invention are as important, if not more important, than the patent itself.

There are three types of patents: utility patents, design patents, and plant patents.

UTILITY PATENTS

The most common patent is the utility patent. Utility patents are granted to the inventor of a new machine or device, a new and useful process, a new composition of matter, or a new and useful improvement of such.

A "machine" or "device" is a man-made tool or product, something that does not already exist in nature. "Useful process" refers to a procedure for making something or performing a task. "Composition of matter" refers to a chemical or organic composition, such as a new kind of cookie dough. A "new and useful improvement" is different from anything else already invented, and not obvious to anyone familiar with the technology involved.

Utility patents are issued for some software. Utility patents are also issued for new methods of doing business, which usually refers to how internet sites work: how a website processes information, or sales, or interactions with visitors ("a useful process"). Many "business method" patents are for nothing more than translating basic business practices into computer code, and getting patents on their systems.

A utility patent will not be granted on a useless device (the government's definition of useless, not mine), on printed matter, on an improvement in a device that would be obvious to a skilled person, or on a machine that will not operate. The government says it never has and never will issue a patent on a perpetual motion machine.

You are required to have a detailed written description or drawings of your invention.

A patent will not be granted if the invention was made known to the public, was in public use, was described in a publication, or was on sale more than a year prior to filing the patent application. So, be sure to keep your invention private and confidential.

DESIGN AND PLANT PATENTS

A design patent covers the appearance of a product: the way it looks, not the way it functions or is constructed. Design patents are similar to trademarks, but the design is part of the product itself. The design can probably be trademarked whether you patent it or not.

Plant patents are for new plant varieties.

LENGTH OF A PATENT

A utility or plant patent is good for twenty years, starting with the date you filed for the patent. The twenty years includes the time it takes for the patent to be approved, which itself can take anywhere from several months to as much as three years. Last year, the U.S. Patent Office received over 600,000 patent applications. So the actual time your patent is valid may be a lot less than twenty years. The twenty-year period can be extended in some cases, if the Patent Office takes more than three years to approve your patent.

A patent may not be renewed or extended. Anyone can use an invention after the patent expires. To keep a patent valid, you have to pay periodic government maintenance fees.

Design patents are good for fourteen years.

APPLYING FOR A PATENT

Applying for a patent can be a lengthy and expensive procedure. The government charges filing, issuance, and maintenance fees, and sometimes fees for printing and claims work. You may need help from a patent attorney or agent. But any dedicated inventor who is willing to study the laws, do the research, and struggle through the forms, will be able to patent his or her own invention at a fraction of the usual cost.

Inventors who are unsure whether their invention justifies the work and cost of going through the regular patent process have two other options:

1. The inventor can file a Provisional Patent Application (a PPA), which is a temporary form of patent. A PPA requires a lot less time, money, and paperwork than a regular patent application, yet offers full patent protection for one year. By the end of that year's time, if things are looking promising, you can apply for regular patent-pending status. But you have to start the patent application process all over again. The PPA itself does not lead to a patent. Should you decide to proceed with the patent, you are spending more time and money, because you took the additional step of filing a Provisional Patent Application. But you do get an extra year's protection. You get the full twenty years, in addition to the PPA's year. The PPA is for utility and plant patents. Design patents are not eligible for the PPA.

2. Inventors who are not even ready to file a PPA can file what the Patent Office calls a "disclosure document," a written explanation of the invention signed by the inventor and submitted to the U.S. Patent Office, which will file and hold it for two years. The document does not lead to a patent, but does offer evidence of the date of conception of the invention.

"PATENT PENDING" AND "PATENT APPLIED FOR"

Products that have federal patent protection from the U.S. Patent and Trademark Office are said to be "patented." A different term, "patent pending" or "patent applied for," means that a patent has been applied for but not yet received. It is a formal notice but offers little legal protection. Some people use "patent pending" even though they haven't applied for anything, either to try to scare off imitators or to impress customers. This is illegal.

OTHER OPTIONS

If filing for and obtaining a patent is a bit overwhelming or too expensive, there are other approaches. Many inventors simply produce and market their invention without a patent, run with it while it's hot, and not worry about someone stealing the idea. Particularly when you are dealing with rapidly changing technology, it's possible your product could become obsolete before anyone has time to copy it.

Many inventors sell or license their ideas to reputable manufacturing companies, companies that will patent the invention on behalf of, or in partnership with, the inventor. Should you approach such a company, have them sign a confidential nondisclosure statement before you show them your idea. Keep detailed, signed, and dated records of your invention.

Be wary of product development companies and invention marketing services, companies that charge you a fee to appraise your invention and make recommendations. Stay away from such companies unless you know them well.

MORE INFORMATION

For more information about patents, contact the U.S. Patent and Trademark Office, Washington, DC 20231. Telephone toll-free (800) 786-9199, or log on to USPTO.gov.

Marcie Hart, inventor, owner of Fat Dog Product Designs, Hesperia, California: "Inventors are a different breed of people. They have the ideas but usually don't want to be bothered with 'the rest.' They just want to get on with the next idea. I really don't think it's the patent process in itself that has given these inventors such a negative attitude. It's the work that's required after the invention that has become so difficult. Inventors have been pretty much locked out of 'Big Business.' The opportunity for success is still there, it's just that the rules have changed. It's because of this 'lock out' that I chose not to beat down the doors of Big Business, but to open my own instead. Opportunity from a closed door. Rather ironic, don't you think?"

Copyrights

Copyrights protect the work of writers, illustrators, artists, designers, and composers.

What can be copyrighted? Literary, dramatic, musical, and artistic works. Writing (with some exceptions listed below). Illustrations. Paintings. Slides and photographs. Movies and videos. Games (physical games and descriptions, not the concepts). Puzzles. Sculpture. Models. Clothing. Jewelry designs. Architectural designs. Choreography and pantomime. Sound recordings. Maps. Software (some software can also be patented). Ads, brochures, and promotional materials.

For a work to be copyrightable, the work must be on a tangible or electronic medium: paper, tape, CD, DVD, video, computer disk or storage device, the internet, or any other electronic format such as downloads and eBooks. Published and unpublished works can be copyrighted.

Your website and any of your work on the internet is copyrighted. Internet copyright is covered in the Online Operations chapter.

Songwriters: Songwriters can copyright not just original songs but also new arrangements or variations on old songs and musical compositions that are no longer covered by copyright or were never copyrighted (in the public domain), such as making changes to ancient folk songs or classical compositions.

If you add words to someone else's melody or if you add music to someone else's words or poem that is protected by copyright, you have created what's called a *derivative work*. You must get permission from the copyright holder to add your contribution to the copyrighted work. If permission is granted, the owner of the copyright may, or may not, allow you to share in the copyright of the new creation. The decision is entirely up to the copyright holder of the original work. You do own the copyright to what you created, independent of the prior work you combine it with. You can copyright your melody, you can copyright your words, and have full rights to your creation. You just cannot combine your work with someone else's without their permission.

If two or more people co-write a song, all of the writers share equal ownership of the copyright and share equally in the income from the copyright, no matter how much or how little each contributed. If one person writes the melody and another writes the lyrics of a song, both writers share equally in the entire song. Royalties are not split between words and music.

Musical compositions have some very specific copyright laws. Full details of the copyright rules are in a free publication, "Circular 50: Copyright Registration for Musical Compositions," available from the U.S. Copyright Office.

WHAT CANNOT BE COPYRIGHTED

You cannot copyright concepts, or ideas in your head, but you can write about concepts and ideas and copyright the writing. You cannot copyright songs you haven't written down or recorded. You cannot copyright a performance, but you can copyright a description of a performance or a recording of a performance.

You cannot copyright an improvisational speech, lists of ingredients or contents, math tables, rulers, standard calendars, blank forms, or height or weight charts. You cannot copyright names, titles, short phrases, slogans, or familiar symbols or sayings.

You cannot copyright databases. Compiled listings of information such as addresses and telephone numbers, stock quotes, directories, or bibliographies cannot be copyrighted.

You cannot copyright *things*, physical objects. A description of a machine could be copyrighted as a writing, but this will not prevent others from making or using the machine.

RIGHTS OF THE COPYRIGHT HOLDER

The owner of a copyright has exclusive rights to print and copy the work, including the right to make photocopies or to scan it into a computer; to sell or distribute copies of the work; to put it on the internet; to dramatize, record, or translate the work; to perform or broadcast the work publicly. A song played on a jukebox in a tavern, or even performed by the local bar band, technically requires permission from the copyright holder.

The owner of a copyright may or may not be the creator of the work. The creator of a work should be cautious when selling some or all rights to his or her work. If a work is specially ordered or commissioned, rights to the work usually go to the person or company paying for the work, not to the creator. Be aware of "work for hire" laws, which automatically give all rights to the employer, none to the creator of the work.

To be entirely clear and legal about copyright ownership, the creator and the commissioner of a work should stipulate in a written contract who owns the copyright. If you are hiring a website designer, or a photographer or videographer to do work for you, be sure your contract states that you, not the person working for you, owns all of the rights to the work.

Copyright law does allow anyone to use small portions of copyrighted material under what's called "the fair use doctrine," without getting permission from or paying the copyright owner. The fair use law was written to allow use of copyrighted material for, to quote the Copyright Office, "criticism, comment, news reporting, teaching, scholarship, and research." What exactly constitutes fair use, and what constitutes a "small portion" has been argued in the courts for years. Sometimes what a user claims is fair use, the copyright owner sees as outright theft.

Artists: The Visual Artists Rights Act protects, in certain cases, original paintings, drawings, sculptures, and some photographs from being altered or destroyed after the works are sold.

ACQUIRING A COPYRIGHT

Copyright in the United States is automatic. Your work is copyrighted the moment you create it. You don't have to put a copyright notice on the work, and you don't have to register the work with the U.S. Copyright Office, although the Copyright Office strongly recommends that you do. Both are covered below.

Under current law, your copyright is good for your lifetime plus another seventy years. The number of years that a copyright is valid has been increased many times, thanks to the Disney

Corporation. Every time Walt Disney's Mickey Mouse gets close to the copyright expiration date, the lobbyists for the Disney Corporation push Congress to extend the copyright protection another twenty or twenty-five years. (That's a true story.)

COPYRIGHT NOTICE

Put a copyright notice on all of your work. Most people don't know that all works are automatically copyrighted. A copyright notice is universally understood. The word "copyright," the symbol ©, your name or whatever name you want the copyright under (you can use a business name or alias or make up a name), and the year of first publication. This will eliminate the possibility that someone will innocently reprint your work, thinking it isn't protected. Some foreign countries also require the words "All rights reserved."

Although the U.S. Office says that a copyright notice should include the year a work was copyrighted, a lot of people leave the year off of copyright notices, usually because they don't want anyone to know how old the work is. An old copyright implies outdated or stale material. The copyright year, however, will help if someone else steals your material and copyrights it as well. The copyright year offers proof that you had the copyright first. If, like Walt Disney, you produce something that will still be selling seventy years from now, the copyright year establishes how long you and your descendants own the rights. However, if you choose to leave the year off of the copyright notice, it does not invalidate or diminish your copyright rights.

REGISTERING A COPYRIGHT

Registration of a copyright is not required by U.S. law. You own your copyright whether you register it or not. But registering your work with the U.S. Copyright Office gives you stronger legal protection, and it's a way of proving that the work really is yours. It costs $35 to file a copyright online, and $85 to file on a paper form. You also must send the Copyright Office two copies of the work.

Full details of the copyright rules are available from the U.S. Copyright Office website, copyright .gov, or call them toll-free at (877) 476-0778, or write to Register of Copyrights, Library of Congress, Washington, DC 20559.

PROTECTING YOUR COPYRIGHT

You don't have to police your copyright, you don't have to be constantly searching for unauthorized use of your material, but if you find someone who is using your copyrighted material without your permission, you have to act promptly. If you do not attempt to stop the unauthorized use, you can lose some of the legal protection for the copyright. You don't have to hire a lawyer and go to court, but you do have to be persistent, continue to state your objections, and keep a record of your actions.

If you license rights to copyrighted material, as many photographers and cartoonists do, check on the licensee to verify he or she hasn't used your work after the term of the license expired or beyond the scope of the license. You are not required by law to monitor licensing usage, but act promptly if you find a violation. And in the case of a wayward licensee, be friendly and non-accusatory. This is not some crook who stole your work. A licensee has already paid you some money and might even pay some more.

CONTRACTS

Business dealings are more likely to be successful and free of disagreements, arguments, misunderstandings, and lawsuits if they include a written contract. This is especially true for someone providing a professional service or doing a multifaceted project. The issues of who does what, when, and for how much, can get dicey without a written contract.

Some Basics

A contract defines your responsibilities and your client's commitment. A contract demonstrates business professionalism and weeds out insincere clients. A contract will protect you from the anguish and frustration of indecisive clients and people who continually change their minds and the extent of the job midstream. It gives your customers a sense of security. Sometimes the only proof you have of the extent of your obligations is your signed agreement. Contracts may help you get insurance or financing.

Don't think of a contract as a means to win or to protect yourself against a lawsuit. The main purpose of a contract should be to clarify an agreement, to make sure all parties fully understand the agreement, not to set up the rules for a fight. Nor should contracts be used to keep crooks in check. It never works anyway. If you don't trust the people you're dealing with, maybe you shouldn't be dealing with them at all.

Contracts should be understandable. No where-ases, heretofores, or legal mumbo jumbo. Avoid words like *he*, *she*, and *they*; it's too easy to confuse who you're talking about. Use names, or "land-lord" and "tenant," "seller" and "buyer." Contracts should be simple and concise yet include full details. A good contract tries to answer all of the questions before they're asked.

Contracts should be signed by both parties: original signatures, not photocopied. Some lawyers suggest you sign in blue ink, so it will be easier to spot as an original. Electronic signatures (if authorized by both parties) are valid, as are the "I accept" buttons nobody reads on websites.

If only one party signs a contract, it is still a legal contract. But only the person signing is bound to the agreement. The person not signing has made no legal commitment.

Some clauses a contract might include:

1. The duration of the contract.

2. A description of the products and services you are providing.

3. All deadlines.

4. Consequences of missing the deadlines or not completing the contract.

5. Amount, terms, and timetable for payment.

6. Conditions under which the contract can be terminated.

7. Wording to the effect that something of value is to be given, and something of value is to be received. This is legally known as "consid-eration," and it should be spelled out in the contract. A contract is not legally a contract unless there is an exchange.

8. If there will be out-of-pocket expenses, the contract should specify who pays the expenses, when and if they are to be reim-bursed, and any dollar limit.

9. Limits to your liability.

10. Whether any rights in the contract can be sold, given, or traded ("assigned") to a third party.

11. A statement that the contract cannot be altered orally. Any changes should be in writ-ing, signed by both parties.

Contracts don't have to be formal, legal-looking documents. Formal contracts sometimes backfire, scaring off a potential customer. A simple letter of agreement, signed by both parties, is a valid con-tract and may be more appropriate. Signed purchase orders are valid contracts.

If your business is a corporation, partnership, or limited liability company, it should be disclosed in the contract. Sign as a representative (president, etc.) of the business, not as an individual, not as "owner." Make it clear that the business, not you personally, is responsible for the contract. This will help limit your personal liability.

Avoid oral contracts. There's an old saying, "A verbal agreement isn't worth the paper it's written on." Although some oral contracts are legally bind-ing, the problem is and always will be that every-one remembers the agreement differently. People's memories are mighty short. They honestly think they agreed to something completely different than what you think they agreed to.

Before I write up a contract, I make a list of the things I want to cover. I take a few days, to make sure I think of everything. I find it helpful to look at other contracts to see how other people wrote theirs. There are books of sample contracts. Trade organizations sometimes have sample con-tracts. Friends in business might let you have cop-ies of their contracts (with names and numbers scratched out). Your accountant may be able to get you samples of contracts. If you are using some-one else's contract, make sure you understand every word. If the legalese doesn't make sense to you, don't use it, or rewrite it so it does make sense.

A note to designers, artists, and others whose work involves intellectual property (writing, art-work, computer programming, etc.): The contract should spell out who owns the rights to your work, and the extent of those rights.

Email Contracts

Email contracts may or may not be legally binding. Different situations—and different judges—have led to different court rulings. Which isn't very helpful, is it? If a contract is important, it's better to be sure it's valid than to trust some judge to make that deci-sion for you.

When you negotiate a contract through email, or make a sales offer, or agree to a purchase, or make any other business commitment, I'd suggest that the email says that what you're sending is a *proposed* contract. If it is agreeable to both parties, it will be followed by a written contract to be signed by both parties. However, sometimes you want to make a deal quickly, or you are facing imminent deadlines, and you don't want to delay the agreement or give the other party an excuse to shop around for alternatives. In that case, you just ask the other party if he or she agrees, and if the other party emails back an agreement, you go for it. And hope for the best, which will most likely be the outcome. But just because the contract comes as an email, don't abbreviate it. Don't leave out any details.

Some businesses use electronic signatures (e-signatures) on emailed contracts that are legally binding, but few people have taken the trouble to get an e-signature, and its unlikely someone will want to get an e-signature just to sign an agreement with you. There are sites that administer e-signatures if you want to learn more about getting one.

Other People's Contracts

If you are asked to sign someone else's contract, it's a whole different ball game. Large corporate vendors and purchasers, government agencies, landlords, banks, leasing companies, professional consultants, and independent freelancers often have their own contracts ready for you to sign, and they probably had talented and expensive lawyers create them.

Make sure you understand and fully agree with every word. Don't be too embarrassed to admit you don't know the meaning of a word. Look it up or ask. Be on your guard; nothing in these contracts is superfluous. Every clause was carefully thought out, to give the best advantage and protection to whoever had the contract prepared. And look out for the word "indemnify." It means that, if there is a lawsuit, you agree to pay the other party's legal expenses. Don't indemnify anyone.

Just because these contracts are printed on fancy paper, are formal, technical, legal, etc., etc., they are not cemented in stone. You can take out your pen and change them, eliminate sections and conditions you don't agree to.

If the contract is important and valuable enough, get a lawyer's help if you feel unsure of yourself. Just don't sign it and hope for the best, which, in this situation, may not be the outcome.

FILING YOUR BUSINESS RECORDS

I read somewhere that 85 percent of all business records, stuck in the filing cabinet or buried in your computer documents, are never looked at again. From my own experience, I can believe it. But it is the other 15 percent of the paperwork that you want or need to locate, and the outside chance of an audit, or a lawsuit involving someone who worked for you eight years ago, that makes an organized filing system a necessity for all businesses.

Every business and financial transaction, every meeting, every action involving employees should be documented and kept for future reference or for proof if you get audited or questioned in some legal dispute. If all documents have their own labeled file, locating them at a later date will be a much easier job.

Storing documents so they are permanent and so you can access them a year, or two years, or ten years later, requires planning. Paper documents, if not damaged or destroyed, will last almost forever. Documents on your computer, on a removable storage device, or on an internet server, may or may not be retrievable in the future, when technology has moved on to the next generation, or the computer

crashed, or the server went bankrupt and vanished. I suggest making paper copies and keeping backup storage for your most important records. And whenever technology brings out a new storage method, take the time to copy your records from the old system to the new one.

Documents to Keep

Here is a list of documents you should keep:

1. All documents that establish and define the business: corporate article and bylaws, partnership agreements, limited liability company agreements, fictitious name statements (DBAs), trademark registrations, and similar organizational records. Keep as long as the business exists.

2. Names, addresses, Social Security numbers, and other pertinent data for all owners and stockholders, including date joined and date departed. Keep as long as the business exists.

3. Record of owners' contributions and withdrawals and all other financial transactions between owners and the business. Keep as long as the business exists.

4. Minutes of corporate board meetings. Keep as long as the business exists. You will find yourself going back to the old minutes many times. If owners ever get in a dispute, old minutes will often provide ready answers.

5. Permits, licenses, insurance policies, and leases. Keep as long as they are in force, but for IRS purposes, keep at least three years.

6. Loan papers. Keep as long as the loans are outstanding, but for IRS purposes, keep at least three years. Actually, it's a good idea to keep loan papers for as long as the business exists. Though a loan may have been paid off several years ago, you may want to show a lender a record of the old loan when you apply for a new one.

7. Invoices, bills, sales receipts, cash receipts, credit memos, and other day-to-day business documents. For IRS purposes, keep at least three years. If your sales documents include customer names and addresses, you may want to keep the records longer if they are the only record you have of your customers. If the documents include customer credit card or debit card numbers, be careful to protect the privacy of the numbers. If discarding the records, destroy them so no one can obtain the information.

8. Complete data on all current and past employees, and I emphasize the word "complete": names, addresses, and contact information, Social Security numbers, date hired, wage rates and dates of raises, payroll withholding, W-4 exemptions, injuries and workers' compensation or disability claims, evaluations, date employment ended and why. Keep as long as the business exists; in fact, keep the records even after you close or sell the business. It is rare, but it does happen that some government agency or court will ask you to produce fifteen-year-old employment records. If this happens, be sure you are legally required to produce the records and be sure you are not violating a law or an agreement of confidentiality by providing the records. I suggest that you contact the employee, if that's possible, and ask for written permission to disclose the documents. You may want to get legal help if the situation looks like trouble brewing.

9. Bank records. For IRS purposes, keep at least three years.

10. Annual financial statements, if you prepare them. Keep as long as the business exists. If you prepare monthly financial statements, keep them a few years. It is useful to compare monthly profit and loss statements for consecutive years to see if there is a pattern or cycle of business activity.

11. Tax returns. Keep at least three years from the date you file the returns, in case of an IRS audit. Some businesses keep their income tax returns for as long as the business exists, though some businesses destroy old returns as soon as the three-year statute of limitations expires. Keep payroll tax returns indefinitely, as explained under #8 above. Keep property tax returns for as long as you own the property. Keep all other tax returns, such as sales tax, inventory tax, and excise tax, at least three years.

12. Financial records. Keep at least three years. Like income tax returns, some businesses keep their financial records for as long as the business exists, and some businesses destroy old records as soon as the three-year statute of limitations expires.

HOW TO AVOID CROOKS AND HOW TO COLLECT WHAT YOU'RE OWED

There are a lot of con artists in the world. Naive small business owners are particularly vulnerable, and every business, I suspect, gets "burned" once or twice. I am not talking about armed robbery or shoplifters or embezzlers. I'm referring to people who offer to buy from you or sell to you or some other business dealing, but are really trying to con you out of goods or money. Pretty quickly you start to recognize these kinds of people, and you learn how to deal, or not to deal, with people you are suspicious of.

This section applies to businesses that extend "direct credit," also known as "selling on account." Direct credit does not refer to accepting credit cards. Direct credit is where you, the business owner, extend credit to your customers. While few if any retail and internet businesses extend direct credit, many wholesale and manufacturing businesses extend direct credit to their customers, as do some print shops and other businesses whose customers are businesses. With direct credit, you have to decide that a customer is, or isn't, trustworthy. And there are untrustworthy lowlifes out there.

In one business I helped set up, which sold books wholesale to bookstores, distributors, and internet book dealers, I developed some safeguards that protected the business from rip-off artists, as well as from people who seemed suspicious but may in fact have been quite honorable. It is important that any procedures you set up appear to apply to everyone you deal with, so as not to offend people who may turn out to be valuable customers.

Here is how I suggest handling a new, untested, and maybe untrustworthy account. The easiest way, of course, is Cash Up Front. We had a written sales policy, just a notice we handed out to most prospective (and unknown to us) dealers and wholesalers. It stated, "We request that your first order be prepaid." As an extra incentive, we offered an additional 5 percent discount for prepayment. Some people offer free shipping for prepayment. This may sound like the end of your problems, but of course it

isn't. All rules are made to be broken, and you will find yourself dealing with people who, for any of a hundred reasons, cannot or will not prepay (maybe they don't trust you). Do you do business with them anyway? Do you take a chance? Sometimes that's what business is all about.

For starters, if you don't know the purchaser, don't ship anything out of the country until you've been paid in full. Many crooks work across borders where it is easy for them to hide and next to impossible for you to collect from them. Do not give out your bank account information for direct deposit, as it can lead to direct withdrawal: They can steal your money. Don't trust any checks you get, even cashier's checks, until you know they've cleared your bank and the issuing bank.

Even within the United States where you have more protections, minimize your risk. Like the cardinal rule of gambling, don't ship more than you can afford to lose. Tell them you will sell them one case of whatever-it-is, so they can "try it out and see how it does," and as soon as they use it up or sell it or whatever it is they're doing with it, and pay for it, you will be more than happy to ship some more. Emphasize that you can fill reorders quickly.

When you get an order (not prepaid) from a company you don't know, look them up on the internet. Do they have a website? Do they have a business phone listing? Not having a business phone doesn't mean the company isn't legitimate; many home businesses are not listed and, likewise, a business listing does not vouchsafe for it either, but it is an indicator whether you're dealing with reputable people. I am immediately cautious of a company without a business phone; we usually stuck to the written policy and demanded prepayment. If you do get the company's telephone number, and the order is big enough to warrant a call, call the company "to confirm the order," maybe inquire how they want it shipped, tell them about your special prepayment offer, and definitely ask if you are going to get paid.

Establishing Credit

When dealing with someone for the first time and extending them credit, be very direct about being paid. Tell them you will be happy to extend credit, but you need their assurance that you will be paid. If you are dealing face-to-face, look the person right in the eye. And get the person to say, "Yes, I will pay this bill." Sometimes they'll say, "Well, this and that corporation extend us credit, we have an AA#1 Dun

& Bradstreet rating, we are an established business, member of the Chamber of Commerce," and various and sundry impressive stuff that is of absolutely no value to you. Just repeat that all you need is their assurance you will be paid. It's a powerful "Yes" when they say it. Even crooks have a hard time going back on their word.

No credit policy should be cemented in concrete. I would not hesitate to extend credit to most large corporations, government agencies, or anyone whose title or company suggests that they are likely to pay. But, an interesting fact I've discovered: The bigger the company, the longer they take to pay. Tell them the bill is due in thirty days, and it's almost guaranteed they won't pay for sixty or even ninety days. Factor this delay into whatever discounts or incentives you offer and in your own cash flow projections.

Collecting Past-Due Accounts

If a bill goes past due, get on it right away. The longer you wait to try to collect it, the less likely you'll collect. Many people have a little money, and they pay as they can until they just call it quits and disappear or file bankruptcy. You want to get paid before this happens, and squeaky wheels get the grease. Email. Telephone once a week. Be friendly and understanding, but be persistent. Don't be hostile or threatening—it will get you nowhere, and that's the truth—but be persistent.

Let people know they can make partial payments. Many people are unable to pay the entire balance at once, so they let the bill languish, unaware they can make partial payments.

And if it finally becomes apparent that you aren't going to get your money, just drop it and forget it. It's bad enough not getting paid, no sense twisting the knife in your own wound with anger and ulcers. If the customer has filed for bankruptcy, put in your claim. If not, turn it over to a collection agency, as long as there is no up-front cost to you. But, either way, you can pretty much figure you won't see any money.

Going to Court

Should you take a nonpaying customer to court? The answer depends on two important factors: (1) Can you collect if you win? Does the debtor have assets such as cash or property, and will you be able to get the assets? Otherwise all you have is one more piece of paper that says the debtor owes you money, but you still don't get the money. And (2) Will your legal fees be more than the settlement? I know, it's the principle of the thing, but how much more money do you want to throw away?

For many types of small businesses, the "credit crooks" are actually rare. And after a few experiences, you can spot 'em a mile away. Something about them always tips you off. Maybe their way of writing an email, everybody has seen bogus emails; or the "hustle" in their voice; or their lack of knowledge how your type of business usually operates; or, always a red flag for us, some stranger talking large quantities and big dollars.

In a way, it's kind of fun, too, sleuthing, feeling the people out—and what great dinner stories. Someday I'll tell you about the guy on the phone from Philadelphia, Mr. Cream Cheese, my wife called him. He was a real pro.

WE OWN IT: EMPLOYEE-OWNED BUSINESSES, COOPERATIVES, AND COLLECTIVES

Some businesses are just that: business, and nothing else. You need to make a living, pay your bills, feed your kids. That's an honest and honorable reason to be in business for yourself. It's why I first went into business. Many businesses, however, have goals beyond just making a living, most often personal satisfaction in what you do, and satisfaction in being able to help others.

And then there are a few special businesses that have another goal: to share a vision of what work means and what working together means. These businesses involve several people with a common idea and a desire to try a different, cooperative approach to business.

The words *cooperative*, co-op, collective, and employee ownership are often used to describe this type of worker-owned business, but the terms mean different things to different people. Often, the terms are used interchangeably (and, as discussed below, sometimes illegally). Some employee-owned businesses are "cooperatives," but most are not. Worker ownership takes many different forms.

A cooperatively owned business is a social organization as much as it is an economic one. The most accepted definition of a cooperatively owned business is one owned and controlled democratically by the workers in the business. The workers are basically business partners, but their goals often are more than just running a successful business, and usually include cooperation, sharing, working with like-minded people, and dividing the income in an open and democratic fashion. Cooperatively owned businesses share all of their financial information with all of the owners.

Legal Structure/Cooperatives

Most worker-owned businesses that call themselves cooperatives are not legally cooperatives at all. Most states have strict definitions of the term *cooperative*. It is usually limited to consumer cooperatives, typically supermarkets owned by the customers; or producer cooperatives, typically agricultural packers and distributors owned by farmers and growers who individually produce a product and then band together to market their products. The term *worker cooperative*, often used to describe cooperatively owned businesses, has no legal meaning in most states, and is often not permitted to be used legally.

Cooperatively owned businesses usually incorporate as conventional corporations, with ownership (shares of stock) restricted to the workers. The corporate bylaws specify how the business is to be run, how wages are to be paid, and how profits are to be shared. The owners are regular employees on the corporation's payroll. The section on corporations in the Growing Up chapter applies to cooperatively owned businesses as well as to conventional businesses. There is, legally, no difference between the two.

Cooperatively owned businesses that don't incorporate are automatically general partnerships, and come under the partnership laws covered under "Partnerships" in the Growing Up chapter. It is usually not a good idea to set up this kind of business as a partnership, because of ownership and liability problems (discussed under "Partnerships").

The term *collective* is not a legal description, although no law prohibits its use in the name of a business.

Employee Stock Ownership Plans (ESOPs)

Employee Stock Ownership Plans, or ESOPs, are used when employees want to take over an existing corporation, usually to rescue companies facing liquidation. ESOPs are usually set up in large companies where large amounts of money are necessary to buy the stock. ESOPs are not used to start new or small, cooperatively run businesses.

Steve Hargraves and Terry Nemeth were two owners of Bookpeople, an employee-owned book distributor: "Everybody who works here owns an equal number of shares in the company. There is a six-month probationary period when someone comes to work here. At the end of that probationary period, if you decide that you want to get involved in an employee-owned company, you have to buy into the company. There's nobody who owns a piece of Bookpeople who doesn't work here. That's part of the bylaws. There can't be outside owners.

"Everybody has the same amount invested. Those that didn't have the money either borrowed or put up a note to be paid off within a year out of their paychecks. If you leave, the company buys back your share. You get back exactly what you put in. There are only as many outstanding shares as there are employees."

Job Structure and Pay

Some worker-owned businesses traditionally operate with the goal of sharing all jobs. This way, owners learn all aspects of their business, and they feel that they are able to make better decisions. Rotating jobs is an equalizing process that allows the less-fun jobs to be shared by all. Everybody has to take turns making executive decisions and emptying the trash cans.

In terms of efficiency, job rotation is often less effective than job specialization. People have different skills and different job preferences. Most cooperatively owned businesses eventually come to the conclusion that job rotation is neither practical nor necessary.

Equal pay for all workers is often a goal of worker-owned businesses. As long as every worker feels good about the equal pay arrangement, as long as none feel they deserve more than the next person, the system will work. Equal pay for all is most effective in businesses that practice regular job rotation. Everyone is the president and everyone is the janitor, so everyone is entitled to the same wage. Such arrangements, however, are rare. Most worker-owned businesses have pay differentials, typically based on the same factors found in most businesses: skills, experience, difficulty of the job, seniority. But one concept almost universal to all cooperatively owned businesses is a fair wage for all workers.

Volunteers

Cooperatively owned businesses, particularly those with a strong social or community mission, often attract volunteers, eager to be part of an organization they admire. Just be warned that volunteer labor may have legal and tax complications and liability risks. Check with your state's employment laws regarding volunteers.

In one recent tax case, volunteers at a business were given some free goods and discounts on purchases as a small thank you for their help. The IRS audited the business and ruled that the free goods and discounts were both, in effect, employee wages, and that the volunteers were legally employees, subject to payroll taxes and all employment laws. Woah! That's getting downright mean, and not usually examined in a normal audit, so I suspect there is more to the story than what was reported. But the ruling stands, just the same, and the business paid dearly. Caution is advised.

A genuine problem with volunteers is liability if a volunteer is injured or becomes ill at the business. Who is legally responsible? Who pays the medical bills? This is an extremely important issue to discuss with your insurance carriers. Does your workers' compensation policy cover volunteers? Does your general liability coverage extend to volunteers? Get the answers in writing.

Work Together

Cooperatively owned businesses are, first and last, people: people who can work together, who understand and respect one another, who can agree on common needs and goals and how they're to be accomplished. It is the people, the workers, who will make or break any business. And it is this "working together" that will require the most work of all.

As "ideal" as cooperative businesses are supposed to be, the people in the ventures are no more ideal than you or me. They have egos, they

have idiosyncrasies, they have minor differences of opinion that, six months later, are suddenly chasms threatening the very existence of the business. There are no hard and fast rules where people are concerned. It all takes what the business likes to call itself: cooperation.

MANAGING YOUR BUSINESS

Volumes have been written on the subject of small business "management." I put the word in quotes because it is such an all-encompassing term. Just about anything you, the owner, does is labeled "management." And just about every study on small business failures blames over 90 percent of those failures on "poor management."

"Poor management" refers to everything from sloppy recordkeeping to lousy business location. If you sell clothing, and the fashions suddenly change, leaving you with unsalable merchandise, it's labeled "poor management": You should have been aware of the market trends and should have made advance preparations to anticipate them. If you expected your business to show a profit the first year, but you wound up with a loss and not enough reserve cash to keep things going, that's another situation they call "poor management."

Read About It

Management is an organic part of your business, interwoven into every aspect of business. It isn't like Step One—get a business license, Step Two—manage, Step Three—update the records, etc. Management is something you can only learn by doing, but a few evenings spent with some good management reading won't do you any harm.

Almost every library in the country has at least ten books on business management. Some of the books are excellent, some are shallow; almost all of them go unread. An interesting SBA study of eighty-one small businesses showed that only one owner in eighty-one read any management literature. Most of those eighty-one businesses failed. There are thousands of defunct businesses, gone belly-up because of the same management errors repeated over and over again. I guess it's just human nature to want to learn from your own mistakes.

You will get the most value out of management books if you read them after you've had several months' experience in your new venture. You will understand much better what the books are discussing, and you will quickly spot the information most valuable to you.

Join the trade organizations for your type of business, and subscribe to the trade magazines. An internet search will locate dozens of organizations that claim to help businesses. Just look out for websites that are primarily trying to sell you something, which unfortunately is what most business-help websites are actually up to. Look for professional, well-known, long-established organizations that offer some real benefits.

The best management advice you can get, however, is from other small businesspeople. Businessmen and -women, I find, love to talk about business. Business is a large part of their lives, and they love to share their experiences and their ideas. You can't get better advice at any price. No accountant or lawyer or college professor knows half of what the person who's doing it every day knows. Strike up acquaintances, get to be friends with businesspeople, find out about the local merchants' organizations and attend their luncheons. Have a little fun, too.

Management is just common sense. As soon as you read or hear advice or a suggestion, you know instinctively that it's right. "Why didn't I think of that?" If it doesn't hit you that way when you hear it, if it doesn't make total sense, don't rely on it. It's probably bad advice, for now anyway, but check back in six months or a year.

Marketing

Keeping a business successful requires ongoing marketing: promoting your business every day, trying to satisfy and keep the customers you already have, and find new ones.

Marketing will always be experimental. Bounce your ideas off other people. Talk to everyone who is interested. Don't hire a consultant.

A common misconception is that marketing means advertising. Advertising is only one element of marketing. Advertising may or may not work, depending on the type of business you have and how talented you are at designing ads. Word of mouth may be your best advertising, and that means always making sure you have satisfied customers.

Think like a customer. Forget how great your business is, and put yourself in the shoes of your customer. What would you want as a customer?

Sometimes, a business will take unsuspected detours as the owner responds to customers' needs. There are many businesses that started out in one direction only to be forced by the actual day-to-day activity of their particular business, and the needs of their customers, to go in another direction entirely.

For many businesses, websites and social media are essential to find and keep customers, but the internet can sure eat up your time. Websites need occasional updating, but social media requires constant attention, regular interaction with visitors. You're not just running a business, you're hosting an online party, something not all business owners enjoy or are good at doing. If you don't enjoy or have time for business-related social media, personally I would not have a Facebook page or Twitter account at all. Better to not have a social media presence than have one that looks abandoned.

One more suggestion: Take all complaints seriously. Most customers don't complain. "How was the meal?" "Fine." They just walk away and never come back. They don't say anything to you, but you

can be sure they'll tell all their friends. If only one customer complains, you can figure at least ten others have the same complaint. If you can solve that customer's problem, not only will you keep that customer, and make him or her one of your best boosters in the bargain, but you'll probably keep many of the others you would have otherwise lost.

Lara Stonebraker, owner, Cunningham's Coffee: "It's important to keep your merchandise rotating in the store, constantly change the position of things. You'd be surprised how many people will say, 'Gee, you've got something new in,' when you know it's been sitting there for two years; you've just moved it from this shelf to that shelf. It has to be displayed in a coherent manner. You have to have all those things that are related together. And you have to give your customers an incredible selection. If you have espresso pots, you have to have them in nine sizes, because people will not be inclined to buy if there is only a choice of two or three. Even if you stock only one of these odd-sized items that you know will not be selling, you still have to have it, just to fill up your shelf, to give the impression that you have a huge variety.

"People will come to your store because they know you have a large selection. A lot of times I know that it's purely psychological, because I know that I will never sell a twelve-cup pot and I know that I will never sell a one-cup pot. But I have to have them there just for the comparison, just so that people will feel that this is a store that has everything, that has all the choices they can possibly get, they don't need to go anywhere else for it. I've seen a lot of stores make this mistake, having only two sizes of something. It just doesn't give you the confidence in the store.

"I do rotating displays on the expensive items every other week. I try to create the kind of display that will make customers stop and look, but not so much that the background will overpower the items you are selling. You can't have too many plants, you can't have things that will distract from your merchandise.

"And you can't have a no-don't-touch atmosphere. You don't want things looking too pretty because people will be afraid to touch them, they'll feel inhibited. Most important of all, you can't have any bare walls. There was a place in San Francisco that opened and the woman just didn't have enough money to buy another cabinet, so she had one wall, the prime wall for display, just blank. Mr. Peet came in and said, 'That's a lovely wall; are you selling walls?'"

THE FUTURE OF SMALL BUSINESS

Since the dawn of economic time, a person with the right idea at the right time and any degree of competence could make a go of small business. Today, even in our shaky economy, with giant corporations getting more and more of the consumers' dollars and with chain stores driving independents out of business, small businesses can and do survive and thrive. Businesses attentive to local and neighborhood needs, and businesses attentive to customers' personal needs, will always have an edge over large, faceless corporations.

Small business owners themselves can help, by patronizing other small and locally owned businesses. Not only does it help the small business environment in general, it keeps the money in town, to be re-spent again in town. What's more, you might meet other local business owners, and exchange help and ideas.

Small business is an ever-changing world, not just the laws, but the entire concept of how to be successful as the world continues to change around us. No business can stand still.

Write or email me if I can be of further help to you:

Bernard Kamoroff
Box 1240
Willits, CA 95490
kamoroff@bellsprings.com

Drive ahead, don't spare the steam, make all the noise possible, and by all means, keep down the expenses.

—P. T. Barnum

INDEX

ABOUT THE AUTHOR

Bernard Kamoroff is a certified public accountant with over thirty years' experience, specializing in small business.

Mr. Kamoroff has worked directly with hundreds of businesses and has been a guest speaker at business, professional, and trade association meetings and conventions.

He has given business workshops and seminars for the University of California, American River College, Mendocino College, Open Exchange, Learning Annex, American Booksellers Association, Marketing Boot Camp, and San Francisco Business Renaissance.

Mr. Kamoroff is the author of five business guidebooks, including *475 Tax Deductions for Businesses and Self-Employed Individuals: An A-to-Z Guide to Hundreds of Tax Write-Offs*, now in its thirteenth edition.

In addition to helping other businesses, Mr. Kamoroff has started and successfully operated three of his own small businesses.

Bernard Kamoroff lives in Mendocino County, California. If you have any questions, suggestions, or comments about *Small Time Operator*, please send them to the author, c/o Bell Springs Publishing, Box 1240, Willits, CA 95490. Or email kamoroff@bellsprings.com.